FREE – RANGE

CHRISTIANITY

....

Graham Hellier

"Why can you not judge for yourselves what is right?"

Jesus — Luke 12:57

This book is an extensive revision of

"The Thoughtful Guide to Christianity"

— which attracted these reviews:

....

This version —**"Free-Range Christianity"** — is more outspoken and occasionally polemical — so, potentially, even more annoying! Nevertheless, it seeks to be constructive. The reader will not agree with everything but may enjoy the journey.

....

Dedication

To Merryn – true companion

To Kirsten, Coel and Struan who have enriched my life

To Ewan, Robin, Reuben and Oscar

May these words help them fly

"They will be strong like eagles soaring upward" Is 40:31

&&&&&&&&&&&&&&&&&&&&&&&&&&&&&&&&&&&&&&&&&&&&&&&&&&&&&&&&

"O give me land, lots of land
Under starry skies above -
Don't fence me in.
Let me ride through the wide
Open country that I love -
Don't fence me in.

Let me be by myself in the evening breeze,
Listen to the murmur of the cottonwood trees;
Send me out for ever, but I ask you, please -
Don't fence me in."

Bob Fletcher and Cole Porter

AuthorHouse™ UK Ltd.
500 Avebury Boulevard
Central Milton Keynes, MK9 2BE
www.authorhouse.co.uk
Phone: 08001974150

First published by AuthorHouse 6/15/2009

ISBN: 978-1-4389-7933-5 (sc)

A CIP catalogue of this book is available from the British Library.

This book is printed on acid-free paper.

"to every cow belongs her calf, to every book her offspring"
Diarmuid, Irish High King
- in a copyright dispute involving Columba – AD561

authorHOUSE®

CONTENTS

This list shows the plain themes; titles in the text are more variable!

CONTENTS

The History of the Church

CONTENTS

CONTENTS

CONTENTS

....

Great God, whom I shall carve from this grey stone
Wherein thou liest, hid to all but me;
Grant thou that when my art hast made thee known
And others bow, I shall not worship thee
But as I pray thee now, then let me pray
Some greater God.
        — source unknown.

INTRODUCTION

A young man had died, a Quaker, a foreigner. Poland was in ruins after the second world war. He had come with other volunteers to help to rebuild a shattered village and there he had fallen ill and died. His family asked if he could be buried in Poland.

They went to the local priest to have him laid to rest in the village churchyard. He said that he was sorry: it was a Catholic burial ground; it was consecrated; his hands were tied; the young man was not even baptised. He could be buried just outside.

So it was that everyone, villagers and volunteers, came to the grave outside the churchyard fence. Simple prayers were said, silence was kept, and there were tears. Quietly they came and quietly went.

That night, some villagers came with torches and set to work. It took them some time. They did not leave until they were satisfied.

It was well into the next day when one of the volunteers discovered what had happened and told the rest. They made their way back to the place. Once more there were tears. The villagers had moved the fence, so that the grave was included within the churchyard.

What was done, in that village in Poland, came from the heart, and in this act the villagers had broken through several barriers. They had questioned the divisions of the sacred and the secular, the priest and the lay, the baptised and the unbaptised.

The churchyard was consecrated ground, blessed and set aside for holy use. We accustom ourselves to sacred times and places, to sabbaths and Sundays, fast days and feast days, to churches and temples, synagogues and mosques, groves and circles of stone. Such is our need and such our experience, but these things should never confine us or enclose us, and should not diminish what lies without. They have no exclusive power, rather, they hold our attention, until we are able to see the great horizons of time and place — time, which is ever the Day of the Lord, and place, that compels us to take the shoes from off our feet. There is no-where and no-when that God is not.

So it is with priests and holy men and women of every kind. We recognise in them something of God and we set them apart. We fence them off to be what we believe we cannot be. They only are called; they alone can lead the religious life; they speak with God on our behalf and mediate the mystery. But all of us are called; we too can speak with the One who is both within and without; we too can discover God in ourselves. Our calling is to mediate God to one another and to handle the mystery with integrity and awe.

So it is with sacraments. How strange that baptism, which should proclaim the generous love of God, should become a legalistic point of entry into the community. How impoverishing that the eucharist, which should celebrate the self-giving of God becomes a sign of exclusion. We, who are called to communion with God, are reduced to 'making our communion' We, who are sent to bring joy to the world, are reduced to 'attending mass' ('missa' is to send). We, who are invited to commit our lives in allegiance to Christ, are reduced to 'receiving the sacrament'. The 'sacramentum' was the sign of allegiance displayed by Roman soldiers on their standards. The Christian sacraments *are* about receiving but, more than that, they are about commitment and action.

It is time to open Christianity up — to ensure that it is free-range — to lift our eyes to the hills and embrace wider horizons. It is true that we are human and comfortable with the close and the familiar. We are at home in our enclosures and are disturbed by those who live 'beyond the pale', but these fences are not sacrosanct. They are temporary until we can trust ourselves as travellers who have no continuing city - Hebr.13:14. Free-range Christianity is not easy. It is challenging and, at times, daunting. It may cause us to lose our bearings or find ourselves in a wilderness, but it is exciting — a venture whose time has come, and it takes us to the places where the wind of God blows freely and unhindered.

The journey of the spirit is the most important we will ever undertake and for that journey we need nourishment. This book offers a rough guide to the Christian faith for anyone within or without the church and a resource too for teachers, preachers and discussion groups. It is for the thoughtful, the honest, and those who welcome truth from wherever it comes.

FUNDAMENTALISM CAN STAND IN OUR WAY

The writer, Bruce Chatwin, tells of the days when his job was to assess modern painting for a firm of art auctioneers. One morning he woke up blind. Sight returned to his left eye but the right one stayed sluggish and clouded. The eye specialist told him that he had been looking too closely at pictures and suggested swapping them for long horizons. I believe that fundamentalism is a form of short-sightedness that comes from peering too closely at a few things. It nails down truth too early and ignores the wide horizons. It is a natural human failing — a coping mechanism. Jonathan Sacks defines fundamentalism as:
" the attempt to impose a single truth on a plural world. What really lies behind it is fear and profound insecurity, and insecurity is always, at bottom, a lack of faith, not the presence of it"

There are fundamentalists in most religions; in political parties and philosophical schools — even in the arts and sciences, whose life-blood is creativity and freedom. Christians can see the dangers clearly enough in other faiths — the ultra-orthodox Jews in Hebron, the Hindu nationalists of the Bajrang Dal, the Wahhabi recruits of Al Qaeda — but it is harder to see the home-grown variety. PTO

One form of fundamentalism looks back to a Bible Conference at Niagara in 1895. It defined five fundamentals: the verbal inerrancy of Scripture, the virgin birth, the divinity of Jesus, the substitutionary theory of atonement, and the bodily return of Jesus. The first is an import without Biblical warrant; the second peripheral to the faith; the third is a credal construct of the early church, and the last two have weak foundations. We will look at these again. Too often, fundamentalists are more exclusive, more legalistic, more judgemental and far less God-centred than Jesus.

Many evangelicals are not fundamentalist as described above and there are many fine and kindly Christians who are fundamentalist by conviction. I do not criticise them but the doctrines that have lent themselves to many evils. Slavery justified, witches burned, women's rights restricted, homosexuals persecuted, AIDS sufferers condemned and genocide excused on the basis of Biblical teaching.
AS IS CATHOLICISM IMMEDIATELY
It is another brand of fundamentalism that is found in the church of Rome. When Protestantism was raising the banner of Biblical infallibility, the Catholic church in 1870 was proclaiming papal infallibility — that in certain circumstances, the Pope speaks on behalf of Christ. The hubris is so breathtaking that many Christians dare not examine closely the history of church leadership down the years. Far from being a symbol of unity, the Vatican has caused division in the Christian family; far from pointing the world to Christ, the Pope himself – white-robed – has become the celebrity focus of adulation; far from advancing the values of the Kingdom, the church of Rome has become an obstacle in its path. It still silences its own critics — Chomiskey, Schillebeek, Curran, Fox, Boff, Küng, Balaswiya — even in recent times the list is long. It prefers its theologians not to debate issues like celibacy, divorce, women priests and contraception. It encourages movements like Opus Dei, Focolare and the Neocatechumenate that by-pass episcopal control and answer directly to the papacy.

Multitudes of Catholics show a humility and generosity that belies the burden of the institution. Many have their doubts and many are content to trust those who lead them. Does it matter then if the institution keeps to old traditions? The answer is certainly yes. The church resists oppression in one area but then fails in humanity — thousands dying because it refuses to endorse both condoms and abstinence in the fight against AIDS. Yes, it does matter.

The Christian church has been a great instrument for good but is also responsible for great evils. We should be our own sternest critics — it should not be left to militant atheists to decry our failings. They have their own fundamentalism — believing that science will explain everything or that Darwinism is the only key to our humanity. What they cannotaccept is the narrow, sometimes inhumane teaching that they have heard from Christians.

Bruce Chatwin recovered his sight when he left for the desert skies of the Sudan, and so began a life-long interest in the nomadic peoples of the world and a love of wide horizons. Free-range Christianity should enable us to see.

LAYOUT

Each double page takes up a single theme and the two sides belong to one another. It is designed for easy access. This imposes serious limitations, because it is clearly not possible to do justice to many of the issues raised, but this is a single book and there are many specialist books for those who wish to explore further.

The layout lends itself to daily reflection for those who wish or for discussion groups to follow part of the book as time allows.

THEMES
Although there is a wide spread of themes, there is much else that could be included. I have chosen those which I believe might most readily interest the reader.

'Provisions' is preparatory and but it underpins much that follows.

'The Jewish Scriptures' is brief but essential. Readers are recommended to go to Jewish as well as Christian sources for a further study of the Old Testament.

'The Christian Scriptures' is a brief treatment of important background material. More light is cast on this in later sections.

'The Life of Jesus' is also brief, because we lack a true biography. This material is supplemented in other sections of the book.

'The Teaching of Jesus' seeks to make good the astonishing lack of thematic material for ordinary readers. Many writers talk *about* Jesus; few deal with what he said.

'The History of the Church' looks critically at some of the 'newsworthy' issues in church history. It cannot do justice to the quieter realities of day to day. Some of the issues appear again later in the book but the emphasis here is on history.

'The Church Today' These themes overlap with what has gone before and with what will come after. It will be only too apparent that my experience is drawn from one Christian tradition and is restricted by geography, culture and prejudice. Readers will bring their own correctives to my partiality.

'Belief Today' I have kept to traditional headings in the Contents list, so that those familiar with the terminology will find their way around. Others may be helped by the connection between traditional language and fresh interpretation.

'Ethics' Attention is drawn particularly to the introduction [see 127] The range of themes cannot be exhaustive but some of the same principles will apply elsewhere.

'Connections' and *'Travelling Together'* These short sections are a reminder that Christianity is not ring-fenced and negative in its dialogue with the rich world of human thought.

QUOTATIONS
These are taken from a great variety of sources and present a great variety of views — some deeply critical of Christianity and the Christian Church. They are not meant to present a coherent point of view and do not necessarily support the adjoining comment. I would urge that they are not passed over lightly — many of these voices are more important than mine. Their words can be savoured and criticised — gathered together in themes, they make a rich resource. Many names

will be unfamiliar so I have given a brief note on each in the name index at the back. Some quotations have been shortened or simplified — I apologise if anyone has been misrepresented and would welcome corrections where mistakes have crept in.

The Biblical Quotations are given in a rather free version of my own. I would not seek to match the beauty of the Authorised Version (largely indebted to the supreme artistry of William Tyndale) or the accuracy of modern scholarly translations. I wish only to explore fresh possibilities in keeping with the purpose of this book. It is strongly recommended that readers have a good modern translation to hand — the comparison will stimulate thought and give opportunity to explore the context of the quotations. The abbreviations will be easily recognisable from the contents list of any copy of the Bible.

A few quotations from the Apocrypha are included (writings not recognised as authoritative by some churches). These include Ecclesiasticus which needs to be distinguished from Ecclesiastes — they are marked *Ecclus.* and *Eccles.* respectively — and the Gospels of Thomas and Philip, which were not incorporated in the New Testament.

INFORMATION AND COMMENT
The information is brief but can be supplemented from other sources. The comment is often personal and reflects my own quest. It seeks to interpret, to challenge or to suggest. Readers are invited to consider all statements in this book in a critical way — never taking agreement or disagreement for granted.

I have kept to the Christian designation of AD and BC rather than the disguised form of CE (Common Era) and BCE (Before Common Era) because several religions and cultures have entirely different dating and would expect traditional Christian use in a book of this kind. (The Year 2000 was 5760 in Judaism and 1420 in Islam.)

CONTENTS AND INDEX
The **Contents** list at the beginning gives a fair guide to the themes covered. **Cross references** are shown throughout the text by the use of squared brackets... [—]. The **Name Index** at the back supplies a little more information where this was available to me. There are some additional lists in the text, see:

58 — martyrs
60 — an 'apostolic succession'
70 — campaigners against slavery
81 — founders of charities
91 — 'front-line' Christians
129 — women leaders

Biblical names are found in the sections on Jewish and Christian scriptures. After the main text, there is a list of **dates** and statistics relating to **Christian denominations** and **world religions**.

Acknowledgements

My sincere thanks to the following:
To the Orion Publishing group for permission to include lines from "Suddenly" by
R S Thomas — Collected Poems, published by J M Dent. [99]

To Faber and Faber for permission to include lines from "Little Gidding" by T S
Eliot — Four Quartets, Collected Poems 1909 -1962. [120]

— and also from "The Transfiguration" by Edwin Muir — Collected Poems.
[125]

I regret that I have not as yet been able to trace the copyright holders for
"Meditation for a Young Boy Confirmed" by Alan Paton.   [109]

I am indebted to the great hand surgeon and leprosy doctor, Paul Brand, for the
interpretation of the Ten Commandments, which underlies my own — see
"Fearfully and Wonderfully Made".   [11]

I owe an unpayable debt to all those from past and present who have provoked and
inspired the original version of this book. My especial thanks go to those who
have given me critical support in its later stages — Tim Bishop, Graham Black,
Anthony Buckley, Donald Eadie, Ralph Fennell, Helen Hammond, Len Moss and
Brenda Watson. Also to Kirsten for her loving support, to Coel for his honest
debate and to Struan for his valued encouragement. The greatest debt is to my
wife, Merryn, for speaking the truth in love and, when needed, bringing me down
to earth. All have helped to shape this book while not necessarily sharing all that is
in it. The final responsibility is, of course, all mine.

PROVISIONS

To find truth is a descent, a journey inwards.   Plotinus

If God were able to backslide from truth, I would fain cling to truth and let God go.
                                                        Meister Eckhart

As for certain truth, all is but a woven web of guesses.   Xenophon

In our infinite ignorance, we are all equal.   Karl Popper

The slenderest knowledge of the highest things is more desirable than the most certain knowledge of lesser things.   Aquinas

If you want the truth to stand clear before you, never be for or against.   Zen Buddhist

The opposite of a correct statement is an incorrect statement but the opposite of a profound truth may well be another profound truth.   Niels Bohr

What I know now is limited. One day I will know as fully as God knows me.
                                                        Paul - I Cor. 13:12

It doesn't matter what you believe; the important thing is belief.   Goebbels

The crowd doesn't have to know. It must believe.   Mussolini

My hosannas are forged in the crucible of doubt.   Dostoievsky

It is not possible to believe everything at the same time.   Keith Ward

Cleave ever to the sunnier side of doubt.   Tennyson

If you want to hear anything from me, you must both give and take reason.   Adelard

We should not be ashamed to acknowledge truth from whatever source it comes to us.
                                                        Al Kindi - Muslim 9C.

Lady, if you have to ask, you'll never know.   Louis Armstrong
    (when asked, 'What is jazz?')

....

Derivations: integrity = honesty, wholeness — to be an integrated
                person. doubt   = moving in two directions   — akin to 'duo'.
                doctrine = teaching...to indoctrinate = to teach uncritically.
                dogma = an opinion (later) a decree.

We can stay at home or range free, open to whatever truth beckons. For this we need integrity: we need to become whole. It involves:

➢ *Honesty* — a complete honesty whether or not it leads to faith. Those who believe in God cannot fear that they will be led astray, for God is Truth. Those who have no belief in God and see religions as ' *a tissue of meaningless mysteries'* (Spinoza) can rest secure in the honesty of their own quest.

➢ *Courage* — that has no fear of doubt. There is a corrosive doubt that is all pervading and keeps us enclosed but there is also honest doubt, and this is an ally, not an enemy of faith.

➢ *Realism* — an acceptance of our limitations — our bias, our clouded vision and our gullibility. Yet realism also requires an acceptance of possibilities, for truth comes to us all, and sometimes with the force of revelation.

➢ *Humility* — a profound humility which is open to all truth from any and every source — from ancient wisdom and modern research, from the unlearned, from the poor, from children, from believer and unbeliever.

➢ *Sharing* — for wisdom is cumulative and in this, as in all else, we do not and cannot stand alone.

➢ *Commitment* — a recognition that this is a journey of the heart. Here too courage is needed but we must not be afraid of commitment, for no one is a spectator, and either we follow the truth we see, or we shuffle along meaninglessly.

➢ *Reason* — this is a sifting tool, not an alternative to belief as some assume. It needs the raw material of perception, of evidence, of hypothesis and of experiment.

Pilate's question, 'What is truth?' still hangs in the air and admits of no easy answer. Likely as not we will find many truths and some of them in conflict with one another. Or we will discover that truth is more like an encounter than a statement, creed or formula. It then carries its own authority and becomes deeply personal. Perhaps there is no truth but our own story and we must give all our powers to this. Or perhaps there is only God's story, as yet unfinished, which we help to create.

....

We godless anti-metaphysicians still take our fire too, from the flame lit by a faith that is thousands of years old — that God is truth, and truth is divine.

Nietzsche

....

Humankind cannot bear very much reality.   T.S.Eliot

Some seed fell on stony ground.   Jesus - Mk 4:5

The most common of all follies is to believe in the palpably not true.   H.L Mencken

The highest knowledge is to know that we are surrounded by mystery.
                                                    Albert Schweitzer

In mathematics, what is certain is useless and what is useful is uncertain.
                                                    Bertrand Russell

*Do I contradict myself? Very well then, I contradict myself. (I am large, I contain
multitudes.)*   Walt Whitman

All theology is paradoxical.   Greek Orthodox

There is nothing God does not wish to be investigated by reason.   Tertullian

Reason is, ought only to be, the slave of the passions.   David Hume

An open mind about the ultimate foundations of reason is idiocy.   C.S.Lewis

He who knows only his own side of the case, knows little of that.   J.S.Mill

Convictions are more dangerous enemies of truth than lies.   Nietzsche

My dear fellow, I wish to thank you. I have been wrong these 15 years.
                                Oxford zoologist to a visiting lecturer

*If God can reveal anything to you by other instruments of his, be as ready to receive it as
ever you were to receive the truth from me.*
                    - the parting words of Pastor Robinson when the Mayflower set sail

*Whoever honours his own sect and disparages that of another, does his own sect the
greatest possible harm.*   *Emperor Asoka 3C.BC*

....

People::   **Hugo Grotius** 1583 - 1645 Christian humanist. He argued for a non-dogmatic, practical faith and sought toleration and church unity. His biblical scholarship anticipated the nineteenth century.

Intolerance is the enemy of truth. The deeper the convictions; the greater the danger of intolerance. More likely, such intolerance betrays an underlying uncertainty. Jung called fanaticism the 'brother of doubt' so our vehemence may say more about our fears than our faith. Intolerance has wrought havoc in Christian history.

Tolerance may also be the enemy of truth. We *should* be intolerant of evil in all its forms. Many German Christians tolerated Nazi ideology and failed to stop their nation's descent into darkness. If we respect truth, tolerance is not enough — especially in the church — however kindly we may be to one another, we cannot abdicate the responsibility to speak the truth as it is given to us.

Paul is already calling down curses on his opponents in Gal 1:6 - 9 and yet it is he (or a disciple of his?) who asks us to 'speak the truth in love' (Eph 4:5). Jesus shows a more open spirit — commending his teaching through questions and parables. But he is outspoken about hypocrisy and the record does not hold back the severity of some of his sayings. When Jesus says, 'whoever is not with me is against me' (Lk 11:23), he is speaking of those who ascribe all that he does to the devil. Elsewhere he says almost the opposite — 'whoever is not against us, is with us' (Mk 9:40) — but he is speaking of someone who is clearly doing good.

Again we must take to the open country. The truth is larger than all of us. It needs no defence — only honest presentation. The tolerant Christian can rest in the patience of God, who does not browbeat or coerce but seeks growth rather than blind obedience. Believers often see themselves as guardians, prepared to fight for the truth — but the truth can fend for itself. It cannot be enclosed in words or institutions to be defended against all comers.

The Church, in its passion for truth, has often demanded assent and been deaf to all criticism. It has gone out to do battle with its opponents but truth has often become the first casualty in the cut and thrust of doctrinal wars.

Conviction and openness are allies, not enemies, in matters of faith, just as in science and in the arts. They enable us to prove what is of worth, to share insight together and to grow in maturity. They allow the Gospel to become good news for others — winning over critics by its inherent appeal.

PROVISIONS

....

We don't have ideology, we don't have theology — we dance.   *A Shinto priest*

Let your religion be less of a theory and more of a love affair.   *G.K.Chesterton*

It is a mistake to assume that God is interested only, or even chiefly, in religion.
                                                                  William Temple

Religion is regarded by the common people as true, by the wise as false, and by rulers as useful.   *Seneca the Younger*

Religion is excellent stuff for keeping common people quiet.   *Napoleon*

Religion is the sigh of the oppressed creature, the feeling of a heartless world and the soul of soulless circumstance.   *Karl Marx*

All religions are the same. Religion is basically guilt with different holidays.
                                                                  Cathy Ladman

The echoes of our own prayers, wishes, laments, that come back to us from the brazen dome of an impersonal world as if they were voices from without.
                                                                  Benjamin Constant

What is natural is divine. What is supernatural is human.   *Max Müller*

True religion, being the greatest thing in life, has been exploited the most.   *Gandhi*

Fanaticism is a very common cause of madness. Most of the maniacal cases that come under my observation proceeded from religious enthusiasm.
                                   William Pargeter - 18C Anglican clergyman & psychiatrist

In science there is no meaning to anything.   *Per Bak*

A religion that is small enough for our understanding is not great enough for our need.
                                                                  A.J.Balfour

Among all my patients in the second half of life, there has not been one whose problem in the last resort was not that of finding a religious outlook on life.
                                                                  C.J.Jung

The fact of the religious vision is our one ground for optimism. Apart from it, human life is a flash of occasional enjoyments lighting up a mass of pain and misery.
                                                                  A N Whitehead

I have come that they may have life in all its richness.   *Jesus - Jn 10:10*

....

It has been said that the greatest contribution of the Hebrew to religion was to do away with it (John Macmurray). The difficulty with the word is that people go on using it. It defies definition and causes much confusion. Eastern languages don't even have a word for it and native Americans protest: *"We don't have a religion; we have a way of life".*

It may be associated with belief in God but you can be Buddhist or Confucian without a Western understanding of belief in God. It can usefully mean any system of meaning and value (*religio = 'that which binds' as in* <u>*ligament*</u>) — any web of ideas about the world and our place in it — which means that all thoughtful people are religious. We all have our ways of viewing the world and making some sense of it, even if there are gaps and contradictions in our outlook. Our optimism or pessimism, our opinions of ourselves and of our neighbours, our vision or our cynicism — this is our religion.When religion is separated from the rest of life or made merely external or confined to one part of us — then it merits the criticism and rejection illustrated in some of the quotations.

Whether or not it is seen to involve everyone, we should be freed from the need to defend all religion as good. It can be irrational and cruel or inspiring and kindly. And any one religion can include some of these elements.

It is unlikely that Jesus (or any other religious leader) set out to found a religion as such. His theme was life itself and his appeal was universal. For convenience, we set boundaries around each system but these are unreal. There is not only considerable overlap between religions but they have deep roots in what has gone before.

Many today prefer to use the term 'spirituality' which moves the focus from the external to the internal and does away with boundaries. Spirituality has a richness and warmth about it — it is both personal and easily shared. Its dangers are vagueness and indulgence. Rabbi Sacks has compared religion and spirituality to prose and poetry — reminding us that we do not spend our lives speaking poetry alone. Even as in marriage a framework of loyalty holds firm in difficult times, so the externals of religion may undergird true freedom of the spirit.

....

Religion is alright as long as it does not interfere with a man's private life.
Lord Melbourne

PROVISIONS

....

Alas we are driven to scale heights inaccessible, to strain our human language in the utterance of things beyond its scope - hence what should be matter for silent meditation must now needs be imperilled by exposure in words.

Hilary of Poitiers 4C

All I have written is as straw compared with what I have seen.　　　Aquinas

Words are fools, who follow blindly once they get a lead, but thoughts are kingfishers that haunt the pools of quiet; seldom seen.　　　Sassoon

How do I know what I think until I see what I say?　　　E.M.Forster

Everything we ever knew about the movement of the sea was preserved in the verses of a song. For thousands of years we went where we wanted and came home safe because of the song.　　　Nootka steerswoman

Sowing alone is not sufficient to make the maize germinate and grow; speech and song must be added, for it is the word that makes the grasses germinate, the fruits grow, the cow go in calf and give milk.

Janheinz Jahn - speaking of the Muntu people

Language isn't something we invented but something we became — something in which we are created and recreated ourselves.　　　Justin Leiber

The limits of my language are the limits of my world.　　　Wittgenstein

What is the prose for God?　　　Harley Granville-Barker

We have only earthenware in which to keep this treasure.　　　Paul - II Cor 4:7

....

We are bedevilled by the changing meaning of words. Consider these originals:
daft = innocent not deranged.
> *silly = simple but with no suggestion of stupidity.*
> *idiot = a private person, not a fool.*
> *pitiful = a person full of pity, not one to be pitied.*
> *— such changes constantly affect religious terminology.*

....

What a dreadful pity that the bother at the tower of Babel should have got language all mixed up, but for that, everyone would always have spoken French.　　　*- a lady overheard by Voltaire at Versailles.*

Language evolves. It is ever-changing, personal to each one of us, and it helps to define our experience. When that experience is profound, we are 'lost for words' and have to fall back on what is clearly inadequate, or keep silence.

Words can have different levels of meaning — appealing to both the intellect and the imagination. The truth conveyed can then be of different kinds; for example, the story of the Good Samaritan may be historically untrue yet deeply true in its teaching.

When we speak face to face, the tone, the inflection, the turn of the mouth, the raised eyebrow all help to interpret the words. The written word leaves a more limited record. Surely, for example, Jesus had a sense of humour; ordinary people were happy to listen to him, he was attractive to children and welcome at parties. He spoke of those who overlooked a camel floating in their soup (Mt 23:24) and laughingly mocked his fisherman disciples — 'you haven't even caught a tiddler!' (a literal translation of Jn 21:5).

We need to have a feel for the language of the time. It was deliberate hyperbole, but no more than that, which led Jesus to talk of a disciple needing to 'hate his mother and father, his wife and his children' (Lk 14:26). Even on the cross he showed concern for his own mother.

Some see an unbroken chain of God's revelation with the words guaranteed at each link: God speaks → the hearer understands the message → it is faithfully transmitted → it is written down accurately → it is translated faithfully → it is copied without mistakes →
it is understood correctly after the passage of centuries ....
No doubt God *could* do this but would God choose a different path from all other learning and knowledge? The treasure *can* be held in 'earthenware' — in fallible people — if God's Spirit is at work in us.

Christians believe in God's revelation in the person of Jesus. The words of the New Testament witness to the Word and he, in turn, is witness to the nature of God himself.

....

Imagine the Lord talking French! Aside from a few odd words in Hebrew, I took it completely for granted that God had never spoken anything but the most dignified English.
                                                                Clarence Day

....

Truth did not come into the world naked, but it came in types and images.
                                                          The Gospel of Philip

The Jews told in mythological images that which belies all mythology.
                                                          Leo Baeck

*The likeness of that which is below is to be found above, for everything is from above
and from below there is nothing.*   Odes of Solomon 1stC.AD

And don't believe in anything that can't be told in coloured pictures.
                                                          G.K.Chesterton

A picture may instantly present what a book could set forth in a hundred pages.
                                                          Turgenev

All thought is symbolic. Thought first constructs symbols, which it substitutes for things.
                                                          Henri Delacroix

*If I can't picture it, I can't understand it. Imagination is more important than
knowledge.*   Einstein

*Compared to the mind-bending ideas of modern science, religious beliefs are notable for
their lack of imagination.*   Steven Pinker

Many a night have I been practising to see.   William Herschel - astronomer.

*What is referred to as a conflict between science and religion is very often a conflict
between science and art.*   John Macmurray

Thank God I have no imagination.   Constable

Art, since it begins with the infinite, cannot progress.   Whistler

The fool sees not the same tree as the wise man sees.   William Blake

....

Science uses symbolism constantly — the universe as a 'sphere' or evolution
as a 'tree'. Like all symbols, they can mislead and must be understood for what
they are. When physicists want to study the structure of the atom, they use a
whole series of models, each useful for describing some aspects of its
behaviour. They treat it as if it were a gas confined to a small spherical
volume, as a drop of liquid, as a minute solar system, as a cloudy crystal ball,
and so on.   [see 146]

The streets of London were said to be paved with gold but we are more likely to find Yorkstone slabs. A great deal of language is symbolic but it's not always obvious to us. We know when we are on top of the world or down in the dumps, but we must remind ourselves what we mean if we talk of God as up, or think of him as out there. Judaism prohibited carved images of God but the mind holds its own images, and idolatry lurks round the corner unless we appreciate our own limitations. The deeper we delve into any area of knowledge, the more picturesque our language becomes.

Calvin described the early Genesis stories as 'baby-talk' [8-10]. The same thing could respectfully be said of much early science teaching — which in one sense has to be unlearned at university. At least science is better than theology at keeping a tight rein on its symbolism; too often religion seems to dissolve into the fairy-tale.

Culture matters a great deal. It is easy for a European to be lost in the crowded skies of Indian religion, so we cannot expect to enter easily the world of first century Palestine. Jesus' disciples found it hard at times to tell content from wrapping — 'Can you not see that I was not talking about bread?' says Jesus in Mtt 16:11. That is, he was using the word 'bread' in a symbolic way — and this, soon after the 'feeding' of the multitude [24]. He faced similar misunderstanding from Nicodemus when he talked of being born again — Jn 3:4 [42], and from his disciples when he spoke of swords —Lk 22:38.

How astonishing the charge made by Steven Pinker (opposite). Some Hebrews preferred the golden calf to the mystery of the unseen God (Gen 32/33), and people today readily 'literalise' — stripping down poetry and reducing it to prose. This ill prepares us for John's Gospel as he has no inhibitions when it comes to recruiting a parable or event to press home his message. He uses both the stories of the wedding at Cana and the cleansing of the temple with little regard for historical detail, because he wishes to show that Jesus reformed the religion of his day and brought new life into old truths.

Christian symbolism is embedded in the European imagination, for stained glass, frescoes and mystery plays were the bible of the poor and illiterate, needing to appeal to all the senses. Such symbols are rungs on a ladder that leads to understanding. They appeal to the heart and to the imagination. They should not be confused with rational explanation but nor should they be discarded lightly.

....

Derivation: symbol = 'to bring together'.

....

They saw God and ate and drank. Ex 24:11

Anyone who does not believe will not experience, and anyone who does not experience will not know. Anselm

Christianity is not plausible. One must become a Christian. Kierkegaard

We feel within us a being that is not ourselves; we see born within us real revelations that do not come from ourselves. Lemba (African)

I regard religious experience as a very risky thing to do, because it can destroy your brain. Marvin Minsky

I use emotion for the many and reserve reason for the few. Hitler

The strongest arguments prove nothing so long as the conclusions are not verified by experience. Roger Bacon

It did not suit God to save his people by arguments. Ambrose

All I have written seems to me like so much straw compared with what I have seen.
Thomas Aquinas - on finishing the 'Summa Theologica'

All I know is: I was blind and now I can see. Jn 9:25

"The brush in my hand, my dustpan, the stairs, seemed to come alive with love. I seemed no longer me, with my petty troubles, but part of this infinite power of love, so utterly and overwhelmingly wonderful that one knew at once what the saints had grasped"
The Religious Experience Research Unit

One of thousands of records held at Oxford University. The unit was founded by the biologist Sir Alister Hardy. He believed that data supplied through human consciousness is vital to true biology. He found 'religious' experience to be common inside and outside of the churches and across a wide diversity of people. It often showed the following :

- an element of surprise — encountered in the ordinary
- a sense of unity with all that is — a feeling of eternity
- a sense of awe before a greater presence
- a deep sense of joy and peace
- a certainty of spiritual reality
- freedom from fear — even the fear of death.

Although the experience usually lasted for a few moments, the feelings associated with it stayed long after. A sense of faith and purpose was carried over into the rest of life. This often led to practical service for others.

The wilder shores of religion are alive with strange happenings — dramatic conversions, charismatic phenomena and mystical ecstasy. These defy easy analysis and explanation. Because they may lead us astray, we seek the safety of cold logic and calculating reason, hoping that these will help us to be more objective.

We have always to decide whether to trust or distrust our experience and maybe it is wise to do both. We can add checks and balances — comparing our experience with others for example — but ultimately we cannot deny ourselves. The experience of love or wonder may come *before* understanding or it may follow *from* understanding.

Whether all experience is supplied by our environment, or whether it can be created from within, is much debated. Some philosophers of the mind (including classical Buddhists) deny that there is a unifying personality at all and it has been suggested today that consciousness is an evolutionary quirk — 'due to imperfections in our hard-wiring' (Dennet and others). We are also faced with parallels to mystical experience, which have clearly been induced with the help of drugs or caused by brain disorders.

Christians, together with the followers of other world faiths, discover an inner world every bit as real as that which is without. This is the realm of the Spirit, where God is more likely to touch our lives than by intervening from without. The San people of the Kalahari have two special dances; one — *the Dance of the Little Hunger* — expresses the life-long need for food; the other — *the Dance of the Great Hunger* — speaks of the need for spiritual fulfilment — for that 'which neither the food of the earth nor the way of life possible upon it can satisfy' (Laurens van der Post).

The sense we have is more than 'mere' feeling — it is a drive to seek the infinite: to discover 'God within'. St Francis, Meister Eckhart, Julian of Norwich, Ignatius of Loyola and Teresa of Avila are but a few of the Christian mystics who have sought to make this inner pilgrimage. Others of more practical bent concentrate on living out the Christian life and finding its validity in the fruit it bears.

....

You should make a point of trying every experience once, except incest and folk-dancing.
                                                                                                    Scots - anon.

THE JEWISH SCRIPTURES

The Holy Scripture, is as a whole, rough-hewn, unfinished, and unsystematic; it preserves the 'fragments of a great confession'.
Leo Baeck - quoting Goethe's reference to his own work.

I take the Bible too seriously to take it literally.
Karl Barth

Now I don't know if it happened this way or not but I know the story is true.
- a native American storyteller

The earliest writings of the Tenakh (the Old Testament) are not placed first, although early fragments may be included within the books - e.g. Miriam's Song in Ex 15.

The first five books contain the Torah — the Jewish **LAW** and the bedrock principles which were the foundation of all else. These are the laws of a nation tailored for different times and circumstances but the values remain.

The books which follow (Samuel, Kings, Chronicles) outline crucial parts of Jewish **HISTORY,** with tales of heroism and shame told with unusual honesty.

The **PSALMS** are the songs of the people — a hymnbook drawn from many generations.

JOB is a powerful poetic drama on the theme of suffering.

The **SONG OF SONGS** is love poetry and **LAMENTATIONS** a cry of grief.

Proverbs and Ecclesiastes are **WISDOM literature** of down to earth practicalities and philosophic reflection.

DANIEL is subversive literature, coded in imagery, to encourage stiffer resistance against an invader.

Much of the rest records the teaching of the **PROPHETS** (Isaiah, Jeremiah etc.) who continually recalled the people and their leaders from legalism and ritual to the claims of justice and mercy.

The **APOCRYPHA** ('hidden') refers to books not originally included in the Hebrew canon. These are later writings and 11 of them were incorporated in the Roman Catholic Bible in 1546.

The doors of interpretation are not closed.
Maimonides

Words: **oral** = *spoken.*
scripture = *writing.*
manuscript = *hand written.*
canon = *a rule or reed used for measuring.*
Bible = *books - from Byblos where papyrus was harvested to make paper.*

The Hebrew traditions were forged in the desert, the wilderness, the open country. At times they evoked a world of freedom and compassion; at other times they are dogged by superstition and savagery.God help us if we have to take everything as the very word of God. In earlier days, these were oral traditions. They were encapsulated in poetry, songs, stories and memorable sayings. The identity of the people and the education of their children depended on the finely trained memories of the storytellers.

When the traditions came to be written down, the scriptures became the record of the faith, hopes and fears of a nation. The Jewish scriptures are the literature of a whole people.

Both oral and written material could be shaped and re-shaped time and again. Original manuscripts rarely survive and those we have are marked by a long process of copying, editing and translating. This does not render the material valueless — but it does mean that the reflections of those who came later are embedded in the tradition. Today we use all the resources of linguists and historians to aid our understanding of the texts and to uncover these layers of meaning.

In time, a people or community often agree on the 'canon' of writings which carry most authority for them. The Jewish canon was probably confirmed at Jamnia in AD90.

Although the Christian church helped to preserve the great heritage of Jewish literature and values it as Christian scripture also, it does not own it — it remains the literature of the Jewish people, to be used with respect, discrimination and thankfulness. Christians can only gain by sitting at the feet of Jewish scholars. [see 161]

It is a profound mistake to approach these writings as though they should speak with one voice. All human life is to be found there — faith and despair, love and hate, generosity and jealousy, certainty and doubt. It should be no surprise, therefore, to find different views of God expressed, reflecting the tumult of this varied experience. There is, nevertheless, a growing understanding of human life and of God's claim upon all humanity. God speaks to us in many ways and through many voices.

....

If you knew the whole Bible by heart, what would it profit you without the love of God?
Thomas à Kempis

....

God created earth and sky. The earth was desolate, darkness was everywhere, and God's spirit hovered over the water.   *Gen 1:1*

The solid stable world of matter appears to be sustained by an underlying sea of quantum light.   *Bernard Haisch - astrophysicist*

Bewildered at empty space, I ask the great grey earth: who controls the rise and fall?   *Mao Tse-Tung*

Then even nothingness was not, nor existence.
The One breathed windlessly and self sustaining.
There was One then, and there was no other.
At first there was only darkness wrapped in darkness.
All this was only unillumined water.
That One which came to be, enclosed in nothing,
arose at last, born of the power of heat.
In the beginning desire descended on it —
that was the primal seed, born of the mind.
But after all, who knows, and who can say
whence it all came, and how creation happened?   *The Rig Veda - c1500 BC*

When sweet and bitter mingled together, no reed was planted, no rushes muddied the water, the gods were nameless, natureless, futureless.
        Babylonian - c.1200 BC

We cannot profound into the hidden things of nature, nor see the first springs and wheels that set the rest a-going.   *Joseph Glanville - 1665*

A supreme intellect has monkeyed with the physics.   *Frederick Hoyle*

The world originates from Brahman by thought.   *Sankara - Hindu*

The universe can be best pictured, although still very imperfectly and inadequately, as consisting of pure thought – the thought of what we must describe ... as a mathematical thinker .... its creation must have been an act of thought.
        James Jeans - astronomer

God suspends the earth in empty space.   *Job 26:7*

If there be but one righteous man, the world is granted its existence.
        Rabbi Yohanan

....

God is alive – he just doesn't want to get involved anymore.   *... graffiti*

Two stories of creation are brought together in Genesis — the first ends at 2:3. They are not artless stories but vehicles for profound teaching and they used the imagery (often Babylonian) which lay to hand. The first speaks of an evolving creation, using 'days' as periods of time (just as we might speak of 'stages' of evolution, even though we don't imagine the world to be a building). Other images include water to represent chaos, wind for the spirit of God (the words are the same in Hebrew) and seven days representing fulfilment

Though the story may be influenced by ancient parallels, like the Mesopotamian story of *Enuma Elish*, the teaching is significantly different in that:
> - there is one sovereign, creating God
> - the sun and moon are not gods but part of the created order
> - the world is not sacred but created and functional
> - all creation is good (some believed that matter is evil)
> - God's power is of a different order to human creativity (emphasised by the words 'Let there be ...')
> - humanity — male and female — has particular significance.

[see 104]

Further notes:

> - Creation includes the making of space and time.
> - The word translated 'hovered' (in v.2) implies quivering or vibrating. It can be compared with the first ripples before the Big Bang or the concept of OM in Hinduism.
> *"God sings out his creation in sounds and rhythms".*   Jurgen Moltmann
> - A day of 24 hours was reckoned from dusk — so 'evening and morning' rather than 'morning and evening'.
> - The 'vault' imagery seems to reflect belief in a solid sky, with rain coming through the 'windows of heaven', as well as up from the springs of the ground. We should *not* assume that the original storytellers took this literally.
> - The repetitions remind us that this was poetry — and not straight history. In fact, the order of events is close to what we believe today. No doubt the storyteller would be happy to re-arrange the fourth day, as it is the teaching that is important not the framework. (The 'lights' may be placed here because of their significance in ordering the agricultural seasons.)
> - In v.26 the phrase 'let us make' may be a remnant of a polytheistic story or, more likely, is a conventional way of talking of the court of heaven.

....

It will no longer be said, 'Parents have eaten sour grapes and the children's teeth jar'.
Everyone will be answerable for his own wrong doing.   Jeremiah - 31:29

Because of their sin, no one will have a sure hold on life.   Isaiah - 7:13

They pretend to be wise but they have made fools of themselves.   Paul - Rom 1:22

I could be bounded in a nutshell and count myself a king of infinite space were it not
that I have bad dreams.   Shakespeare - Hamlet

Until we know that we exist in our own right, we can't make our way in the world at
all, yet this really is the basic error of us all: that in truth man is one with the universe
and until he achieves that wholeness and re-absorption, he is never fully aware of what
he is or what life is.   David Stafford-Clark

The line separating good and evil passes right through every heart.
       Alexander Solzhenitsyn

....

The Garden of Eden - Gen 2:4 - 3:24.

And who is so stupid as to imagine that God planted a garden in Eden eastward, and put in it a
tree of life, which could be seen and felt?

       Origen 3C

The *serpent* is associated with both wisdom and temptation but also with rebirth and
therefore immortality — because it sloughs its skin. It is not here identified with the
devil.
The *tree of life* (note that there are 2 trees) may symbolise that true life/eternal life is not
possible until the earlier stages of creation have been won through.
Nakedness is a symbol of innocence. It is only when alienated from God that shame
enters the story and humans are also alienated from themselves. There is no suggestion
that sexuality is the problem.
The story is clearly edited and re-edited from older material, some drawn from other
cultures.

Evil came about because of the imperfections of a world in the making, rather than
because of the fall of an originally perfect cosmos.   Irenaeus 2C

....

The whole trouble with you is you won't listen to what the whole trouble with
you is.   *Lucy in the Peanuts cartoon - Schultz.*

"Adam. where are you?

The answer is both "hidden in the garden" and "staring at us in the mirror" These early stories in Genesis are part of a marvellous inheritance. There is artistry, imagination and insight here and, to be honest, not a little ambiguity and uncertainty. We have more than one layer of text and more than one layer of meaning.

Think of it as a house. Starting in the basement, there are fragments of 'Aesop-type' questions: *how did snakes lose their legs? why do we wear clothes? how did everything begin? why are things not as they should be? why do we die?* A succession of such questions will lead to the hoariest of all — where did Cain's wife come from?

Better to leave them to it and escape to the ground floor, where exploration is more profitable. At this level, we can take it as a straightforward story but it is worth noticing what is *not* said. The snake, which was both feared and reverenced in the Middle East, is not identified with the devil. Work is not seen as punishment, for Adam is first given the garden to till. The male is not depicted as superior to the female, for this deformed relationship is seen as one of the consequences of the rift between humanity and God.

On that ground floor level, it does seem that we are dealing with the first human couple but we can ascend to another level, as the storyteller is no mean artist and clearly gives permission to explore more deeply. He does this by giving the man a representative name: 'Adam' means 'humanity' and has the same root meaning as 'dust'. 'Eve' may mean 'life'. Then there are the trees with symbolic, not botanical, names and the great rivers suggest that the garden may represent the known, inhabited world. (The 'Gihon' is the Nile.)

We are not therefore talking of distant history, or of a primal catastrophe, but humanity as it is before God. We are Adam and Eve — we all experience temptation but we court danger when we no longer respect God's created order and try to redefine good and evil to suit ourselves — forgetting that God 'has the final word'. Then we have to live with the consequences — illustrated in Genesis by the distortion of the marriage relationship and the abuse of the earth itself. In Hebrew thought, everything that happens is ascribed *directly* to God, whatever the intervening causes. We can amend this and say that: when alienated from God, we exile ourselves from each other, and from our environment — we 'cast ourselves out of the garden'.

PTO

FALLING SHORT

If we approach the story of Eden with a prosaic mind, we find ourselves in collision with the scientific understanding that there has never been a world without desire and death, devouring and being devoured. But we have not fallen from an idyllic state. The story is applicable to every time — this is the human predicament. We could say that we are still being created. As Paul says:

"Up to the present, as we know, the whole created universe in all its parts groans as if in the pangs of childbirth."   – Rom 8:22

Some Christians will be upset at this point, because this clearly calls into question a historical 'Fall'. In this teaching, there is an age of harmony, then an act of human disobedience, and then a lost humanity until Jesus redeems the world and salvation can come.
Some of today's 'worship songs' enshrine this of travesty of God's work in history:

            "The world was in darkness in sin and in shame;
               mankind was lost and then Jesus came."

The doctrine of the Fall is not scriptural but largely originated with the thinking of Augustine, who lived over 300 years after Jesus. Augustine relied on a misleading translation of Rom 5:12. This reading forces the conclusion that all human beings were made to sin because Adam sinned. The true translation should read: *"death came to all humanity because all have sinned"* — it is not that 'Adam' caused everyone to fail. Adam and Eve are already mortal — it is spiritual death that threatens. A truer Christian perspective rests on the teaching of Jesus, where there is no idea of a Fall but there is an understanding, both stern and compassionate, of human failings.

Better to drop the idea of a Fall and to say what we mean. To sin — as the Hebrew word implies — is to fall short, even as an arrow falls short of its target. We may or may not be to blame. What we do is partly determined by others or by our past but we are always able to answer God's questioning 'where are you?'. God is creating real people. Note that he does not curse the couple — he clothes and resettles them!

[see 35, 111]

The issue of evolution will concern us later but let us first sum up the main themes of the stories — that God is creator of all that is, that the world is fundamentally good, that it may be used but that there are serious implications for us if we abuse what is given.

....

Cain and Abel

The Lord asked Cain, 'Where is your brother Abel?'
'I don't know', Cain answered. 'Am I responsible for him?'
The Lord said, 'What have you done?'   *Gen 4:1-16*

The story of Eden is not isolated. We are invited to ponder a world out of
joint, raw and immature. In the story of Cain and Abel, the brothers are
representative figures (so it is idle to ask where Cain's wife came from!).
The classic themes of jealousy, murder and guilt see a family destroyed
and society threatened. The very ground again seems cursed and yet it is
not God that curses Cain. The punishment is real but the often misquoted
mark of Cain is a protective one — the guilty are not beyond the pale in
God's sight.

Here also is the age-old clash of hunter and settler, herdsman and farmer.
How many times have we seen wire strung across the prairie as the day of
Cain supplants that of Abel? Possibly too, there is allusion to human
sacrifice — of blood spilled into the ground to ensure fertility. This is
human life — raw and divisive — far from the peace of Eden.

The Flood

Noah was a good man, the one blameless man of his time, and he walked with
God. God saw that the world was corrupt and full of violence and said to Noah, 'I
am going to make an end of the whole human race'.
                                        Gen 6:5 - 9:17
The storytellers move on to speak of global destruction. Perhaps there were
folk memories of a disaster (one line of research has shown that the waters
of the Black Sea rose 6' a day for 2 years around 5,600 BC) but, if so, these
are taken up into a greater theme. Has the earth a future? Can evil threaten
creation itself? The waters take on a new destructive meaning, as the
consequences of sin seem to overwhelm the order set by God. In the
beginning, chaos — symbolised by water — was set at bay in the story of
creation. Now, it is unleashed again — compare Gen 1:7 and 7:11.

We who have feared a nuclear holocaust might well use different imagery
but the questions still confront us. The storyteller puts his faith in God.
Although at first sight it is God who seems to permit (and therefore decree)
total destruction, it becomes clear that, on the contrary, he is working to
save all that is good. Not only the line of humanity itself but also

the whole living world is safeguarded — as symbolised by the rainbow. Understanding this as a parable not only disposes of the literalist problems but also avoids the demeaning view of a god who bungles his creation the first time round, then destroys most of humanity, and finally discovers that Noah's line is no better than that which went before.

The Tower of Babel

They said, 'Let us build a city and a tower that fills the sky, then we will be famous'. And God came to see the city and tower.   *Gen 11:1-9*

Undaunted, the editors now include the story of the tower of Babel. This late story is likely to have been modelled on the city of Babylon and its, great tower, which was the seat of imperial and religious authority. The Israelites had been exiled to Babylon and the tower, for them, was the symbol of tyranny. The question this time was, 'Are there limits to human injustice — to the arrogance which seems to challenge God himself. The answer implies that the very evils on which tyranny is reared — greed, rivalry, suspicion, fear and pride — will ensure its downfall. An old fable about the origin of languages is pressed into service to symbolise the themes of unity and disunity.

['Babylon' = 'The Gate of God' — akin to the Hebrew 'Bethel'.]

~~~~~~~~~~

We can now trace the common threads. It is *our* story, that is being told — we choose between Eden and Babel. The destructive potential is there to shatter human community and threaten God's purpose, but evil cannot stand against good. It is a 'kingdom at odds with itself'.. Jesus - Lk 11:17.
....

You may come this far but here your surging waves must stop.
        God speaking of the sea (the realm of chaos) — in Job *38:11*

Cautionary note:
All such interpretations as these are speculative. What we do know is that the stories are not the earliest texts in the Bible and that the Babylonian stories on which they draw are highly symbolic. We also know that the stories of today's primitive (first) peoples are rich in meaning. I would claim that the above are closer to the originals than the literalist interpretations so often fed to us.

These scriptures are full of great stories. They fill the pages of children's books but are rarely explained. A brief look at three more is in order.

Parting the Red Sea   Ex 14:15f.

Strictly, the 'reed sea' — shallow lakes, where 'a strong east wind' can make a difference and where the chariots of the Pharaoh can get bogged down. The story has grown in the telling and why not? The miracle is in the man. Moses, with his Egyptian upbringing and desert skills takes advantage of natural disasters stemming from the failing Nile waters. We can dismiss the desolate view of a God who is motivated by destructive revenge. Later rabbinic comment has God silencing the celebrations over the Egyptian dead with the words: *"Were not these my children too?"* This is also the message of —

Jonah and the Whale   — see the book

It's always good to start at the end. God has compassion on the people of Nineveh. This is the great capital of the oppressor, and Jonah, despite being God's messenger, wants nothing to do with them. The whale may represent the forces of chaos from old legends or the ruin that has overtaken Israel or maybe simply a device for getting Jonah to the right place! Whatever the detail, the book is a blast against exclusive nationalism and a triumphant assertion of the universality of God.

The Fiery Furnace & the Lions' Den   Daniel 3 & 6

This is *samizdat* literature, akin to that produced in Stalin's Soviet Union to attack his tyranny. Ostensibly the writings appeared to be historical, dealing with Peter the Great or other figures from the past. In fact, as many would realise, they were dealing with contemporary issues. The writer of Daniel uses fragments of history but, for Nebuchadnezzar, read Antiochus IV, who ruled Judaea after the break-up of Alexander the Great's empire. He proscribed Jewish worship, desecrated the Temple, made circumcision illegal and hunted down anyone who resisted. These events provoked the wars of the Maccabees. The message of the book is apparent — stand firm, face persecution, endure and God will be with you through the fire.

Such interpretations are hardly new to scholars. Why then, are so many churchgoers left in ignorance?

Listen, O Israel: God is one; and you must love the Lord your God with your whole being — all your heart and all your soul and all your strength.

Deut 6:4 (& see Ex 20)

1. You shall have no other gods.
    — there can only be one ultimate reality.

2. You shall not make a carved image.
    — i.e. to worship. All images of God necessarily diminish him.

3. You shall not make wrong use of the name of God.
    — condemning all hypocrisy and the abuse of religion for lesser ends.

4. Remember to keep the sabbath day.
    — as a sign that work should not dominate life and that time should be set aside to appreciate life's richness, enjoy God's creation and realise our human partnership with God as the key to fulfilment.

5. Honour your father and your mother.
    — ensuring that the gifts of each generation are passed on to the next.

6. Do not commit murder.
    — safeguarding human life. Hebrew has one word only for kill / murder. The latter is assumed here because the laws allowed for capital punishment.

7. Do not commit adultery.
    — to protect family life and personal integrity.

8. Do not steal.
    — because this places material things above human relationships.

9. Do not give false evidence.
    — prohibiting perjury and therefore safeguarding justice. It can equally cover slander and racist abuse.

10. Do not covet.
    — true contentment must abandon envy.

....

The way that I have set out for you is not too difficult for you or out of reach. It is not way above your heads so that you say, 'Who will explain it to us so that we can keep it?' It is not far off so that you say; 'Who will find it for us?' It is very near to you, on your lips and in your heart ready to be kept.

Deut 30:11

.... the Hebrew speaks of 'words' rather than 'commandments'

1. I am the reality behind all that you know. Know me, the source of your life, and you will discover yourself and much else besides.

2. Do not misunderstand or misrepresent me. Face up to the mystery of my being. I am far greater than you imagine. When you are ready I will reveal myself to you.

3. You are invited to share in my purpose. In its fulfilment you will be fulfilled but do not try to use me for your purposes. In betraying me, you will betray yourself.

4. Make time for all that life has to offer. Do not allow the routine of every day to narrow your horizons.

5. Honour your parents. The future can only be built on the past. You will not always agree with them but love must begin at home.

6. Value human life — for what it is and for what it can become.

7. Marriage is the deepest relationship you can enter. Be true to it. It can enrich your life and make society strong.

8. Respect property for in so doing you respect others. Share the gifts I have given.

9. Justice is the framework, that makes love possible. Never lose sight of the truth or you will lose your way.

10. Practise contentment. Envy will sour your relationships and take away your own happiness.

I have given you freedom to choose that you might become strong and enjoy what is good. Do not be surprised that I, who made you, know your needs, and do not take these words lightly lest you destroy yourself.

....

Moses was educated in Egypt and may have used earlier law codes in establishing the principles of a new nation. The codes do not have to be literally written by God for them to be God-given.

If you wish to know real life, keep the commandments.

***Jesus** - Mtt 19:17* [see 34 & 49]

....

*Leave your own country, your relatives and your ancestral home and go to a country
that I will show you.*   God to Abraham - Gen 12:1

Go, lift up the child, and hold him in your arms — I shall make him a great nation.
                                              God's promise concerning Ishmael - Gen 21:18

You have not held back your son, your only son.
                                                          God to Abraham - Gen 22:12

*You shall no longer be Jacob (he supplants), but Israel (God fights), because you have
striven with God and with men and you have prevailed.*   Gen 32:28

Who am I, that I should be able to bring the Israelites out of Egypt?
                                                              Moses to God - Ex 3:11

Warn them and tell what such a king will be like.
                                                          God to Samuel - I Sam 8:9

*Once Saul had made his throne safe, he fought his enemies on all sides and everywhere
he was victorious.*   I Sam 14:47

Saul conquered thousands, but David tens of thousands.   I Sam 18:7

David grew more and more powerful, for God was with him.   II Sam 5:10

Would that I had died instead of you! O Absalom, my son, my son!
                                      David mourns the son who rebelled against him - II Sam 18:33

Your wisdom and your prosperity far surpass all that I had heard.
                          The Queen of Sheba (southern Arabia) to King Solomon - IKings 10:7

....

Even though I walk in deepest darkness,
I will not be afraid of anything,
For you are with me,
Your club and your crook give me strength.
I will always find generous hospitality
And a welcome with you.   **Ps 23**

*The 23rd Psalm is believed to have been written by David when he was being hunted
down by Saul.*

....

Christians and Muslims as well as Jews look to **Abraham.** He was a tribal chief and semi-nomad, whose family travelled from the flood plains of modern Iraq towards Egypt. His outward journeying was not unusual but he also represents an inner pilgrimage from the moon cult of Mesopotamia to the high monotheism of the Hebrews — a pilgrimage marked by his absolute trust in God.

Perhaps it was that high monotheism which allowed the Hebrew storytellers to record the faith and follies of their ancestors with such honesty. Abraham is not idealised — he exposes his wife to humiliation and does grave injustice to his first son, **Ishmael,** and his slave mother. His faith in God is dangerously fundamentalist, when he is prepared to sacrifice his son and heir, **Isaac,** yet he is generous to his nephew, **Lot,** compassionate towards the stricken city of Sodom and he becomes the founder father of a people's faith.

The Hebrew line is traced through Isaac to **Jacob,** but the shadow brother, Ishmael, is still given a future in the purpose of God and Arab peoples look back to Abraham through him. Jacob too is no saint, cheating his brother of the inheritance and sowing future tragedy by his preference for **Joseph** among his own sons.

In the years ahead, first Joseph, and then the whole people, experience slavery, until their liberation under the leadership of **Moses.** This great but reluctant leader uses providential disasters and the knowledge gained from his Egyptian upbringing to confound the Pharaoh and then goes on to lay the foundations of a new nation.

The exodus from Egypt and the harsh life of the desert forge a unique understanding of one God, which the later trappings of civilisation threaten, but never destroy. Military success and the desire to be like other nations lure the Hebrew people into establishing a monarchy.

The first king — **Saul** — was a good military leader but became unstable, and destructively jealous of **David** who later succeeded him. David was cast in heroic mould and created a new kingdom with its capital in Jerusalem. He was capable of great wrong but inspired great loyalty. Politically speaking, this was a golden age in Jewish history. David's son — **Solomon** — brought even greater wealth and power through his control of the rich trade routes which crossed this strategic area but his autocratic and oppressive regime brought unrest and civil wars, which began a long period of decline.

....

God has spoken, how can I keep silent? Amos - 3:8

If I say, I will not speak for him any more, then I find that my very soul is on fire and I cannot help myself. Jeremiah - 20:9

Why did I come out of the womb to see only sorrow and hardship, and to end my days in shame? Jeremiah - 20:18

Can horses gallop across boulders? Can the sea be ploughed with oxen? Yet you have made justice into a destroyer. Amos - 6:12

When Israel was a youth I loved him; I called my son out of Egypt. Hos 11:1

Your rulers are criminals and associate with thieves. They love to be bribed. They deny the rights of orphans and ignore the widow's plea. Isaiah - 1:23

Spare me your songs; I cannot endure your music. Let fairness be spread like a river in flood and justice sweep down like a torrent. Amos - 5:23

Even if you defeat the whole Chaldean army, and only the wounded are left lying in their tents, even they will rise and fire this city. Jeremiah - 37:10

By his suffering my servant will bring many to God — he shall see the result of his work and be content. Isaiah - 53:11

A branch will grow from the stump of Jesse, and a fresh shoot will spring from his roots. On him the spirit of the Lord will rest. Isaiah - 11:1
(.... Jesse is the father of David.)

They will no longer need to teach one another to know the Lord. All of them, from the highest to the lowest will know me, says the Lord. All wrongdoing shall be forgiven and all sin forgotten. Jeremiah - 31:34

Act justly, live kindly, and walk humbly before God. Micah - 6:8

There will be no hurt or harm in all my holy mountain; for the land will be as full of the knowledge of the Lord, as the waters cover the sea.
Isaiah - 11:9

Dry bones, hear God's word. I will put breath into you and you will live.
Ezek 37:4

....

The prophets are the glory of Israel. Lacking status and pedigree, driven by their calling, they speak for God to the conscience of the nation. No king or queen can be above censure, no injustice lie hidden and no religious authority can escape scrutiny, as long as there is a prophetic voice in the land. The prophets often came from among ordinary people and spoke for them — becoming the voice of the voiceless. They brought deep insight and vivid imagery to their preaching. Sometimes they become visionaries of the future but their message was first and foremost powerfully contemporary.

1050 BC - **Samuel** established the vital role of conscience in matters
of faith.
1000 BC - **Nathan** was prepared to challenge even King David when
he broke the laws of God.
850 BC - **Elijah** called for a faith founded on national justice.
750 BC - **Amos** vehemently upheld the rights of the poor.
750 BC - **Hosea** out of his own family crisis came to a deeper
understanding of the love of God.
700 BC - **Micah** attacked economic and religious abuse.
700 BC - **Isaiah** spoke of God's judgement and holiness.
600 BC - **Jeremiah** saw God's judgement and promise in the rise
and fall of nations.
600 BC - **Ezekiel** proclaimed the hope of national renewal.
550 BC - a later prophet looked to the coming of the Servant of God
— his writings are included in the collection we know as 'Isaiah', particularly
ch.40-55.

No other nation can furnish such voices. Uncomfortable men, with psychic intensity, they held faith and action together despite the loneliness, persecution and doubt that they often suffered. They compelled a hearing, often using visible signs — Jeremiah wore a cattle yoke round his neck to signify inevitable defeat at the hands of imperial power. Yet he — known since as the 'prophet of doom'— bought a field as a sign of hope when the nation lay in ruins.

Although passionately bound up with their own people, the prophets also rise to a vision of the whole world brought into the purpose of God — with the Philistines, Egyptians and Persians also seen as God's servants. The later chapters of Isaiah picture one ideal servant — *a light to lighten the Gentiles* — being the nation or individual, yet to come, through whom all nations would be blessed.

THE CHRISTIAN SCRIPTURES

Do you not know that so much reading of Scripture ruins the Catholic religion?
Pope Paul V to the Venetian ambassador.

But, if you want to risk it, which text is the right one?

EDITING: Biblical writings are often compiled from various sources. For example, Matthew used Mark's Gospel and added fresh material. Teaching like the Sermon on the Mount was pieced together and set in a typical situation. Luke adds much of the same teaching to Mark but it is more interspersed with narrative and contains more of the parables.

ADDITIONS: Mark 16:9-20 appears to have been added to Mark's Gospel sometime later — perhaps to replace a lost ending. Jn 7:53 — 8:11 seems to be a free-floating tradition which appears elsewhere (or nowhere) in different manuscripts.

DISCREPANCIES: Among many discrepancies are those in the genealogies - Mt 1 and Lk 3:23; in the list of disciples - Mt 10:2 and Lk 6:13; and in the Beatitudes - Mt 5:3 and Lk 6:20.

MISTAKES: e.g. Mt 27:9 refers to Jeremiah but the quotation is from Zechariah.

MISTRANSLATION: Lk 16:23 was translated 'compel them to come in' and this was used by Augustine to justify compulsion in religion, but Jewish scholars judge that the original should be translated 'urge them to come in'.

READING BACK: It must be questionable whether Jesus spoke the words in Jn 10:8 and in Mt 25:41, considering that he prayed for his enemies from the cross. Mt 18:17 also seems out of keeping and Jn 8:44 could well reflect Jewish-Christian hostility from a later period.

PARABLE? The cursing of the fig tree — Mt 11:12-14 + 20-24 — appears to be a miracle out of all proportion, and not in tune with the rest of the record. Luke omits it but does relate a parable which could have been mistaken for a factual account — Lk 13:6f.

IN OR OUT? The Christian canon rested on finely balanced judgements made in the 4th and 5th centuries AD. In fact there has never been complete agreement among the churches as to which books should be included in the Bible.

....

When the Spirit comes, he will help you to know the truth.   *Jn 16:13*

The New Testament, like the Old, is a collection of books but whereas the Jewish scriptures originate over several centuries, the Christian writings span scarce 50 years. **Paul's letters** came first, with the earliest around 50AD. **Mark** is probably the first gospel and both **Matthew** and **Luke** use it in addition to other sources. **Acts** appears to be a sequel to Luke's gospel. **John** was written years later and offers a distinctive interpretation of Jesus' life. **Revelation** uses the imagery of Daniel and reflects a time of persecution. It is coded literature akin to the underground 'samizdat' of the Soviet Union.

These writings are in the Greek spoken at the time but show some traces of the Aramaic that was Jesus' native tongue.

Authorship is problematic. A disciple of John, for example, would not wish to put his own name to a gospel that drew on John's teaching. It became urgent to write more down when it was realised that Jesus was not returning immediately and that the apostles would not be alive for much longer.

Translation is a difficult art. There are shifting meanings, even within a language, and no translator can capture every shade of meaning. The New Testament was translated from Greek to Latin to English. Modern English translations work directly from the Greek but try to take account of Aramaic and Hebrew idioms.

Parts of the scriptures have now been published in over 2,000 languages.

There is no cause for dismay in the textual difficulties outlined here. God is not baulked by human fallibility. On the contrary, if the scriptures were uniform, their authenticity would be in doubt. *The letter can kill — it is the Spirit which gives life (see IICor 3:6).*
God works then and now in human lives. *We are the text.* We can respect scripture whilst approaching it with honesty, making allowances for the limitations of the writers and of ourselves The Bible has been subject to the most meticulous and searching examination ever given to any sources. It can be approached critically and yet remain a profound source of inspiration.

If the King's English was good enough for our Lord and Saviour, Jesus Christ, it's good enough for our kids.   *A Tennessee State legislator.*

THE CHRISTIAN SCRIPTURES

....

Many writers have tried to draw up an account of the events that have taken place among us — and so I, in my turn, as one who has researched the whole course of these events in detail, have decided to write the story for you, your Excellency, in the proper order.   *Luke - introducing his gospel.*

He knew how to distil truth from fact.   *Emile Rieu - speaking of Luke*

All inspired scripture has its use for teaching the truth.   *Paul - II Tim 3:16*
(speaking of the Jewish scriptures, as the New Testament did not yet exist.)

The Lord has more light and truth yet to break out of his holy Word.
John Robinson, pastor - parting words to the Pilgrim Fathers 1620.

There is as much healing power in a Beethoven sonata as in some excerpts from the Bible.   *George Bernard Shaw*

Many psalms are left out as highly improper for the mouths of a Christian congregation.
John Wesley - issuing an expurgated Psalter.

If only the farmer with his hand on the plough sang some of it to himself, the weaver said something of it to the beat of the loom, and the traveller shortened his way with stories of this kind!   *Erasmus, translator*

The Bible is government of the people, by the people, for the people.
John Wycliffe, translator - who originated this phrase

No women, prentices, journeymen, servingmen, husbandmen nor labourers shall read the Bible.   *- decreed in England - 1543*

If God spare my life, ere many years I will cause a boy that driveth the plough shall know more of the Scriptures than thou dost.
William Tyndale, translator (martyred 1536) - to a fellow priest

Veda is eternal: the creator causes seers to see them, perfect in all their sounds and accents.   *Ramanuja - concerning the Hindu scriptures*

The history, the lives and the cultures of the indigenous peoples are God's first book. The Bible is God's second book, given to help us read the first.
Pablo Richard Consilium 20C.

....

Arguments about scripture achieve nothing but a headache.
Tertullian, theologian - 160-220 AD.

Jesus used the Jewish scriptures to nourish his own faith and yet he clearly sifted them to sort the wheat from the chaff. His attitude was one of critical reverence — with the authority of tradition measured against the authority of his own relationship with God — an authority which enabled him to say, 'but I am telling you ...'.

Paul's words to Timothy are an echo of Genesis 2:7, where God breathes into humanity the breath of life — that is He 'inspires'. All inspiration is of God — the artist, the musician, the scientist and the prophet — all draw from the same source. Many conservative Christians, place enormous and unjustified weight on this text, believing that inspiration brings the assurance that someone or something cannot err. Would that it were so! Apart from this, they argue from the particular to the general using passages like Mk 7:5-13. They ignore the qualifications that Jesus himself makes to his scriptures, for they long for the kind of certainty that most Muslims find in the Qur'an or the Mormons find in the Book of Mormon.

The Bible is a record of human searching and discovering — and a record too of God revealing himself in human experience. It is not itself the word of God but God's word can be heard through human words.

A Swiss Calvinist declaration of 1675 affirmed that the very grammar and vowel pointings of the Bible were divinely certified. With such a belief, some see themselves to be on safe ground, otherwise we may be lost in the uncertain swamp of speculation and metaphor. The difficulty here is that, even if we had the original manuscript fully guaranteed, there is no such thing as a plain, literal meaning. All language is based on comparison, metaphor and symbol. It has its own history and meaning, not only for different times but also for different readers. In fact, we bring our own history to the text and read in and out of it as we will.

We must accept that 'at present we see only puzzling reflections in a mirror' — ICor 13:12 — *but the mirror can reflect reality*. Truth is self-authenticating — it carries no hallmark but the Spirit of God is promised to help us in our recognition.

....

Criticisms of the Bible fall away as unimportant in those moments when, for all its fallibility, some eternal truth blazes into vision and I catch a glimpse of God.
                                                                    Leslie Weatherhead

THE WORD OF GOD ?

We recognise that the writers are committed, not so much to present the kind of notebook accuracy expected of a contemporary reporter, but rather to draw out the significance of the stories that have been handed to them. Even when committed to paper, the copying of texts by hand gives opportunity for amendment and the translation from one language to another may mean that words are misunderstood or carry a different meaning. Even today's translators and ourselves as readers cannot be altogether objective — we all bring our assumptions to the text. It is not only vain to seek a fixed, unfailing word of God in this dynamic process; it is to misjudge the ways of God. The Creator, then and now, entrusts his truth into the hands of fallible humanity. This is its risk and its glory.

So when we read the scriptures, we will find different opinions — as between Paul and James in the matter of faith; and we will find discrepancies and bias — as when the writer of John's Gospel shows his antipathy to 'the Jews'. We will find difficulties over translation. In other words, the Gospel is carried in earthen vessels as pointed out by Paul in 2Cor 4:7. Some seek a solution in saying that we must take the Bible as a whole and so secure the guarantee that we seek. Certainly it is useful to see the greater picture but infallibility is not on offer. The Bible, however valuable, is the gathered literature of a nation and speaks with many voices.

In the New Testament, Jesus is often described as 'the word of God' Too often this phrase has been transferred from Jesus to the records of those who witness to Jesus. In recent times, this move has become embedded in churches where it has become customary to say 'This is the word of the Lord' after a Biblical reading (A practice I believe to have been introduced by Archbishop Ramsay). There are several reasons why this is to reduce the Christian vision to a shrunken, more pagan version of Christianity.

Christians do not need to abominate shellfish (Lev.10:10) or to sell their daughters into slavery (Ex 21:7) or to stone those who work on Saturday (Ex.35:2). They can only abhor the killing of homosexuals (Lev 20:13) and the justification of genocide found in ISam 15:3.

No arguments about context or the times being different can really bypass the problem if the Bible is *the* Word of God. It is astonishing that we give good reason for militant atheists like Richard Dawkins to describe the God of the Old Testament as: *"a vindictive, bloodthirsty, ethnic cleanser ..."* and much else besides.

The Bible shows development and diversity in the human understanding of God. Take, for example, Luke's use of Mark's gospel. He clearly uses a great deal of Mark's text but he alters it in significant ways. He is unhappy with the reference to the anger of Jesus in Mark's account of the healing of a leper – 1:40f. —softening the words — Lk 5:12f. The same motivation makes him change the reference to anger in the healing of the man with the withered arm in Mk 3:5 — see Lk 6:8f. His view of Jesus is altogether more gentle than that shown in Mark's writing. More significant is his omission of the cry of dereliction from the cross.

This is the early stage of a development that will one day take much of Jesus' humanity away. Even the treatment of the disciples shows a protective instinct. Peter is spared Jesus' rebuke, they are not described as complaining during the storm on Galilee, and Luke glosses over their desertion of Jesus.

Another instance of development within scripture can be taken from the letters ascribed to Paul. These letters are clearly not all by Paul and there is evidence of editing within the letters. The most authentic documents contain rather convoluted passages about women. He stresses the different roles of men and women and requires that women conform to the dress codes of the time but he does not clearly state that men are superior to women. In his missions, he shows great respect and gratitude to many women as equal colleagues in Christian witness. By contrast, in those texts that are likely to be post-Pauline, there is a clear lack of equality between men and women, although respect is still to the fore and, if obedience is expected of wives, so is self-sacrifice expected of husbands.

The same changes have been suggested in the attitude toward slaves in these letters. There seems to be a strong case that more conservative ideas were re-asserting themselves against the early radicalism of the Christian movement.

Jews don't read the Bible. We sing it, argue with it, wrestle with it, listen to it, and turn it inside out to find a new insight we had missed before ... I believe this is what God wants. He wants us to be, in a certain sense, co-authors of His book. The Bible isn't a book to be read and put down. It is God's invitation to join the conversation between Heaven and Earth that began at Mount Sinai and has never since ceased.   *Jonathan Sacks*

PALESTINE:

Palestine was a key part of the Levant — the richest part of the Roman Empire. About the size of Wales, it straddled the great highways from Europe to Africa and the rich trade routes which brought the wealth of Arabia and the East through Petra and Damascus. The name derives from the Philistines, who inhabited the coastal strip.

In the South lay **Judaea** — as tawny, dignified and fierce as the lion that was its symbol. Its history was written in its stones. Here was disaster and triumph, loyalty and betrayal. All the passion and conflict of Jewish identity swirled about its ancient capital, Jerusalem. To it came hundreds of thousands of Jews from the great cities of the Mediterranean to celebrate the Passover until the hills were lit by their campfires. Four times Jerusalem had been besieged in living memory and, even then was living on borrowed time.

To the East lay the **Ghor** — a great rift in the earth's surface that runs deep into Africa. Here lies the Dead Sea — its surface 400m below that of the Mediterranean. Its sterile waters and shores speak of disaster and divine punishment. From the mountains opposite, Moses viewed the land he would never know for himself, and he died in the desert that forged Israel's faith.

To the West lay the sea whose name **Mediterranean** means 'the middle of the earth'. From here came the Philistines whose memory lingers in the name, Palestine. On its shores Herod the Great built the Roman city of Caesarea in honour of his master.

In the centre of the country lay **Samaria** - its fertile plain rich with grain. The Samaritans were despised by the Jews, reflecting old divisions of North and South, and the resentment against the displaced peoples who were settled there by the Assyrians when the Jews were taken into exile. In religion they followed a branch of Judaism centred on Mount Gerizim — a place said to be sacred before Jerusalem. The capital was called Samaria but was re-named Sebaste.

To the North lay **Galilee** - disparaged as 'the circle of unbelievers' and distrusted by the orthodox of Judaea. This was the most beautiful and prosperous part of Palestine — its hills wooded and fruitful, its valleys watered, and the Sea of Galilee (Gennesaret) thronged with Greek cities, fishing villages and military camps. It was cosmopolitan, open to the Empire and beyond — a ferment of people and ideas.

....

Galilee, Galilee, you have always hated the law.   Rabbi Jochanan 1C.AD

The Priests: An exclusive caste, believed to be the descendants of Aaron and Zadok. Some 20,000 in number, they served the vast organisation of the Temple by rota — 1 week in 24. The higher clergy formed a hierarchy that made up the core of theocratic government — i.e. where civil and religious affairs are identical.

The Levites: These were Temple assistants — of the tribe of Levi.

The Pharisees: They were a reforming party who, based on the synagogues, had challenged priestly power, fostered learning and sought to recover the law as the basis of faith and social justice. Not only priests and scribes but also anyone could become a Pharisee. As with other 'puritan' movements, some in time became legalistic and censorious but others were known for their wisdom and their defence of the poor. Some were sympathetic to Jesus — e.g. Lk 13:31.

N.B. The gospel records later emphasise Jesus' criticisms of the Pharisees — criticisms that were paralleled in other Jewish sources.

The Scribes: They were an intellectual aristocracy who studied and developed the law, controlling education and appointing judges. The best known scribes were spoken of as 'doctors of the law' and included the great rabbis:
- **Hillel** — who died aged 100 in 10AD. Jesus, may have heard him, when he was a teenager — being born c.5BC [21]
- **Shammai** — his stern rival
- **Gamaliel** — grandson of Hillel, a gentle, moderate man — see Acts 5:34-40
- **Jochanan ben Zakkai** — a fierce, exclusive thinker
- **Yossi** — a Galilean, and famous interpreter of the prophets.

The Sadducees: The Establishment of priests, landowners, merchants and officials who were realists in politics, accepting, or attracted by Greek culture and Roman rule. In religion they were staunch defenders of the scriptures against the continually developing tradition of the scribes and Pharisees.

The Zealots: Militant nationalists who rebelled against the Romans.

The Essenes: or 'pious ones' — who went 'back to the desert' and led withdrawn lives in monastic communities. They sought ritual purity and avoided blood sacrifice. Men and women lived separately.
The Dead Sea scrolls were probably hidden when the Essene community at Qumran was occupied by the Tenth Legion in 68AD.

THE OCCUPATION

The Roman occupation began when Pompey was invited to take control of the country in a time of appalling civil war (63BC). Over subsequent years there was a succession of risings and massacres. In the time of Jesus there was relative stability but strong currents of hatred and violence were always close to the surface.

Partly by preference, but partly due to fierce Jewish resistance, the Romans governed with a light hand between bouts of severe repression. Troops were garrisoned at Caesarea on the coast and in adjoining Syria. When reinforcements were needed in Jerusalem, they were sent to the Antonia Tower next to the Temple, with their standards covered to hide the idolatrous symbols of Caesar. Some Roman coins were minted without the Emperor's face for the same reason.

The local troops numbered something over 3,000 — with 5 cohorts of infantry and 1 of cavalry. These were led by prefects or tribunes with centurions commanding some 90 men. They were auxiliaries chiefly composed of Greeks, Syrians and Samaritans.

God made manifest and saviour of the world.
- inscription on the statue to Augustus in Ephesus.

How have I played my part in the comedy of life?
- the words of Augustus on his deathbed - 14 AD

Men who do not think me a god are worse than criminal.   *Caligula - 41 AD*

The most distinguished non-Roman in the whole world.
Pliny - of Herod the Great.

The people of the land were the 'out-castes' — the illiterate commoners who did not or could not observe the laws. They included incomers and also Galileans (see Jn 7:49).
The latter *'have no conscience, they are anything but human'* — according to Rabbi Hillel, who was in most things liberal and enlightened.

Notes: *Caesar — a family name of Julius, adopted by his successors.*
Augustus — a title - one who is august or majestic.
' diaspora' — Jews living in cities across the Roman Empire. Once refugees from invasion and war, there were more Jews living abroad than inside Palestine.

Augustus (= Octavius) 31BC -14AD. Master of Rome after the defeat of Antony. Architect of the 'Pax Romana' (the 'Peace of Rome') which gave stability to the Empire. He kept the facade of a republic and refused divine honours in his lifetime. Capable, and frugal in his private life.

Tiberius 14 -37AD. A morose figure who often withdrew from public life.

Herod the Great 37- 4BC. An Edomite Arab who achieved power in Palestine through ruthlessness and personal friendship with successive Roman emperors. He was therefore able to win privileges for the Jewish people, including exemption from military service and the right of Jews in the diaspora to remit taxes to the Temple. He was a great administrator and saved Palestine from famine in 24BC. He commissioned many great buildings, making Jerusalem 'by far the most famous city of the whole East'. Soaring above all else was the new Temple — built largely in 19-10BC but never altogether finished. Its platform alone rode as high as many a cathedral today. Herod suffered from arterio-sclerosis in his later years, which were marked by bouts of insanity and murder.

Herod Antipas — his son, who ruled Galilee from 4BC to 39AD, when he was banished to Lyons.

Herod Agrippa I — son of Antipas, who was briefly king over a united Palestine 41- 44AD.

Herod Agrippa II 53 -100AD, before whom Paul was summoned.

Pontius Pilate Roman Procurator of Judaea 26-37AD but under the authority of the Legate of Syria, with responsibility for keeping the peace. He clashed with Jewish leaders on several occasions and is said to have committed suicide after his recall to Rome, following a massacre of Samaritans.

Caiaphas High Priest 18 - 36AD but his predecessor, Annas, was still powerful. This was a political appointment.

The Sanhedrin was the Jewish government, though ultimately subject to Rome. The old nobility, the priestly hierarchy and the scribes made up its membership of 71. Herod the Great had executed 45 members in 37BC and substituted his own nominees.

....

The Family

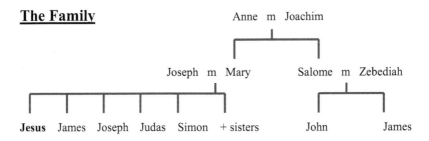

Anne m Joachim

Joseph m Mary   Salome m Zebediah

Jesus James Joseph Judas Simon + sisters   John   James

Nazareth, where Jesus was brought up, was not remote. It was near Sephoris — Joseph could well have assisted in its rebuilding as a colonial town. And it was not so far to the great desert road from Ptolemais to the East or from the Road of the Sea which ran down the coast to Egypt. In his boyhood, from the nearby hilltops, Jesus would have seen throngs of merchants, soldiers and other travellers, as well as an endless line of crosses on the roadside, bearing the bodies of executed rebels.

In his schooling, he would have learned the Shema (Dt 6:4f), the Hallel (Ps 113-118), Gen ch1-5, Lev ch1-8 and a personal text to make his own. His father would be an all-round craftsman — making yokes, doorframes, footbridges and furniture.

The Twelve

Peter   = 'the rock' (Cephas) - a nickname given to Simon.
Andrew — his brother.
James — son of Zebediah.
John — his brother.
Philip
Bartholomew — which means 'son of Talmai'.
Matthew — also known as Levi.
Thomas — the Twin.
James — the Little. Son of Alphaeus.
Thaddaeus — also known as Lebbaeus.
Simon — also known as the Canaanite, and as the Zealot.
Judas — surnamed Iscariot (surnames were not fixed at this time).

……..**Twelve** is a symbolic number representing all Israel…….
……

Derivations: *disciple = learner*
            apostle = one sent out i.e. the disciples became apostles.
            evangelist = one who carries good news

Jesus was one of a large family and probably became the breadwinner for some years after his father's death. **James** and **John** were cousins, living in Bethsaida and their family was in partnership with that of **Simon (Peter)** and **Andrew**. Several disciples may first have been followers of **John the Baptist** — also related to Jesus. **Matthew** was a customs official in Capernaum. Of the twelve, perhaps only **Judas Iscariot** came from the South — from Judaea. Iscariot may originate from the village of 'Kerioth' or may link Judas to the 'Sicarii' — an assassin branch of the Zealots who were dedicated to driving the Romans out.

Salome is one of several important women supporters and followers, who included **Peter's mother-in-law**, **Mary** — mother of James and Barnabas (Joses), **Joanna** — wife of Chusa, who was steward to Herod, **Mary of Magdala**, and **Mary** and **Martha** down in Bethany.
It was not possible for women to travel widely or therefore to be members of the twelve but their support was clearly no less crucial.

Jesus' brothers do not support him until after his death, when at least two become evangelists. **James** became a respected leader of the Christian community in Jerusalem for over 20 years and became known as James the Just.
* **Judas** committed suicide after betraying Jesus — c.30AD
* **James bar Zebediah** was executed by Herod Agrippa — c.42AD
* **Andrew** is said to have been crucified by Herod Agrippa
* **James bar Joseph** was stoned to death — c.61AD. *(bar = 'son of')*
* **Peter** was executed in Rome after the Great Fire in 65AD.

Little is known of the others in later life. **Philip** is associated with Asia Minor, **Bartholomew** with Armenia, and **Thomas** with India.
Matthew may have recorded some of Jesus' teachings in Aramaic.

Mary, Jesus' mother, may have moved to Ephesus with **John bar Zebediah**. John lived and wrote until he was over 90 years old. By tradition, Mary's mother was **Anne**, but this is not Biblical. **Jude's** grandsons were said, by the historian, Eusebius, to have been brought before the Emperor, Domitian (81-96AD), but he released them as worthless, manual labourers.

References: Mt 13:53, Jn 7:3-5, Mk 3:21 & 31, Jn 1:15-40, Mt 27:56 (cp. Mk 15:40 and see Mt 20:20), ICor 9:5, 15:7, Gal 1:18f, Acts 15:4-34 , 21:18,19.

.... **from Paul's letters** ....

To Galatia: *The good news you heard me preach is not of human origin. No one taught it to me. Jesus, chosen by God, has passed it on to me.* (1:11)

To Rome: *Do you imagine that God is God only of the Jews?* . (3:29)

('This man made himself strange to the commandments.'
- from a Jewish commentary on the Book of Ruth, believed to refer to Paul.)

To Galatia: *The life I now live is not mine, but the one chosen by God lives in me; and my present life is lived by faith in God's son, who loved me and gave himself for me.* (12:20)

('The boundary of Judaism was crossed by Paul at the point where mystery wanted to prevail without commandment, and faith without the law.' Leo Baeck

To Philippi: *By race an Israelite, by birth a Hebrew, by practice a Pharisee — but all this I have written off because of Christ.* (3:6)

To Ephesus: *Believe this — that you are saved by God's choice, not by your own efforts.* (2:8)
(Though linguistic evidence casts doubt on Paul's authorship.)

To Philippi: *God is at work in you, inspiring both the will and the deed (2:13). My friends, I do not claim to have achieved it yet.* (3:13)

To Rome: *The good that I want to do, I can't; but what I don't want to do, that I do.* (7:19)

To Athens: *What you worship but don't know, I will reveal to you.* (Acts 17:23)

To Corinth: *God's foolishness is wiser than human wisdom.* (ICor 1:25)
I came to you without pretending to be eloquent or wise. (ICor 2:1)
If I have no love, I am a badly struck gong or discordant cymbal.
(ICor 13:1)
To Rome: *I am convinced that nothing in life or death, present or future — no power, no force, no height, no depth — nothing in all creation is capable of separating us from the love of God in Christ Jesus.* (8:38f)

....

Note: Paul's letters have themselves been edited and may well show elements of later ideas.

Paul was a rabbi and tentmaker, who came from the Greek university city of Tarsus and then studied under Gamaliel in Jerusalem. He became a fierce persecutor of the Christians until, overwhelmed by a personal experience of Christ, he became the first Christian missionary to the Gentiles (the non-Jewish world).

Strikingly, the language of Paul came to shape Christian orthodoxy even more than the words of his master. Some believe that he betrayed the simple gospel of Jesus. Some think that he successfully interpreted the gospel for a wider world and demonstrated to it the significance of Jesus. Some think that he lost touch with the very practical realism of Judaism and created a new romantic religion — *"the first corrupter of the doctrines of Jesus"* — Jefferson.

We have a record of some of his teaching in the letters he wrote between 50 & 62AD to the Christian communities that he had established. In them he is responding to immediate needs and current controversies. He writes out of intense conviction, frequent hardship, recurrent illness and the persecution that ultimately brought him to execution in Rome.

His achievement was monumental. He won the respect of other Christian leaders and of the Roman authorities. He successfully overcame the conservative attempts that would have restricted the new faith within the confines of Judaism. His tireless travelling, world vision, remonstration and encouragement strengthened his missionary colleagues and inspired the young communities that would one day change the Empire.

The letters we have today are a few surviving examples of his writing and they too have been edited, but alongside some contradictory and difficult material, there are incomparable passages and inspired ideas that are close to the heart of Jesus' teaching. It is faith which is triumphant in his teaching, made possible by the unconquerable love of God — faith set forth as the foundation of the divine commonwealth to which we are called.

'I see that our voyage from here on will be dangerous ..... '
Luke recalls his diary of Paul's voyage to Rome in Acts 27. The British Navy made a study of this voyage, taking into account the vessels of the time, the winds and currents, and they took similar soundings off Malta. The conclusion was that the narrative is entirely credible.

THE LIFE OF JESUS

His name is not so much written as ploughed in history.   *Emerson*

Jesus was born in Bethlehem of Judaea during the reign of Herod.   *Mt 2:1*

About that time lived Jesus, a wise man, if man he may be called, for he did wonderful works — a teacher of those who joyfully received the truth.
Josephus d.100AD

He (Jesus) practised witchcraft, seduced Israel and led her astray and to transgression.
The Talmud

This man could have developed only on the soil of Judaism. Here alone, in this Jewish sphere, in this Jewish atmosphere of trust and longing, could this man live his life and meet his death — a Jew among Jews.   *Leo Baeck*

Whoever denies that Jesus is the Christ is a liar.   *I Jn 2:22*

Whoever slanders me will be forgiven.   *Jesus - Mt 12:32*

Typical of men as no other man is typical. His nature is essentially ours —   and our nature is essentially his.   *Victor Gollancz*

The son is the mirror of the invisible God; coming first in all creation. Through him everything was created, both visible and invisible. The whole universe has been created through him and for him. He exists before all things, and all things are held together in him. He is the head of the body, the church. He is its origin, the first to return from the dead, to become in everything supreme. For all the fullness of God is poured into him.
Paul - Col 1:15f.

He was too big to be nailed to the wall
Of a stone chapel, yet still we crammed him
Between the boards of a black book.   *R S Thomas*

I believe there is no one lovelier, deeper, more sympathetic and more a perfect person than Jesus. Not only is there no one else like him, but there could never be anyone like him.   *Dostoevsky*

Since he was, no time has been without him, nor has there been a time which was not challenged by the epoch that would consider him its starting point.   *Leo Baeck*

A truly human person in a world of partial humans.   *Keith Ward*

In the presence of Jesus, all men know themselves.   *Oscar Wilde*

That Jesus was a real figure in history is beyond reasonable doubt. If he was not historical, there had to be one such as he. The New Testament records have been subjected to exhaustive examination by scholars of every point of view. It would be difficult to argue that they are the product of romantic imagination. Yet, inevitably, there is sufficient uncertainty and embroidery to feed the wilder speculations that sell so well in the bookshops of today.

His family was village provincial, neither poor nor rich, but his education would be good, and cosmopolitan Galilee was an education in itself. The mission of John the Baptist was the occasion for Jesus' life to change from that of a craftsman to that of itinerant preacher. But Jesus was not an ascetic like John nor did he follow the Essenes in their secluded rituals and exclusive view of the world.

He became known as a healer and teacher, with an inner authority and a clear sense of vocation. He was seen to walk with God and to be content to be a servant to all. He called his followers to be citizens of God's kingdom and recalled them to an ancient faith. To do this he had to assault the pretensions of self-seeking religion and to free the faith from the shallow and legalistic. Many people at first were sympathetic and supportive — including some of the Pharisees.

Ever since the time of King David, Jewish teachers had looked for another such leader or 'messiah'. The disciples came to believe that Jesus was the messiah, but he warned them not to see in him a leader destined to overthrow the Roman yoke. His eyes were for a greater kingdom. Later, some would say that he was God appearing as a man but the Gospels are clear — he was limited in knowledge and subject to weariness, doubt, anger and fear — as the creed says, *he suffered under Pontius Pilate and was crucified, dead, and buried.*

He often spoke of himself as 'son of man' — a phrase which simply meant 'human'. There is a more specialist use of 'son of man' in some Jewish literature as one who represents the true Israel — an ideal or perfected humanity and therefore, as it were, present in the mind of God from the beginning. Perhaps Jesus was a true man in a world of half men. Until we too attain our humanity, we are challenged by what he was.

....

Since he was, no time has been without him, nor has there been a time which was not challenged by the epoch that would consider him its starting point.

Leo Baeck

As you do not know how a living spirit comes to the body inside the womb of a pregnant woman, even so you do not know the work of God, the maker of everything.
Eccles 11:5

Providence has sent him to us as saviour, and he will end all war and order all things. The day of his birth has brought the world the glad tidings.
an inscription referring to Caesar Augustus - 9BC

Christmas is a cosmic celebration of the beginning of something that we cannot adequately describe. It is a liturgy that sings of the new covenant between the God of eternity and man in history.
Pope Paul VI

The birth stories are a powerful overture to the great gospels of Matthew and Luke that, like so many good overtures, conveys in a nutshell the message which is later to be developed.
Hans Küng

BC/AD: A 6C Roman monk placed Jesus' birth at the end of the Roman year 753. This became AD = Anno Domini /The Year of our Lord. We now place Jesus' birth around 5BC.

Angels = 'messengers' were widely spoken of by a people who would not presume to suggest that God had spoken to them directly.

The Wise Men or magi, belong to the Zoroastrian scholarly class in the Middle East, known to study of astronomy, astrology, ancient texts and world events. Akin to Celtic druids; the Celts originated from the same area. The gifts are symbolic of royalty, worship and suffering. **Frankincense** — *boswellia carteri* — may have come to Egypt from the Himalayas in 1570BC (and see Ex 30:34f). **Myrrh** — *balsamodendron myrrha* — is grown in Arabia and India. It was used to anoint the dead. **The star** has led to much speculation. Conjunctions of Saturn and Jupiter in 7 & 6BC. were succeeded by a comet in 5BC. Astrology suggested a link with Israel. The word we translate as 'stood over the place' — Mt 2:9 — is said to be a technical term used of comets where the tail appears to be vertical. Fragments of history may underlie this account but the storyteller is concerned with symbolic truth. not historical exactitude.

Herod was paranoid enough to murder two of his own children at this time. [see 17]

The birth stories are not found in Mark, John or Paul. They are a reflection by some of Jesus' followers on the significance of the man they had *already* come to know. They are an overture, that introduces later themes: of good news for the poor and powerless; of the call of God; of suffering and exaltation to come.   [see 59, 97]

Was there ever such a misconceived (!) story as that of the virgin birth of Jesus? It devalues history, undermines the incarnation and distorts human sexuality. It illustrates clearly the difficulties that we are contending with in this book. With this story a fence was erected around the man Jesus, a veritable 'cordon sanitaire' that almost sets him beyond our reach.

Luke and Matthew may have taken the story literally, yet Luke, who never met Jesus, may have created it as an imaginative way of drawing out his significance. The disciple, Matthew, is unlikely to have written the Gospel that appears under his name — the name only became associated with it much later. The Gospels, being written 70 to 100 years after Jesus' birth, are likely to reflect folk-belief that was already gathering around genuine memories.

What would give rise to the belief of a virgin birth? As long pointed out by scholars, the Greek Jewish scriptures mistranslate Is.7:14, where King Ahaz is told, according to the Hebrew:
"A young woman is pregnant and will give birth to a son".
The Greek translator wrote:
"A virgin will conceive and bear a son".

Christians searched the Jewish scriptures for prophecies that could be linked to Jesus as the Messiah. It was an easy step to transfer this promise to Jesus' own birth. Add to this, that those who were familiar with Greek culture and wished to commend Jesus in the Gentile world, would know that stories of virgin births were commonplace. The gods were believed to visit humanity and beget outstanding leaders, including Perseus, Plato, Alexander the Great, not to mention the Buddha and Krishna in eastern belief. Virgil, the Roman poet, celebrates the young Augustus in the words:

"Now is the Virgin herself made known and the reign of Saturn on earth; now is a child engendered by heaven".

PTO

A VIRGIN BIRTH ?

The Jews shared no such beliefs and were largely uninfluenced by the devaluation of human sexuality found in Greek philosophy. When they do refer to virginity, it is laden with the promise of fertility; see for example, Jer 31:21 - *"Come back, virgin Israel, come back to your cities and towns"* - which is a call to restoration and prosperity after the Exile in Babylon. More than that, they readily spoke of the involvement of God's Spirit in every birth.

The story of the virgin birth causes immediate difficulties in the gospels of Matthew and Luke. Matthew is anxious to show Jesus as a descendant of David and ultimately of Abraham (Mtt 1:1f.). Luke pushes the same ancestry further back (Lk 3:23f.). If the authors took the virgin birth story literally, such genealogies are redundant — and arguments about 'adoption' are surely special pleading.

Nor would Mary's ancestry help, as it was the common belief that a child came from the male seed and that the mother simply nurtured the child in her womb. Jesus therefore has to be a fresh human creation — *"A second Adam to the fight and to the rescue came"* — as Newman's hymn puts it.

The writings of Mark and Paul are thought to be earlier than the above gospels. They appear to know nothing of a virgin birth. This is no slight omission. Such a birth is either of the utmost significance or it is unnecessary. Not only does Mark show no awareness of the story, but he tells us that Mary, with the rest of her sons, at one point came to fetch Jesus home, believing him to be mentally disturbed (Mk 3:21, 31f.). If a choice has to be made between this account and that of the virgin birth, it is surely the latter that can be questioned. Growing reverence for Mary would have censored the former, unless it was a strong and genuine recollection.

The writer of John's Gospel must have known of the story, if, as the scholars generally believe, it was not written until sometime after the rest. His view of Jesus appears to be the most developed, as we have seen above, yet he makes no use of an event that would have proclaimed in the most dramatic way his divine origin.

Non-believers will naturally point out that a virgin birth flies in the face of human experience and medical knowledge. Believers would be wise not to scour the world for marginal possibilities or to take refuge in the assurance that God can do what he will. For Christians, God can indeed act as he thinks fit but why should he overturn his own laws, and why would he in this case?

The issue can be stated quite simply: did God reveal himself through human life as we know it? If so, we can talk of incarnation — God revealing himself, even being present in some sense, in normal human life. If the fulness of God cannot rest in this humanity, then the fulness of God cannot rest in us (see Col 1:19 and Eph 3:19). If Jesus was a fresh creation, we can hardly follow him. He is born with an insuperable advantage. He would not be human as we know humanity — and he would not therefore be *"tempted in all points as we are"* — Hebr.4:15. Our genetic inheritance, our physical and psychological being is essential to the humanity we wrestle with. The great fourth century theologian, Augustine, makes the dilemma starker, for he argues that our inheritance has been corrupted from the days of Adam. The church's emphasis upon the virgin birth has arisen in part from the need to protect Jesus from this corruption. The problem was compounded by teaching that Mary too was made immaculate to ensure that the 'cordon sanitaire' was fail-safe (though what of Mary's mother?).

No! Let us take the fences away. Jesus was born in the normal course of things. He enjoyed no special privilege, no inherent advantage — and yet he speaks to us of God, as few, perhaps none others, have been able to do. He persistently diverted attention away from himself — *"Why do you call me good?"* — and towards God, though in his obedience, his love and his suffering, he showed us the nature of God more than words alone can describe.

It is a fundamental misjudgement to portray God as operating on two tracks: the first, that of Creation, in which he failed, and the second, that of Redemption, by which we can be saved. On this view, humanity in God's original creation becomes hopelessly corrupt and, save for one family, has to be wiped out in the Flood. Even afterwards, corruption sets in again and God's chosen people, the Jews, go astray and have to be sidelined. The whole scheme has to be air-lifted from disaster by the descent and ascent of a saviour-god, Jesus. This is indeed a shrunken vision, born of short-sightedness. It is capped by treating the scriptures as a package of faith formulae designed to guide us to the one saviour. Let us then believe in the incarnation without reservation and recast our understanding of it

[see 102]

THE LIFE OF JESUS

Put God's kingdom and his justice before everything.   *Jesus - Mt 6:33*

The baptism:
During a mass baptism of the people, when Jesus too was baptised and was praying, it was as though heaven opened and the spirit of God descended on him like a dove, and there was a voice which said, *You are my dear son; I am more than pleased with you.*   Luke - 3:21,22

In the wilderness:
For forty days Jesus lived in the wilderness, led by the Spirit and it was as though a devil tempted him. During that time he fasted, and at the end of it was very hungry. The devil said to him, 'If you are God's son, you can tell this stone to become bread'. Jesus answered, 'It is written that people need more than bread'.

Next the devil showed him in an instant all the kingdoms of the world. 'I will give you all this power,' he said, 'and the glory that goes with it. You have only to recognise me and it will all be yours.' Jesus answered him, 'It is written that you shall serve God alone'.

The devil took him to Jerusalem and set him on the high parapet of the temple. 'If you are the God's son,' he said, 'jump; for scripture says 'God's messengers will keep you safe and they will support you in case you injure yourself.' Jesus answered him, 'It has been said, *You are not to try to put God to the test.*
Luke - 4:1f.

....

It is good to be without vices, but it is not good to be without temptations
                                                   Walter Bagehot

1.Baptism was a dramatic sign of conversion — a deliberate commitment to live by new principles and therefore of dying and rebirth. Jesus identifies with John's reform movement, though John defers to him — Mt 3:13f.

2.The language is traditional and symbolic, rather than literal. It describes a deeply personal experience of calling, insight and choice. Jesus himself may have summed up 6 weeks in the wilderness in 3 vivid scenes for the benefit of his disciples.

3. The devil is a conventional folk-figure associated with times of testing.

4. Fasting is to be found in many faiths. Modern medical experiments suggest that it can be an aid to clear thinking after the first two or three days. After some forty days body fats are used up and the body deteriorates. (Liquids are essential at all times.) Forty may itself be a symbolic number.

....

I can resist everything except temptation.   Oscar Wilde

For Jesus this is a time of personal call which will demand everything of him. He seeks time and solitude to work out what it will mean. He does this in the wilderness, the open country and does not feel compelled to accept previous teaching in a fundamentalist way. The 'temptations' can be interpreted in personal terms as if Jesus was more than human but the suggestions made here relate more closely to his future ministry.   (see Luke 4)

BREAD: The first temptation has Deut 8 in mind. The testing and preparation of the Hebrew people centres on the teaching that
'people need more than bread — they need God's truth to live by' v.3. It becomes a recurrent theme of Jesus' teaching. Bread represents material needs — no doubt including physical healing — which was a vital part of Jesus' ministry, but our spiritual needs are vital also, as it is the truth of God which gives meaning and depth to life.
Surely life is not just food: the body is not just clothes.   *Jesus - Mt 6:25*

Just as Jesus had to set aside his hunger, so his work will concern itself not just with food and clothing or even physical disease, but with the fullness of God's kingdom. These are not contradictory goals.

POWER: To 'worship the devil' is not about satanic ritual. It is to adopt ends or means which fall outside the good which God intends. Jesus had to face the attraction of power —

Realising that they meant to seize him and to proclaim him king, he went into the hills by himself.   *John - 6:15*

This is a temptation that has destroyed many whose ideals were once sincere enough. Jesus chose 'to worship God' — that is, to follow God's way in everything.

SUFFERING: Here, Jesus faces up to the reality of what might happen to him. He knows well the comforting words of Ps 91 but he accepts that for him there may be a harder road to travel.

If it is possible, let me avoid this cup and yet — not what I want but what you want.   *Mt 26:39*

Jesus decides in this time what his ministry will be, what his methods will be, and what the consequences are likely to be. When Peter, or other friends, or enemies try to draw him away in future, he remains obedient, 'even to the point of death'
                                                                        — Phil 2:8.

The healing stories:

	Matthew	Mark	Luke	John
A man with skin disease	8:2	1:40	5:12	
The centurion's servant	8:5		7:1	
Peter's mother-in-law	8:14	1:30	4:38	
Two mentally ill	8:28	5:1	8:27	
A paralytic	9:2	2:3	5:18	
A girl in a coma	9:18	5:22	8:41	
A case of haemorrhage	9:20	5:25	8:43	
Two blind men	9:27			
The dumb man	9:32			
A useless arm	12:10	3:1	6:6	
Speech and sight	12:22			
The Canaanite girl	15:21	7:24		
The epileptic boy	17:14	9:17	9:38	
Two blind men	20:29			
A man possessed		1:23	4:33	
A deaf mute		7:31		
A blind man		8:22		
Blind Bartimaeus		10:46	18:35	
A crippled woman			13:11	
A case of dropsy			14:1	
Ten with skin diseases			17:11	
The high priest's servant			22:50	
The official's son				4:46
A crippled man				5:1
Blind from birth				9:1

Leprosy: The terrible results of untreated leprosy arise because the skin is desensitised. The fear of infection led to social exclusion, which could be more dehumanising than the disease. The Greek word used here may include other skin diseases.

Evil spirits: The popular belief in evil spirits covered a wide range of disorders that appeared to be caused by invasion from outside. We might now speak of viral infections and mental disorders, but we still meet with baffling conditions both in scientific and pre-scientific societies. Jesus may have shared the culture of his time but in neglecting ceremonial washing, touching lepers, and spending time in the wilderness, he lived more freely than most. In healing, it may have been essential to accept the presuppositions of the disordered.

The healings are well attested. Those denying them are left with the immense difficulty of explaining how an ordinary man came to have such an extraordinary impact. Even if details are misremembered or embroidered, the overall witness has an authentic ring — see:

> - the Aramaic phrases — *talitha cumi* & *ephphatha* - Mk 5:41, 7:34
> - the use of clay and spittle — Jn 9:6 (both can have relieving properties)
> - the practical details — e.g. Mk 5:43
> - the interrogation of the blind man — Jn 9
> - the inverted image suggested in Mk 8:24
> - the medical terminology of Luke, the doctor — Col 4:14.

The writers are restrained in the use they make of these stories and testify that healing was not Jesus' first priority. He does not seek popular acclaim as a healer nor claim uniqueness for this ministry.

The cures are not presented as automatic or as overriding the will of the victim. Many of the examples given would now be described as psychosomatic and we are ever more aware of the power of belief in the use of placebos. This equates with what Jesus himself said constantly about the effect of faith in healing, so that to talk in this way, does not diminish these stories one whit. It is as though Jesus (or God through Jesus) helped to release healing power from within. Doctors today rarely hold the narrow view that gives patients no role either in the illness or the cure. Yet we should not assume it is 'all a matter of psychology'. Jesus' experience that 'power had gone out of him' — Lk 8:46, is not unknown today.

The causes of disease may relate to us, or to others, or to none. The healing may need our faith, or that of others, or come unheralded. The paralytic — Lk 6:6-10 — is of particular interest as guilt can be a potent source of paralysis. The assurance of forgiveness is here accepted and physical liberation follows as a matter of course. This does not mean that disease is all a consequence of sin — see Jn 9:1-5 — nor should we conclude from Mt 13:58 that the absence of healing is *always* due to lack of faith.

There will have been many who were not healed, then as now, and 'death comes to us all'. It would seem wise to beware of delusion and fraud but nevertheless to accept both the gifts of faith and the skills of doctors and nurses, who likewise do the work of God.   [131]

....

He healed the blind and the lame but he never did teeth!   anon.

....

It is a generation without God which wants signs.   *Jesus - Mt 12:39*

Whoever trusts me will do greater things still.   *Jesus - Jn 14:12*

For he who believes, a miracle is not necessary.
For he who does not believe, a miracle is not enough.   *An Italian archbishop*

I can see no reason at all why God should not suspend or change the average course of
events.   *Victor Hess - scientist and Nobel prize winner.*

They will take no notice if someone does rise from the dead.
Abraham in Jesus' parable - Lk 16:31

A common man marvels at uncommon things; a wise man marvels at the
commonplace.   *Confucius*

The Christian religion not only was at first attended with miracles, but even at this day,
cannot be believed by any reasonable person without one.
David Hume

Following alleged miracles in the St Medard cemetery in Paris, 1732, Louis XV had
this sign placed upon the locked gates:

**BY ORDER OF THE KING, GOD IS FORBIDDEN TO WORK MIRACLES IN THIS
PLACE.**

....

If miracle is believing the impossible, then there is no such thing as a miracle. The
New Testament Greek speaks of *mighty works, wonders* or *signs.* Our task is to
ask, 'What things are possible?'. In Nature grain does multiply, water turns to
wine and life is born out of death. There is endless scope for wonder in the world
about us and many will read in Creation signs of the living God.

With God, all things are possible, and our knowledge is far from complete, but
would God suspend his laws? Are there laws we have not yet grasped? We have
so much more to learn about the relationships of mind and body; energy and
matter.

Like the early Church, we should approach the 'Nature' miracles with care and
insight:
> ➢ the story that the boy Jesus made birds from clay, which then flew away,
>   was in an early writing left out of the canon
> ➢ the story of the fig tree was possibly misunderstood, perhaps coming
>   from an original parable — Mk 11:13f / Lk 13:6f.

> ➤ the story of the coin in Mt 17:24f could have altered in the telling, influenced by 'St Peter's fish' which, like a magpie, collects shiny objects
> ➤ the account of the wine at Cana — Jn 2:1f — is told only by John in a richly symbolic story, where the quantity and quality of the wine represents new life
> ➤ the catch of fish — Lk 5:1f. & Jn 21:1f. — may or may not be judged 'miraculous'. There is a link with Jesus' invitation to the disciples to become 'fishers of men' — Mt 4:19.

In 1938, a Church of England Commission recognised that many Christians feel it to be *more* congruous with the majesty of God if the laws of Nature serve his purpose without exceptions on the physical plane. Why operate two systems of activity — one being sporadic, apparently arbitrary and therefore unjust? The New Testament writers are concerned with the meaning of these stories and Jesus did not present himself as a 'miracle-worker' nor teach that faith could be built on such signs.   [see 117]

"Walking on water?"

        "There was no longer any sea"   *Rev.21:1*

This must be one of the most disappointing texts in the Bible! But it would have been a relief to many Hebrews had they lived long enough to read it. They were not seafarers and were often at war with those who crossed the Mediterranean to their coasts.

We have started at the wrong end of the Bible and need to go back to the beginning:

        "The spirit of God brooded over the waters"   *Gen 1:2*

The picture we are given in this story of creation is one of disorder, out of which God brings order; of chaos, out of which springs the universe we know. The sea is a tumultuous image of chaos — the waters exist above and below this new space in which God is at work. We can take the picture given as literal or symbolic or both. The powerful poetry of the book of Job reflects this moment of birth:

> *"Who supported the sea at its birth,*
> *when it burst out of the womb in flood*
> * — when I wrapped it in cloud like a blanket*
> *and swaddled it in dense fog,*
> *when I established its boundaries,*
> *locked the doors against it*
> *and said: 'You may come this far but no farther;*
> *here your surging waves must stop'?"*

        Job 38:8f.

THE MIRACLE WORKER

The story of the Flood also depends on more than one level of meaning. In the basement level are real memories of catastrophic floods. One line of research has shown that around 5,600 BC the Black Sea rose nearly two metres every day for two years. We know too that the Tigris-Euphrates basin has suffered terrible floods. Let those who will, be side-tracked into taking the whole story literally. But the editor merges two different accounts together — accounts that do not agree as to how many pairs of animals enter the ark or as to how long the rain lasts. The literalist cannot explain the problems of space, feeding, hygiene, manpower available etc. Above all, he cannot cope convincingly with a God who fails signally in his first creation and has to start all over again with a single family salvaged from the ruin — one that later proves to be as fallible as before.

We can safely leave the basement for the ground floor. Here we find that the Biblical narrative draws in part on older stories from the culture of Mesopotamia — the *Epic of Gilgamesh* and the even older *Atrahasis*. The latter resembles Genesis in containing a prior account of the making of humanity from clay. In the Gilgamesh epic, the hero, Utnapishtim, builds a great ship to escape the anger of the gods, who destroy Shuruppak in a great flood. Here too we find the release of birds. The gods repent of their anger, admire the ingenuity of Utnapishtim and grant him eternal life because he restores the ritual sacrifices:

"The gods smelled the savour,
The gods smelled the sweet savour,
The gods crowded like flies above the sacrificer".

When we leave the ground floor for the upper storey, we are in a different world. The Hebrew storyteller speaks of the one God, whose dignity and power is evident. A vital issue is posed — "Can evil threaten creation itself?" The waters pour in from above and below:
"All the springs of the great deep burst out, the windows of the heavens were opened"

Gen.7:12

Chaos, held back in the act of creation, returns and could overwhelm everything. We, who fear an environmental or nuclear crisis today, face the same issue, at least as far as this earth is concerned. The answer given in the story is that God is at work to save all that is good — not only humanity, but all living creatures. It is artlessly (?) told in ancient imagery but is no less powerful for that.

We now turn to the New Testament. where the 'nature miracles' challenge the thoughtful reader. In one story, Jesus calms a storm. The setting is convincing. Jesus is with his fishermen friends, out on the open water, when a storm erupts down the slopes of the desert plateau. A further story tells of Jesus walking across the water to meet his disciples who are battling with headwind and a heavy sea:

"When the disciples saw him walking on the lake they were so shaken that they cried out terrified: 'It is a ghost!"   Mtt 14:26
Then, in a sequel, provided by Matthew alone, Peter tries to emulate his master but fails dramatically when his faith falters.

The literalist, on the ground floor, takes these stories as a further demonstration of the divine power of Jesus but, even apart from our natural scepticism, there is a serious difficulty. Matthew believes that Jesus held back from trying to use such power (Mtt 12:39). Luke shows Jesus, in the temptation story, refusing to use such means. Why, we can ask the literalist, should Jesus walk on water when there was no life-threatening emergency? Once more, we pass to the upper storey. There we can look back to Psalm 107:25f:

"At God's command the storm wind rose and whipped up the waves. The seamen were carried to the sky, then plunged down into the troughs, they were tossed perilously here and there, they swayed and staggered as though they were drunk and all their skill meant nothing. So they cried desperately to God and he brought them out of their distress. The storm sank to a murmur and the waves of the sea were stilled".

The fishermen disciples were well used to storms on the sea of Galilee but what of the storm that assailed them when Jesus' enemies closed upon him? Was it not Jesus who walked his path of destiny even through ' the springs of the deep'? And when the test came, was it not Peter, who had sworn never to leave his master, who found that his faith had failed him — even to shouting at a servant girl that he had never known the one he called his master?

This exploration is done. It is but an illustration of our freedom once the fences are down but remember two things. Our language world is prosaic — flat and factual — the Biblical authors wove their stories with sacred imagination. In days before print, they had to appeal to the visual and easily memorable. We know that a two-thousand- year old storm can scarcely touch us but few of us will escape things troubling and fearful. It is then that such stories will speak.

PTO

THE MIRACLE WORKER

"Five thousand eat bread"

"Give us today our daily bread". Mtt 6:11

When Jesus included these words in his template of prayer, his hearers' would readily associate it with the story of desert survival, when the Hebrews were sustained by eating manna:

"On the surface of the desert fine flakes appeared, fine as hoar-frost on the ground. When the Israelites saw it, they said to each other: 'What is that?' because they had no idea. Moses said to them: 'This is the bread that the Lord has given you to eat'." Ex 16:14

The 'bread' had to be collected daily because it soon deteriorated. This manna may well have been the sweet substance exuded by the tamarisk shrub that is still collected today and called 'man'. There is a probable pun in the above as the word for 'what' in Hebrew ('What is that?') is very similar to the word 'manna'.In the Bible it is clear that manna comes to have wider significance and represents the whole of God's provision for his people. We use the word 'bread' in this way — *"on the breadline", "the breadwinner"* etc.

So in the New Testament it is no surprise that bread is the very staff of life and Jesus' sayings come over the more powerfully. See, for example, the extensive passage - John 6: 30f.

With this key we can begin to unlock the difficult stories where Jesus feeds thousands of people:

(Mtt 14:15, 15:32, Mk 6:35, 8:1, Lk 9:12 and John 6:5).

The literalist, on the ground floor, will try to take them at face value. God can do this whenever he wishes, and, as C.S.Lewis suggested, doesn't he do it all the time in Nature's seedtime and harvest? Once more we have to ask why God should work in a twin track way — establishing his laws and then ignoring them. And we can ask whether the emergency was so great as to require such an extraordinary exercise of power. Jesus said:

"It is a generation without God that wants signs" Mtt 12:39

It will not do for some to say that Jesus is deliberately demonstrating his divinity, for Jesus is recorded as saying:

"Whoever trusts me will do greater things still" John 14:12

Once more we note that the temptation story appears to rule out any manipulation of Nature, particularly as it would lead many more thousands to seek out Jesus for all the wrong reasons. We are also left with an intriguing question. Miracles wouldn't normally lead to over-supply, so why were there considerable left-overs ?

We are fully justified in leaving the ground floor arguments and going to the upper storey. We are reminded that:

"Mankind shall not live by bread alone but by every word that comes from the mouth of God"   Mtt 4:4 - and see Deut 8:3

Here also we can look more closely at the details given in the various accounts. We discover that the seating arrangements were highly organised, that men alone took part, and that the numbers relate to them as would be true of synagogue worship and public assemblies. The accounts speak of 12 baskets being left over in one case and 7 baskets in another. Twelve is a common representative number for the whole of Israel and seven or seventy was used to indicate the nations of the world. There are suggestions too that one of these events followed hard on the death of John the Baptist and that there were (quite plausible) attempts to declare Jesus a king.

It does not take a great leap of the imagination to suggest that we have here a symbolic use of bread, as indeed in our eucharist services. Jesus could well have addressed large groups of those who had joined the movement for national renewal that John had instigated, but who now had lost their leader. These could include some kind of commitment and commissioning but, for Jesus, clearly not an overt political movement. These occasions could have been misunderstood when passed on in the oral tradition. The exchange in Mtt 16:5f. lends weight to a less literal interpretation:

"How can you fail to see that I was not talking about bread/"

The literal interpretation not only presupposes that Jesus performs a major miracle to meet a minor need but, far more important, that he would come close to undermining the whole basis of his ministry as suggested in the Temptation story. This applies whether or not *that* story is taken literally. If he actually forswears turning stones into bread, how can he then turn bread into bread on one or two arbitrary occasions? If this temptation is taken to indicate that he will not place material need foremost in his ministry, how can he then do so in these instances — and attract further crowds as a consequence?

....

One who sits in the shade does not know the sun's heat.　　　　　　　Nigerian proverb

Jesus said, ' I tell you, no prophet is valued in his own country.' .... They drove him out of the town, and took him to the brow of the hill on which it was built, meaning to push him over the edge. But he walked straight through the whole crowd, and left them.
　　　　　　　　　　　　　　　　　　　　　　　　　　　　　　　　　Luke - 4:24,29

The scribes and the Pharisees began asking among themselves, 'Who is this fellow with his blasphemous talk? Who else besides God can forgive sins?'
　　　　　　　　　　　　　　　　　　　　　　　　　　　　　　　　　Luke - 5:21

He moved into the territory of Tyre. He found a house to stay in, and would have liked to remain incognito.　　　　　　　　　　　　　　　　　　　　　　Mark - 7:24

Be on your guard against the insidious influence of the Pharisees and Herod.
　　　　　　　　　　　　　　　　　　　　　　　　　　　　　　　　Jesus - Mark 8:15

Some of the Pharisees came and warned him, 'You had better leave and be on your way; Herod wants to kill you'.　　　　　　　　　　　　　　　　　　Luke - 13:31

The chief priests and the Pharisees convened a meeting of the Council. 'This man is producing many signs,' they said, 'and what are we doing about it? If we let him go on like this the whole population will believe in him, and then the Romans will come and destroy our temple and nation.' But one of them, Caiaphas, who was high priest that year, said, 'You don't understand the situation at all; you do not realise that it is more to your interest that one man should die for the people, than that the whole nation should be destroyed.' So Jesus no longer went about openly among the Jews, but left for a town called Ephraim, in the country bordering the desert, and stayed there with his disciples.　　　　　　　　　　　　　　　　　　　　　　　　John - 11:47f.

He began to teach them that this son of man had to be put to death. He spoke about it plainly.　　　　　　　　　　　　　　　　　　　　　　　　　Jesus - Mk 8:31

The chief priests, scribes and elders came to him and said, 'What is your authority for acting like this? Who gave you such authority?'
　　　　　　　　　　　　　　　　　　　　　　　　　　　　　　　　Mark - 11:27

As they sat at supper Jesus said, 'Believe me: one of you will betray me — one who is eating with me.'　　　　　　　　　　　　　　　　　　　　　　Mark 14:18

....

The question, 'Why was Jesus crucified?' is sometimes removed from history on the grounds that this is God's cosmic confrontation with sin. The drama is conducted at a higher level, as though between God and the devil, and human beings are but the supporting cast. But it may be more profitable to explore the reality of history and then, perhaps, see this as representative of a greater drama.

John the Baptist was executed by **Herod Antipas** and Jesus had associated with John. He had to avoid Herod's jurisdiction at times — perhaps spending some months in Tyre. Jesus' social teaching and popularity could both have threatened Herod's ambitions.

The high priestly family of **Annas** and **Caiaphas** was noted for its corruption. The 'bazaars of Annas' were the outlets for the vast business enterprise of sacrifice, centred upon the Temple, and this was challenged by Jesus. Caiaphas had every reason to preserve his profitable liaison with Rome. The Sanhedrin had been subverted with political appointees and there were hundreds of priests who stood to lose if the Temple traditions were abandoned.

Pilate might have accepted Jesus as innocent , though we know that he could be ruthless at times — but he had to watch his back. His task was to keep the peace and he knew well how stubborn the Jews could be. A previous confrontation, over Roman soldiers displaying images of Caesar on their standards, had led to thousands of protestors in a massive sit-down demonstration in Caesarea. Despite threats of death, they kept it up until their cause was won. Another possible reason for the favourable portrayal of Pilate is that the story was told and retold in the 40s when King Agrippa I was in charge, not a Roman governor. It was Agrippa who had James bar Zebedee killed and Jesus' followers were under violent persecution. They may have seen direct Roman rule as the better of two evils.

In any event, there was genuine **religious opposition** to Jesus. He overthrew conventions regarding foreigners, Samaritans and women; he was compromised by the company he kept; he was cavalier in his attitude to the laws of purification and the sabbath; he questioned the value of a dearly preserved national identity going back to Abraham, and he could have been involved in subversion. Above all, untrained as he was, he took it upon himself to reinterpret old authorities and was alleged to claim divine authority for himself.

In the final week it was Jesus who threw down the gauntlet in a way which could not be ignored.

THE LIFE OF JESUS

....

It is a good thing to sit alone and keep silence, because he has taken this yoke upon himself.   *Lam 3:28*

I have a baptism to face, and I can think of nothing else until it is over.
                                                                                   Jesus - Lk 12:50

I am willing to lay down my life.   *Jesus - Jn 10:17*

She has anointed my body already for burial.   *Jesus - Mk 14:8*

Unless a wheatgrain falls into the soil and dies, it remains a seed and nothing more.
                                                                                   Jesus - Jn 12:24

There is no greater love than this, that someone should give his life for his friends.
                                                                                   Jesus - Jn 15:13

This is the cup the Father has given me. Shall I not drink it?
                                                                                   Jesus - Jn 18:11

My life pours out of me like water and all my bones are undone.   *Ps 22:14*

He suffered because of our wrongdoing and was crushed because of our injustice.
                                                                                   Isaiah - 53:5

This, my body, is broken for you.   *Jesus - ICor 11:24*

In this, the world stands judged.   *Jesus - Jn 12:31*

Never should I forget that nocturnal silence which deprived me, for all eternity, of the desire to live. Never shall I forget these moments which murdered my God and my soul and turned my dreams to dust.
            Elie Wiesel - writing of his experiences in Auschwitz and Buchenwald

One day the Gestapo hanged a child. Even the SS were disturbed by the prospect of hanging a young boy in front of thousands of spectators. The child who, Wiesel recalled, had the face of a' sad-eyed angel,' was silent, lividly pale and almost calm as he ascended the gallows. Behind Wiesel, one of the prisoners asked: 'Where is God? Where is He?' It took the child half an hour to die, while the prisoners were forced to look him in the face. The same man asked again: 'Where is God now?' And Wiesel heard a voice within him make this answer: 'Where is he? here He is — He is hanging here on this gallows.'
                                                     - retold by Karen Armstrong

....

The physical nature of the crucifixion need not detain us — the flogging, the degradation and the torture. Death is normally from suffocation, when the body is too exhausted to lever itself upwards to allow another breath. Jesus refused drugged wine and died fully aware but relatively quickly. The spear thrust was to confirm death, so that the body could be removed before the sabbath began at dusk.

— see Mt 27:27f... Mk 15:15f... Lk 23:26f... Jn 19:16f...

These 'passion narratives' have pride of place in the records. They are vivid and moving — not the least because the awful culmination of Jesus' ministry becomes by God's act an unexpected triumph.The significance of this death is not easy to express. The imagery of animal sacrifice is not meaningful today nor the idea of transferred guilt. The suggestion of a ransom payment to the devil is crude at best and we can scarce be satisfied with the idea of God visiting undeserved punishment upon his son. Such are distortions which come from isolating Jesus' death from his teaching. He:

> ➤ *identified with the oppressed and suffering, sharing their pain and degradation*
> ➤ *accepted the consequences of human injustice without anger or bitterness*
> ➤ *stayed faithful to God to realise a Kingdom where dignity and justice could prevail*
> ➤ *showed how to love and forgive and so open the way to peace.*

Christians saw that God himself was revealed in this death — the death of one who was the very characterisation of God. What Jesus was, God is, and they saw how God approaches humanity with limitless love and confronts all that is destructive and evil by taking the pain upon himself. The way of Jesus exemplified God's way of loving, God's way of forgiving and God's way of salvation.

This contrasts with the Buddhist call to detachment and the Hindu acceptance of the inevitable laws of karma. It goes further than the Muslim proclamation of God's mercy. Muhammad revered Jesus but could not accept that he was really crucified or that his dying could be a revelation. For Christians, it *is* a revelation. A revelation of God's love and a spur to discipleship. It is neither the fact of Jesus' death that is vital nor the manner of it; it is the love that triumphed in death — the love of God himself.

....

God was drawing the world to himself.   *Paul - IICor 5:19*

....

Why do you search for the living among the dead ?　　　　　　　*Lk 24:5*

The women told everything to the eleven and to the others. But the story seemed to them to be nonsense, and they would not believe them.　　　　*Luke - 24:9,11*

They will not be convinced even if someone does rise from the dead.

Jesus - Lk 16:31

Do you believe because you have seen me? Happy are they who do not need to see me.

Jesus - Jn 20:29

He has come back from the dead and has gone on before you.　　　*Mt 28:7*

Why do you Galileans stand looking up into the sky?　　　　*Luke - Acts 1:11*

It was not possible for death to hold him.　　　　　　*Peter - Acts 2:24*

We cannot physically inherit the Kingdom of God.　　　*Paul - ICor 15:50*

Indwelt by the spirit of holiness he was revealed in power as son of God by being raised from the dead.　　　　　　　　　　*Paul - Rom 1:4*

He was clearly seen in the flesh but equally clearly known in the spirit.

Paul - ITim 3:16

Faith is the evidence of invisible reality.　　　　　　　*Heb 11:1*

The Easter event is not determined by the empty tomb, but at best illustrated by it.

Hans Küng

We may very simply test our understanding of the Resurrection of Christ by putting to ourselves the following question: 'Do we wish that there had been at the time something corresponding to an impartial scientific enquiry, and that there had been better attestation to the Resurrection on the part of disinterested outside observers; or do we realise that such attestation would be quite helpless to prove the thing that Christians really believe, and that only the testimony of those within *the faith could here be of any avail?'*

John Baillie

....

Jesus was a typical man; they always say they will come back but they never do!
anon.

What happened to Jesus' body is not recoverable. Theories of theft, resuscitation, hallucination and fabrication are all fraught with difficulty, but so is the claim made by Jesus' followers. Science gives no grounds for believing in a crude form of resurrection. We may speculate about matter and energy, dimensions of reality and even interpenetrating universes but proven answers are not available to us.

Paul writes; *"God revealed his son within me"* Gal 1:15 and uses words more akin to spiritual vision than physical sight Stating that *"flesh and blood cannot inherit the kingdom of God"*, he could hardly believe that Jesus' flesh and blood did so. The word 'body' in the New Testament conveys more than our word 'physical'. It is a way of emphasising the full reality of Jesus' continued existence over against the bloodless, thinned-down, shadowy world of Hades.

The Christian faith does not depend on the bare fact of disappearing bones nor would such evidence convince the sceptic. Two contrasting Greek words are used in John 16:16 — *"in a while you will see me no more but soon after that, you will see me.* The first word concerns physical sight; the second, spiritual insight. What we have is a mixed, fragmentary testimony witnessing to an experience that changed lives.

(see Matt 28, Mark 16, Luke 24, John 20 & 21)

The early Christians testified to the living presence of Christ after his death. They were convinced by experience, and despite fears, doubts and disillusionment, were willing to live and die in this faith. Even some of Jesus' brothers, who 'had no faith in him' (Jn 7:5), became convinced — James becoming a leader of the church. The resurrection comes not from Jesus but from God and the experience of the risen Jesus is scarcely distinguishable from the experience of the Spirit or that of God himself. Paul's emphasis is that Jesus was raised into God, rather than back to life on earth. [see 116]

The Transfiguration — Mt 17:1f. — has been compared to a resurrection experience. It may be best understood as a mystic vision, where the deepest intuitions of the disciples are expressed symbolically. Jesus' death was seen to be foreshadowed in the Law and the Prophets. The cloud is a traditional sign of the presence of God.

The Ascension — Acts 1:1f. — is a familiar model of exaltation. Once again we have to go behind the words to find the conviction that God has endorsed all that Jesus was and did. Other New Testament writers do not separate it from the Resurrection.

Immortality — usually refers to the soul surviving death but the Christian conviction is that the whole person is raised to life.

THE TEACHING OF JESUS

Whoever can listen, let him listen.   *Jesus - Mt 11:15*

Earth and sky will pass but what I say will remains.   *Jesus - Mk 13:31*

Humanity needs more than bread; it is more important to know God's will.
                                                  Jesus - Mt 4:4, quoting Dt 8:3

I shall speak in parables — things kept secret from the beginning of the world.
                          Ps 78:2. Matthew applies these words to Jesus - Mt 13:35

Men must be taught as if you taught them not.   *Alexander Pope*

*No man can reveal to you aught but that which already lies half asleep in the dawning
of your knowledge.*   *Kahlil Gibran*

*Wear the yoke. See for yourselves how slight were my labours compared to the great
satisfaction I have found.*   *Jesus, son of Sirach - Ecclus 51:26*
            (Rabbis used this image in reference to the law)

*Wear my yoke and let me teach you, for I am gentle and seek no power over you. My
yoke is comfortable and my load light.*
                  Jesus – son of Joseph, who may well have made yokes - Mt 11:29

Dry your eyes if you are weeping now, for you will laugh.   *Jesus – Luke 6:21*

*What have we to do with tales and laughter? I judge that not only extravagant jesting is
to be condemned, but all jesting.*   *Bernard of Clairveaux*

He deserves paradise who makes his companions laugh.   *The Qur'an*

Dry your eyes if you are weeping now, for you will laugh.   *Jesus - Lk 6:21*

....

Choosing foundations:
Everyone who comes to me and hears my words and acts on them ... is like a
man building a house who dug deep and laid the foundations on rock. When
the river was in flood, it burst upon that house, but could not weaken it,
because it had been soundly secured. He who hears and does not act is like a
man who built his house on soil without foundations. As the river burst upon
it, the house collapsed and fell with a great crash.   Jesus - Lk 6:47f.

Note: We know the teaching of Jesus only through those who interpreted it for us.
This should be borne in mind throughout this section.

Jesus is widely accepted as a great teacher. Judaism held its teachers in high honour and Jesus drew upon a rich Jewish tradition as well as being a master in his own right.

He used poetry and parable as an artist uses paint, probably working and re-working material, often adapting it to different audiences. We should not assume that any parable or saying had a single fixed form. He surely spoke with humour — a quality that is strained away by translation and sober piety. In his teaching he pictures a camel floating in soup and a man walking along the street oblivious to the plank that was projecting from his eye. His stories include the bothersome neighbour, the fed-up judge and the rascally accountant, and it was surely with a smile that he used phrases like — *'If you, bad as you are, know how to give good things to your children...'.* Unlike John the Baptist, his presence was welcomed by young and old on social occasions so there is enough to make us pause, in case we become too earnest in our understanding of his words.

Jesus knew that his listeners would hear (or not hear) according to their character and situation. He sought a thoughtful response, where each could make his or her own discoveries, often leaving a question in the air or a story to be mulled over at leisure. His harshest words were for those with closed minds.

Yet he spoke with authority, as one who knew at first hand. He said that his teaching would give a foundation for life and was food for the human spirit — as comfortable as a well-made yoke. Above all he believed that his words were given to him by God and that his own authority was grounded in that of the Author of all truth.

The parables: It is important to understand what these are and what they are not:
- they are designed to be highly memorable for people who relied on memory much more than we do.
- they are based on familiar characters — a housewife, a shepherd, a father, an employer, a traveller, or a farmer.
- they invite listeners to be involved, to make the situation their own and judge the truth for themselves.
- the furnishings of the story must not be pressed.

When we encounter the words of Jesus, we do not judge them by a philosophical system; they meet us with the question of how we are to interpret our existence.
Rudolph Bultmann

God gives you his light to shine into the depths of your own soul.   Prov 20:27

This people pay me lip service, but their hearts are not in it.
        Isaiah 29:13 (quoted by Jesus Mt 15:8)

All you need to say is 'yes' or 'no'.   Jesus - Mt 5:37

Don't show off your religion in front of others.   Jesus - Mt 6:1

How can you offer to take the speck of dust out of your brother's eye when you have a plank in your own?   Jesus - Lk 6:41

The man I kiss is the one you want.   Judas - Mt 26:48

Our within should be as our without.   Jewish

Hypocrisy is the shadow cast by idealism, and the higher the idealism, the longer the shadow.   D C Somervell

Hypocrisy is the homage vice pays to virtue.   La Rochefoucauld

Men never do evil so completely and cheerfully as when they do it from religious conviction.   Blaise Pascal

You must not misuse the name of God.   Ex 20:7

The fruit depends on the tree:
There is no such thing as a good tree producing bad fruit, nor yet a bad tree producing good fruit. Every tree is known by its fruit: you do not gather figs from brambles or pick grapes from thistles. Good people produce good from the store of good within themselves.
        Jesus - Lk 6:43f.

An enquirer came to Rabbi Shammai and asked if the whole Law could be summed up whilst standing on one leg — and was met with a blow from a ruler. He made the same request to Rabbi Hillel, who replied, 'What is unpleasant to yourself, do not to your neighbour'.

Derivations: 'sincere' = without wax. Unscrupulous traders in the Roman markets used to disguise cracks in earthenware vessels by the use of wax.

In Jesus' teaching sincerity is perhaps the essential condition for all else. What is in the human heart is what matters. The danger for us all, especially in religion, is hypocrisy. Time and again Jesus' harshest words are for religious leaders whose piety is a pretence.

Matthew records an extended assault on scribes and Pharisees in ch.23. Some years before many Pharisees had given their lives to prevent the Jewish nation and faith from being engulfed by Greek culture. They called on their people to be separate and distinct (the word 'pharisee' means 'the separated'). Now, they had fragmented into several groups — Shammai and Hillel were resolute opponents, said to disagree on over 300 points of law.

The best Pharisees were often self-critical — aware of pitfalls common enough in human nature. The Jewish Talmud lists seven kinds of Pharisee:

> ➢ *the 'what do I get out of it?' Pharisee*
> ➢ *the 'I look the part' Pharisee*
> ➢ *the 'oh my poor head' Pharisee, who walks with his head down so as not to see a woman, and therefore bangs into a wall*
> ➢ *the pestle-Pharisee, who goes about so bent that he looks like a pestle*
> ➢ *the 'what is my duty so that I may do it?' Pharisee*
> ➢ *the 'I do one good deed a day' Pharisee and*
> ➢ *the real Pharisee who acts out of love for God.*

The *Assumption of Moses* (Jewish) condemns *'these vile and impure men who claim to be the only pure, the only righteous beings, but who are nothing but monsters of pride'.* Such sins are not limited to any one group, as we know well in our own hearts. Some Pharisees listened to Jesus and warned him when he was in danger (Lk 13:31). Nicodemus was a Pharisee who tried to secure a fair trial for Jesus and later became a follower (Jn 7:50, 19:38f.). And there was a scribe who was said by Jesus to be 'not far from the Kingdom of God' (Mk 12:34).

Jesus therefore called for that quiet, genuine commitment which results in transparency, trustworthiness and helpfulness. It was the Society of Friends which took most literally the plain yes or no suggested by Jesus, even to refusing to take oaths in court. We may not go that far but can still be impressed by the trust that Quakers earned over the years — a trust that underlay their success in business and in resolving conflict.

....

Listen closely, O Israel, God is one, and you must be one in loving him with all your heart and all your soul and all your strength.   *- Dt 6:4*
      (This Jewish teaching was certainly fundamental for Jesus)

Have we not all have one father? Has not one God made us?   *Malachi - 2:10*

When you pray, say,'Our Father ...'   *Jesus - Mt 6:9*

Philip said, 'Lord, help us to see the Father' — Jesus answered, 'If you have seen me, you have seen the Father'.   *John 14:8*

My Father is always working.   *Jesus - Jn 5:17*

If you would imitate God, be gracious to the ungracious; for the sun shines on the wicked, and the sea is open to pirates.   *Seneca*

Your heavenly Father provides sun for good and bad alike, and rain for innocent and guilty.   *Jesus - Mt 5:45*

....

The loving father: (see Lk 15:11- 32)

The story of the prodigal (wasteful) son and that of the good Samaritan can lay claim to be among the best known stories in the world. The loving father is the main character and represents God. The story mirrors the human condition before God who shows respect for all his children:

> ➢ he gives us freedom and responsibility,
> ➢ he does not impose himself but loves unconditionally,
> ➢ when we waste our inheritance, he suffers with us,
> ➢ when we 'return home', he meets us with generous joy,
> ➢ when we are loyal but lack love, he seeks to open our hearts to others.

There is no *scheme* of salvation here, no legalism and no obstacles to reconciliation. This *is* the Gospel of Christ.

Notes:
1. the elder son would receive 2/3 and the younger 1/3 of the land.
2. becoming a swineherd is degrading.. Jews did not eat pork.
3. the son does not get a chance to finish his rehearsed speech.
4. the ring implies restoration to sonship.
5. the older son would have been away in the hill country.
6. 'everything I have is yours' — the elder son would inherit the remaining two thirds of the land.

Jesus did not leave us any teaching about God which would satisfy a modern sceptic. The reality of God was not an issue. What we have is the expression of a profoundly personal relationship between Jesus and God, expressed in the use of the intimate term — *abba* —father. Jesus' first recorded words at 12 years old showed his consciousness of being about his Father's business, and his last words in death were 'Father, I give my spirit into your hands'. He readily turned to God in moments of crisis or exaltation, and often withdrew to quiet places to pray, teaching his followers to do the same.

For him, God was the supreme Creator — who feeds, clothes and cares for all living things. He is all goodness and always accessible, providing for the deserving and undeserving alike. Unsurprisingly, as the source of all, his claim is absolute, yet at the same time, he is patient and forgiving. Nevertheless, there may be some whose hearts are closed to any move that God makes.

As with us all, Jesus had to speak in anthropomorphic terms (using human imagery to describe God), yet there is no confusion. If real goodness can be found in ordinary people, how much more, insists Jesus, must this be true of God. And when human possibilities are exhausted, there is still the unlimited resource of God to bring about renewal. In any case, God is spirit and can only be worshipped 'in spirit and in truth'　　(Jn 4:24).

The Gospels are clear that Jesus knew himself to be called by God to fulfil whatever was to be asked of him. God was at work in human affairs and Jesus saw himself as a servant of God to be used on behalf of a Kingdom yet to come, but already at hand. Although several parables speak of a landlord or king who was absent for a time, the implication is not that God has left his people but that he gives responsibility to humanity to realise the values of the Kingdom, as a true commonwealth where justice shall prevail.

It is appropriate to spell the word 'God' with a capital letter when referring to belief in one supreme God, whatever the religion. Those who write that Christians or Muslims believe in 'a god' indicate their own scepticism rather than the belief they would describe.
Some translators and hymn writers use 'Yahweh' but such a name today suggests one god among others and therefore misleads. The name 'Jehovah' is a fiction created in 1520. It was guesswork, because early Jewish scholars had added the vowels of the Hebrew for "Lord" to the consonants of the written, but unspoken, name of God. 'Yahweh' is a closer approximation to the original.

I against my brother
I and my brother against our cousin
I, my brother and my cousin against the neighbours
All of us against the foreigner   *Bedouin proverb*

You must love your neighbour as you love yourself.   *Lev 19:18*

Be to others as you would like them to be to you.   *Jesus - Lk 6:31*

He embraced the whole world as his city and extended his acquaintance, his society,
and his affection to all mankind.   *Montaigne - of Socrates*

Do nothing to others, which, if done to you, would cause you pain.   *Hindu*

Do not hurt others with that which pains yourself.   *Buddhist*

No one of you is a believer until he loves for his brother what he loves for himself.
                                                    Muslim

Look on other men as you look on yourself.   *Sikh*

Do not to any creature what you would not like done to you.   *Jain*

The golden rule is that there is no golden rule.   *George Bernard Shaw*

Great Spirit, help me never to judge another till I have walked two weeks in his
moccasins.   *Sioux*

Do not wrong or hate your neighbour. It is not he whom you wrong — you wrong
yourself.   *Shawnee*

If anyone does not welcome you, shake the dust of that house from your feet.
                                                    Jesus - Mt 10:14

The neighbour praises selflessness because he derives advantage from it.   *Nietzsche*

The Good Samaritan
A man was travelling from Jerusalem to Jericho when he was attacked by robbers and
left half dead. A priest going the same way saw him, but went past on the other side. A
Levite did exactly the same. But a Samaritan took pity on him. He bandaged his
wounds, bathing them with oil and wine. He lifted him on to his donkey, brought him
to an inn and looked after him. The next day he produced two silver pieces and asked
the innkeeper to look after him, promising to make up the amount, if he should spend
more.
Who do you think was a true neighbour to the man who was robbed?   Lk 10:25-37

At the heart of Jesus' teaching about human relationships lies the story of the Good Samaritan. Its very familiarity can mean that we miss some of its power. The details are memorable:

> the barren road from the high plateau to Jericho was notorious for thieves and it was unwise to travel alone.
> the priest and Levite cannot plead Temple duty or ritual as an excuse — they are travelling away from Jerusalem.
> we might expect them to live up to their vocation but their livelihood was inherited and did not depend on their beliefs.
> it was dangerous to stop, and could have been a trap.
> the care given is impressive — oil to soothe, alcohol to sterilise, and the acceptance of continuing responsibility.

This part of the message is clear enough but there is more to the story. The Samaritans were despised by strict Jews. Today's bitter ethnic disputes can give us a glimpse of the deep distrust and mutual contempt that divided the two peoples. Traditional stories were often built around 3 characters — the priest, the Levite and the good Jew. Jesus substituted the Samaritan — to some of his hearers, this would have been offensive. The story therefore condemns racism. There are two neighbours to love — the one in need and the racially despised.

We are here on earth to do good to others. What the others are here for, I don't know.
W H Auden

....

The Rabble: (see Jn 7:49)
The Samaritans tend to be lumped together with other 'people of the land' who attracted the contempt of the learned and those who practised the required rituals. Many were very poor and illiterate. Such people were seen as ignorant —their work prevented them from obeying the ramifications of the Law or paying the tithes demanded.They were all commonly referred to as 'sinners'. The Talmud defined them as those who 'did not eat their bread in a state of ritual cleanliness'. Even Hillel asserted, 'they have no conscience, and they are anything but human'. Rabbi Jonathan forbade intermarriage as equivalent to mating with a beast. Rabbi Eleazar recommended 'quartering' - even on the Day of Atonement.
Jesus mixed freely with everyone — Samaritans, women, Gentiles, the immoral and the poor.
The majority of the people were glad to listen to him.   - Mk 12:37

Love your neighbour, but don't pull down the hedge.   *Swiss proverb*

....

Gold is a pitfall to those who are obsessed with it. A wealthy man does well if he is not tainted by it.   *Ecclus 31:7*

Wherever you keep your treasure, there will be your heart.   *Jesus - Lk 12:34*

How much better off would you be if you won all the money in the world and lost — yourself?   *Jesus - Mk 8:36*

I had no shoes to my feet. I grumbled. I met a man with no feet.   *Indian*

Even when someone has more than enough, that does not guarantee him life.
                                                                                                              Jesus - Lk 12:15

The love of money is at the root of all evil.   *Paul - ITim 6:10*

They are to be rich benefactors and ready to give generously. Then they will know what life really is.   *Paul - ITim 6:18*

She clothes her stones in gold and leaves her sons naked.
                                                        Bernard of Clairveaux - speaking of the Church

Money is like muck — not good except it be spread.   *Francis Bacon*

Only those riches should be sought that can be got justly, distributed cheerfully, and left contentedly.   *Francis Bacon*

....

The Pauper
There was a wealthy farmer who had gathered a good harvest. He wondered to himself: 'What shall I do? I don't have the space to store my crop. I will pull down my barns and make them bigger. I will put everything in them and I will say to myself, *You have plenty put away, enough for many years, take life easy — eat, drink, and enjoy yourself.*' But God said to him, 'You are a fool, tonight you must die, and who will get the money you have made?' So it is with the man who accumulates wealth for himself, but remains a pauper in the sight of God.   Jesus - Lk 12:16f

....

What's a thousand dollars? Mere chicken feed. A poultry matter.
                                                                                                              Groucho Marx

In Jesus' teaching money and possessions are neither good nor evil but the place they occupy in our lives and the use they are put to matter a great deal. He challenges us to decide what is real wealth, and to use wisely 'the wealth of this world'.

Ultimately there is a choice between God and money (Lk 16:13) and God and his Kingdom must come before all else. But this is not a self-denying choice, as our true interests lie in discovering that there is more to life than material wealth. We are shaped by the priorities we choose — therefore it matters where our heart is.

If Jesus asked his disciples to give away their money, it does *not* follow that he asks everyone to do the same. The disciples had a particular vocation to fulfil. The rich young man wanted to be a disciple and, for him, money was an obstacle. We cannot make a general rule out of the challenge that Jesus put to him (Mt 19:16f). More likely, as with Zacchaeus (Lk 19:2f), we have to work out our own way of life.

The difficult parable of the dishonest steward —Lk 16:1f — rests on the recognition that human relationships are more important than money. It may be that the steward is making a poor beginning in learning to value others but it is a beginning. Jesus no doubt implied that most of us could do so much more in sorting out our priorities.

The issue then lies between the love of money, and the love of God and our neighbour. The rich farmer has no thought for the poor, nor does Dives (Lk 16:19f) have any compassion for the beggar at his gate. In resolving this, we determine what we ourselves become.

Care is needed in interpreting Jesus' parables. He may appear to be speaking of material wealth but money may symbolise something else. He is not speaking of material possessions when he says:
More will be given to those who have and everything will be taken away from those who have nothing. (Mt 25:29). A talent was then a measure of silver. We now use the word for personal abilities precisely because of this parable. We are expected to make the most of our God-given gifts or they, and we, will wither.

[140]

A tourist went to visit the famous Polish rabbi, Hafez Hayyim. He was astonished to see only a table and a bench in the rabbi's simple home.
'Rabbi, where is your furniture?' asked the tourist. 'Where is yours?' replied Hafez.
'Mine? But I'm only a visitor here'.
'So am I' said the rabbi.

....

Hate evil, love good, and ensure justice in the courts.   Amos - 5:15

He has given the hungry good things to eat but sent the rich away with nothing.
                                                                                    Mary - Lk 1:53

He has sent me to bring good news to the poor.   Jesus - Lk 4:18 (Is 61:1)

You will be happy if you long to see what is right.   Jesus - Mt 5:6

You have neglected the main demands of the law — justice, mercy, and trust.
                                                                                    Jesus - Mt 23:23

When you throw a party, ask the poor, the disabled, the lame and the blind.
                                                                                    Jesus - Lk 14:13

Anything you did for one of my friends, however unimportant, you did for me.
                                                                                    Jesus - Mt 25:40

He who is generous to the poor gives to God.   Prov 19:17

Poverty and wealth both come from God   Hannah ISam 2:7

If you are poor, be glad, for God's kingdom is for you.   Jesus - Lk 6:20

Will not God give justice to his own?   Jesus - Lk 18:7

If anyone slaps your right cheek, turn and offer him the left.   Jesus - Mt 5:39

This was a formal insult - equivalent to 'throwing down the gauntlet'. Jesus might now say, 'don't be drawn!'. Like God, be slow to anger (Neh 9:17). After all, pursuing justice for oneself is not the same as seeking it for another.

We had shown that anyone who slapped us on our cheek would get his head kicked off.
                                                                                    Nikita Krushchev

Has this house, which is called the house of God, become a den of thieves?
                                                                                    Jeremiah - 7:11

God's house shall be called a house of prayer for all nations — but you have made it a den of thieves.   Jesus - Mk 11:17

....

To Jesus, justice is not based on an abstract rule of equality, but on God's provision for all his people. The poor belong to God's Kingdom — they are part of the family. It is the poor who are blessed, not their poverty. Those who are preoccupied with their riches, shut themselves away from the Kingdom.   [also 143]

When Jesus criticises the leaders of his day, he challenges their hypocrisy. They failed to act on behalf of the needy. Worse still, they contributed to the problem by legalistic demands, heavy taxation and corrupt courts. Jesus' anger was powerfully demonstrated in his challenge to those profiteering in the Temple courts — (Mk 11:15f). Money-changing was necessary, because of the varied coinage circulating in Palestine, the diversity of visitors, and the need to offer coins free from images of other divinities — Caesar was claimed to be divine. The problem is exploitation, particularly of foreigners, and there is a wider challenge of misdirected religion, echoing the passionate anger of Jeremiah long before — see Jer 7.

Strikingly, Jesus did not publicly oppose the Roman occupation. Perhaps it was because he knew that the odds were too great. More likely he believed that his mission was profounder and more far-reaching. Certainly he dealt with Romans as fellow human beings who were doing their duty and not as representatives of an imperial power, which in any case he believed to be limited by the authority of God. In the end, his teaching conquered Rome.

Martin Luther King criticised white moderates for preferring a negative peace, which is the absence of tension, rather than the positive peace, which is the presence of justice.

....

Justice There was once a wealthy man, who used to dress in purple and the finest of linen, and feasted magnificently every day. At his gate lay a poor man called Lazarus covered in sores. He would have been glad to satisfy his hunger with the left-overs from the wealthy man's table. Dogs used to come and lick his sores. One day the poor man died and was carried away by the God's messengers to be with Abraham. The wealthy man also died and was buried ......

                    Jesus - Lk 16:19f.

Note: Such a story is commonplace in Judaism and can even be found centuries before in Egypt. The scene was drawn from traditional imagery and should not be taken as a literal description of heaven and hell [117]. Although the message is about redress in the next life, it is clearly meant to challenge conditions in this life (see especially v 31).

....

I will place my law in their very hearts.   Jeremiah - 31:33

The ark of the covenant carries those who carry it.   Jewish

Do not suppose that I have come to do away with the law and the prophets; I did not come to do away with them but to complete them.   Jesus - Mt 5:17

No one puts fresh wine into old wineskins; if he does, the wine will burst the skins, and both wine and skins are lost.   Jesus - Mk 2:22

You know what the law says about murder. But believe me; God will judge a man who is even angry with his brother.   Jesus - Mt 5:21

The rules about the sabbath are as mountains hanging on a hair, for scripture is scanty and the rules many.   The Mishnah (Jewish) on Hag 1:8

Wasn't it right that she should be set free on the sabbath?   Jesus - Lk 13:16
(Legalists criticised Jesus for healing on a day when no work should be done.)

The sabbath was made for people, not people for the sabbath.   Mk 2:27

If you obey and fulfil the commandment of God, it is as if you fulfilled yourselves.
                    Rabbi Hanina

The letter kills but it is the spirit which gives life.   Paul - IICor 3:6

Live by the commandments; do not die by them.   The Talmud

The foreigner who practises the law is the equal of the High Priest.   Rabbinic

The law of love is the ultimate law because it is the negation of law.   Paul Tillich

The law was our guardian to lead us to Christ.   Paul - Gal 3:24
(strictly this referred to a slave who took a child to school in Roman cities.)

The law, taken abstract from its original reason and end, is made a shell without a kernel, and a body without a soul.   John Lilburne 1642

....

One day Jesus saw a man out at work. It was the sabbath. Nobody was supposed to do any work on the sabbath. 'Sir,' said Jesus, 'if you know what you are doing, you are a very happy man. If you don't — if you just don't care what you do and when you do it — you really are breaking the law about the sabbath'.
                    — found in some old manuscripts of Luke's Gospel.

Jewish civil and religious law was one and the same. We think of civil law as detached and separate but this is, in part, mistaken. Our civil law rests on our morality, which, in turn, rests on our beliefs. Jesus shows his respect for the Law and what lies behind it but he challenges the forest of regulations which obscured its essence.

It has been said that beliefs are passed on like coconuts — the husk needs cracking.The records show that Jesus was criticised for cracking the husk — for the company he kept, the lesser rituals he neglected, and for his interpretation of the sabbath law, which was the touchstone for much else. The sabbath law was humanitarian in origin. It created space apart from the daily grind — space for family, for reflection and for vision. It was 'made for man' and not meant to enforce conformity for conformity's sake. Jesus healed on the sabbath because, by so doing, he fulfilled the law — restoring its original purpose. We shall see in the Sermon on the Mount how Jesus shows again and again his concern for the quality of our humanity. It is the purpose of the Law that counts.

Jewish law was overlaid by Roman law. The people resented this double burden and was near to revolt. Jesus accepted what God had permitted and was not involved in civil disobedience.

Christians may find helpful the words of a contemporary Jewish rabbi on the Law:
These by no means insignificant precepts acquire their religious worth by seeking to bind life to God with innumerable 'ties of love'. These statutes do not seek to lead man away from his own environment; they leave him to his work and his home where they connect him with God. They demand the inner presence of the soul during the action of each hour. Each morning, noon and evening, each beginning and each ending, has its prayers and worship. The atmosphere of the house of God, the halo of religious devotion, is spread over the whole of existence; each day has its lesson and its consecration; the Law has prevented Judaism from becoming a mere religion for the Sabbath. And similarly it has overcome sacraments with their separation of holiness from life, by its introduction of holiness into life.
                              — abridged from Leo Baeck - 'The Essence of Judaism'.

We have several set forms which are held as law, and so held and used for good reason, though we cannot at present remember that reason.
                              Chief Justice Fortescue - 1458

....

Change your ways for God's kingdom is here.
                                        John the Baptist - Mt 3:2 (and Jesus - Mt 4:17)

I did not come for the sake of the respectable, but for sinners.   Jesus - Mt 9:13

If you were blind, you would not be guilty, but as you claim to see, you become guilty.
                                                                        Jesus - Jn 9:41

You surely cannot mean me?   Judas - Mt 26:25

If I had told them nothing, they would not be guilty.   Jesus - Jn 15:22

Whoever is innocent of all wrong may cast the first stone.   Jesus - Jn 8:7

Everyone who does wrong gives himself up to slavery.   Jesus - Jn 8:34

I see the better way and approve it; I follow the worse.   Ovid

The stain of sin is not something positive - it is like a shadow.   Aquinas

The future of mankind depends on recognition of the shadow.   Jung

Each of us takes his place in the centre of his own world. But I am not the centre of the world and God is. This is my original sin.   William Temple

Go away, Lord, for I am a sinful man.   Peter - Lk 5:8

Only when you have been blessed with a harvest of fish will you know that you are a sinner.   Walter Brueggemann

....

Humility before God

Two men went up to the temple to pray, one was a Pharisee and the other a tax-collector. The Pharisee stood up and this was his prayer: 'God, I thank you that I am not like other men — greedy, dishonest and adulterous — or, for that matter, like this tax-collector. I fast twice a week; I pay tithes on all that I get.' But the other kept his distance and would not even look up to heaven, but blamed himself, saying, 'God, have mercy on me, sinner that I am.' This man, I tell you, and not the other, went home in peace.

                                                        Jesus - Lk 18:10f.

Notes: 1. the tax-collector was a 'quisling' , who collaborated with the Romans. Jesus exaggerates the contrast to make his point.
            2. 'acquitted' — i.e. his relationship with God is restored.

The church has been far more concerned about sin than Jesus was. Most of the teachings we have are in John's Gospel. Not only that, but the word 'sinners' has to be understood aright — Jesus refers to the 'righteous' who are not, and to 'sinners' — who are only sinners in the sense that they are thought to be so by the strictly orthodox.

The word 'sin' now carries a heavy freight but in the Bible, it often means 'missing the mark', as an archer's arrow may fall short of the target. There are all sorts of reasons why people may fall short — why we all fall short, and we may or may not be to blame. There are terrible sins that deserve condemnation — evils of child abuse, torture, genocide — but there is failure arising from the chains that have been forged by inheritance, circumstance and communities. This kind of sin is akin to sickness as it carries no personal blame.

Jesus dealt kindly with those typically regarded as sinners but condemned the self-righteous who exploited others and lacked both understanding and humility. We have a paradox here — those sure of their righteousness may need to be 'convicted of sin', but those who know feelings of guilt only too well, need release and the chance to make a fresh start. It is a bitter and distorted religion which deliberately reinforces guilt — the hymn-writer, Augustus Toplady (*"Rock of Ages"*), preached that everyone committed 630 million sins by the time they were 20 years old.This is not the voice of Jesus. The commandments may show where we fall short but Christ came to save, not to condemn.   [see also 'The Rabble' 31]

William Temple describes a traditional view of sin (see opposite) but this should be treated with caution. Young children are self-centred but should not be condemned as sinful. We are all self-centred in some sense and how could it be otherwise? To put it more strongly, has not God created our 'self'? Is he not still creating it? Jesus teaches us to love our neighbour *as ourselves* and when the lost son *'comes to himself'* he is on the road to salvation — Lk 15.   [see 9,112]

Sin is therefore of three kinds:

  ➤ evil that flouts the fundamental order established by God.
  ➤ inadequacy or falling short.
  ➤ self-righteousness, which raises barriers between ourselves and God —
     and ourselves and others.

The first cries out for repentance and radical change. The second, the recognition that God allows us room to make mistakes. The last needs a fresh humility, which will allow us to grow again.

THE TEACHING OF JESUS

....

If you forgive those who wrong you, then God, your Father, will forgive you.
Jesus - Mt 6:14

Even if someone wrongs you times without number and is sorry for it, you are to forgive him.
Jesus - Lk 17:4

You know that they used to be told, 'An eye for an eye, a tooth for a tooth.' But I tell you: Do not turn against those who wrong you.
Jesus - Mt 5:38

Father, forgive them; they have no idea what they are doing.
Jesus - Lk 23:34

Whoever opts for revenge should dig two graves.
Chinese proverb

No man ever forgets where he buried the hatchet.
Ogden Nash

God of forgiveness, do not forgive those who created this place. Remember the nocturnal procession of children — all so wise, so frightened, so beautiful.
Elie Wiesel – on the 50th anniversary of the liberation of Auschwitz

I don't think its vengeance that people should want. I think what they should work for is the truth.
Aung San Sun Kyi - under house arrest in Burma

There is a hard law — that when a deep injury is done to us, we never recover until we forgive.
Alan Paton

He who cannot forgive others breaks the bridge over which he must pass himself.
George Herbert

Jesus never meant to produce guilt feelings and leave people alone with them but to invite them to an inner, radical and total conversion — a homecoming of the whole person to God.
Hans Küng

We are all formed of weaknesses and errors; let us naturally pardon each other's follies.
Voltaire

....

The debtors: There was once a king ....   Jesus - Mt 18:23f
Notes: 1. v34 should not be used to support a doctrine of everlasting torment.
2. the debts consist of 100 denarii and 60 million denarii — the latter would need a 5 mile baggage train of 8,600 carriers, each with a sack 60lb in weight.!

....

Always forgive your enemies. Nothing annoys them so much.   Mark Twain

In current usage, forgiveness tends to be a one-sided letting off. Jesus, however, asks for changed lives and a restored relationship. He encourages his followers never to hold someone's offence against them — knowing that restoration may be impossible if they make no move. So it is with our relationship with God. He is ever the same, never affronted, never withdrawing from us, but we have to turn to him, even as the straying son had to decide to return home.

Repentance in the Bible is a practical word. It isn't feeling sorry — it is a change of mind and direction. It is the way we face which decides whether we have a future. In the Lord's Prayer, Jesus makes our forgiveness conditional on our willingness to forgive others. This is not an arbitrary condition. We cannot close ourselves up in one direction and be open in another — forgiveness, like love, has to flow freely. As we judge others, so we will judge ourselves.

To understand forgiveness as restoration makes it possible to ask forgiveness for the sins of the past. It is natural for us to carry regret and guilt for past failure but God can heal the blame and hurt of old wrongs. We cannot change the past nor can it be forgotten but we can be restored to new life and this will spur us both to seek new relationships and to fight the obvious evils which beset human life.

Jesus speaks of one sin that cannot be forgiven — the one against the Holy Spirit (Mt 12:31f). His critics had dismissed the evident good of his healing miracles as the work of the devil. In this way black and white are reversed, good and evil change places. But these things are given. It is not for us to *decide* what is good and what is evil but to *recognise* which is which. Such things belong to the moral order established by God. If we insist on being perverse, what can God do? We shut ourselves away and stifle all renewal.

Ultimately, it is a matter of love and not a legal issue. The woman who anointed Jesus (Lk 7:36f) was already free because of her love.
As Peter says, 'love makes up for a great deal' (IPet 1:8)   [114]

Rabbi Leo Baeck is quoted frequently in this book as one of the great Jewish voices of the last century. He was leader of the German Jewish community in the 1930's and was sent to Theresienstadt concentration camp. Russian troops arrived at the camp on the very day on which Leo Baeck was due to be shot. He set himself to save the lives of the camp guards — first arguing with the Russians, and then, when the guards were handed over to the inmates, persuading his fellow Jews not to seek vengeance. He later went to the USA and died in 1957, aged 80.

....

With God, anything is possible.   *Jesus - Mt 19:26*

You must not presume to examine God.   *Dt 6:16 - quoted by Jesus - Mt 4:7*

As you have believed it could happen, so let it happen.   *Jesus - Mt 9:29*

If you have faith, you can say to a mountain, 'Move!' and it will move.
                                       Jesus - Mt 17:20
    (Jewish teachers often spoke of faith as an 'uprooter of mountains'.)

Lord, I have faith, help me where faith falls short.
           - the distraught father of an epileptic boy to Jesus - Mk 9:24

I have therefore found it necessary to deny knowledge in order to make room for faith.
                                                 Kant

I don't believe, I know.   *Jung*

Faith is one of the world's great evils, comparable to the smallpox virus but harder to eradicate.   *Richard Dawkins*

To the sphere of religion belongs the faith that the regulations valid for the world of existence are rational, that it is comprehensible to reason. I cannot conceive of a genuine scientist without that profound faith.   *Einstein*

Faith[perishes if it is walled in or confined. If it is anywhere it must be everywhere, like God himself.   *Austin Farrer*

It is not that faith is difficult. It is that listening to the voice of reality is difficult, and faith is the courage to live with that difficulty.   *Jonathan Sacks*

An illogical belief in the occurrence of the improbable.   *H.L.Mencken*

Faith is the assertion of a possibility against all probabilities.   *Stauffer*

I believe in the sun even if it does not shine;
I believe in love even if I do not feel it;
I believe in God even if I do not see him.
                            - words found in the Warsaw Ghetto

Faith consists in a man's lying 'constantly out upon the deep with 70,000 fathoms of water under him'.   *Kierkegaard*

....

LIVING BY FAITH

Faith is a quality that Jesus discovered time and again — in Jews and non-Jews. It was a quality which made healing possible   (see Mt 9:22 & 29, 15:28, Mk 10:52, Lk 7:1f). Such illness, and the healing too, may be psychosomatic, but this is not a term of dismissal. In one way or another, it can be possible to draw on the power of God to bring healing to mind and body. See also:

- ➢ the woman who suffered from haemorrhages - Mk 5:25f.
- ➢ the two blind men - Mt 9:25f.
- ➢ blind Bartimaeus - Mk 10:46f.
- ➢ the girl who was possessed - Mt 15:21f.

Even though Jesus expected that faith 'could remove mountains', it does not necessarily mean that it is a peculiar religious quality. We all have to walk by faith rather than sight — we all have to trust. Is there an artist, a scientist, a politician, a mother, who does not have faith. So it is with us all. The issue is rather, in what do we place our faith or trust? Faith needs a worthy object, and our lives need a sense of direction.

Jesus awakened faith in all of life's possibilities — that love could be realised, healing discovered, enmities overcome and goodness established. He showed that it was possible to have faith in God, in oneself, and in the future.

There is no sense in which faith is ultimately opposed to reason, nor is it 'believing the impossible'. On the contrary, it is believing the possible — and trusting in God, for whom all things *are* possible. Faith is reason grown courageous with the confidence that right will triumph.

....

The fig tree has no blossom,
the vines no fruit,
the olives fail,
the orchards yield nothing,
the fold is empty,
and there are no cattle in the stalls.
Even so I shall exult in the Lord
and rejoice in the God who saves me.

Habakkuk - 3:17f

....

We walk by faith, not by sight.   Paul - II Cor 5:7

....

Give to everyone who asks; do not turn away from anyone who wants to borrow.
Jesus - Mt 5:42

Everyone who hears my words and lives by them is like a man building on rock.
Jesus - Mt 7:24

He whose wisdom is greater than his deeds is like a tree whose branches are many but whose roots are few.
The Talmud (Jewish)

Prove that you are different by the fruit you bear.   *John the Baptist - Mt 3:8*

Beware of false prophets — you will be able to tell them by their fruits.
Jesus - Mt 7:15

You are saved by trusting in God's love for you; it is not your own doing. It is God's gift, not a reward for what you have done. There is nothing to boast about; we are God's craftmanship, created in Christ Jesus to live the life of good works for which God has designed us .
Paul - Eph 2:8

What good is it, my friends, for someone to say he has faith when his actions do nothing to show it? Can that faith help anyone? Suppose a brother or sister is in rags with not enough food for the day, and one of you says, 'I wish you well, keep warm, and have a good meal' but gives no practical help; what good is that? Faith without action is useless.
James - 2: 14-16,20

It is not good works which make a good man, but a good man who makes good works.
Luther

All that is necessary for the triumph of evil is for good men to do nothing.
Edmund Burke

The sky is immense but it grows no grass.   *Yoruba proverb*

In the end we always believe according to what we do.   *Leo Baeck*

One who claims to be a saint, and goes about begging — touch not his feet! He whose livelihood is earned through work, and part given away in charity — such a one, Nanak, truly knows the way of God.   *Adi Granth (Sikh)*

....

Muhammad once overheard one of his followers say, 'I will loose my camel and commit it to God.' 'Friend,' said the prophet, 'tie your camel and commit it to God.'

The way of Jesus was practical — he went about doing good. He believed that his Father was always at work and that he must work too (Jn 5:17), so that when he had to face death, he knew that he had done what was asked of him. He had little time for shallow sentimentalism. When a woman supposed that Mary's happiness was in nurturing such a son, he insisted that true happiness consisted in hearing the word of God and keeping it. (Lk 11:27).

Jesus would perhaps have had little time for debating as to whether faith or works is more important. Both are the gift of God and, like John the Baptist, he used the metaphor of fruit. Whatever our faith or belief might be, we are judged by what we do — a good tree cannot bear bad fruit and a poor tree sound fruit —Mtt 7:16f. In the parable of the sheep and the goats, it is deeds that are the basis of judgement and which reveal the reality of the faith professed:

....

You did it for me.
The son of man will separate everyone into two groups, as a shepherd separates the sheep from the goats. He will place the sheep on his right and the goats on his left. Then the king will say to those on his right, 'Enter the kingdom that has been waiting for you since the world was made. For when I was hungry, you gave me food; when I was thirsty, you gave me drink; when I was a stranger, you gave me hospitality; when naked, you clothed me; when I was ill, you came to my help; when in prison, you visited me.' Then these good people will reply, 'Lord, when did we see you...?' And the king will answer, 'The truth is: anything you did for one of my brothers here, however insignificant, you did for me.'
(The king then condemns those who did nothing).
                                        - see Mt 25:31f. for the full parable.

Notes: This parable is again cast in largely traditional form and is not meant to teach about heaven and hell.
        — in a later section, we will look at the place of Jesus in Christian teaching. For now, it is sufficient to note that those who help the needy are serving God.

Pushed to extreme, this could mean that belief is of no importance at all. The difficulty there is that the interplay between belief and action, what we are and what we do, is much more complex. Nevertheless, there is a serious message here for the way in which Christians understand others who act with humanity and love.   [126]

....

Then the Lord God said, 'It is not good for this man to be alone; I shall make a partner suitable for him.'   Gen 2:18

A man leaves his father and mother and joins himself to his wife, and the two become one.   Gen 2:24

They are no longer two individuals: they are physically one. Therefore no one must separate what God has joined together.   Jesus - Mt 19:6

It was because you were so unreasonable that Moses gave you permission to divorce your wives but it was not the original intention.   Jesus - Mt 19:8

If a man divorces his wife for any reason, except for unfaithfulness, he forces her into adultery.   Jesus - Mt 5:32

Whoever divorces his wife and remarries is guilty of adultery against her. It is the same if she divorces her husband.   Jesus - Mk 10:11

If a man looks at a woman with lust, he has already committed adultery with her in his heart.   Jesus - Mt 5:28

If a man divorces his wife and turns her out, says the Lord God of Israel, he overwhelms her with cruelty.   Malachi - 2:16

God created the first human being half male, half female. He then separated the two parts to form a man and a woman.   Midrash - Jewish

The altar itself weeps over the husband who repudiates his wife.

Rabbi Shammai

As a wife, you may be the salvation of your husband; as a husband, you may be the salvation of your wife.   Paul - ICor 7:16

Never marry but for love; but see that thou lovest what is lovely. Nothing can be more entire and without reserve; nothing more zealous, affectionate and sincere; nothing more contented and constant.   William Penn

Once more, go and give your love to a woman loved by another man, an adulteress; love her just as I, the Lord, love the Israelites.   Hosea - 3:1
(God, instructing Hosea to restore his own wife, who has been unfaithful to him.)

....

I married beneath me — all women do.   Nancy Astor

Jesus is less concerned with legislation about marriage and divorce and more with the ideal of marriage as suggested in Genesis. Any falling away from this ideal is a matter of sin (in the strict sense of falling short) but not necessarily of condemnation.

His questioners appear to draw him into the differences between Rabbi Hillel and Rabbi Shammai. Hillel was more liberal and would permit a man to divorce his wife for various reasons. In this, Jesus gives him little support. As for wives:
- they were not allowed to divorce their husbands in current law
- it was very difficult for a single woman to find any security or income, except for widows, who were given support by the community.

Adultery in the Jewish tradition was not necessarily defined as extra-marital relations but as the breaking into an existing marriage. *Let no one break up what God has joined together* — this particular statement is not about a couple divorcing but about someone else invading their marriage. Jesus' reference to the 'lustful eye' has little to do with sexual admiration or attraction as such; it is forceful language that comes under the tenth commandment. It is wrong to covet another's wife (or husband?) and seek to separate them from one another. *What God has joined together* can well refer to the love and loyalty that has developed between two people, and not to the ceremony as such.

There is no specific teaching on pre-marital sex. Betrothal had very clear rights and obligations in Jewish tradition. Sexual relations may not have been normal before full marriage, but nor is it likely that such acts would have been regarded as sinful.

A case of adultery.

A woman was brought to Jesus who had been caught in the act of adultery. He was asked whether she should be stoned according to the Law. Jesus replied, 'Let whoever has done no wrong throw the first stone at her.' Her accusers quietly go away.   Jn 8:53f

Notes: 1.this passage does not appear in some old manuscripts. When it
         does, there is no agreement as to where. Yet it seems so authentic
         in its spirit.
         2. it is wonderfully told: Jesus spares some of the woman's
         humiliation by not looking at her; he even acts in the same way
         towards the accusers. Significantly, it is the eldest who move away
         first.   (But where was the man?)

....

Teach us what we should say to God — we cannot find the words for we are in
darkness.   *Elihu - Job 37:19*

Go into a room by yourself and pray to your Father in confidence. Your
Father knows what your needs are, so you don't need to go on and on.
                                                        Jesus - Mt 6:6,8

As for how you pray, the words do not matter if they are sincere. Turn your prayer book
upside down and face the infinite.   *Victor Hugo*

You will receive if you ask; you will find if you seek; the door will be opened if you
knock.   *Jesus - Mt 7:7*

Real worshippers will worship the Father honestly and with their whole being.
                                                         Jesus - Jn 4:23

The people worship me with empty words and pay me lip service but their hearts are far
away, and their religion is only a human construction, learned by heart.
                                     Isaiah 29:13 (quoted by Jesus - Mk 7:6)

To ask that the laws of the universe be annulled on behalf of a single petitioner
confessedly unworthy ...!   *Ambrose Bierce*

It would be utterly absurd for a man who was troubled by the scorching sun at the
summer solstice to imagine that by his prayers, the sun could be shifted
back to its springtime place among the heavenly bodies.   *Origen*

....

Jesus was surrounded by the rhythms of prayer — in his family upbringing
and in the community. His own practice was inspired by a deep sense of
intimacy with God. He sought times of quiet in solitary places and the great
crises of his life were marked by prayer.
When others asked for help in praying, he stressed sincerity, allowing that it
was right to bring requests to God, as long as these did not fall back to become
empty repetition.

The Lord's Prayer:

It was customary for a Jewish rabbi to provide a helpful pattern for prayer.
Jesus drew **the Lord's Prayer** from the rich resources of his own people. It is
as Jewish as it is Christian - Mt 6:9f & Lk 11:2f. The Aramaic discloses the
poetry of the original.

Our Father — *a prayer for people as a community rather than as individuals. It uses a homely image combining love and respect, as in the story of the lost son.*

in heaven — *this carries a sense of eternity, beyond space and time.*

Hallowed be your name — *'hallowed' = honoured, but characteristically used of God as it is linked with 'holy'. The 'name' represents God as he is revealed to us.*

Your kingdom come — *i.e. the reign of God both in the present and in its final fulfilment.*

Your will be done — *implying acceptance and commitment, as Jesus did himself in Gethsemane (Mk 14:36).*

On earth as in heaven — *emphasising that the world has a full place in God's purpose. The translation 'in earth' may have been more correct-- praying that the spiritual may be incarnate in the material.*

Give us today our daily bread — *recognising our dependence upon God for all material necessities.*

And forgive us our sins — *strictly 'debts' as a symbol of sins. We ask for God's love and help whatever our failings.*

As we forgive those who sin against us — *not a bargain but a realisation that love can only be received in generosity of spirit.*

Save us from the time of trial — *the meaning is close to that shown when Jesus faced arrest and told his disciples, 'pray that you may be spared the test.' (Lk 22:40 and see ICor 10:13).*

and deliver us from evil — *a prayer for protection from all that destroy the human spirit. (the translation 'the evil one' is influenced by early Christian commentators rather than found in the Greek),*

for the kingdom, the power, and the glory are yours now and for ever.
A traditional doxology added later in worship.

Amen.   *More than a formality — it implies assent.*

Notes: 1. some manuscripts add, 'May your Holy Spirit come upon us and cleanse us' after the words 'who art in heaven'.
2. the version used here is one of the revised versions in current use.

....

Stand in awe of the Lord your God and serve him alone.   Dt 6:13 qu.Mt 4:10

You are the salt of the earth. But if salt becomes tasteless, how is its taste to be restored?
                                                                          Jesus - Mt 5:13

Whoever does not take up his cross and follow me is of no use to me.   *Jesus - Mt 10:38*

Wear my yoke and learn from me, for my yoke is comfortable and my load easy to carry.   *Jesus - Mt 11:29*

The least significant among you all is the most important.   *Jesus - Lk 9:48*

I have called you friends.   *Jesus - Jn 15:15*

You received without charge; give without charge.   *Jesus - Mt 10:8*

What does anyone gain by winning the whole world and losing his true self?
                                                                          Jesus - Mk 8:36

There must be no limit to your goodness, just as there is no limit to your heavenly Father's goodness.   *Jesus - Mt 5:48*

God has chosen what is foolish to shame the wise.   *Paul - ICor 1:27*

As a flame in a windless place that flickers not, so is the devoted.   *The Bhagavad Ghita*

There's but the twinkling of a star between the man of peace and war.   *Nicholas Butler*

He bade me give my possessions to the poor and follow him. But he possessed nothing; therefore he knew not the assurance and the freedom of possessions nor the dignity and self-respect that lie within.   *Kahlil Gibran*
(speaking for the rich man who turned down the offer to become a disciple - Lk 19:16f.)

Go and win disciples from all nations.   *Jesus - Mt 28:19*

They declared that their offence was summed up in this, that they met on a stated day after daybreak, and addressed a form of prayer to Christ, as to a divinity, binding themselves by a solemn oath, not for any wicked purpose, but never to commit fraud, robbery, theft; never to break their word, or to deny a trust when called upon to deliver it up; after which it was their custom to separate and then reassemble to eat together a harmless meal.

   Pliny's report to the Emperor Trajan, after interrogating Christians. c103AD.

We do not need to assume that discipleship follows a single pattern. A variety of personalities and a variety of gifts means that *God's wisdom is shown to be right by all her children* (Lk 7:35). Peter draws a distinction between the teaching meant for Jesus' immediate followers and that meant for everyone (Lk 12:41).Some disciples needed to be free to travel and could encounter opposition. Jesus' instructions for them were both demanding and practical (see the missions of the twelve and the seventy two — Lk 9:1f and 10:1f.) They would have to leave family and possessions. Jesus urged them to face up to the hardships and the risks — (Lk 14:25f and Mt ch.10). What he says is severe: ..... *If anyone comes to me and does not hate his father and mother, wife and children, brothers and sisters, even his own life, he cannot be a follower of mine.*

The heightened language should not be pressed too literally. We know that Jesus showed concern for his own mother, even when he was dying. The words may, however, reflect some of the pain of his own family's incomprehension. At one point, they believed that he was 'out of his mind' — Mk 3:21. In any event, the message is clear that even blood ties cannot have the greatest claim upon us.

For other disciples, the call may have been different. Those healed were often restored to their families. Zacchaeus presumably continued as a tax collector, and the centurion as a soldier. Mary and Martha were as different as sisters can be, and, in future, would have different parts to play. The twelve were in training to become apostles — 'sent out' to witness to the Kingdom. They were raw, but chosen for what they could become. Jesus will have had good reasons to choose Judas, whose qualities could be used for good or ill. Perhaps all our deepest traits can either strengthen or betray? We all need to accept the shadow side of our own nature.   [126]

Making the most of our gifts.

A king, who was going away for a while, gave his servants sums of money to trade with. On his return, one who made ten times as much was handsomely rewarded. So was one who made five times as much, but a third servant reported that he had been afraid to do anything with it. He is condemned as a scoundrel.

Lk 19:12-26

Note: This would be typical of a hard-headed ruler and the saying that follows: 'he who has will be given more; whoever has nothing will lose even what he has' would be unjust if the story was about money, but Jesus is speaking of the gifts and possibilities that God has given to us — and that is a different matter. It suggests risk, rather than playing safe.

....

A conversation at night. A Pharisee and member of the Sanhedrin, called Nicodemus, is in conversation with Jesus:

<u>Nicodemus:</u> *Rabbi, we know that you are a teacher sent by God; for no one could do these things unless God were with him.*

<u>Jesus:</u> *Believe me, nobody can see the kingdom of God unless he has been born again.*

<u>Nicodemus:</u> *But how can somebody be born when he is old? Can he go back to his mother's womb and be born again?*

<u>Jesus:</u> *Believe me, no one can enter the kingdom of God unless he is born from water and spirit. Flesh gives birth only to flesh; it is spirit that gives birth to spirit.*

Jn 3:2f
....

Notes: 1. 'water' probably refers to baptism as a sign of human choice — but the real transformation comes from God.

2. See also John 7:50 and 19:39 regarding Nicodemus. The Talmud refers to a Christian called Nicodemus (the same?) living in Jerusalem in 70AD.

....

You have been born again, not in a physical but in a spiritual way.   IPet 1:23

Think of yourselves as dead to sin but alive to God.   Paul - Rom 6:11

If anyone is united to Christ, there is a new creation.   Paul - IICor 5:17

I shall put a new heart and a new spirit into you.   Ezekiel - 36:26

Repentance makes man a new creature; hitherto dead through sin, he is fashioned afresh.   *- from a Jewish midrash on Ps 18.*

The teacher causes the pupil to be born a second time by imparting to him sacred learning. The second birth is the best; the father and mother produce the body only.   *Apastamba Dharma Sutra (Hindu).*

Die before you die.   *Muhammad*

If you want to become full, let yourself be empty; if you want to be reborn, let yourself die.   *Lao Tzu*
....

In John's Gospel there is detailed teaching on the need for a new birth but the theme is touched on in other Gospels:
* when Jesus speaks of good and evil depending on the heart
* where good fruit can only come from a good tree
* where the Kingdom of God is seen as within as well as without
* where baptism becomes a vivid parable of death and new birth
* when the disciples are told to be 'as little children'.

In John introduces the idea of new birth in his prologue:
To those who put their trust in him, he gave the right to become children of God, born not of human stock by the physical desire of a human father, but of God. This teaching may have links with Mithraism and other Greek mystery religions but here it has a clear Christian character.

Such rebirth does not depend on ritual or sacrament, nor should be seen as a rigid requirement demanded at one point in the Christian life. It is part of the ever-renewing work of the Spirit of God — gentle or dramatic — reformatory or revolutionary — it defies all attempts to reduce it to a formula. It may include the pain of beginning a challenging new life but above all, it is a promise of growth and a witness to the transforming power of God, which breaks free from pessimism and fatalism time and again.

Unsurprisingly, the same message is written deep in 'Nature'. The unfolding of the universe and the evolution of life on earth is a story of dramatic breakthroughs and fresh emergence. Ever-growing complexity leads to a sudden twist or turning and a new consciousness is born. Nature rarely looks back. So it is with human beings who can indeed be 'born again', whatever their inheritance. Every year Spring reminds us that God can bring new life to the old and the young, to the lost and the confused, to the living and the dying. [see 124]

Regeneration or the renewal of our first birth is something entirely distinct from sudden conversion or call to repentance — it is not a thing done in an instant, but is a certain process, a gradual release from our captivity and disorder, consisting of several stages and degrees, both of death and life, which the soul must go through before it can have thoroughly put off the old nature.

William Law

Make me a new person O God: and refresh my spirit.   *Ps 51:10*

....
.

Humanity needs more than bread. The word of God is as vital.
Jesus - Mt 4:4 (quoting Dt 8:3)

I have come so that people might live life to the full.   Jesus - Jn 10:10

Enter by the narrow gate, since the road that leads to destruction is wide and spacious,
and many take it; but it is a narrow gate and a hard road that leads to life, and only a
few find it.
Jesus - Mt 7:13

What is life?
It is the flash of a firefly in the night.
It is the breath of a buffalo in the wintertime.
It is the little shadow that runs across the grass and loses itself in the sunset.
Chief Isapwo Crowfoot - native American

Life's but a walking shadow, a poor player
That struts and frets his hour upon the stage
And then is heard no more.
Shakespeare

Know that the life of this world is but sport, and a play, an adornment, and something
to boast of among yourselves.
Muhammad

Everybody's hurrying but nobody's going anywhere.
Vernon Cooper - native American

Thou hast conquered, O pale Galilean, and the world has grown grey at thy breath.
Swinburne

Life is the structure replication of enzymes ensured by exactly reproduced nucleic acid
molecules.
- one scientific definition

My understanding of the soul is that it is the almost infinitely complex, dynamic,
information bearing pattern carried by the matter of my animated body.
John Polkinghorne

All sentient beings, if only they were able to realise it, are already in nirvana.
Asvaghosa (nirvana is the Buddhist word for the final indescribable state).

The water that I shall give will be a wellspring of water welling up and bringing eternal
life.
Jesus - Jn 4:14

....
.

Jesus invites us to discover true life in all its joy and exhilaration, free from distractions, and from the substitutes which fail to satisfy. The problem of giving our all to wealth, or power, or sex, or food, is not so much what these are in themselves, but what they cannot give to us. The lost son in Lk 15 [30] finds that he has wasted several years of his life and so it is with many who fail to find the 'narrow gate' (Mtt 7:14). The narrowness is not that of a repressive and blinkered outlook — it is the reality that there is only one sure way of meeting the destination for which we are born — and many ways of missing it.

The secret lies in a clear vision of God's way. We are 'to eat to live, not to live to eat', and so it is with many such pleasures. If this leads to a grey world, we have got it wrong. Jesus was a welcome guest at feast and fireside — not a killjoy, and not an ascetic like John the Baptist.

It is in this light that we must be careful about the way of denial and renunciation. Christians are often exhorted to forget themselves in the belief that the self is only associated with selfishness. But the lost son 'came unto himself' and returned home. We are allowed to love ourselves and asked to love our neighbours in the same way. It is in mutual sharing that we discover our true selves.

To the biologist, life may be a bonus created by material complexity, or it may not be such a latecomer after all but have lain hidden. In all this it still remains a profound wonder and however explained, is never explained away. Even our test tubes cannot create life, although they may one day put together the material that is capable of receiving life. Does matter create life, or give rise to it, or does life create matter, or exist alongside it? Ultimately we may not know of what we speak.

Eternal life should not be conceived as wholly other than the natural life that we now experience. It is more the fullness of that which we have only begun to experience. As yet we are half-formed creatures, somewhat faceless and stumbling in the way. Then we shall come to our full humanity, as measured by the stature of Christ (Eph 4:13). Then we shall walk with a sure step before God.   [see 106]

....

Not life, but a good life, is to be chiefly valued.   *Plato*

....

.

Why did I come from the womb to see nothing but sorrow?   Jeremiah - 20:18

Shall we accept good at the hand of God, and not evil?   Job - 2:10

God may bring grief, yet no one is more full of compassion. He does not willingly bring grief to anyone.   Lam 3:32

There is bound to be trouble but it shall not go well for the person who causes it.   Jesus - Lk 17:1

O Jerusalem, Jerusalem — many times I have longed to gather your children, as a hen gathers her brood under her wings; but you would not let me.   Jesus - Mt 23:37

It is not because he or his parents sinned.   Jesus - on a man born blind - Jn 9:3

Do you imagine that the people who were killed when the tower of Siloam fell on them were more guilty than everyone else? No, I tell you.   Jesus - Lk 13:4

Two sparrows are sold for next to nothing, but not one of them falls to the ground without your Father knowing.   Jesus - Mt 10:29

Once Jesus was approached by a leper and he was filled with anger.
     (because of the man's suffering?) - Mark -1:40

Be compassionate as your Father is compassionate.   Jesus - Lk 6:36

Jesus wept.   Jn 11:35

Happy are those who suffer for what is right.   Jesus - Mt 5:10

This son of man has to endure great suffering.   Jesus - Lk 9:22

He was overwhelmed with dread.   Mark - 14:33

He trusts God does he? Well God can have him if he wants him.   Mt 27:43

Jesus cried out,'My God, my God, why have you deserted me?'   Mt 27:46
     (In his agony, Jesus was remembering Psalm 22 and Psalm 31:5)

Father, I give myself into your hands.   Jesus - Lk 23:46

....

Much of Jesus' ministry was concerned with the relief of suffering and he could be moved to anger by it. We are left no explanation for the existence of suffering, nor does Jesus tell us how to reconcile it with the goodness of God. For him, God's love is unquestioned — but the sparrow still falls to the ground, Jerusalem still faces destruction, and Jesus still has to confront the cross.

He did teach that:
> ➢ there is no automatic link between sin and suffering
> ➢ natural disasters should not be considered as punishment
> ➢ we are answerable for the suffering we bring about
> ➢ suffering in a good cause is to be praised
> ➢ we should be compassionate.

Jesus' sense of vocation was influenced by the redemptive vision of the suffering servant in Jewish prophecy:
> ➢ he identified himself with his own people in baptism
> ➢ he gave himself to the sick and distressed
> ➢ he accepted the cost of speaking out for truth and justice.

Yet in his acceptance of suffering, he met hate with love and injustice with forgiveness.

The Suffering Servant — extracts from Isaiah 53.
(This originally referred to the nation of Israel or one who represented Israel.)

He was despised, shunned, racked by pain and afflicted by disease.
We despised him as one to be ignored, who counted for nothing.
Yet it was our trouble he was bearing, our pain he was enduring.
We thought it was God striking him down with disease and misery
but it was our wrong that was wounding him, our sin crushing him.
The pain he bore restored us to health and his wounds healed us.
We strayed like sheep, each going his own way,
and God allowed it to fall upon him.

He was badly treated, yet he put up with it and was silent.
Like a sheep to the slaughter, like a ewe before the shearer, he was silent.
He was arrested, sentenced and taken away,
and who thought twice about it — how he was cut off from the living, brought down to death because of our wrong-doing?

Therefore he shall be one with the great
and share the reward with the strong.
because he faced death and was willing to be thought a criminal.
He took upon himself the sin of many and asked forgiveness for them.

....

I took them in my arms; I led them and my love bound them to me, and I lifted them like a little child to my cheek.　　　　　　　　　　　*Hosea - speaking of God - 11:3*

If you just love those who love you, is that to your credit? Anyone can do that — love one another as I have loved you.　　　　　　　　　　*Jesus - Lk 6:32 & Jn 13:34*

When you helped the least important of my brothers, you helped me.
　　　　　　　　　　　　　　　　　　　　　　　　　　Jesus - Mt 25:40

Whoever, O monks, would wait upon me, let him wait upon the sick.
　　　　　　　　　　　　　　　　　　　　　　　Gautama - the Buddha

When you love all things, you love the Lord.　　　　　　　*Tulsi Das - Hindu*

This is how much God loved us — he gave his only son, so that instead of destroying themselves, people should trust him and discover what life really means.
　　　　　　　　　　　　　　　　　　　　　　　　　　　John - 3:16

We cannot say that God has any such ambiguous, unstable, and mixed set of feelings such as I call love in myself. Thank God that God does not love as I do!
　　　　　　　　　　　　　　　　　　　　　　　　　H.N. Wieman

I can say that what the world needs is Christian love.　　　*Bertrand Russell*

We are shaped, fashioned, by what we love.　　　　　　　　　　*Goethe*

Confusion comes from thinking of people's genes as their true self, and the motives of their genes as their deepest, truest, unconscious motives. From there it's easy to draw the cynical and incorrect moral that all love is hypocritical. Genes are not puppetmasters. They act as the recipe for making the brain and body and then they get out of the way.
　　　　　　　　　　　　　　　　　　　　　　　　　Steven Pinker

Nothing that is worth doing can be achieved in our lifetime; therefore we must be saved by hope. Nothing which is true or beautiful or good makes complete sense in any immediate context of history; therefore we must be saved by faith. Nothing we can do, however virtuous, can be accomplished alone; therefore we must be saved by love.
　　　　　　　　　　　　　　　　　　　　　　　　Reinhold Niebuhr

In my medical experience as well as in my own life, I have again and again been faced with the mystery of love, and have never been able to explain what it is.　　*Jung*

This is what love is: not that we loved God but that God loved us.　　*I Jn 4:10*

....

At the heart of the Jewish faith lies the love of God for his people (and their answering love). This passed into Christian understanding, which sees it revealed in the life and death of Jesus.

The various Greek words for love as used in the scriptures should not be distinguished too rigorously as the meaning flows from one to another. It is true that *agape* comes to have a special resonance for the love experienced in the Christian community but it is not a rarefied, purer love to be contrasted with baser human affections. It is a practical love that asks for our wholehearted commitment to each other. In evolution and in everyday experience, both altruism and true egoism have a part in God's purpose.

Paul's incomparable words in I Cor 13 follow closely the character of Jesus and reflect his life and teaching:
- love is unconditional like the father towards his lost son
- it is unlimited, symbolised by the cup that runs over. It can go the extra mile, turn the other cheek and always forgive
- it transcends the law by fulfilling its deepest intent
- it saves the righteous from self-righteousness, the good from 'do-gooding', and charity from being patronising
- it crosses all boundaries and all religious systems. It is a mark of the presence of God, named or unnamed
- it has its source and inspiration in the nature of God

My speech may be elegant and inspired,
but if there is no love there, I am nothing but empty noise.
I may see everything and know everything;
I may have enough faith to do anything;
but if there is no love there, I am nothing.
I may give everything to the needy, I may even give up my life,
but if there is no love there, I gain nothing.

Love is patient and kindly. Love envies no one, is neither boastful nor conceited nor rude; it is never selfish and never takes offence.
Love does not keep a tally of wrongs, takes no pleasure in the faults of others but is happy for the truth to be known. Love can bear anything — its belief is never shaken, its hope never shattered and its endurance never in doubt.   Paul — I Cor 13

After liberation from an extermination camp, a woman survivor was found trying to save a Nazi family's baby from the avengers. An army chaplain, who came on the scene, embraced her and asked her, 'How did you manage to preserve such love?' She replied, 'I didn't — it was love preserved me.'

....

All that I am comes from God.   *Jesus - Jn 8:42*

Peter answered: 'You are the son of the living God — the one that God has chosen.'
Jesus gave clear instructions to his disciples not to say that he was the Messiah.
                                                                              Matthew - 16:16,20

Only the Father knows the son and only the son knows the Father except for those to
whom the son wishes to make him known.   *Jesus - Mt 11:27*

By talking about God as his own father, he seemed to claim equality with God. Jesus
insisted that the son could do nothing by himself.   *John - 5:18*

About that day or hour, no one knows when that will be — not even the son; only the
Father knows such things.
                                          Jesus - probably referring to the end of the world - Mk 13:32

This son of the earth has nowhere to sleep.   *Jesus - Mt 8:20*

Whoever says a word against the Son of Man will be forgiven.   *Jesus - Mt 12:32*

Why do you call me good? Only God is good.   *Jesus – Mk 10:18*

I am with you like a servant.   *Jesus - Lk 22:27*

Happy is he who does not find that I am an obstacle to faith.   *Jesus - Lk 7:23*

To welcome you is to welcome me, and to welcome me is to welcome the one who sent
me.   *Jesus - Mt 10:40*

I am the way, the truth, and the life. No one comes to the Father except by me.
                                                                           Jesus - Jn 14:6

Thomas said, 'My Lord and my God!' Jesus said,'Happy are those who can believe
without seeing me.'   .   *John - 20:28*
(A deliberate contrast with Domitian's command to address him as "our Lord and our
God"?)

Jesus cried out, 'My God, my God, why have you deserted me?'
                                                       Jesus - Mt 27:46 - quoting Ps 22:1

I am going to my Father and your Father, to my God and your God.
                                                                           Jesus - Jn 20:17

....

"God is not a baby three days old"

The speaker is Nestorius, an eloquent firebrand of a priest from Antioch, who became bishop of Constantinople in 428 AD. He was not averse to burning down the meeting houses of his doctrinal opponents and to attending councils with a posse of armed men. We shall separate his character from his teaching and concentrate on the latter. In many a carol, we meet the opposite point of view:

"Let earth and heaven combine, angels and men agree, to praise in songs divine the incarnate Deity, our God contracted to a span, incomprehensibly made man".

In this magnificent hymn by Charles Wesley (who else could include a word like 'incomprehensibly'?), we echo the great words of the Nicene Creed — *"God from God, Light from Light, true God from true God   ... for us and for our salvation he came down from heaven".* Then the old questions suggest themselves: was God then divided or did he absent himself from his role as sustainer of all things or did he surreptitiously continue his creative work from the feeding trough in which he was born?

And then the boy? We may excuse the twelve year-old worrying his parents on their visit to Jerusalem but what of the eight year-old who wouldn't come in when called or who thumped his younger brother, James? Was he 'mild and obedient' and unbelievably good as another carol declares? We might even ask whether any parent would want such a son — there is an extra-Biblical writing that suggests that Mary and Joseph deferred to him in everything!

If so, any idea of incarnation is diminished not enhanced. Should not the Christian message involve real humanity with all its raw passion and possibilities? We can of course retreat to that refuge of the faithful: "It is all a mystery" but before we do so, let's explore 'Jesus on Jesus'.

What does Jesus tell us about himself?

He accepts the term *Messiah* (*'one chosen by God'*) but carefully guards his own interpretation of its meaning. He often uses the term *Son of Man* but this can mean simply 'human'. Where it shadows the prophetic figure in the book of Daniel, the meaning is far from clear. In any case, Jesus does not put denial of the Son of Man on the same level as denial of the Spirit of God — Mt 12:31.   PTO

JESUS ON JESUS

He certainly claims an active and intimate association with God - and frequently speaks in terms of a father/son relationship, but it is accompanied by a humility, which disclaims any form of equality or identity and he taught his followers to pray to God as 'Father' as well.. His critics may accuse him of claiming equality and Thomas may see God in him but this tells us nothing of what was in his own mind.

He often deflected attention from himself and when addressed as 'good master', he responded:

"Why do you call me good? Only God is good".   Mark 10:18

He taught that some things are known only to God. When questioned about the end of the world, he replied:

"About that day or hour, no one knows when that will be — not even the son; only the Father knows such things".   Mark 13:32

He sees that some might find faith in God difficult because of him:

"Happy is he who does not find that I am an obstacle to faith".   Luke 7:23

Many of his reported sayings testify to his sense of closeness to God and he accepts the term 'son' but when challenged on the very point that he is actually claiming to be God, his answer is perfectly clear:

"By talking about God as his own father, he seemed to be claiming equality with God. Jesus answered this charge by insisting that the son could do nothing of himself". And again: *"All that I am comes from God"*
                    John 5:18, 8:42

In Jesus' farewell speech to his disciples as presented by John, there is the definite statement:

"The Father is greater than I".   John 14:28

Add to these testimonies, the cry of desolation from the cross:

"My God, why have you deserted me?"   Mark 15:34

— add also the parting words in John 20:17:

"I am going to my Father and your Father, to my God and your God".

This is far too strong a witness to counter with the few sayings that are usually pressed into service by 'Nicene' Christians. One of these is often taken out of context:

"I and my Father are one"   John 10:30

Jesus is being accused of blasphemy — of claiming to be God. He responds with the strange quotation from Psalm 82:6, where God appears to be addressing lesser or perhaps defunct gods:

"Though you are gods, all sons of the Most High, you shall die as mortals die".

Jesus is said to apply this to those who question him:

"It is those to whom God's word came, who are called gods".   John 10:35

At the very least, it is a confusing passage and makes John 10:30 problematic. Taking John's Gospel as a whole, the teaching appears to be that there is a unity of will and purpose, of word and deed between Jesus and God — but not an ultimate statement of the nature of God.

Then there are the 'I am' passages in John's Gospel — *"I am the bread of life / the light of the world / the way, the truth and the life / the resurrection and the life "* ... which are said to reflect the divine name in the great Hebrew text, Ex 3:14:

"God answered, 'I AM that I am' - tell them I AM has sent you".

It may be that John is conscious of a possible link as this is more typical of his style than of the other gospel writers. It is certainly too tenuous a link to build on it a claim by Jesus to deity. The one reference that may point to a definite association with the revelation given in Exodus is in John 8:58 — *"Before Abraham was born, I am"* but Jesus has already referred to his obedience to God and the most that can be read into this saying is that Jesus believes in his own pre-existence. It is important to note at this point that John may well be expressing his personal belief rather than recording what he knows Jesus to have said — but even if these are all Jesus' words, there is little to suggest that he believed himself to be God.

....

....

The kingdom of God is here.   Jesus - Mk 1:15

The Pharisees asked him, 'When will God's kingdom come?' Jesus answered, 'You cannot tell by looking when the kingdom of God will come. You can't say, Look, here it is! or There it is! For the kingdom of God is already with you.'   Jesus - Lk 17:20
(the natural meaning of the Greek is 'within you' but the reading 'among you' is a possible alternative.)

You are very near to the kingdom of God.   Jesus - to a scribe - Mk 12:34

You need to be reborn to see the kingdom of God.   Jesus - Jn 3:3

Put God's kingdom and his justice before everything else.   Jesus - Mt 6:33

You have been allowed to know the secrets of the kingdom of heaven.
                                                    Jesus - to his disciples - Mt 13:11

The kingdom of heaven is like:
   - a mustard seed / yeast / a treasure / a fine pearl / a net -
                                                                 Jesus - Mt 13

When you pray, say 'Your kingdom come; your will be done.'   Jesus - Lk 11:2

My kingdom is not what you think.   Jesus - Jn 18:36

I shall not drink wine again until that day when I drink it fresh with you in the kingdom of my Father.   Jesus - Mt 26:29

His disciples said to him: 'On what day will the Kingdom come?' Jesus said: ' It does not come with looking. No one will say, " Here it is !" or, "There it is !" But the Kingdom of the Father is spread out upon the earth, and men do not see it.'
                                                    The Gospel of Thomas

The Kingdom is inside of you and it is outside of you. When you come to know yourselves, then you will become known, and you will realise that it is you who are the sons of the living Father.   Jesus - the Gospel of Thomas
(- a gospel, not accepted in the New Testament canon but still of interest.)

It is not an announcement of something which will descend from another world. It is rather a demand and a certainty arising from the very depths of life's significance.
                                                                 Leo Baeck

....
...

The Kingdom lies at the heart of Jesus' teaching. He announced it at the synagogue in Nazareth. It is a living community of all those everywhere who carry out God's work. It is not 'of this world' (as one translation of Jn 18:36 has it), with institutions and boundaries, but rather the heart of all true community — its members stretching way beyond the church. It is at hand, but has to be realised. There should be no surprise that Jesus speaks of it in different ways at different times — now but not yet — a gift for which we pray and yet a reality which we must help to bring about. Herbert Butterfield, reviewing Christianity and history, compares history to a Beethoven symphony — 'the point of it is not saved up until the end'.

In the politics of Palestine, it was easy to slip into speaking of a Jewish kingdom free from the yoke of Rome, but Jesus' teaching challenges all conventional kingdoms. It speaks of freedom, not coercion, service not power, community not hierarchy, and Jesus himself is the most unlordly of lords and unkingly of kings — our free use of such terms in speaking of Jesus hides the challenge and masks the emphasis of his teaching that the kingdom is the kingdom of God. Matthew prefers the term 'the kingdom of heaven' but this is only because he reflects the Jewish reticence at using the name of God — it does not imply a physical reality in the sky or a state existing only beyond death.

The character of the Kingdom takes in all of Jesus' teaching and is paralleled in John's gospel by the references to eternal life, that is, life in its fullness. No one should be marginalised or forgotten; no one should suffer oppression or injustice; no one should be burdened by guilt or anxiety. It is a realm of faith and hope, love and forgiveness, healing and reconciliation. The narrowness, superficiality and self-righteousness of what often passes for religion will be left behind. It is therefore beyond price and a blessing full of possibility for all people. Jesus himself the proof of it. It is for men and women to choose it and take it upon themselves.

Not yet ? A Russian youth who had become a conscientious objector was brought before a magistrate. He told the judge of the life which loves its enemies, which does good to those who abuse it, which overcomes evil with good. 'I understand,' said the judge, 'But you must be realistic. These laws you are talking about are the laws of the kingdom of God; and it has not come yet.' The young man straightened, and said,'Sir, I recognise that it has not come for you, nor yet for Russia or the world. But the kingdom of God has come for me. I cannot go on hating and killing as though it had not come.'

You know how to read the weather from the appearance of earth and sky — why can't you see what is happening around you?   Jesus - Lk 12:56

When he saw the city, he broke down and said, 'If only you had known the way that leads to peace! But no; you cannot see it. The time will come upon you, when your enemies will besiege you; they will surround you and trap you at every point; they will utterly destroy you — you and your children within your walls, and not leave one stone standing on another, because you did not seize the chance that God was giving you'.
                                                                      Luke - 19:42

He began to teach them that the son of man had to face great suffering at the hands of the elders, chief priests, and scribes; and be executed, but then rise again.
                                                                      Jesus - Mk 8:31

Now I am in turmoil, and what am I to say?' Father, save me from this hour'? No, this is why I came to this hour.   Jesus - Jn 12:27

Whoever is not with me is against me, and whoever does not gather with me scatters.
                                                                      Jesus - Mt 12:30

I have come to set the world on fire, and how I wish it was already burning! I have a baptism to endure, and I cannot wait until it is over! Do you suppose I came to create peace in the world? No indeed, I have come to bring conflict.   Jesus - Lk 12:49

The villagers would not welcome Jesus because he was going to Jerusalem. When James and John saw this they said, 'Lord, do you want us to call down fire from heaven to destroy them?' But he turned on them, 'You do not know,' he said, 'what you are saying'.
                                                                      Luke - 9:53

Many women grieved for him. Jesus turned to them and said, 'Daughters of Jerusalem, do not weep for me; weep for yourselves and for your children. If these things are done when the wood is still green, what will happen when it is dry?   Luke - 23:27,31

Peace is my last gift to you, my peace, such as the world cannot give.   Jesus - Jn 14:27

He who has come through the fire will not fade in the sun.   Hindu proverb

Derivations: crisis = a moment of decision — of judgement..
          apocalyptic = hidden. Imaginative writers sought to reveal the hidden future in a style of literature well known in Jesus' time. It was pessimistic about the present and described coming judgement and salvation with dramatic symbolism.

During Jesus' ministry, the country was gathering for a crisis. Revolt was simmering and there were periodic violent clashes — not least that involving Barabbas only days before the crucifixion of Jesus (Mk 15:7). The national crisis was seen by many as a world crisis — perhaps the end of human history — and Jesus may have shared this foreboding. He constantly urged his followers to prepare for the testing which was to come and which would destroy their nation. When Luke came to write his gospel, the Jewish people may have already risen against Rome. In 70AD Jerusalem was taken by Titus and utterly destroyed.

The gospel writers also faced persecution in their time and the sense of deepening crisis was very real to them. Every such time was seen as a time of God's judgement and Mark's account in ch.13 mingles the devastation of Palestine with prophecies of the end of the world. Yet, even here, Jesus speaks of the birth pangs of a new age and of stretches of history still to come. [see 123]

Jesus' ministry was surely, in part, an effort to win the nation to reform and renewal before it was too late. His strategy is two-fold. In the first place, unlike the zealot nationalists, he sought acceptance of the realities of occupation. He taught people:
> ➤ to go the extra mile, when forced to carry a soldier's pack
> ➤ to deal with 'quisling' tax collectors as human beings
> ➤ to pay proper dues to the Roman authorities.

In the second place, he precipitated his own challenge to the authorities on behalf of the poor and oppressed. He rode into Jerusalem in a manner that deliberately fulfilled prophecy and symbolically called for political and religious reform by confronting the corrupt trading in the Temple courts. Given the vast throngs which converged on Jerusalem at Passover time (not unlike Mecca today) and the heightened tension which this generated, his actions could not fail to herald a final confrontation — see Mt 21:1-13.

Cry out in triumph, daughter of Jerusalem! Your king is coming to you - unassuming and riding on a donkey, on a colt, the foal of a donkey.
.......When that time comes, there will no longer be any trader in the house of the Lord of Hosts.   *Zech 9:9,14:21*

My house shall be known as a house of prayer for all nations.   *Is 56:7*

The Sermon on the Mount (Mtt ch 5-7 & Lk 6:20f) is, in part, a commentary on the Ten Commandments — Deut 5 [see 11]. These are examples of Jesus' teaching, gathered by the gospel writers:

On God: Jesus emphatically endorses the Shema — Mk 12:29 — and links it with 'You must love your neighbour even as you love yourself' — Lev 19:18.

On images: 'God is spirit — those who worship him must worship him sincerely and honestly' — Jn 4:24.

On hypocrisy: Jesus' harshest words are reserved for religious hypocrites — e.g. Lk 11:37f.

On the sabbath: 'The sabbath was designed for people, not people for the sabbath' — Mk 2:27.

On parents: Jesus condemns those who shelve their responsibilities towards their parents by a form of financial evasion — Mk 7:9f.
(but see Mt 12:46 and 19:29)
On murder: The problem, says Jesus, is in the heart, where anger and contempt originate — Mt 5:21f.

On adultery: Jesus stresses the sin of breaking up another's marriage — Mt 19:6.   [see 39]

On stealing: This is dealt with in the wider context of greed — e.g. Lk 12:13f.

On perjury: Again it is the wider principle of honest dealing which Jesus teaches — Mt 5:33f.

On envy: Jesus calls for true priorities in life — putting God's kingdom first — Mt 6:25f.

I did not come to do away with the law. As long as there is earth and sky, not a letter, not a comma, will disappear from the law until all that must happen has happened.
Jesus - 5:17 [34]

The sabbath is delivered unto you, and you are not delivered to the sabbath.
Rabbi Simeon ben Manasya

The Beatitudes:

Happy are those in need. The kingdom of God is for them.

Happy are those who sorrow, for they will be given courage.

Happy are the gentle, for the whole earth will belong to them.

Happy are those who hunger to see justice prevail; they shall be satisfied.

Happy are the kind-hearted, for kindness will be shown to them.

Happy are the pure in heart, for they shall see God.

Happy are the peacemakers; they shall be called the children of God.

Happy are those who suffer in the cause of right, for the kingdom belongs to them.

There are two versions of The Beatitudes (or 'Blessings') — Mt 5:3f & Lk 6:20,21. The emphasis is different , with Luke stressing physical needs, but both are true to Jesus' teaching. He was not prone to thinking that material welfare was everything or to 'spiritualise' out of this world. The English 'poor in spirit' (Mt 5:3) does not do justice to the Jewish reference to those in material poverty whose hearts are turned towards God. It is the rich who often become closed off to the call of God.

Jesus gives us a character sketch of those who are blessed now and in the future. They are sincere and open hearted, compassionate and gentle in their dealings; they are peacemakers; they long to see justice done and are willing, if need be, to suffer for what is right. In a sentence, they reflect the nature of God and therefore are more able to realise his Kingdom. The world's future rests upon such as these.

God's spirit is with me; he has sent me to give good news to the poor. Jesus - Lk 4:18

These verses are not about happiness or blessing but a call from the man from Nazareth to my forefathers to get their hands dirty as a result of their thirst for justice and peace. Peace does not need contemplators but actors and workers.
Elias Chacour — Palestinian Christian

He will not break a bent reed or snuff out a smouldering wick; he will secure justice.
Isaiah 42:3 - looking forward to the Messiah

A man's reach should exceed his grasp or what's a heaven for? Browning

Jesus does not give the Jewish scriptures unquestioning authority. He modifies the strict meaning of the law on tithing (Mt 23:23, Deut 14:22) — the law is to benefit the poor, not burden them. In the same way he questions the sabbath laws, where he places humanitarian considerations above what the scriptures say: *"The sabbath was made for man, not man for the sabbath"* Mk 2:27). He modifies the dietary and purification laws, saying that we must look to the heart and not to outward observance.

Jesus moves away from the Jewish tradition in his treatment of women. It is true that women were honoured but there was still a bias towards men. Woman is the temptress in Eden and is one of man's possessions in the last commandment (Gen 3:12, Deut 5:21). The wife can be divorced more easily than the husband (Deut 24:1 then see Mtt 19. There was bias in the law on adultery, in that a married man could be unfaithful as long as his partner was unmarried but a married woman was subject to capital punishment irrespective of her partner. Jesus protected the woman who was brought to him for judgement.

John the Baptist had come near to undermining the whole idea of God's covenant with his people — *"God can make children for Abraham out of these very stones"* (Luke 3:8). Yet Jesus endorses John and by his easy relationships with Samaritan, Roman and Greek, challenged all exclusiveness. He recognised faith and goodness in non-Jews as in Jews and taught: *"By their fruits, you shall know them"*. Neither race nor place was central to his thinking. Even Jerusalem and its Temple would be superseded, as he told the Samaritan woman (John 4:21-23). This, despite the promise in II Chr.7:16: *"I have chosen and consecrated this house that my name may be there for ever"*. The scriptures suggested that God's favoured people would be specifically blessed — *"If you obey the voice of the Lord your God ...the Lord will open to you his good treasury the heavens, to give the rain of your land in season"* (Deut 28:1,12) but in contrast, Jesus taught:*"He sends his rain upon the just and unjust alike"* (Mtt 5:45).

The most dramatic change is Jesus' injunction to "love your enemies", whereas his scriptures are laden with God's curses upon the enemies of the Hebrews (e.g. Deut.30:7, Psalm 109). Jesus rebuked his disciples for wanting to call down fire from heaven upon the Samaritan villagers (Lk 9:54).His teaching is to bless even those who persecute you. The basis of this change is his own insight into the boundless goodness of God (Mtt 5:43f.).

The same compassion is evident in his approach to suffering. The scriptures time and again imply that disease and suffering arise because sinfulness causes God to withhold his blessing (e.g. Ex 15:25f. Deut.30). Jesus denied this when confronted with the man born blind (Jn 9:1-3) and when he was questioned about the fatalities caused by the collapse of a tower (Lk 13:4).

It is often overlooked that Jesus response in the Temptation story overturns the belief that God will keep those who serve him safe from all harm. The psalmist eloquently declares his belief in God's protective mercy in Psalm 91:12. but Jesus refuses to endorse this, knowing that suffering may have to be faced This is a radical departure from the scriptural witness

To sum up so far; Jesus did not simply accept the teaching of his own scriptures or interpret them in a narrow, literalistic way. He did not assume that they must be the word of God to be obeyed without question. Even if we take the words: *"not a letter, not a dot will disappear from the law"* as undoubtedly his, he can only be referring to God's deeper purpose as it underlies the texts which had come down to him. What we see here makes more understandable some of the opposition he encountered.

This can help us in our approach to the Old and the New Testaments. Jesus uses his personal judgement, informed by his knowledge of the Father, hence the recurring — *"but I say to you"*. Can we use the same criteria? At first sight that would seem arrogance on our part. We are not Christ. How can we presume to interpret scripture — and if we do, how can we avoid the obvious trap of picking and choosing to suit ourselves? There are grounds for believing that we not only *can* do so but *should* do so. Jesus himself asked the crowds: *"Why can you not judge what is right?"* (Lk 12:57) and invited his followers to judge by the fruits borne — not necessarily by the beliefs expressed. As for insight into the very purposes of God, he promised that the Spirit would guide us in our need (Jn 16:13).

....

Note: Many Jews, then and now, would have agreed with much of the above teaching. Jesus' strictures stood against some of the unbending fundamentalists of his time.

THE HISTORY OF THE CHURCH

*The birth and rapid rise of the Christian Church therefore remains an
unsolved enigma for any historian who refuses to take seriously the only explanation
offered by the Church itself.*   C F D Moule

History is not a fate but a revelation and a creation.   Leo Baeck

There is your Temple — God has abandoned it.   Jesus - Lk 13:35

*On the day when the Temple was destroyed, there fell an iron wall, which
had raised itself up between Israel and the Father.*   Rabbi Eleazar - c.80 AD

Solomon, I have surpassed you.   - the Emperor Justinian
(- on the completion of the Church of St Sophia in Constantinople)

Jesus came preaching the Kingdom of God and what we got was the Church.   - 19C

*No one can have God for his Father unless he has the Church for his Mother.
There is no salvation outside the Church.*   Cyprian

*I should have no faith in the gospel if the authority of the Catholic Church did not
induce me.*   Augustine

Every part of the Church shines but the poor go hungry.   Bernard of Clairvaux

*In the day to day business of exhorting, teaching, marrying, baptising,
shriving and praying, the Church in these centuries was deploying powers to
drill a barbaric world into civilisation, yet we have almost no direct
information about the process.* J M Roberts - re the centuries following the fall of Rome

*The Church was the custodian of culture and the teacher of all men, the
vehicle and vessel of civilisation itself.*   J M Roberts - re Europe in 1500

*English religion was in the main a free and healthy function of that old -
world life, nicely guiding itself between superstition and fanaticism on the
one side and material barbarism on the other.*   G M Trevelyan - re 1700

*It is the Church of the saints and martyrs and prophets that has the demand upon your
allegiance — not the Church which has been corrupted by wealth and worldly power.*
                                                                     A R Vidler

....

History will be kind to me for I intend to write it.   Churchill

In the centuries following Jesus' death, the new church expanded rapidly and found itself facing the 'problems of success'. It had to create an organisation, co-ordinate its diversity of ministries and decide on the nature of its authority. At times it lost sight of the kingdom of God:

- ➤ the community of mutual service developed a strict hierarchy
- ➤ the faith which proclaimed direct access to God created a new priesthood — just as the Jews had abandoned theirs
- ➤ those who had valued men and women equally, accepted the subordination of women
- ➤ those who had valued both slaves and free now reinforced a system of slavery and bishops took on the trappings of kings.

Later still, in Europe at least, there would be further betrayals — a spirit of legalism would return, coercion would be justified, and blood would be spilled on behalf of the Prince of Peace.

It took time, of course, for a centralised, imperialist church to bring the free Christian communities into the one iron cage of teaching and power. To this end, theology was re-cast. Paul's imagery of the church as the body of Christ — Rom 12:4f. ICor 12:12f. — was transformed and the church, identified with the hierarchy, became Christ's new incarnation. The church claimed to control access to salvation and the hold the keys to eternal life. Even the teaching that God's Spirit could lead the church into new truth was hobbled by the belief that the church could not be wrong, as Christ was already manifest in it. Was such betrayal inevitable? All human institutions have to organise their life and all depend on human beings who are fallible — the church no less so. Once it became a mass movement, once it held responsibility, once Imperial Rome had fallen and people looked to the church for help — could it have been otherwise? And then as now, it was subject to manipulation from outside, to be used and abused by rulers and people alike.

Yet thousands have found inspiration and compassion within the church and a multitude of saints and servants have enriched the world. As a holding place for the hurting, as a community of pilgrims with a vision, as a provisional community reflecting a greater Kingdom, the church — within and without the walls — has endured and its faith has burned afresh for each generation. In these pages we look at some of the best and some of the worst features of the history of the Church.

Pentecost: *The Feast of Pentecost had come. They were all met together and it was as though the Spirit swept through the house and flamed among them, inspiring each of them with the very presence of God.* Acts 2

Only a profound and shared spiritual experience was able to transform the disciples and turn utter defeat into an exaltation that took them across the Roman world. Although Luke's language is stretched to cover an extraordinary experience, he is still careful to show that he is not talking about literal wind and fire.

The feast is that of harvest — Ex 23:16. The word 'Pentecost' means '50th day' — referring to the days since the Passover. Judaism later linked this feast with the giving of the Law on Sinai and suggested that God proclaimed the law simultaneously in every nation. There are links also with the Babel story [10]

Paul discusses the phenomena of 'tongues' at length in I Cor 12 -14. Luke refashions the experience to take account of the rich layers of symbolism but it was the inspiration that mattered more than anything else. [103]

Pentecost today: *The leprosy doctor, Paul Brand, describing a visit to Vellore hospital in India, by the Abbé Pierre — renowned for his work among the beggars of Paris:*
"Lunchtime guests would stand and say a few words. Our students were lighthearted and ornery. If any guest talked longer than three minutes the students would stamp their feet and make the person sit down. Abbé Pierre started speaking in French and I strained to translate what he was saying. He began slowly but soon speeded up, like a tape recorder turning too fast, with sentences spilling over each other. I was extremely tense because I knew the students would soon shout down this great, humble man. Worse, I was failing miserably to translate his rapid-fire sentences. He spoke faster and faster, and we shrugged helplessly.

Three minutes passed, and I stepped back and looked round the room. No one moved. The Indian students gazed at Pierre with piercing black eyes, their faces rapt. He went on and on, and no one interrupted. After twenty minutes he sat down, and immediately the students burst into the most tremendous ovation I ever heard in that hall".

Completely mystified, I asked, 'How did you understand? No one here speaks French.' One student answered me, 'We did not need a language. We felt the presence of God and the presence of love.'

The first church was a marginal group of families together with sympathisers. They were mostly Galilean fishermen, craftsmen and peasants — probably known as Nazarenes from the beginning. Their poverty and insecurity was offset by the support they gave one another and by their certainty as to the living significance of Jesus. Women were prominent among them and they soon grew to include Greek as well as Aramaic speakers; Samaritans as well as Jews — and, in due course, foreigners.

There was an expectation about them, a sense of being used by God at a crucial time. They shared a spiritual horizon that influenced their outlook on marriage, vocation, life and death. They met in each other's houses and worshipped in the Temple. There was no hierarchy or priesthood but the practical sharing out of tasks to be done. It is unlikely that they (or Jesus) thought that they were founding 'a church' but they practised baptism and celebrated their communion with one another in a simple meal — believing that Jesus was present with them.

The Jewish bedrock of monotheism, faith, and respect for the scriptures was a shared inheritance but boundaries were falling away and they debated long about the sabbath, dietary and purity laws, circumcision and their expectations of non-Jews. Each step brought greater risk of conflict with the authorities.

In the early years, Stephen was stoned by an angry crowd but more serious persecution came at the hands of King Agrippa. In AD43 Peter was briefly imprisoned and James bar Zebedee was executed. The leadership of the movement was assumed by James – Jesus' brother – who gained a high reputation but was himself stoned to death in AD62. The future largely lay with new Christian communities scattered across the wider Empire.

The Great Supper: (see Luke 14:15f.)

In speaking of God's kingdom, Jesus used a challenging parable of a feast where all made excuses for their absence. The host invited the poor, the disabled, and the discarded to take their places — 'Scour the highways and hedgerows and urge folk to come. I want my house to be full', he commanded.

A list of **selected dates** can be found before the main index. Readers are encouraged to look at the unfolding vista of church history against the background of other significant events. **'Companion'** = to break bread with.

....

My kingdom is nothing like the kingdoms of this world.   Jesus - Jn 18:36

Give back to Caesar what belongs to Caesar and to God what belongs to God.
Jesus - Mt 22:21 - perhaps echoing the Jewish saying:
'Give to God what is God's, for you and whatever is yours belong to God'.

Everyone should accept the authority of government, for all authority comes from God.
Paul - Rom 13:1

In the west the church began to overshadow the state, while in the east, the state
overshadowed the Church.   J.W.C.Wand

We decided that it was right that Christians and all others should have freedom to
follow the kind of religion they favoured.   Constantine - 313

We have decreed that the sacred see of the blessed Peter shall be gloriously exalted above
our empire and earthly throne.   - the 'Donation of Constantine'
—which was claimed to be the Emperor's decree but, long after, shown to be a forgery.

As the temporal power has been ordained by God for the punishment of the bad and the
protection of the good, we must let it do its duty throughout the whole Christian body,
whether it strikes popes, bishops, priests, monks, nuns, or whoever it may be.
Luther - to the Christian nobility - 1520

Be it enacted that the king our sovereign lord, his heirs and successors, shall be taken,
accepted, and reputed the only supreme head in earth of the Church of England.
Henry VIII - The Act of Supremacy - 1534

If any person above the age of 16 shall obstinately refuse to repair to some church to hear
divine service ... and being therefore lawfully convicted, shall be committed to prison.
Elizabeth I - Act Against Puritans - 1593

Conscience ought not to be constrained nor people forced in matters of religion.
James II - The Declaration of Indulgence - 1688

A Church always tries to be the Church of the many and in the end it yields to the
temptations of power.   Leo Baeck

We repudiate the false teaching that the State can and should expand beyond its special
responsibility to become the single and total order of human life.
The Barmen Declaration - the Confessing Church - Germany 1934

....

The Christian movement has always had to define its place within, or over against, the State [79]. Sometimes Christian groups have rejected the State, refused to acknowledge its sovereignty, and lived apart. Such groups may find peace, or may suffer persecution.

In contrast, a powerful Church has sometimes sought to establish a theocracy where governments bow to the laws of God and the rule of the Church. From Rome to Geneva, St Petersburg to Madrid, these attempts have profoundly affected our history but have now largely given way to a more pluralist spirit.

Dictatorial governments have sought to control the Church — making ecclesiastical appointments, installing government advisers and sometimes reordering a whole organisation, with sanctions to ensure compliance. The efforts of communist and fascist states in recent times are not new in church history. When such states are avowedly atheist, they create new religious myths, dogmas, hymns and symbols. How could it be otherwise?

Establishment is in part, compromise but, in part, a recognition that the interests of religion and politics are inevitably intertwined. The establishment of the Church of England gives Crown and Parliament some authority over it, whilst that of the Church of Scotland safeguards its autonomy. Establishment may no longer be a restriction on freedom of thought but it can suggest that non-members are second-hand citizens. Christians too may lose their prophetic role — willing if need be to criticise governments.

Separation, as in the United States, arose from the conviction that it was vital to protect the state from interference by the church and to protect the church from interference by the state. The Founding Fathers, deist and Christian, had seen how much damage the entanglement of church and state had caused in Europe. We can go much further back, for it is Ibn Rushd, 12C, who was designated as "the founding father of secular thought in Western Europe".

An attractive model for the Church today is that of the servant — where, as with Jesus, all pretensions to power are given up. The Church eases back to become the churches — communities within the community — there to serve society by example and love.

Men are free when they belong to a living, organic, believing community.

D H Lawrence

....

.

*Kings look down on their subjects; and the powerful style themselves benefactors. It
must not be that way with you.*   Jesus - Lk 22:25

*When the Holy One saw Abraham, He said, 'Lo, I have discovered a rock (petra) to
found the world upon.'*   Rabbinic legend

*You are Peter, 'the rock'. It is on such rock that I will build my church, and even death
shall not stand in its way. I will give you the keys of God's kingdom.*
                                    Jesus - Mt 16:18

If the Church is founded on Peter, it is not founded on his person but on his faith.
                                    Pope Benedict XVI

*As I follow no leader save Christ, so I communicate with none save your Beatitude, that
is, with the chair of Peter. For this, I know, is the Rock on which the Church is built.
This is Noah's ark, and he who is not found in it shall perish when the flood
overwhelms all.*   Jerome to Pope Damasus - 376

*To the throne of old Rome, the Fathers gave privileges with good reason, because it was
the imperial city. And the 150 bishops gave equal privileges to the most holy throne of
New Rome (Constantinople).*   Canons of the Council of Chalcedon - 451

*We desire to love all men, but he whom you call 'pope' is not entitled to style himself the
'father of Fathers' and the only submission we can render him is that which we owe to
every Christian.*   Dionoth - a Celtic Abbot - to Roman Church emissaries c.600

The First See shall not be judged by any.   Nicholas I 865

*The Roman Pontiff ... has supreme, full, immediate and universal ordinary power in
the Church, and he can always freely exercise this power.*   Code of Canon Law

*It is the wholly reliable teaching of the whole Church that is operative in the judgement
of the universal primate ...*

> ➢ *that Anglicans be open to and desire a recovery and re-reception under certain
> clear conditions of the exercise of universal primacy by the Bishop of Rome;*
> ➢ *that Roman Catholics be open to ... the offering of such a ministry to the whole
> Church of God.*
>   .   *'The Gift of Authority' – an Anglican-Catholic statement 1999*

The best way to acquire real dignity is to wash one's own underwear.   Francis Xavier

....

The Year: 1870   **The Place: Rome**

Distinctly wet, the cardinals straggled in for the crucial session of the
First Vatican Council. Outside the sky was lit by lightning. The
oppresssive heat had triggered off a storm of rain which would climax in a
roll of thunder as the final vote was taken. Some seats were empty. The
Archbishops of Milan and St Louis, with many of the representatives of
major sees in France, Germany and Austria-Hungary were no longer
present. Fifty seven delegates had left the previous day to avoid
embarrassment.

The darkness within the hall so matched the darkness without, that a
large taper had to be brought before Pius IX could read the decree of papal
infallibility. Only the text itself can capture the severity of the language as
well as the loftiness of the claims:

*"We teach and declare that by the ordinance of the Lord the Roman Church has the
pre-eminence of ordinary authority over all others, and that this authority of jurisdiction
of the Bishop of Rome, which is truly episcopal, is direct: to it the pastors and faithful of
every rite and rank - both individually and altogether - are obligated by hierarchical
submission and true obedience, not only in matters of faith and morals but also in such
matters as concern the discipline and leadership of the church spread throughout the
earth, so that through the preservation of unity both of communion and of the same
confession of faith the church of Christ with the Bishop of Rome may be one flock under
the supreme Shepherd (cf. John 10:16). This is the teaching of the Catholic truth, from
which no one may deviate without harm to faith and salvation....*
*If the Bishop of Rome speaks ex cathedra, in other words if he decides in exercising his
office as pastor and teacher of all Christians by virtue of his supreme apostolic authority
that a doctrine of faith or morals is to be maintained by the whole church, then by
means of the divine support promised him in blessed Peter he possesses the infallibility
with which the divine Redeemer willed to see his church equipped in the definition of
doctrines of faith or morality; therefore such definitions by the Bishop of Rome are of
themselves unalterable, and are not based on the assent of the church.*

*If anyone - which God forbid - should undertake to contradict this our definition: let
him be excluded".*

Lightning still lit up the sky as the Te Deum was sung and the
assembled cardinals fell on their knees.   PTO

POWER AND PAPACY

Cardinal Guidi had wished to see specific reference in the papal decree to the counsel offered by bishops, who manifested the tradition of the churches. Pius IX was deeply annoyed and blocked the move with the words; "I am the tradition".

Nothing demonstrates more clearly the break with Jesus' teaching than the church's adoption of an imperial structure. An 'emperor of the church' cannot be representative and is often seduced by power. He becomes a witness to the absence, rather than the presence, of Christ.

There have been popes who were wise and humble men and those, like Gregory the Great (590 – 604), who used their power for the good of many, but others have been ambitious and flagrantly corrupt. There have been competing popes, reflecting nationalist factions within the church. The early history of the bishops of Rome is lost to us, but it is not a serious loss, as spiritual tradition cannot rest on physical transmission. The first certain date of a Roman 'pontificate' is 222. The words attributed to Jesus in Mt.16:18 were used to underpin what became a mighty edifice, but the text reflects a later time than that of Jesus, and its import is far from clear. Even Augustine (5C) did not link this text with the Roman See. The reference to 'keys' is a common rabbinic image for all teachers — it is the *teaching* that has the power to lock or unlock the truth. There is a rabbinic legend telling that: *"When the Holy One saw Abraham, He said: 'Lo, I have discovered a rock (petra) to found the world upon' "*.

We have a doctrine that grows by degrees, prompted by more ambitious popes, each fresh claim carrying the tide further up the beach until the high watermark is reached. Unlike the tide, however, doctrines become dogmas and don't retreat again. The far-reaching consequences can hardly be underestimated. They contributed to the great divisions between the Orthodox and Protestant churches. The spiritual riches of Rome, the good it has brought many peoples and the witness of its great throng of servants and saints is overshadowed by the claims made by Rome. The Orthodox churches find this whole way of thinking inimical. Their institutions are organised on more national lines and less emphasis is placed on correct doctrine. One nineteenth century spokesman for the Russian Orthodox Church — Alexey Khomiakov — taught that the Church has nothing to do with authority; she is the Divine grace inhabiting free and reasonable creatures, who share in its gifts only as long as they live in charity and peace with one another and obey the voice of the Holy Spirit.

Step by step the Roman Church departed from both scripture and early Christian history — becoming neither catholic nor apostolic. 'Peter' became a rock on which Christian unity foundered.
Protestants sit more loosely to their institutions but they can be seduced by charismatic figures who interpret the scriptures for them. Jesus would hardly have approved the frozen hierarchies of a our older institutions or the messiahs of tele-evangelism.

We should take down the fences and do away with the divide between orthodoxy and heresy. We should acknowledge all Christians as seekers; for even when we feel that we have arrived, we find that it is but a staging post upon the way. Let there be full freedom of thought and expression with a simple commitment to keep company with one another. Quakers have long known this and have much to teach us.

Offices in the Church should be for the exercise of gifts. All are equal. All are valuable. Each leader and pastor should draw his or her strength from below and from the Spirit, whose coming and going is unfettered. It is said that the leadership of the old Celtic church was like that of a skein of wild geese travelling overhead — each taking its turn at the front of the arrowhead, then falling back to bring up the rear. A reluctant leadership thrust upon them by forerunners moving back to enjoy the slipstream of others! Jesus clearly envisaged a new community, not patterned on the characteristics of earthly kingdoms:

"In foreign nations, kings hold sway over their subjects; and those in authority take the title 'Benefactor'. It must not be like that with you; on the contrary, the greatest among you must not be above the newest member, the one who rules like the one who serves".   Luke 22:25

Recently popes have emphasised that they are 'servants of the servants of God' and some have strengthened conciliar authority but, from 1917, all appointments of bishops have to be approved by the Vatican, internal critics can be summarily silenced, and the 'princes of the church' can be summoned to Rome at short notice. The celebrity standing of the pope remains seductive and very far from the servant model of Jesus. The church, as an institution is transient — it should turn people toward God and leave aside its pomp and show.

....

*You are said to have publicly condemned the Apostolic and Latin Church. And the chief
reason... is that the Latin Church dares to celebrate the commemoration of the Lord's
passion with unleavened bread. What an unguarded accusation is this, what an evil
piece of arrogance! As a hinge, remaining unmoved, opens and shuts a door, so Peter
and his successors have an unfettered jurisdiction over the whole Church ... because the
highest See is judged by none.   Pope Leo IX to the Patriarch of Constantinople - 1053*

*Always to be ready to obey with mind and heart, setting aside all judgement of one's
own; the true spouse of Jesus Christ, our holy mother, our infallible and orthodox
mistress, the Catholic Church.   Ignatius Loyola 1534*

*We ask God then out of His supreme goodness to reform our Church, as being entirely
out of joint, to the perfectness of its first beginnings.   The Lollard Conclusions - 1394
         (the Lollards were followers of the early reformer, John Wycliffe)*

*For some years before Luther, there was in the church almost no religion left.
                                                    Cardinal Bellarmine*

*King Henry has incurred the penalty of deprivation of his kingdom and that they have
been sundered for ever from all faithful Christians and their goods — we smite them
with the sword of anathema, malediction and eternal damnation.
                                              Pope Paul III of Henry VIII - 1535*

*We permit those of the so-called Reformed Religion to live and abide in all the towns of
this our Realm ...free from inquisition, molestation or compulsion.
                              Henry IV speaking of the Huguenots - withdrawn by Louis XIV*

*That all and every Jesuits and other priests ordained by any authority derived, or
pretended, from the see of Rome, shall within forty days next depart out of this realm of
England.   Elizabeth I - 1585*

*The Catholic or universal Church, which is invisible, consists of the whole number of
God's elect. The visible Church consists of all those throughout the world that profess the
true religion. There is no other head of the Church but the Lord Jesus Christ. Nor can
the Pope of Rome in any sense be head thereof
                        The Westminster Confession of Faith - Presbyterian - 1643*

I live and die a member of the Church of England.   John Wesley - 1790

*We declare that ordinations performed according to the Anglican rite are utterly invalid
and altogether void.   Pope Leo XIII – 1896*

The papacy is the scandalon which prevents Christian unity.   Eamon Duffy

....

The divisions of the Christian Church may be a sign of sickness or of health. They can come about through rivalry, intolerance, ignorance or narrow-mindedness, but they can equally be a sign of growth, insight, vitality and renewal. The early churches sought strength by looking to Jerusalem, Antioch, Alexandria and Rome for guidance and came to be ruled by 'a battalion of bishops' (Tertullian).

The fourth and fifth centuries saw the elaboration and consolidation of eastern orthodox Christianity, where the sacraments created a sense of mystical brotherhood, where saints were honoured rather than the hierarchy, and where the devotional reading of the Bible was encouraged. To this day the Orthodox Churches (a fifth of all Christians) hold to the language and practices of this time.

Rome, however, became the centre of the western church, more legalistic, and more centralised. Cultural and economic factors were contributing to the progressive alienation of East and West. As always the rifts are rarely as simple as the documents suggest but papal claims and intransigent personalities brought about the Great Schism between Rome and Constantinople — catholicism and orthodoxy (1054), which has only recently shown signs of healing.

When the mediaeval Church of Rome cried out for reform, it was men like **Francis of Assisi**, **John Wycliffe** and **Jan Hus** who were the prophets of the time, but it may be that the imperial style Church was broken by the numbers of common clergy in the 16th century who chose disengagement as the only path to reform. Politics and humanist thinking helped **Martin Luther**, **John Calvin** and others to break the mould, and the Protestant Churches — Lutheran, Reformed and Baptist were the result. Subsequently, new movements — Quakers, Moravians, Methodists, Pentecostalists and others — have continued to appear.

The Church of Rome set out to reform from within with some success but religious and political warfare and the claims of the papacy made internal change and improved relationships with other churches hard to achieve.

The Anglican Church, born in part out of the self-aggrandisement of Henry VIII, has long sought to act as a bridge and holds within itself some of these divisions but the issue of the ordination of women priests has made this role harder. New strains between churches are now emerging, for example, between Northern and Southern hemispheres over the issue of homosexuality. [93]

"Wherever there is a creed, there is a heretic round the corner or in his grave."
A N Whitehead

In the year 386 AD, at Trier in Gaul, Christians burned Christians for the first time. Priscillian and his followers were certainly 'unorthodox' — breaking with conventions, renouncing the world, and berating the churches for their luxury and vanity. Angry churchmen were scandalized that laymen and clerics were treated equally and that the sexes mixed freely. Despite protests by Martin of Tours, the heretics were consigned to the flames. Though rarely advocating such extremes, the champions of orthodoxy often show this darker side. This is Athanasius in the 4C:

"An Arian is a wicked thing in truth and in every respect his heart is depraved and irreligious. For behold, though convicted on all points and shown to be utterly bereft of understanding, heretics show no shame, but as the Hydra of Gentile fable, when its former serpents were destroyed, gave birth to fresh ones, contending against the slayer of the old by the production of the new, so also are they hostile and hateful to God."

A decade before the burning of Priscillian, Epiphanius had compiled his *Panarion* — listing sixty Christian heresies and demonstrating his passion for 'correct' doctrine. He stood in the hard tradition of Christian intolerance that looked back to Irenaeus of Lyons (c130 - c200). Irenaeus, in his work, *"Against Heresies",* showed particularly resentment at the way that heretics made use of scripture:

"They endeavour to adapt with an air of probability to their own peculiar assertions the parables of the Lord, the sayings of the prophets, and the words of the apostles, in order that their scheme may not seem altogether without support."

There was something noble in the momentous effort to define orthodoxy. There was a deep concern for the true faith, for the secure grounding of truth, for the assurance of salvation. But there was also arrogance: a presumption that we could encompass the divine, penetrate the mystery and set forth the nature of God. The earliest creeds had not been used as weapons. They were, as the word 'credo' suggests, of the heart as much as of the mind — a free expression of the faith of the community. They were variable and varied — not dogmas in our modern sense. 'Heresy' indicated choice (*'hairesis'*) and out of that rich diversity came both insight and inspiration.

What changed? It appears that the zealot wing of the Christian movement converged with the interests of the State. The Emperor Constantine brought relief to beleaguered Christian churches but he also brought patronage, wealth, prestige — and therefore danger. Pagan cities already had an *episcopos* / overseer, who was responsible for civic religious ritual. Some of them became Christian overseers, even if they had to be hurriedly baptised first. The office held opportunity for aggrandisement, with corruption, intimidation and sheer thuggery far from unknown.

Emperors had often been successful generals and they brought the same military mindset to the battle for Christian uniformity. This is Theodosius in an edict to the prefect of Illyricum in 381:

"The observation of the Nicene faith, handed down from our ancestors, and affirmed by the testimony and declaration of the divine religion, destined to be continued forever, will be maintained. The contamination of the Photinian error, the poison of the Arian sacrilege, the crime of the Eunomian heresy, and the unspeakable, from the monstrous names of their authors, prodigies of the sects will be banished from hearing."

This policy was strongly supported by Ambrose of Milan and Augustine justified it —
"What does brotherly love do? Does it, because it fears the short-lived furnaces for the few, abandon all to the eternal fires of hell?"

How far the church had travelled from the days in which a thousand flowers could bloom. With what assurance truth was set against untruth; orthodoxy against heterodoxy. Now the means of salvation was mapped out and the fear of damnation instilled into would-be dissenters.

But what of the great ecumenical councils? Surely they were widely representative, dedicated to wise counsel and led by the Spirit as a trustworthy guide for generations to come? We must not discount what was good in these assemblies but nor must we ignore what was shameful. The *Council of Nicaea* (325AD) was summoned by the Emperor Constantine, who accounted himself to be the thirteenth apostle. Church leaders were 'dazzled' by his gifts and lavish hospitality.

The credal formula was drawn up by Eusebius of Caesarea, though he himself was regarded as a heretic by the 'Alexandrian' bishops. We repeat a revised form of the creed today but would be justifiably embarrassed to include the anathemas that were attached to it.   PTO

HERESY

No western bishops attended the *Council of Constantinople* (381AD) —
called by the Emperor Theodosius to secure a uniform church and empire.
Those attending had to be approved by the Emperor. It was said that the
churchmen *"screeched on every side ... (like) a mob of wild young men."*
The final session was chaired by a pagan senator in order to keep the
peace. The *Council of Ephesus* (431AD) was called by the Emperor
Theodosius II. Cyril of Alexandria presided. He *"arrived early and bullied
his way to success."* Later arrivals formed a separate council and
excommunicated him. The *Council of Chalcedon* (451AD) was called by
the Emperor Marcion and all documents were vetted by imperial officials.
The western church was scarcely represented.. The Council's decisions
were violently disputed for years afterwards.

These were the four key ecumenical councils, now spoken of with
dutiful reverence. It is a matter scarce to be believed that their conclusions
and creeds should be regarded as authoritative and untouchable by many
Christian churches 1500 years later. The councils and the imperialism of
church and state were to shatter the unity and mission of the Christian
movement. Chalcedon became the launchpad for the persecution of
Christians by Christians.

The truth of these things has been airbrushed out of Christian history and
omitted from the textbooks. Still we meet with statements such as:*"We can
say that, almost invariably, disagreements over heresies were settled in a
non-violent way."* We can say it, but it is not true. *"How many thousands"*,
wrote a bishop after the *Council of Chalcedon*, *"have been killed for Christ
in Alexandria, Egypt, Jerusalem ... What country, what city, does not
recall the deaths inflicted since then to the present day, among the lambs
of Christ, and the sentences of exile and confiscation of property."*
Ramsay Macmullen gives a rough count of 25,000 deaths for the two and a
quarter centuries following Nicaea, and lists relevant sources. The West
Syrian Church went underground for a time and many of its members fled
Byzantine territory. The violence disfigured each side in these disputes and
bishops were far from being the focus of unity. Henry Chadwick affirms
that episcopal elections were normally a source of unrest and disorder.
Some hundreds of bishops were deposed, many were exiled, a few had
their tongues cut out or were sent to the mines.

*"No wild beasts are such enemies to mankind as most of the Christians in their
deadly hatred of each other"*
Ammanianus Marcellinus c.361.

When Islam began its rapid expansion, the churches were riven by differences of doctrine and practice and many that had suffered Byzantine intolerance welcomed the relief that Islam afforded. Co-operation between Christians, Jews and Moslems brought a new cultural world into being. Science, philosophy, medicine and theology prospered, particularly because Christian scholars were able to translate the learning of Greece, Persia and India into Arabic. It was only when a new Muslim fundamentalism arose and Arab rulers also sought state uniformity that the heartlands of the Christian faith were lost to Islam.

The western church then inherited the mantle of Roman power and pursued the quest for orthodoxy with all the passion of the Roman legal mind. Choice could not be countenanced. Just as the earlier churches had developed teachings of Jesus' divinity and of the Trinity that were not fully supported by scripture; so now the church of Rome developed novel doctrines of the church, papacy and the place of Mary, the mother of Jesus. It assumed the right to define what should be believed.

The consequences have been severe. Further divisions among Christians; needless barriers between the Christian and other great movements of thought and faith; a loss of vision for the world as a whole. Our understanding of scripture has suffered too — we scarcely notice how we wrest the text to fit the template of orthodoxy. Still we seek to constrain by creed and covenant. Still we insist that revelation uses only the channels that we have laid down. But we do not have to be fearful for the truth. We do not have to appoint ourselves as its guardian. We can dare to trust the freedom of the Spirit to reveal truth in whatever guise it comes. Is the Church strong enough or must we sacrifice integrity in order to keep the peace? In 457AD the Emperor, Leo I, asked the bishop of Militene whether he wanted to call a council. He answered carefully:

"We seek to uphold the Nicene creed but avoid difficult questions beyond human grasp. Christian theologians soon become heretics."

"All the Christian confessions of faith — both old and new — must be held in honour, but something else is more important for being a Christian. Jesus nowhere said, 'Say after me', but rather 'Follow me.' That means that Jesus did not first require a confession of faith from his disciples, men or women, but rather called them to utterly practical discipleship. The important thing is not to say 'Lord, Lord' but 'to do the will of the Father who is in heaven' ".   *Hans Küng*

SCOTS PORAGE

We cannot begin to do justice to the numberless Christian thinkers who were vilified and persecuted as heretics but we can select just one — a Celtic scholar, whose Latin name was Pelagius.

Jerome, who first translated the Hebrew Bible into Latin, was a Croatian who became a papal secretary in the year 386 and later moved from Rome to live in Bethlehem. He was a pugnacious character, prone to making insulting remarks about the man whom he said was 'made heavy by Scottish porridge'. He was referring to Pelagius.

Like many heretics, he is abused and misrepresented in Christian writings. Bede, the historian of the early British church, quoted Prosper of Aquitaine in condemning Pelagius:
> *"A scribbler vile, inflamed by hellish spite,*
> *Against the great Augustine dared to write."*

So who was he and what did he believe? There is a difficulty in answering, because his writings were deliberately destroyed and we know him chiefly through his critics. Therefore the following, like porridge, has to be taken with a small pinch of salt.

He was probably Irish (then known as Scots!) and his Celtic name was Morien. He was said to be the son of Argad the Bard and came to live in Caerleon, not far from Cardiff, — an important Celtic centre of learning — which is one reason why the Romans built their camp there. There was much more coming and going between Britain and the Mediterranean in those days than we might imagine and Morien was one of the early 'peregrines' who went to Rome to study law. [A 'peregrine' was one who travelled 'through the fields'. Our word 'pilgrim' derives from it.] He arrived in Rome in the year 382 or thereabouts and became well known as a scholar and leading theologian. Augustine of Hippo called him *'that most excellent Christian'*. Like Augustine, he sought social reforms — he challenged the rich and privileged, condemned public executions, and encouraged women to read and interpret the scriptures. His massive Biblical commentary and his Confession were in use for centuries after and the latter was used by Alcuin to instruct the Emperor Charlemagne.

Why then a heretic? Apparently because Morien opposed the growing authoritarianism of the Roman Church and because he and Augustine fell out over crucial matters of doctrine. The Roman Empire was disintegrating at this time. Christian leaders had to flee to North Africa when the Vandals took Rome in 410 AD.

Church and state were trying hold together against the forces of anarchy. Uniformity in politics and doctrine became the overriding aim and dissidents were subject to exile or persecution.

Augustine was developing his fierce theology of original sin, with no salvation outside the Church. The fall of Adam became 'The Fall' — infecting the whole human race, physically and spiritually, so that no-one was born innocent. Free will was no more and all stood helpless and condemned before God. The one hope was that God would elect some to salvation, for which the Church and its sacraments were essential.

In contrast, perhaps reflecting his Celtic Christian background, Morien saw Adam only as an example of human sin. He insisted that every baby was born innocent and that infant baptism was not essential, even if desirable. He upheld free will and the moral responsibility of each individual before God. The potential was there to live without sin (akin to Wesley's doctrine of sanctification). Even the pagan could come to salvation. He was not *"'opposed to the Augustinian primacy of God's grace"* as is wearily asserted by many writers. He was opposed to those who spoke of grace as though it were a matter of arbitrary condescension, like the favour of the Roman Emperor. Morien stressed 'prevenient' grace — that we are created and sustained by the grace of God that ' goes before' and inspires all that is good in us. All our ability, our willing and our doing are *"totally from God alone"*. Our calling is to develop a four-way love — for God, for self, for our neighbour, and for our enemy.

His teaching was accepted by two church councils in the year 415. In 416, two further councils pronounced him 'heretic' i.e. non-orthodox. In 417, the pope exonerated him but in 418, he was again condemned. Nineteen bishops resigned because of that decision. A dark uniformity had prevailed over diversity. The Emperor exiled him. We don't know whether he continued to live in North Africa or whether he returned to a cottage in the Welsh Marches to enjoy his porridge! Certainly church emissaries from Rome kept coming to Britain to root out this terrible heresy — widespread, no doubt, because it belonged to the traditions of Celtic Christianity. All Christians who have broken free from the darker aspects of Augustinian thought can surely honour him today as a great British theologian — especially as most of us would agree with him, rather than with Augustine!

The time is coming when anyone who kills you will think that he is serving God.

Jesus - Jn 16:2

Stephen — the first martyr after Christ — stoned in the year AD 35 *'Lord, do not hold this against them.'*
- see Acts 6 & 7

Polycarp — was Bishop of Smyrna in Roman Asia. Born in AD 69, he is believed to have met the Apostle John. He was arrested during a pagan festival and burnt for refusing to curse Christ. - 155
'Eighty and six years have I served him, and he has done me no wrong; how then can I blaspheme my king who saved me ?'

Pothinus — was Bishop of Lyons and died two days after suffering mob violence. A slave girl — **Blandina,** died with others in the arena.
'Pothinus, more than ninety years of age and feeble in body, asked by the Governor, 'Who was the God of the Christians?', said, 'If you are worthy, you shall know.' Whereupon he was pulled about without pity.' - 177

Alban — an early British martyr, was beheaded for sheltering a Christian priest and refusing to recant his new faith.
'I confess Jesus Christ, the Son of God, with my whole being.' - 309

Jan Hus — burnt at Constance for seeking the reform of the Church.
'What I taught with my lips, I now seal with my blood.' - 1415

Thomas More — executed for upholding papal authority against Henry VIII - said on mounting the scaffold. - 1535
'I pray you see me safe up, and for my coming down, let me shift for myself'

Thomas Tomkins — a Shoreditch weaver, burnt for asserting that the sacrament was but a token and a remembrance. He quoted Jesus:
'O Lord, into thy hands I commend my spirit.' - 1555

Admiral Coligny — a Huguenot leader, who died in the St Bartholomew's Day massacre in Paris.
'Oh my brother, I now perceive that I am loved of God'. - 1572

Theobald Stapleton — a Dominican priest, killed by Puritan soldiers in Cashel, Ireland.
'Your cruelties will be to me a blessing, and death itself a great gain'. – 1650

Religion is like a nail, the harder you strikeit, the deeper it goes. Yaroslavsky

Elizabeth Atwater — one of 135 missionaries who died along with their children in the Boxer rebellion, China.
'I do not regret coming to China, but am sorry to have done so little.'   *- 1900*

Maria Skobtsova — an Orthodox nun who helped Jewish escapees and was transported to Ravensbrück. Witnesses say that on Good Friday, she voluntarily joined a group condemned to the gas chambers so as 'to help them to die'.   *'Love one another, as long as it is to the end and without exception'.*
- 1945

Dietrich Bonhoeffer — a pastor who was hanged for his part in a plot to kill Hitler. *'I'm travelling with gratitude and cheerfulness along the road where I'm being led'.*   *- 1944*

Martin Luther King — leader of the American civil rights movement who was shot on the balcony of an hotel.
'I won't have any money to leave behind. I won't have the fine and luxurious things of life to leave behind. But I just want to leave a committed life behind'.
- 1968

Janani Luwum — Anglican Archbishop of Uganda, murdered by the dictator, Idi Amin, for defending justice.
'While the opportunity is there, I preach the Gospel with all my might'.   *1977*

Oscar Romero — Archbishop of El Salvador. who was shot whilst saying Mass in a hospital chapel. He was a voice for justice in a time of military repression.
'Martyrdom is a grace which I do not deserve.'   *- 1980*

Jerzy Popieluszko — a Catholic priest, murdered by the secret police for supporting the reform movement in Poland.
'You must speak of evil as a disease if you are to serve God'.   *- 1984*

These are a few, a very few, of a great multitude. Martyrs are found in every generation. Few sought death, and in one sense, death is almost incidental. They sought to live their faith to the uttermost. Countless others showed the same courage and compassion and survived. Such witness lies beyond words. They were their own creed and lived their liturgy.

....

All these died in faith. They themselves had not enjoyed the things which have been promised but they could see them coming and welcomed them.
- Hebr 11:13

There are three things free to a country and its borders: the river, the roads and the place of worship. These are under the protection of God and his peace.
                    Dynvall Moelmud - who codified the laws of Cambria - ? 450 BC

The Celts never shut the doors of their houses: they invite strangers to their feasts and when all is over, ask who they are and what is their business.
                                        Didorus Siculus - 60 BC

They lecture on the stars and their motion, the magnitude of the earth and its divisions, on natural history, on the power and government of God - and instruct the youth on these subjects.   *Caesar - of the druids - 55 BC*

The Apostles passed beyond the ocean to the isles called the Brittanic Isles.
                                    - claimed by Eusebius - c 330

The glory of Britain consists not only in this, that she was the first country which in a national capacity publicly professed herself Christian but that she made this confession when the Roman Empire itself was pagan and a cruel persecutor of Christianity.
                                            Sabellius - 3rd C.

(The reference is to a National Council of Celtic tribes held by Lucius before his death in Gloucester in 156 - he is said to have had contact with Eleutherus, Bishop of Rome but the account may be legendary.)

Triads of the Druids:

There are three primeval unities and more than one of each cannot exist: One God, one Truth, and one point of Liberty where all opposites preponderate.

The three primary principles of Wisdom: Wisdom to the laws of God; concern for the welfare of mankind; suffering with fortitude all the accidents of life.

The three things God alone can do: endure the eternities of infinity, participate of all being without changing, renewing all things without annihilating themt.

There are three men that all ought to look on with affection: he that with affection looks on the face of the earth; he that is delighted with rational works of art; and he that looks lovingly on little infants.

Note: These are said to belong to early oral tradition - the dates are very uncertain.

An African proverb runs: 'Until lions tell their story, tales of hunting will always glorify the hunter'. We still see Celtic / British people through Roman eyes and need a more balanced view.

The Celts migrated to Britain from the Black Sea area. In language, culture and religion, they show links with Semitic peoples. The druids were their wise men, and the bards their historians. Some of their teaching lent itself to a Christian interpretation and their faith could be seen as a preparation for the new truth in much the same way as Christians see the Old Testament.

Part animist, part polytheist, the sun, as the source of light and power, with its infinite circle and perfect harmony, was the symbol of the High God (Archaeologists are prone to believe that earlier people were incapable of symbolic thought — which is certainly not true of today's more 'primitive' people. We should not jump to the conclusion that they worshipped the sun.) The circle symbol is picked up in the cross-section of a leek, the emblem of Wales — with its infinity of circles.The oak tree, with its trunk, crown and outstretched branches, was used as a threefold symbol of the enduring God. The broad shafted arrow, now only seen on trig points, was a sign of the power of God — purposive, but unlimited in its follow-through.

There is little evidence of conflict with this older faith. Places of worship and centres of learning were converted from the old to the new and many druids accepted Christian teaching. It may be that the practice of human sacrifice had been abandoned before Christianity arrived.

Many Britons in Roman occupied areas died in the Diocletian persecution of 290. There is a wealth of evidence that the new faith was firmly established in the areas beyond Roman influence — having spread via sea routes, rather than with the Roman army. Significantly, Celtic Christianity reflected the Eastern traditions which the Roman church had been moving away from. The date of Easter, the slave tonsure, the greater equality of women, the grass-roots monastic structure, and the more symbolic approach to scripture, all testify to an early introduction. The monks were missionary, not cloistered — seeding the church into new areas by sending out groups of 12 with a 'papa'. Worship was sacramental in the widest sense, close to Nature and often held in the open air.

....

Note: The Galatians were Celtic settlers in Asia Minor.

50

37 A legend suggests that **Judean refugees** were given land at Glastonbury.
43 Claudius' invasion of Britain. (Caesar's in 54 BC was more exploratory)

51 Roman defeat of **Caradoc** (Caratacus) in Powys.

100

120 Britain incorporated by treaty into the Roman Empire.

150

156 Tradition that a **National Council** of tribes accepted Christianity.

200

200 Origen writes that Christianity had 'even reached Britain'.

250

290 Diocletian Persecution in which the bishops of London, York and
Carlisle are said to have died.

300

304 Death of **St Alban** — some believe that this happened in 209.
313 Peace of Constantine — legalising Christianity. Proclaimed in York.
314 The Council of Arles (in Gaul) — attended by three British bishops.

350

382 Morien (Pelagius) — a young British scholar — moves to Rome and
becomes well known as a theologian there and in North Africa.
397 Ninian → Whithorn, Galloway — missionary to the Picts and Irish.

400

410 Rome falls to Alaric the Goth. Britain now independent.
432 Maelwyn (Patrick) — possibly trained by Caranoc at Whithorn, and
afterwards in Gaul — begins his mission in Éire.

450

490 Celts defeat the Angles at **Mons Badonis.**

500

540 David born — became a pupil of Paul the Aged, who had worked with
Ninian. Worked among the Saxons and then at Mynyw, Wales.

550

547 The **Yellow Plague** and further invasion caused mass flight of Britons to
the South West and Brittany.
563 Columcille (Columba) moved to Iona — having founded several
monastic bases in Ireland

600

597 Augustine — sent as a missionary to the Angles. After some early
success, his work became limited to Kent.

635 Aidan moved to Lindisfarne from Iona and evangelised the Anglo-
Saxons.

650

664 The **Synod of Whitby** — secular rulers accept the Roman Church.

Names and dates are seasoned with a touch of imagination!

Ninian 360 - 432 who founded Candida Casa in Galloway, was taught by:

  Martin 335 - 397 at the greatest Celtic centre of all in Tours. He was taught by:

    Hilary 315 - 367 of Poitiers — who was banished for a time to Phrygia (Turkey), where he was taught by:

      Basil of Caesarea 330 - 379 — the father of Eastern monasticism. Taught by:

Athanasius 296 - 373 Bishop of Alexandria who supported the monasteries of:

  Pachomius 290 - 346 on the River Nile. He would have consulted regularly with:

    Alexander d. 328 Bishop of Alexandria, who would have known:

      Eusebius 260 - 340 historian and Bishop of Caesarea and pupil of:

        Pamphilus 240 - 309 who ran a theological school in Caesarea. Pupil of:

      Origen 185 - 254 theologian, who was taught by:

Clement of Alexandria 150 - 215 He travelled widely and would have known:

  Irenaeus 130 - 200 He became Bishop of Lyons after the death of his teacher:

    Pothinus 87 - 177 who had died as a martyr. He was a disciple of:

      Polycarp 69 - 155 also martyred. Irenaeus states that he knew:

John d.96 - the Galilean fisherman who lived to a great age in Ephesus. Disciple of:

JESUS

The Celtic Church   The rapid growth of the Celtic Church is witness to the fact first, that it was not dependent on the Roman occupation, and secondly, that it drew strength from earlier religious traditions in Britain. Its inspiration came via Martin of Tours who inherited the ideal of service from Hilary and Basil the Great. Basil had founded hospitals, hostels for the poor, schools and workshops in Caesarea. He believed that, 'the chief austerity is selfless love of the needy'.

The Celtic monks combined service with education, cultivation, copying the scriptures and prayer. Centres in Éire included Armagh f.450, Aran - 484, Clonard - 520, Clogher - 525, Moville - 540, Clonfert & Bangor - 559. Columba founded monastic schools at Derry, Durrow, Kells, Kilmore, Boyle, Swords, Rechra, Raphoe, Drumcliffe, Glen Columcille and Iona. Students from the continent came to Ireland 'like a swarm of bees.' Women were as active as men in many of these communities, and clergy could be married.

....

My life and death are in my neighbour.

St Antony - giving up life as a hermit after 20 years - 305

A race of filthy animals, to whom one is tempted to refuse the name of men.

Edward Gibbon on hermits

A monk must live under the rule of one father, and in the society of many brethren, that he may learn humility from one, patience from another, silence from a third, gentleness from a fourth. He is not to do as he likes. He is to eat what he is told to eat, he is to have only what is given to him, he must do the work which is set him, he must be subject to those he dislikes. He must go to bed so tired that he will fall asleep on the way.

Rule of Columbanus

Let no one presume to give or receive anything without the leave of the abbot, or to retain anything as his own. He should have nothing at all: neither a book, nor tablets, nor a pen - nothing at all.
Idleness is enemy of the soul. And therefore, at fixed times, the brothers ought to be occupied in manual labour.
All guests are to be received as Christ himself.

Rule of St Benedict

The brothers shall possess nothing, neither a house, nor a place, nor anything. But as pilgrims and strangers in this world, serving God in poverty and humility, they shall confidently seek alms, and not be ashamed, for the Lord made himself poor in this world for us.

Rule of St Francis

I have built a church in the city of Khanbalig (Peking), where the king has his chief residence. I have baptised up to this time about 6,000 persons. I am old and grey, more from toil and trouble than from age, for I am 58 years old. I know the Tartar language and writing, and have now translated the whole New Testament and psalter.

John of Monte Corvino (Franciscan) - 1307

The Act for the Dissolution of the Monasteries (1536) abolished a few nests of corruption together with the greatest network of social and educational welfare that England had ever known.

Norman Davies

I shall be 70 when I take the veil. It is inside the convent walls that I acquired the peace for which I have been longing all my life and the hope which I had lost.

Svetlana Allilulyeva - daughter of Stalin

....

Words: Hermit = a desert dweller.   Monk = (originally) one who lives alone.
           Friar = brother   Nun = mother, then, an unmarried woman.

Monasticism is many things. It is the solitude of the desert where God can be sought in singleness of heart. It is the turning from the unreality of the world, as in Indian religion, to an alternative reality. It is a refuge from social or personal crisis. It is a perpetual re-living of religious experience.It is living in a disciplined community of faith. It is a base for mission and service.

Pachomius and his sister established 11 communities in Egypt by the year 346. **Basil** adapted these desert communities to the cities and made them great centres of welfare for the poor and sick.His rule is still common in Orthodox Christianity. **Columbanus** was part of the great outpouring of Irish monks to the continent, who founded 550 communities in Gaul alone. He was personally responsible for Luxeuil (France), St Gall (Switzerland), and Bobbio (Italy), among others but the severity of his rule created a preference for that of **Benedict**, which was more suited to a settled community.

Francis went to live among poorer people in 1209. His order of 'God's jesters' combined simplicity, prayer and service. In time his friars spread to Africa and the Far East. **Dominic** trained his friars — the 'hounds of the Lord' — to teach and combat heresy. Both monks and friars posed problems for the church hierarchy, because of their independence and tendency towards innovation.

Tragically, in the West, sin was associated with sex, and celibacy valued, not just as a positive opportunity for service, but also as a defence against sin. The 'religious life' was held up as a model of sanctity beyond the reach of others. But the repression of sexual instincts could, and did, lead to distortion and abuse.

Women had a valued place in early communities but nuns were later rigidly enclosed. When, in the 17C. Mary Ward founded the Institute of the Blessed Virgin Mary as an active order of charity, the Church was horrified. She was imprisoned and her nuns literally dispossessed. Other new orders were sent back to the cloister to await more enlightened times.

There were all kinds of recruits. In 12C. Cluny many monks were there because they had been given or abandoned to the monasteries due to deformity or backwardness. This is one of many reasons why laxity and corruption could become a serious problem. Today, recruits are not so easily found in prosperous societies and difficulties remain. For all that, the best communities present an inspiration and a challenge to more conventional society.

....

.

Who can find a good wife? She sees that her business goes well. She helps the poor. She has strength and dignity. She talks good sense.   *- from Prov 31*

Women are excused from the duties that begin: 'Thou shalt'.   *The Talmud*

His disciples were astonished to find Jesus talking to a woman.   *John - 4:27*

    In Christ it does not matter whether you are a man or a woman.
    While every man looks to Christ for leadership, a woman looks to her husband.
    The husband may find God through his Christian wife, and the wife through her Christian husband.
    As in all gatherings of God's people, women should keep silent.
    Wives, give way to your husbands.   *Give way to one another.*

.... ***Paul*** *- Gal 3:28. ICor 7:14, 11:3, 14:34. Eph 5:21,22*

Adam came first; and it was not Adam who was deceived.
         I Tim 2:13 (many scholars believe this letter to come from a later time.)

You are the devil's gateway. You destroyed God's image, man.   *Tertullian*

She who does not believe is a woman and should be designated by the name of her sex, whereas she who believes progresses to perfect manhood. She then dispenses with the name of her sex.   *Ambrose - Bp. of Milan - 4C.*

He for God only, she for God in him.   *Milton*

Man is more courageous, pugnacious and energetic than woman, and has a more inventive genius.   *Darwin*

Men have authority over women because Allah   has made the one superior to the other.   *The Qur'an 4:34*

The woman may not be killed in any way, neither by slaughter, nor by poison, nor in water, nor in fire, but shall die in their own lawful bed.
      Adomnán's 'Law of the Innocents', signed by Celtic kings in the 7C.

I would have given the Church my head, my hands, and my heart. She did not know what to do with them. She told me to go back and do the crocheting in my mother's drawing room.   *Florence Nightingale*

....

When God made man, she was having one of her off days.   *— graffiti*

MEN AND WOMEN: **62**

The Jewish scriptures reflect a patriarchal society, where the laws of property and divorce are weighted in favour of men. Yet Sarah, Rebekah, Rachel, Miriam, Deborah and many others are important figures in Israel's history and Prov 31 shows that a woman's place was not simply in the home — though this was the centre of Jewish life *and faith*. Our individualism does not equip us to judge a society where the family is all and the man is the public face of the family — his duties emphasising his total responsibility.

The story of Eden is misinterpreted. The rib symbol (Gen 2:22) speaks of interdependence and equality. The reference to the husband as master (3:16) is given as a mark of *disorder* - a falling away from God's purpose. ITim 2:8-15 is tendentious.

Jesus ignored restrictions in the public life of women. They were prominent among his followers. — Luke 8:1-3 — and he treated them with respect. Some of the twelve disciples have less importance. Mary Magdalene was the first witness to the resurrection and is was later counted as 'apostle to the apostles'.

Paul *appears* to be a mass of contradictions. He chose to remain single, unlike some apostles (Acts 21:5) but he compared marriage to the relationship between Christ and his followers. In his most authentic writings, he taught full equality within the church.
ITim 2:8-15 tells against this, but the letter was almost certainly not written by him and 14:33-36 is thought to be a late insertion in the first letter to Corinth.We are dealing with edited material.

It seems that early idealism was lost and that patriarchy re-asserted itself, just as it did in later years when Junia — *"prominent among the apostles"* — in Rom 16:7 was changed by churchmen from female to male — no doubt, because she destroyed the case for an all-male priesthood. The ten women mentioned, with appreciation, at the end of Paul's letter to Rome are clearly Christian leaders — 'co-workers'.

The growth of asceticism devalued human sexuality and cast women in the diabolic role of temptress. Unlike the Celtic and Orthodox Churches, Rome came to prefer celibacy for its priests and imposed it in 1059, despite extensive protests. The Reformation broke away from celibacy but not from male authority. Even the struggle for women's emancipation in the 19 C. gained little support from the churches, except within the Christian socialist movement. [see 129]

....
.

I am the Lord's servant, let it be as you wish.   Mary - Lk 1:38

As by her disobedience Eve was the cause of death for herself and for the human race, so the obedient virgin becomes a cause of salvation for herself and the human race.
                                                                    Irenaeus - 2C.

Nestorius: *Do not make a goddess of the Virgin!*
Cyril: *We have not made a divinity of her who must be numbered among the creatures. She belongs to humanity as we do.*   - as related by Cyril - 4C.

Mary was the temple of God, not the God of the temple.   Ambrose - 4C.

Mary has given you this brother (i.e. Jesus). But perhaps you fear the divine majesty in him? Do you want an advocate close by him? Appeal to Mary. The Son will grant the Mother's request and the Father the Son's.   Bernard of Clairveaux- 12C.

The most blessed Virgin Mary in the first instant of her conception, was preserved immune from all stain of original sin.   Pius IX - 1854

She is Divine Wisdom in the created world. She covers the world with her veil.
                                                            Sergius Bulgakov - 20C. Orthodox

The divine Maternity raises her to a dizzy height and places her immediately after God in the vast scale of beings. Her greatness borders on the infinite.
                                                            Gabriele Roschini - 20C. Catholic

From the universal consensus of the Church may be drawn a sure and certain argument for affirming the Assumption. It is a truth revealed by God.
                                                            Munificentissimus Deus - 1950

Do not call me saviour and co-redemptress. Do not honour me as if God were not enough for you.   - imagined by Adam Widenfeldt - Catholic jurist - 1673

Do you not see what they are doing in the streets of Jerusalem? Children gather wood, fathers light fires, women knead dough to make special cakes in honour of the queen of heaven.   Jer 7:17

Mariology, as it has been developed further and further, has alienated Christians from Jews, the church from the New Testament, Protestant Christians from Catholic Christians and Christians generally from modern men and women.
                                                            Jurgen Moltmann

....

Our information about Mary is slender:

> ➢ she quietly accepts the role given to her — Lk 1:26f.
> ➢ she pressurises Jesus at Cana — Jn 2:1f.
> ➢ she doubts Jesus' sanity — Mk 3:21, 31f.
> ➢ she witnesses the crucifixion (only in John's gospel).

In the 4 C. Mary was spoken of as *Theotokos* = 'bearer of God'. The emphasis was on the divinity of Jesus rather than on the nature of Mary. At the Council of Ephesus, however, in 431 this title was formally proclaimed and the intention was to honour Mary herself.

This was perhaps the beginning of a long development, which continues to this day. How can we account for this?

> ➢ Ephesus, where Mary was said to have lived with John, was the centre of the worship of the Mother-Goddess — Artemis (Diana). Local factions notoriously manipulated the Council held there in order to exploit pagan religion
> ➢ asceticism devalued sexuality and made a virtue of virginity. The focus was moving from God's action to Mary herself
> ➢ Jesus was becoming a less accessible figure — more judge than brother — so Mary became a compassionate substitute
> ➢ the mechanistic view of hereditary sin made it necessary to put a 'cordon sanitaire' around the incarnation — so Mary is said to have been conceived without the taint of original sin.

Mary therefore becomes, as in a distorting mirror, a reflection of the false turnings taken by church teaching. The process continues in the declaration that Jesus ensured her bodily assumption into heaven — and today, by the massive petitions to the Pope, asking that she be formally declared *Co-Redeemer* with Christ. Popular demand has been an ever-rising tide in this development.

It is a long time since St Antony misused Rom 8:32 and spoke of Mary who 'did not spare her own son, but gave him up for us all'.

No wonder that Muhammad understood the Christian Trinity as *Father, Mother and Child.* And it is long enough since the Dominicans believed that the Franciscans were falling into heresy because of their assimilation of Mary to Christ. Perhaps Mary, with her hope and doubt, faith and pain, should be freed from the devotional pedestal onto which she has been placed.   [see 21]

....

Do you not see what they are doing in the streets of Jerusalem? Children gather wood, fathers light fires, women knead dough to make special cakes in honour of the queen of heaven.
                                                                              Jeremiah - 7:17

....

When the Lord your God leads you into the land; when he drives out many nations before you... you must destroy them.   *Dt 7:1*

A Christian glories in the death of a Muslim because Christ is glorified.
Bernard of Clairveaux
(— said to be the first Christian theologian to preach holy war.)

Whoever for devotion alone, not to gain honour or money, goes to Jerusalem to liberate the Church of God can substitute this journey for all penance.   *Urban II*

The whole world desired to go to the tomb of our Lord in Jerusalem. First of all went the meaner people, then the men of middle rank, and lastly, very many kings, counts, marquesses and bishops.   *- contemporary*

With drawn swords our people ran through the city; nor did they spare anyone, not even those pleading for mercy. The horses waded in blood up to their knees, nay, up to the bridle. It was a just and wonderful judgement of God.
A crusader, on the taking of Jerusalem - 1099

Such a slaughter of pagans, no one has ever seen or heard of; the pyres they made were like pyramids.   *- an eyewitness*

Pseudo-prophets — who by stupid words misled the Christians, and by empty preaching induced all sorts of men to go.   *- a German monk*

The best kind of struggle ("jihad") is against yourself.   *Muhammad*

The Muslims and Franks are bleeding to death. The country is utterly ruined and good lives have been sacrificed on both sides. The time has come to stop this.
King Richard

.

....

THE KNIGHTS:

The **Knights of St John** grew out of the **Hospitallers** who ran a hospital in Jerusalem from 1023 for poor and sick Latin pilgrims. This was similar to many on the pilgrim routes of Europe. It became a military order committed to the defence of Jerusalem. When the Holy Land was lost, they moved to Rhodes and then Malta. Knights of such orders took vows of poverty, chastity and obedience, and continued to serve pilgrims as well as fight the Saracens in the Middle East and Spain. The **Templars** were founded by Hugh de Payen, and sought to be 'lions on the battlefield but lambs at home'.
The **Teutonic Knights** fought in Eastern Europe to 'convert' the Prussians and Lithuanians.

Honest savagery may have been preferable to the fanatical movement that unleashed waves of destruction in the Middle East.There was, however, some justification. The Arabs had respected the Holy Places — especially Jerusalem — and allowed pilgrims access to them. The Turks and Mongols who replaced them and took Jerusalem in 1078 showed no such respect and denied all access. There was a difficult fault line between Islamic and European civilisations — and ignorance on both sides of the faiths that came into collision. (The Qur'an was not available in Latin until 1143.)

The tragedy of the Crusades engulfed moderate Arabs, Christian heretics and Eastern Christendom. The Normans had moved North to Britain and South into Italy and the Viking warrior spirit lived on. The Popes saw opportunity to extend their influence and perhaps re-unite Christendom. Kings and nobles saw a chance to win wealth and glory. Preachers, like Peter the Hermit, capitalised on the millenarian fever, which fed on drought and pestilence, and gathered thousands of the poor to hasten the Messiah's coming.

Urban II preached the first Crusade in 1095, urging that it would be a goodly thing to die in the city where Christ had died. The massacre of men, women and children, which followed the taking of Jerusalem, contrasted with the peaceful take-over by Caliph Umar in 638.The second Crusade was launched when the Saracens captured Edessa in 1144. The third followed the loss of Jerusalem to Saladin in 1187. The fourth was guided by Innocent III and ended by sacking the Christian city of Constantinople.

Muslims were deeply divided in religion and politics. There were atrocities on both sides but Saladin — in the treatment of prisoners, for example, — was truer to his faith than many chivalrous Christian knights were to theirs. There were saner voices — Anselm, Peter Damian and Francis of Assisi were among those who condemned the Crusades. The Bishop of Spiers, the Archbishop of Mainz and Bernard of Clairveaux at least denounced the persecution of the Jews that accompanied them — but such voices were drowned out in the clamour of the times. Credit then to Abelard of Bath who travelled Muslim lands at that time in order to learn not fight.

The legacy of the Crusades was to be enduring. Orthodox Christians were left with a deep distrust of Rome, Islamic civilisation was weakened, the rights of minorities in Jerusalem were trampled, and Christian-Muslim relationships were poisoned for generations. [162]

....

You do not realise what you are saying.   Jesus - Lk 9:55

A servant of the Lord must be kindly towards everyone, easy-going and gentle.
                                                                      Paul - IITim 2:24

*We order those who follow the law to assume the name of 'Catholic Christians'. The
rest, whom we declare to be mad and insane, have to bear the shame of being called
heretics.*   Emperor Theodosius - 380

To put a heretic to death would be a crime inexpiable.   Chrysostom - 4C.

She did not seek to make windows into men's souls.   Francis Bacon
      — speaking of Elizabeth I and her moves towards greater toleration.

Expel the mangy sheep from the fold.   Jerome - 4C.

*It is a much more serious matter to corrupt faith, than to forge money. If forgers of
money are justly put to death, with much more justice can heretics also be put to death.*
                                                                      Aquinas - 13C.

*In those days flourished John Wycliffe. This man strove to surpass the skill of other men
by subtlety of knowledge, and to traverse their opinions.*
               - an English chronicler - 1382. Wycliffe's writings were burned

They simply cry heresy, but no author is free from heresy, whether ancient or modern.
                                                                      Luther - 16C.

I would burn a hundred innocents if there was one guilty among them.
                                                                      Conrad Tors – 16C

Even if my own father were a heretic, I would gladly gather wood to have him burned.
                                                                      Paul IV - 1542

I do not desire to be the ruler of heretics.   Philip II of Spain - 16C

*We ought always to hold that the white which I see is black, if the Hierarchical Church
so decides it.*   Ignatius Loyola - 16C.

*A true Bolshevik ... would be ready to believe that black was white and white was black,
if the Party required it.*   Iurii Piatakov

*Heresy and schism were invented merely to deprive mankind of the benefits of private
judgement and liberty of conscience.*   John Wesley - 18C.

....

The Inquisition was the culmination of the totalitarian spirit of Church and State, which prevailed for centuries after the Emperor Justinian (525-565). When established by the Lateran Council of 1215, it was simply a way of enquiring into suspect teaching as a matter of church discipline. Later it became an instrument of both church and secular control, and involved spies, torture and burning.

Torture was regulated by Innocent IV in 1252. Burning at the stake was used before and after the Inquisition — sometimes with official sanction, sometimes by lynch mobs. There was clerical opposition at times and Gregory VII excommunicated the people of Cambrai for causing such deaths.

The Spanish Inquisition was instituted by the Crown as a means of uniting and controlling the former kingdoms of Castile and Aragon, following the defeat of the Moors. A large number of semi-converts from Judaism and Islam had resulted in a climate of toleration but Sixtus IV empowered Ferdinand and Isabella to organise the Inquisition in their domains and in 1483 Torquemada (a Jewish convert) became Grand Inquisitor, heralding the worst excesses of the time. Jews were expelled altogether in 1492 and, over 20 years, some 2,000 Christian heretics were burned at the stake.

The Reformers attacked the Inquisition fiercely, helped by the availability of printing. But critics need to keep a balanced view here. Extensive files available in Salamanca show that in Valencia torture was employed in 2% of cases and that strict rules of evidence applied. For this reason fewer witch-burnings took place in Spain than elsewhere [see 60]. Luther, Calvin and Zwingli were all prepared to sanction execution by burning (as does, in one form, the United States today), but it is difficult at times to separate political repression from the suppression of ideas.

Ideas are potent, and in our day, the struggle for freedom of thought goes on. The Church had rarely championed such freedom and its pursuit of heretics had so compromised and blinded it, that it was in no position to restrain absolute rulers who were determined on uniformity. The fact that it justified such extremes on the grounds that the unrepentant would go to hell, only highlights the distance it had travelled away from the teaching of Jesus.

....

Words: Inquisition = enquiry.   Heretic = one who thinks otherwise.

....

If Galileo had only known how to retain the favour of the Jesuits, he would have stood in renown before the whole world — and he could have written what he pleased about everything, even about the motion of the earth.
                                        Fr Grienberger - contemporary Jesuit astronomer

To derive from the Bible knowledge of truths which belong only to human sciences, and which are useless for our salvation, is to apply the holy Scripture to a purpose for which God did not give it, and so to abuse it.   Descartes

You fixed the earth so that it will never be moved.   Ps 104:5

Nor is God less excellently revealed in Nature's actions, than in the sacred statements of the Bible.   Galileo

I should think that it should be the part of prudence not to let anyone usurp scriptural texts and force them in some way to maintain any physical conclusions to be true, when at some future time the senses may show the contrary.   Galileo

Be of good cheer, Galileo, and come out publicly.   Kepler
    (who took refuge briefly from his Protestant critics by staying with the Jesuits)

Scripture does not refrain from over-shadowing its most essential dogmas by attributing to God qualities very far from, and contrary to, His essence.   Galileo
    (Fr Lorini changed 'over-shadowing' to 'perverting' in a hostile submission to the Inquisition.)

To propose that the earth is not the centre of the world is equally absurd and false philosophy and theology, considered at least erroneous in faith.
                                        Galileo's judges - 22.6.1633

Unfortunately, I have to answer for all the idiocies that thirty or forty thousand brothers may, and do, actually commit.
    Fr Maraffi - Preacher General of the Dominicans, in an earlier apology to Galileo.

The Archbishop has told many that Galileo was unjustly sentenced by the Holy Congregation, that he is the first man in the world, and that he will live for ever in his writings.
    - a witness speaking of the Archbishop of Siena — from the files of the Inquisition

....

In 1633, Galileo, one of the world's most renowned scientists, was humiliated before the Roman Inquisition, and forced to recant his work. He had sought to confirm the work of Copernicus published in 1543. Copernicus was a Dean of the Church, who had dedicated his treatise to Pope Paul III. It suggested that Ptolemy's geometry made more sense if the sun, and not the earth, was the centre of the universe. Astronomers, like Tycho Brahe, opposed Copernicus, and Catholic thinkers treated his work with scepticism.

Galileo was also a convinced Catholic and said that he found more encouragement within the Church than from his fellow academics (an observatory had been established in the Vatican 50 years before). His views were not heretical, as the Church had no official view on the matter. However, it had recently recovered the classical teachings of Aristotle and the Renaissance climate was reluctant to question the marriage of Greek and Christian thought created by Aquinas.

Modern commentators suggest that it was the central position of humanity that the Church wanted to safeguard but, in fact, theologians saw God as the centre of the universe and not humanity — earth was the *lowest* part of Creation. There was concern, however, to defend the perfection of Creation and some felt that Galileo's discovery of sunspots was an insult to God. In any case, common sense was against these absurd innovations — or so most people believed.

It was the middle-ranking Dominicans and Jesuits who led the attack. They wove a case out of partial misrepresentations:

• that Galileo was presuming to interpret scripture
• that he had flouted judicial instructions
• that he published his 'Dialogues' without authority.

Pope Urban VIII was now a bitter man, whose political ambitions were collapsing. He felt betrayed by Galileo, who had been his friend, and authorised the inquisition. Under threat of torture, Galileo recanted.

Friends made sure that his life sentence became 5 months as the personal guest of the Archbishop of Siena, and then 'house arrest' at his own farm, where he continued working on mechanics and gravity. Nevertheless, the thought police had won and science was set back in Italy and elsewhere for many years. In 1744 Benedict XIV authorised the publication of the 'Dialogues'. In 1993 the Vatican quashed the original judgement. [see 153]

I know respecting this voyage that God has miraculously shown his will. I hope in our Lord that it will be a great benefit to Christianity.
Columbus – after landfall in the Bahamas, 11 October 1492

Not only the Christian religion but nature herself cries out against a state of slavery
Leo X on reports from the Indies – 1516

We should realise the truth, that in forty years, some twelve million of souls have died unjustly and tyrannically at the hands of Christians.
Bartolomé de las Casas – 1552

Being thus arrived in a good harbour and brought safe to land, they fell upon their knees and blessed the God of heaven, who had brought them over the vast and furious ocean.
William Bradford – the 'Mayflower' – Nov. 1620

We were entertained with all love and kindness and with as much bounty, after their manner, as they could possibly devise. We found the people most gentle loving and faithful, void of all guile and treason, and such as lived after the manner of the Golden Age …. a more kind and loving people there cannot be found in the world, as far as we have hitherto had trial..
Arthur Barlow – Virginia colonist - meeting local natives – 1584

Brutish savages, which by reason of their godless ignorance, and blasphemous idolatry, are worse than those beasts which are of a most wild and savage nature.
Robert Gray – Virginia colonist – of the same people – 1590

Pursue them to extermination, or drive them beyond our reach.   *Jefferson*

Tell me what the natives of the whole extent of America have gained by the commerce they have had with Europeans?   *James Cook 1773*

The first commonwealth in modern history to make religious liberty a cardinal principle and maintain the separation of church and state on these grounds.
Sydney Ahlstrom on Rhode Island – 1633

The form of government established in the Providence Plantations is DEMOCRATICAL, that is to say, a government held by the free and voluntary consent of all, or the greater part of the free inhabitants. All may walk as their conscience persuades them, every one in the name of his God.
- agreed at Rhode Island - 1647

Only now can we begin to measure the extent of the holocaust of disease and genocide that the coming of the Europeans meant for the American nations, both north and south. Now too, we can acknowledge the complicity of Catholic and Protestant Christians in a disaster that overwhelmed around 100 million people. We do not romanticise the pre-Columban civilisations but we should mourn the richness and diversity of what was lost and is still being lost. A few Christian voices, including popes, spoke out for the rights of 'Indians' and the Jesuits in Paraguay and beyond abolished the death penalty and established schools, hospitals and free services for the poor, but missions elsewhere sometimes became centres of forced labour and enforced conversion.

Anglicans were in Virginia from 1607 but rarely questioned a society that was built on black slavery. In time, Anglican loyalty to the Old World was a handicap during the struggle for independence. In the north, Catholic influence had spread from New France, which became a royal dominion in 1663, but numbers of immigrants were small and the fortunes of French Canada rose and fell with those of the Jesuits. (The society was suppressed for 10 years after Canada was ceded to Britain.)

The formative influence in the 17th century came from the Protestant colonies strung from Maine to Georgia. The immigrants reflected European religious conflicts and brought the Puritan revolution to the New World, spearheaded by the Scots-Irish of whom 12,000 per year were arriving by the 1740s. The Reformed outlook, which could be narrow and censorious, also provided the foundation ingredients of America — vigorous optimism, a sense of covenant, civic responsibility, hard work and an emphasis on learning (Harvard was established in 1636, Yale in 1701, and Princeton 1746).

Congregationalism provided a training ground for democracy. Roger Williams' classic defence of religious freedom on the grounds of 'soul liberty' – 1644 – guided the Providence Plantations, and William Penn's 'holy experiment' in Quaker Pennsylvania (1681 – 1750s) left a permanent mark on the great institutions of the United States. The revivals of the 18C and the spread of Enlightenment values were surprisingly merged in the work of Jonathan Edwards (1703-58), so that even the 'secularised' Fathers of the Constitution could build in 1788 on foundations well laid..

[see also 69, 71]

The Year: 1492   **The Place: Hispaniola**

The Admiral strode forward to grasp one of the ropes that pulled the rough but impressive cross upright. It lurched, swayed, then thudded into the socket. Columbus formally claimed the land for the Spanish crown and was satisfied that none of the Arawak-speaking people objected. This was scarcely surprising, as none spoke Spanish, and none had any idea that their lands were being taken from them and passing into the hands of a sovereign several thousand miles away. Similar scenes were solemnly enacted as Columbus went from island to island. He later described the people he met:

'They have no iron or steel or weapons, nor are they capable of using them, although they are well-built people of handsome stature, because they are wondrous timid. . . . They are so artless and free with all they possess, that no one would believe it without having seen it. Of anything they have, if you ask them for it, they never say no; rather they invite the person to share it, and show as much love as if they were giving their hearts'.

This was the people who would soon bear the full cruelty of an onslaught that could later be justly described as the American holocaust. As the conquest gathered pace, the short declaration used by Columbus was fixed into the formal words of the *requerimiento*. The natives were soon to be manacled and brought forward to be informed of the truths of Christianity and the necessity to swear allegiance to the Pope and to the Spanish crown. After this, if the 'Indians' refused, or even delayed in their acceptance, the statement continued:

' I certify to you that, with the help of God, we shall powerfully enter into your country and shall make war against you in all ways and manners that we can, and shall subject you to the yoke and obedience of the Church and of Their Highnesses. We shall take you and your wives and your children and shall make slaves of them, and as such shall sell and dispose of them as Their Highnesses may command. And we shall take your goods, and shall do all the mischief and damage that we can, as to vassals that do not obey and refuse to receive their lord and resist and contradict him'.

It is estimated that Hispaniola had a population of 8 million at this time. Within four years, some three million had died from slaughter, disease and despair. By 1,535 the native population was more or less extinct. For the Americas, this was only the beginning.

Christians today will be appalled by the above but may not so easily recognise the roots of such atrocity. There is a confusion of faith and political power. True enough, it may well be that religion was being used by those motivated by imperialist greed. It is also true that elements within Church teaching lent themselves to such abuse. We see again the fanaticism of those who divide God's world between the faithful and the infidel - and are determined to convert or conquer in the name of God. Because the stakes are seen to be so high — no less than eternal salvation — all humanitarian considerations are cast aside and extreme measures justified.

It remains only to close the eyes to any evidence of virtue among the people to be subjugated. Any sign of friendship, affection and generosity is taken to be evidence that the devil himself can be dressed as an angel of light in order to deceive the faithful.

Once again we have a reductionist Gospel. Salvation is a matter of submitting to Holy Church and to those powers which rule by divine right. The reward is acceptance, redemption and heaven itself. To refuse is to suffer eternal damnation — better therefore to 'compel them to come in'.

We must now guard against swinging to the other extreme. It is not true that such atrocity is typical of the Church and its missions. It is one end of a spectrum, which, at the other, is marked by respect, openness and sharing. There were many Christian voices raised against the American holocaust. Many Dominicans and Jesuits sided with the oppressed when there was no one else to speak for them. The best known voice is that of Bartolomé de Las Casas — the 'Apostle of the Indies'. He had sailed with Columbus on the third voyage and spent some fifty years campaigning in Hispaniola and Spain on behalf of native Americans. The shame is that he could do little more than chronicle the unfolding tragedy. He had no such qualms about importing slaves from Africa.

....

When Pope John Paul II visited Peru, five hundred years later, he was presented with a Bible. Nothing unusual in that, save for the words that accompanied it:

'John Paul II, we, Andean and American Indians, have decided to take advantage of your visit to return to you your Bible, since in five centuries it has not given us love, peace, or justice. Please take back your Bible and give it back to our oppressors, because they need its moral teaching more than we do'.

....

You shall not allow a witch to live.   Ex 22:18

To believe in witches or werewolves is unChristian.   *Wynfrith (Boniface)*
- c.730
To disbelieve in witchcraft is the greatest of heresies.
                                          'The Hammer of the Witches' - 1486

The Bible teaches us that there are witches, and that they must be slain.
                                                       Calvin - 16C.

*Witches are commonly old, lame, bleuried, pale, fowle, and full of wrinkles, in whose
drowsie minds the divell hath gotten a fine seat.*
                         Reginald Scot (who opposed the persecution) - 1584

Witchcraft grows with heresy, heresy with witchcraft.   *Thomas Stapleton - 1594*

*Witches are multiplying on the land like caterpillars in a garden. I wish they all had but
one body, so that we could burn them all at once.*   *Henri Boguet - 1602*

*Now my dearest child, you have all my acts and confessions, for which I must die. It is
all falsehood and invention, so help me God.*
                         Johannes Julius (a victim) - to his daughter - c.1630

*Most, of all that ever were taken, were tormented - and this usage was the ground of all
their confessions.*   *Sir George Mackenzie – 1678*

....

A modern parallel could possibly be made with Wanatchee, Washington
State, in the 1990's. 43 adults were charged with 30,000 counts of child abuse.
Most, if not all of these, were later agreed to be false.

Studies of the witch craze among the **Shona** people in Southern Africa
(1950's/60's)
suggest that freely admitted experiences referred to dreams brought on by
neighbours' suspicions.

Today's witches in Britain are linked with a revival of interest in old sources
of wisdom. These cults are usually benign, seeking freedom, wholeness,
inclusiveness and closeness to Nature. The rituals owe a great deal to
practitioners like Gerald Gardner. They draw more on traditions of magic
than of religion. Unlike early paganism, today's witches stress a duality of
opposites and have little to do with wealth, war, or sacrifice. Their eight-fold
calendar of festivals was not used by any people known.

Between 1450 and 1700, some 40,000 to 100,000 witches are said to have been burned at the stake or beheaded in Europe.

In the first 1,000 years of Christianity, witchcraft was not a serious issue and eastern Christianity has never been associated with witchhunts. In 10C Europe, most scholars and bishops believed witchcraft to be impossible and leading churchmen in England, France and Rome opposed the persecutions almost throughout. The 'Canon Episcopi' condemned literal belief in demonic nocturnal experience, and this was re-affirmed at the Council of Treves (1310).

The intellectual context was created by the growth of rationalism and by the reaction of dark unreason with its stress on the devil, and the contrast drawn between the Kingdom of God and the Kingdom of Satan. The Dominican friars and the Cathars were in the forefront of such belief, followed by the leaders of the Reformation and the Counter-Reformation. Interestingly it was the Renaissance and the age of reason which brought back the Roman laws against sorcery and the legalisation of torture.

The latter created a self-perpetuating terror. Victims were compelled to denounce others and a great fear gripped society. Critics — religious and secular — were swept aside or even swallowed up, as magistrates, judges and priests became victims in their turn.

Unhealthy attitudes towards women and sexuality played a part. The feminine was symbolised either by the 'pure virgin', or by the 'seductive hag'. It is true that some 20% of those executed were men, and that many women were among the accusers, but the apparatus of persecution was male.

There seems to be little evidence that witches represented the survival of pagan religions. Prejudice against those who do not conform, fear engendered by war and plague, and delusion all played a part. Some critics were convinced by coherent accounts of satanic experience made quite voluntarily. It is now suggested that false memories may be responsible or perhaps a fungal disease of grain causing hallucinations. Physicians, philosophers, scholars and humanist popes were all caught up in the prevailing hysteria. In the 17C, Friedrich von Spee, a Jesuit, and Thomas Ady – *A Candle in the Dark* – condemned the persecution of witches.

In England the Witchcraft Act of 1736 made *accusations* illegal but allowed imprisonment for those *claiming* to practise the art.

....

.

If I have infringed the rights of slave or slave girl when they brought a complaint against me, what shall I say if God summons me before him? Did not the same God create us in the womb? *Job 31:13*

If a man knocks out the tooth of a slave or a slave girl, he must let the slave go free. *Ex 21:27*

Welcome him not as a slave, but as more than a slave: as a dear brother.
Paul to Philemon - v.16

The ugliest and stupidest slaves come from Britain. *Cicero*

These are the souls for whom Christ died, and for our conduct towards them we must answer before that Almighty Being who is no respecter of persons.
John Woolman - 1757

Loosing the bonds of wickedness and setting the oppressed free is evidently a duty incumbent on all professors of Christianity. (see Isaiah - 58:6)
- declaration of the first anti-slavery society - Philadelphia - 1775

The vilest trade under the sun. *John Wesley to William Wilberforce*

All manner of dealing and trading in slaves to be utterly abolished.
House of Commons - 1807

The dark night of slavery closed in upon me, and behold a man transformed to a brute.
Frederick Douglass (a former slave)- 1834

Didn't my Lord deliver Daniel,
And why not every man? *Negro Spiritual*

Some 1800 years ago Christ was crucified: this morning, perchance, Captain Brown was hung. These are two ends of a chain.
Henry Thoreau on John Brown whose 'soul goes marching on'- 2 Dec.1859

If slavery is not wrong, nothing is wrong. *Lincoln - 1864*

....

"There is a poor blind Samson in this land,
  Shorn of his strength and bound in bonds of steel,
Who may, in some grim revelation, raise his hand,
  And shake the pillars of this Commonweal,
Till the vast Temple of our liberties
  A shapeless mass of wreck and rubbish lies"
.

Longfellow - 1842

Judaism safeguarded slaves from abuse by *over*-compensation — not 'a tooth for a tooth' but 'freedom for a tooth' (Ex 21:27). Christians knelt alongside their slaves and sometimes bought their freedom Was it unimaginable to oppose slavery altogether? Paul advised the escaped slave, Onesimus, to return to his master, yet appealed to Philemon to treat him as a brother — *'there is no such thing as slave or freeman. All are one in Christ' — Gal 3:28.* Ignatius, facing martyrdom in AD107, warmly remembered Onesimus, bishop of Ephesus — perhaps the same?

Mediaeval popes justified slavery — in 1455 Pope Nicholas V licensed King Alfonso of Portugal to *"reduce to perpetual slavery all the inhabitants of Africa"*. Benedictines kept slaves until 1864. Through ignorance and lack of vision, the church reflected society. Bartolomé de las Casas defended the rights of native Americans yet kept African slaves. There were exceptions: Patrick 5C was said to be *"the first human being in the history of the world to speak out against slavery"*.

The Reformation and Enlightenment slowly undermined the institution of slavery. Even so Europeans, with the help of Arab and African slavers, captured 30-60 million Africans, of whom some 12-15 million survived the forced marches and the passage across the 'Green Sea of Darkness'. This cancer still lies on the soul of Africa and on the conscience of Christians. The struggle is far from over. In India enlightened Hindus and Jesuits campaign against the virtual slavery inherent in the caste system and, world-wide the traffic in human beings is as lucrative today as that in drugs. [see 114]

[see 114]

A roll of honour of those who opposed slavery would include:
The Popes - **Paul III, Pius V** and **Urban VIII. William Ames** - 17C. Calvinist. **Richard Baxter** - 17C Puritan. **John Locke** - 17C. Christian rationalist. **Charles Montesquieu** - humanist, **John Woolman, Lucretia & James Mott, John Greenleaf Whittier** and **Levi Coffin** - together with numerous other Quakers. Levi ran the 'Underground Railroad', which assisted escaping slaves. Also the **Amistad** committee in Bristol - founded 1730, chiefly by Congregationalists, **Lord Mansfield** whose judgements in 1772, freed some 10,000 slaves in Britain. **Thomas Clarkson, William Wilberforce** and **Hannah More**, with others, fought the Parliamentary cause for abolition; **Henry Thoreau, Abraham Lincoln** and **Frederick Douglass** and **John Brown** led the American struggle. Nor should we forget the many slaves who fought for liberation.

It is customary now to stress factors which made slavery no longer economic. Such factors are important, and ideals must often wait until their time has come. But there have to be those who will seize the opportunity — and sometimes create it — even to the moving of mountains.

....

Go to the whole world and win disciples for me.   *Jesus - Mt 28:19*

Alas, we were so saddened because they came. They came to make our flowers wither, so that only their flower might live.
                                        Mayan prophet in Chilam Balam de Chumayel - 16C.

Yet more, O my God, more toil, more agony, more suffering for you.
                                                            Francis Xavier - 16C.

Do not bring any pressure to bear on the peoples, to change their manners, customs and uses, unless they are evidently contrary to religion and sound morals.
                            Congregation for the Propagation of the Faith (Catholic) - 1659

The sending out of missionaries into our Eastern possessions is the maddest, most extravagant, most costly, most indefensible project   - the East India Company

I go back to Africa to try to make an open path for commerce and Christianity.
                                                                Livingstone

A people died out but the Gospel had reached them in time.
                                                    - heard at a missionary lecture.

That irresistible urge to come to the aid of everybody, without realising that they themselves are in need of help.   Fr Burgman - missionary in Kenya

Now an atheist, I've been convinced of the enormous contribution that Christian evangelism makes in Africa ... education and training alone will not do. Christianity changes people's hearts. It brings a spiritual transformation. The change is good.
                                            Matthew Parris – the Times – 2009

I cannot understand you Europeans, always leaning over backwards to beat your breasts. You did a good job, don't run it down!   Desmond Tutu

Please take back your Bible and give it back to our oppressors because they need its moral teaching more than we do.
                                        Andean native Americans to Pope John Paul II

The Gospel always includes the responsibility to participate in the struggle for justice and human dignity.   - the World Council of Churches - 1975

The truth is, I was always political — I just changed sides.
                                    - a Brazilian bishop - on the struggle for liberation

....

.

Nowhere is the flawed greatness of the Church shown as clearly as in the tragic ambiguity of its missionary work. There was arrogance and blindness.There was also courage and compassion and fine examples can be found today. No generalisations are possible. Missionaries should not be romanticised nor demonised — nor should the people to whom they went. There is much to honour:

➤ the conviction of the early Christians who changed an empire
➤ the Irish Celts who evangelised from Kiev toTaranto — founding communities, copying both scriptures and the classics
➤ Methodius and Constantine, missionaries to the Slavs, who preached human rights and created a vernacular liturgy
➤ the 13C. friars who travelled to Africa and the Far East, reaching the Great Khan in 1245 and Peking in 1280.

In later times, was it priests or adventurers who hungered for 'God, Gold and Glory'? Certainly many missionaries became emissaries of European civilisation — for good and ill. Some were agents of imperial domination and could speak of '*ruling, civilising and Christianising the silent peoples'* (John Kennaway of the Church Missionary Society 19 C.). Yet Andrew Knight (Quaker) also of the CMS, insisted that no one takes Christ to the 'heathen' for he is there with them.There were no silent people.

The greatest knew that well enough:

➤ **Alessandro Valignano** insisted that the Jesuits who went to Japan in 1579 leave all vestiges of Europe behind
➤ **Bartolome de Las Casas** — Cuba — 1502, fought for the rights of native people
➤ **Matteo Ricci** — China — 1583, became a Confucian scholar
➤ **James Chalmers** — New Guinea, in 1877, deplored the Victorian literature which demeaned native peoples.

The 20C.saw another wave of evangelism with a great deal achieved but the ambiguity still applies in a world of 30,000 missionaries. There can be no return to a world of isolated peoples. The impact of power upon weakness, new upon old, will continue to bring its tragedies in a shrinking world. Sometimes it was a choice between the Bible and the bullet. Today the challenge is whether we can meet one another with the kind of respect which was characteristic of Jesus. Thankfully, many churches see world mission today in terms of mutual sharing.   [see 90]

....

Bring me honey for my eyes and some fat — I am weak; I want to have my eyes and they are missing.   *Poi - an Egyptian artist - c.1220 BC*

I will use my power to help the sick to the best of my ability and judgement; I will abstain from harming or wronging anyone by it.   *Hippocrates - 410 BC*

Having no treatment which would help, they concealed and sheltered themselves behind superstition and called the ignorance sacred.   *- 5C.BC*

I only bandage men's wounds; it is God who heals them.   *Galen - Greek*

May I be the doctor and the medicine for all sick beings and the world, until everyone is healed.   *Buddhist*

Value the services of a doctor — his skill comes from God.   *Ecclus 28:1*

He travelled throughout Galilee, healing all kinds of illness.   *Matthew - of Jesus - 4:23*

From the start Christianity was a healing faith.   *Roy Porter - medical historian*

I bless God, I never have been in so good plight as to my health as I am at this day, but I am at a great loss to know, whether it be my Hare's foot, or taking every morning of a pill of Turpentine, or my having left off the wearing of a gowne.   *Samuel Pepys - 1664*

It is not the clean keeping and sweeping of our houses and streets that can drive away this fearful messenger of God's wrath — but the purging and sweeping of our consciences.   *Lawrence Chadderton - Puritan - 17C.*

When a nation abounds with physicians, it grows thin of people.   *Joseph Addison - 1711*

The greatest earthly blessing that God can give to any of us is health — a newly made grave, poverty, slander, sinking of the spirit, might teach us lessons nowhere else to be learned so well.   *Spurgeon - Baptist - 19C.*

Modern medicine produces what it is intended to produce: a doctor who sees himself as a scientist. It may not produce what is so often needed: someone who can care.   *Ian Kennedy – 1980*

....

Following the example of Jesus, healing was a natural part of Christian ministry from the beginning [23].

- ➤ **Basil**, Bishop of Caesarea (330-379) built hospitals and hostels for the poor, with relief for those at home.
- ➤ **Fabiola** († 399) was famed in Rome for tending the sick and founding many hospices.

Christian doctors gained a wide reputation. Their school at Gondishapur 9 Iraq) became the cradle of Arab medicine. A great Islamic tradition returned the compliment through scholars like **Ibn Rushd** (Averroës), tutor to **Maimonides,** the Jewish philosopher.

In 1136 the Pantokrator in Constantinople included a monastery, an old people's home and a leper house. Monasteries offered hospitality throughout the 'Dark Ages' and often had infirmaries. Their approach was holistic — the cure of bodies and the cure of souls — their herb gardens and liturgies grew together.

By 1225 there were 19,000 leprosaria in Europe and lazarettos for plague victims. In 16C.England, hospitals had to be re-founded to fill the vacuum left by the dissolution of the monasteries — including: **St Bartholomews** for the sick, **St Thomas's** for the disabled, **Christ's Hospital** for foundlings, and **Bridewell** for homeless beggars.

Male elitism in the universities later excluded Jews and women from practising medicine. This was partly offset by the growth in nursing orders such as the Sisters of Charity. By the early 20C. Germany had 26,000 Catholic and 12,000 Protestant sisters and deaconesses. On the negative side, Leeo XII forbade vaccination in 1829 because he thought that smallpox was a punishment from heaven.

For mental illness, **Bethlehem** ('Bedlam') was opened in 1402. In 1751 **William Beattie** founded **St Luke's**, believing that mental illness was as curable as physical.**William Tuke** (Quaker) opened the **York Retreat** in 1796 — to be governed by *'reason, mildness and community'*. Most of the grim reputation of 'lunatic asylums' comes those run for profit in the 19C.and from public ignorance of the great achievements of men like **Gardiner Hill** in Lincoln and **Conolly** of Hanwell. Even today, it is hard to match the vision and humanity of an asylum like **St Francis** Hospital opened in Sussex in 1859.

Christians have no monopoly of caring but this ministry — still continued and expanded across the world — is an outstanding testimony to the faith and love of a great movement for good.

....

Life is a country that the old have seen and lived in. Those who have to travel through iit can only learn the way from them.   *Joseph Joubert*

Let there be schools for reading boys; le them learn psalms, notes, chants and grammar, in every monastery and bishop's house.   *Charlemagne*

To provide education for boys from the remote and barren areas who would otherwise be deprived of education.   *Archbishop Rotherham's school - 1483*

Here I will make supplication that ye would bestow as much to the finding of scholars of good wits, of poor men's sons, as ye were wont to bestow in pilgrimage matters, in pardons, in purgatory matters.   *Hugh Latimer - 16C.*

The charity school is another universal nursery of idleness; nor is it easy to conceive or invent anything more destructive than the giving an education to the children of the lowest class, that will make them condemn the drudgeries for which they were born.
                                                                                      A P Wadsworth - 1763

A preposterous institution replete with folly, indolence, fanaticism and mischief.
                                                                      - a critic of. Sunday Schools in Hull - 1788

My object will be, if possible, to form Christian men, for Christian boys I can hardly hope to make.   *Thomas Arnold - headmaster of Rugby - 1828*

All who will, may send their children and have them educated freely, and those who do not wish to have education for nothing, may pay for it if they please.
                                                                                      Joseph Lancaster - 19C.

I have seen educated men offer their services to a new barbarism:
  ➢ *engineers designing efficient incinerators,*
  ➢ *chemists researching the most appropriate gas,*
  ➢ *mathematicians calculating economic usage,*
  ➢ *managers regulating the supply of victims,*
  ➢ *psychologists helping to allay their fears,*
  ➢ *doctors experimenting on young children.*
To all who teach I ask in the name of God and all humanity, that when you give us better scientists, better engineers, better doctors
— you also give us better people.   - source untraced

....

On teachers: *The refuse of all other callings — to whom no gentleman would entrust the key of his cellar.*   *Lord Macaulay - 1847*

Christianity has had a profound influence on Western education. The ultimate objective was, by reading both the Bible and the 'Book of Nature', to know God. After the fall of Rome, it was,above all, the monks who preserved culture and learning in Europe. The 6C.Irish Renaissance is almost unknown, yet it was:

— **Alcuin,** taught by Colen the Wise, later adviser to Charlemagne, who provided free schools in every community – AD797.
— **Asser,** from St David's, who taught King Alfred and had charge of his educational and legal reforms
— **John Scotus** who became adviser to Charles the Bald.
In the misnamed 'Dark Ages' monks and friars founded schools, colleges, and universities, paving the way for the 16C.Renaissance.

In 13C Britain, cathedrals and wealthier churches employed 'grammar masters' and ensuing grammar schools (such as that which Shakespeare attended at Stratford) offered free education. The first Public Schools — Winchester (1382) and Harrow (1572) were originally grammar schools. Most of those that followed grew from an alliance between the Church and wealthy patrons.On the continent the Jesuit schools, though traditional in theology, pioneered enlightenment education including mathematics and science. Calvinist schools were equally progressive in Geneva.

Parish schools developed in the 17C.and charity schools a little later. The latter provided food, clothes and education for some of the poorest in the towns. SPCK formed or reformed 1,500 schools in 35 years.Sunday Schools, in England from 1780, taught the '3 Rs' to over 1 million children and gave rise to several major football clubs!.

In the 19C.the National Schools and the British Schools were developed according to the methods of Andrew Bell (Anglican) and Joseph Lancaster (Quaker), together with the first training colleges for teachers. By 1851 there were more than 17,000 church schools.

From our vantagepoint, we are aware of the defects and difficulties of some of these earlier schools but the overall achievement was monumental. With the Education Bill of William Forster (Quaker) in 1870, an alliance of progressive churchmen and radical reformers overcame the vested interests and established a universal system of education based on a statutory-voluntary partnership.

Meanwhile the missionary movement was creating thousands of schools across the world. Some were tragically insensitive to local needs but many of them are deeply respected institutions to this day.

....

*First up walked the squire to the communion rail; the farmers went up next, then up
went the tradesmen, then the wheelwrights and the blacksmiths; and then, the very last
of all, went the poor agricultural labourers in their smock frocks. They walked up by
themselves; nobody else knelt with them.*

Joseph Arch - founder of the Union of Agricultural Labourers - 19C.

*In 1840, 57% of working class children in Manchester died before reaching the age of
five. It was common for nine year olds to work for 24 and 36 hours without a break.
They were kept awake with whips. Children of three and four worked standing on
chairs in the lace factories. Four and five year olds crawled through the narrow, hot
galleries of the coal mines.*

Deschner

*Seething in the very centre of our great cities, concealed by the thinnest crust of
civilisation and decency, is a vast mass of moral corruption, of heart-breaking misery
and absolute godlessness.*

Andrew Mearns - 19C.

The Evangelical Revival: *Parliament stopped debating game laws and began to
discuss prison reform. Politics became an exercise in morality; the aristocracy assumed a
high seriousness and devoted themselves to good works. Above all, a middle class, which
might so easily have lost faith in the prevailing political system, found satisfaction in
taking up great moral causes.*

Ian Bradley

The regeneration came in churches, chapels and town halls.

Simon Schama

We have used the Bible as an opium dose for keeping beasts of burden patient.

Charles Kingsley

*The modern class conscious worker contemptuously casts aside religious prejudices,
leaves heaven to the priests and bourgeois bigots, and tries to win a better life for himself
on earth.*

Lenin

It was souls against pounds, shillings and pence.

Richard Oastler

*Once Evangelicalism became generally accepted, it lost its edge; it became merely a
convenient way to divert attention from the real ills of society. Only the outward
conformity remained; respectability replaced commitment.*

Ian Bradley

*[Between 1780 and 1850] the English ceased to be one of the most aggressive, brutal,
rowdy, outspoken, riotous, cruel and bloodthirsty nations in the world, and became one
of the most inhibited, polite, orderly, tender-minded, prudish and hypocritical!*

Harold Perkin

....

In the fourth century, Christians created a social revolution across the empire — opening 'houses for strangers' and 'places for the poor'. In Victorian Britain, Christians brought about another social revolution. **Marx** followed **Kingsley** in describing religion as the opium of the people but Kingsley was being self-critical. It was he and his christian socialist friends — **F D Maurice, Tom Hughes, William Morris, John Ludlow** — who were changing society for the better. It was Methodism, not Marxism that drove the trade union movement and provided articulate leaders - Methodism had 20,000 local preachers and 50,000 class leaders.

The Evangelical Revival and the Oxford Movement fostered strong social concern — pillories were abandoned, animal baiting banned, prisons, asylums and hospitals reformed. Slavery was abolished, temperance promoted and philanthropy encouraged — in the mid-19C this amounted to well over £5 million p.a. — greater than the national revenues of Sweden, Denmark or the Swiss Federation.

John Chapman championed feminism, promoted public health and published Mill, Spencer and Emerson. Charities multiplied and there was a new awareness of children — the NSPCC, Dr Barnado's and the emergence of children's writers witness to this. In the 1880s police court missionaries foreshadowed the probation service and the Salvation Army opened its first night shelters. In 1891 the first 'poor man's lawyer' was made available at Mansfield House.

At the same time, there were strong conservative and reactionary forces in the churches. Some churches were class-ridden and the property class was afraid of disorder and anarchy. Laws were harsh and punishments severe. Factory slavery could go unrecognised by those who fought African slavery — a factory where children were fined for being late on their 10-hour shifts, sent the money to overseas missions. **Richard Oastler** and **Lord Shaftesbury**, like many Christian reformers, found surer allies among radical secularists, than from among some of the 'high and dry' clergy.

Such developments were paralleled by the Catholic Church in countries where it was strong. A great network of Catholic Associations in Germany created a wealth of social initiatives. A warning is in order here — never to confuse the empty shells left behind by an ebbing tide of reform with the vitality and richness of the waters when the tide was at the flood.

[see 140]

....

The King of Righteousness ... hath enlightened our hearts so far as to see that the earth
was not made for you to be lords of it ... but it was made to be a common livelihood for
all.   *Gerard Winstanley*

A couple of flitches of bacon are worth 50,000 Methodist sermons.   *William Cobbett*

Our divine old Poor Law was a kind of sacred compact between the nation and
Almighty God.   *Rev Joseph Stevens - Methodist*

The system of forcing able-bodied paupers to provide for themselves through the terror of
a well-disciplined workhouse.   *- favoured by Rev Robert Lowe - Rector*
       (— the emphasis is on 'able-bodied' - and the dilemma is still a real one.)

The whole science of Political Economy is full of those exquisite adaptations to the
wants and comforts of human life, which bespeak the skill of a master
hand, in the adjustment of its laws, and the working of its profoundly constructed
mechanism.   *Thomas Chalmers - Presbyterian*
       (— thinking of the operation of the free market.)

They reduce the man to want and then give with pomp and ceremony.
                                                                 William Blake - on industrialists

Some people find it easier and more agreeable to take than to make. This temptation
marks all societies, and only moral training and vigilance can hold it in check.
                                                                 David Landes - historian

It is due to the religious emotions of the country that the avarice of the capitalist has
been kept in check.   *President of the TUC - 1892*

The genuine honesty of most British merchants had been one of the causes of our great
commercial prosperity.   *G M Trevelyan - historian*

From each according to his abilities, to each according to his needs.   *Marx*

Religion is the opium of the people.   *Marx*

The heart of the matter lay in the making of a new kind of man — rational, ordered,
diligent, productive. These virtues, while not new, were hardly commonplace.
Protestantism generalised them among its adherents.   *David Landes*

....

The relief of the poor has been a universal obligation on Christians and had been expressed through monasteries and churches for centuries. After the dissolution of the monasteries in England, the obvious need and Puritan pressure created 'little commonwealths'. These typically had a workshop, school, storehouse and hospital — with profits going to the poor. The 16C. Poor Law sought to provide work for the willing but punishment for the idle. Profits made in the workshops went to the needy and begging was made illegal on the grounds that it should be unnecessary.

Then, as now, it was difficult to find a just balance between showing compassion and encouraging independence. The Reformers — Crowley, Latimer, Ridley and Cranmer — called for more of the church's wealth to be used for the poor. But in the 17C. it was the self-help of the friendly societies, which did as much for the poor as philanthropy or the parish dole.

In the eighteenth century, SPCK provided workhouses that originally were far from the later harsh regimes — intended by the 1834 Act to force the poor to fend for themselves. The appalling results brought swift reaction from more radical Christians — among them, Rev Andrew Mearns, Rev Samuel Beckett, William Booth (of the Salvation Army) and Joseph Rowntree (Quaker).

The blind side of Christian charity was a disregard for the economic structures that produced constant poverty. Charity was an ambulance service but few questioned the ways of industry and trade, which had brought great reward at great cost. The influence of the Protestant ethic is contested, but Calvinist industry and integrity had done much to fashion business practice. Alongside the greed and exploitation were high ideals and commitments that offset some of the worst excesses of industrialisation. The achievement of employers like Robert Owen and the great Quaker pioneers — Cadbury, Rowntrees and Lloyds — was to set fresh standards by which future industry would be measured. Recent financial crises have starkly illustrated how these standards have been betrayed and how crucial they are to human welfare.

By the 20C a significant number of nonconformist MPs were in Parliament determined to ensure that the state was concerned for working conditions, pay and employees' rights. The church was as divided as society in the politics of it all, but there was a great deal of underlying agreement as to the values that mattered.   [see141]

....

Search out able, God-fearing men, honest and incorruptible, and appoint them over the
people.   *Jethro to Moses - Ex 18:21*

In those days there was no king in Israel and everyone did whatever he wanted.
           Judges 17:6

Those who have authority exercise it on God's behalf.   *Paul - Rom 13:1*

Pay to Caesar what belongs to Caesar, and to God what belongs to God.
           Jesus - Mt 22:21

Let Caesar have his due and us, the free Commons, ours.   *John Lilburne*

That the king can do no wrong is a necessary principle of the English constitution.
           Sir William Blackstone

The poorest man in his cottage may bid defiance to all the forces of the crown. It may be
frail, its roof may shake, the wind may blow through it, the storm may enter, but the
King of England cannot enter.   *William Pitt - 18C.*

It is unjust, devilish and tyrannical for any man to assume power to rule over any sort
of man without their free consent.   *John Lilburne - 17C.*

We leave to others the passions and politics of this world.   *Thomas Chalmers*

Our religion has established, as the supreme good, humility, abjection and contempt for
human affairs.   *Niccolo Machiavelli*

There are three property birthrights of every Briton: five British acres of land, the right of
armorial bearings, the right of suffrage in the enacting of the laws — the male at 21, the
female on her marriage.   *Celtic oral tradition*

The Bible is the government of God, of the people, by the people and for the people.
       John Wycliffe (who coined the phrase) - 14C.

Working class politics was largely the creation of people steeped in religion and the
Bible.   *Thomas Laqueur - 18C.*

Democracy lives on implicit Christian inspiration.   *Henri Bergson*

Let men be good and government cannot be bad. If it be ill, they will cure it.
       William Penn – 1681

....

Born in a patriarchal age, the Biblical tradition favours neither anarchy nor tyranny. Law and administration there must be but it is answerable to God. The new Hebrew nation hesitated before establishing a monarchy, and the prophets strove to ensure that it did not become absolute. Nathan's confrontation with Israel's greatest king — II Sam ch.11/12 — could well be unique in court literature.

Jesus can be recruited neither for nor against the Romans. His well known saying - *Give to Caesar what belongs to Caesar and to God what belongs to God* - should read 'give *back* to Caesar' according to Jewish commentators. A Jewish parallel adds - *for you and whatever is yours are God's.* (See Mt 22:21.) Paul, as a Roman citizen, is aware of the virtues of government but less alive to its vices (unlike the writer of Revelation).

Democracy owes a great deal to Athens, whose elite was elected by free male citizens, but early Christianity included women and slaves. It threatened to turn the world upside-down until the church was seduced by power and Roman imperialism. Yet we should not judge the Church of Rome through democratic eyes. What choices were available? For centuries it strove for law and order in a harsh world, which could have descended into anarchy. However, in later centuries it leaned towards monarchy, even dictatorship, and the papacy resisted the lower clergy who called for reform.

Luther firmly supported and was protected by established government, being pessimistic about human nature. The fact that church members were discouraged from political involvement meant that in later years many German Christians were looking the other way when Hitler came to power. **Calvin** believed that all institutions were under judgement and yet established the ideas and platform for democracy. He believed that everyone was responsible for political conduct and the running of the Reformed churches became a good training ground for democratic government. **Zwingli** promoted a 'civic' society with majority voting.

In England, the path to democracy was charted by such middle of the way thinkers as **Richard Hooker, Roger Williams, John Milton** and **John Locke.** In America **Thomas Jefferson** is rightly honoured but he was closely advised by the Calvinist **James Madison.** [143]

....

Democracy is the worst form of Government except all those other forms that have been tried from time to time. *Churchill*

....

His kingdom endures generation after generation.   Dan 4:34

The preservation of things by God does not take place by some new action, but by a continuation of the activity by which he gives existence, an activity which is outside space and time.   Aquinas - 13C.

I can remember the very spot in the road, whilst in my carriage, where to my joy, the solution occurred to me.   Darwin- on the forking of the' tree of life'

The life of such a man as Charles Darwin is in truth a standing proof of the existence of God.   J S Haldane

From death, famine, rapine, and the concealed war of nature, we can see that the highest good which we can conceive, the creation of the higher animals has directly come.   Darwin

My theology is a simple muddle. I cannot look upon the universe as the result of blind chance. Yet I can see no evidence of beneficent design, or indeed of design of any kind in the details.   Darwin

In my most extreme fluctuations, I have never been an atheist in the sense of denying the existence of God.   Darwin

Extinguished theologians lie about the cradle of every science as the strangled snakes beside that of Hercules.   Thomas Huxley - 1860

The last few years have witnessed the gradual acceptance by Christian thinkers of the great scientific generalisation of our age — the Theory of Evolution.   Lux Mundi (Anglican) - 1890

God did not make things, we may say; no, but He made them make themselves.   Frederick Temple

It was a few theologians and many scientists who dismissed Darwinism and evolution.   James Moore- biographer of Darwin

We might expect as the products of evolution our ancestors would be selfish, but it was their ability to work together and support each other which made them more successful than any other.   Andrew Whiten

Darwinism appeared and under the guise of a foe, did the work of a friend.   Aubrey Moore   19C theologian and scientist

....

.

Date: 30 June 1860   Place: The Athenaum, Oxford

— the British Association for the Advancement of Science

This was a great duel. In the blue corner, "Soapy Sam" Wilberforce, the bumbling bishop, who, clearly out of his depth, tried to make a mock of his opponent. In the red corner, Thomas H Huxley, the young champion of rational science. The contest to be fought over Darwin's theory of evolution. Over 700 packed into the room, the whole of the west side crowded with ladies who came to watch the fray.

The bishop of Oxford spoke for half an hour with *"inimitable spirit, emptiness and unfairness"*, finishing with a flourish by enquiring as to whether Mr Huxley was descended from an ape on his grandfather's or his grandmother's side. Huxley whispered to his neighbour, *"The Lord hath delivered him into my hands"*. Rising from his seat, he replied that he would rather have an ape than a bishop for his ancestor.

The effect was tremendous. One lady fainted and the rest waved and fluttered their handkerchiefs. The clash between science and religion and finally come and the Church was soundly defeated.

Like religion, science has its mythical stories. Revision is in order .....

The debate was of high quality according to the report in the "Athenaum". Wilberforce and Huxley *"have each found foemen worthy of their steel, and made their charges and counter-charges very much to their own satisfaction and the delight of their respective friends"*. Wilberforce (son of William, the anti-slavery campaigner) was shrewd and knowledgeable. A few days later, the "Quarterly Review" published a formal review by him of *"The Origin of Species"* and Darwin described it as:

"uncommonly clever, it picks out with skill all the most conjectural parts, and brings forward well all the difficulties. It quizzes me quite splendidly".

Scientists were deeply divided. Wilberforce was advised, in part, by the eminent scientist, Sir Richard Owen, Superintendent of Natural History at the British Museum. Scientists had a particular difficulty in judging far-reaching conjectures as scientific, when the evidence would necessarily be slow to emerge. PTO

DARWIN

Theologians were divided. Frederick Temple, later Archbishop of Canterbury, welcomed the new ideas at the closing service of the British Association. A recent biographer of Darwin, James Moore, believes that: *"it was a few theologians and many scientists who dismissed Darwin and evolution"*.

What was important was that the new ideas were open to vigorous debate. A new breed of professional scientists were in a sense challenging the clerical amateurs who dominated the university establishment. At this time in England, not a few scientists found the requirements of Anglican orthodoxy stifling. The Roman church also was inhibiting free thinking. it was time for a new generation to assert its independence. As for those theologians who contested the new theory of origins, what did they fear? Why were they concerned? Bishop Wilberforce spelled out his own anxieties and to these we will now turn.

First, we can notice some surprising omissions. He does not emphasise problems arising from the interpretation of Genesis. In fact, the literalness of the creation stories had been argued for some time, for it was Biblical scholars rather than scientists who had provoked that debate. Nor is there a problem about time — that the history of humanity is taken much further back than many believed. Often mentioned in this connection is the 17C Archbishop Ussher's calculation of the age of the world using the Biblical narrative. He had suggested 4004 BC. It is easy now to scoff at such a reckoning but the contemporary palaeontologist, Stephen Jay Gould recently criticised: *"lamentable small-mindedness, based on a mistaken use of present criteria, to judge a distant and different past"*. He describes Ussher's work as: *"within the generous and liberal tradition of humanistic scholarship"*. Nor again was Wilberforce anxious about the idea that there is a self-acting power in nature. Some will be surprised that the Christian thinker, Gregory of Nyssa wrote: *"God created only the germs and causes of life, which then slowly developed over long periods of time"* — because Gregory lived from c330 to 395 AD (alternatively ascribed to Augustine).

What Wilberforce did set out was the following:
"Man's derived supremacy over the earth; man's power of absolute speech; man's gift of reason; man's free will and responsibility; man's fall and man's redemption; the incarnation of the Eternal Son; the indwelling of the Eternal Spirit, — all are equally and utterly irreconcilable with the degrading notion of the brute origin of him who was created in the image of God, and redeemed by the Eternal Son"

How far do Christians today share these difficulties? How many touch upon the substance of the faith?. We may query man's 'derived supremacy'. Few would defend the exploitation of the earth but we may wish to talk in terms of stewardship. If human supremacy is an all-too-obvious fact, then it appears to make little difference as to whether it came about through evolution or not. Similarly, our gifts of speech and reason are scarcely devalued if we can show that there are antecedents in the rest of the animal world.

   The question of free will and consequent responsibility are a matter of serious philosophical debate then and now. Some use Darwinism to support their stand that the universe is meaningless, save in that we struggle to invent some meaning:
"An impersonal, unreflective, mindless little scrap of molecular machinery is the ultimate basis of all the agency and hence meaning, and hence consciousness, in the universe".

 Yet the same philosopher, Daniel Dennett, effectively contradicts this claim when he says: *"What makes us special is that we, alone among species, can rise above the imperatives of our genes".* The fact is that determinism, which rules out free will, is not a necessary consequence of evolutionary theory, for science simply doesn't have the tools to settle this debate.

   Jacques Monod wrote that: *"Pure chance, absolutely free but blind, is at the root of the stupendous edifice of evolution"* but we don't have to agree. We have long known that: *"time and chance happen to us all"* (Eccl 9:11). Indeed the role of chance in genetic mutation appears to show that it operates deep within living processes but that that is but part of the story. Matt Ridley notes that: *"stasis too is the hallmark of evolution".* There is remarkable stability, a landscape of order, a means of selection and a development over long periods of time that no amount of random shuffling alone could achieve.

It is the whole system that exhibits the marks of direction and purpose. The proponent of 'chance alone' may try to call in an infinite number of universes, arguing that our universe could be thrown up without any suggestion of design — but that is his speculation, an argument that has no scientific basis, and certainly no evolutionary support. In this we are all amateurs and have to wrestle with faith and mystery.

....

.

His blood be upon us and on our children.   Mt 27:25
(notoriously used as a justification for anti-semitism.)

May the Nazarenes and heretics perish as in a moment, and be blotted out of the book of
life.   (Nazarenes = Christians)   — *a Jewish prayer - c.90AD*

The synagogue is not only a whorehouse and a theatre, it is also a den of thieves and a
haunt of wild animals.   *Chrysostom - 4C.*

Many of those preparing to join the Crusade to Jerusalem decided they would first rise
up against the Jews. And so, on the 6th February in Norwich, all those Jews found in
their homes were slaughtered.   *- contemporary - 1190*

We Christians can hardly believe that a Jew's foul mouth is worthy to speak the name
of God in our presence.   *Luther*

Whoever makes the assertion that Christ was a Jew is either ignorant or insincere.
                                          Houston Chamberlain - 1899

Jews and mosquitos are a nuisance that humanity must get rid of in some
manner — I believe the best would be gas.   *Kaiser Wilhelm II - 1919*

The Church has always regarded the Jews as parasites. I am merely doing what the
Church has done for 1,500 years.   *Hitler to Bishop Berning*

Our relationship with the Third Reich is one of absolute and implicit trust.
                                 Ludwig Müller - leader of the German Christians

We repudiate the false teaching that the State can expand beyond its special
responsibility to become the single and total order of human life.
                       The Barmen Declaration of the German Confessing Church

We learned that we were totally and nakedly alone, that we could expect neither support
nor succour from God nor from our fellow creatures. Therefore the world will forever
remain a place of pain, suffering, alienation and defeat.   *Richard Rubinstein*

Those we loved came to the edge of a wilderness. And it opened and drew them in.
                                          Rabbi Friedlander

Never shall I forget the faces of the children, whose bodies I saw turned into wreaths of
smoke beneath a silent blue sky. Never shall I forget those flames which consumed my
faith forever.   *Elie Wiesel*

....

Jesus and his disciples were Jews but growing tensions led to the separation of Christian Jews from the synagogues. Some Jewish factions persecuted Christians — the stoning of Stephen and the execution of James, the brother of Jesus. In the 60s, Jews distanced themselves from Nero's attacks on Christians who, in turn, did not support the Jewish rebellions against Rome. After 90AD ritual cursing of Christians was added to the synagogue services.

These divisions influence the New Testament text. The enemies of Jesus are 'the Jews' (e.g.John 8:37f), though John mentions 'Israelites' favourably, and could be thinking of Judeans as distinct from Galileans (see Jn 7:1,13). Anti-Jewish texts (also Thess.2:14f.) supported the distortion found in sermons, plays and literature up until modern times. All the weaponry of ghettoes, badges and pogroms existed before Hitler, much of it fashioned by the church..

Many sane and courageous voices have spoken against anti-semitism but the record remains appalling:
- the Emperor Theodosius II (401-450) made synagogues illegal
- in 638 the Toledo synod ordered the forcible baptism of Jews
- Jews were expelled from England — 1290, and Spain — 1492
- the papal record is mixed. Innocent III condemned the Jews but Innocent IV and Gregory X denounced anti-Jewish hysteria. Pius XI spoke against the rise of Nazism but critics are still trying to assess the strategy of Pius XII.

As so often, political and religious factors are confused:
- the York massacre of 1190 is believed to have been instigated by local landowners, who were in debt to Jewish financiers
- the Christian reconquest of Spain allocated land to Jews and allowed new synagogues to be built but the Jewish community favoured the losing side in the subsequent civil war.

In the Holocaust (Jews refer to the 'Shoah' = 'destruction') six million died in 'the kingdom of the night'. This story must be told often, yet never can be told. Many Christians bear the guilt for what they did *not* do 'for the least of these my brethren'. Through it all, Jesus was surely nearer to his people than many of his followers were.

In an isolated kingdom, the grain harvest turned poisonous. It made everyone mad. The king turned to a trusted counsellor, 'We must all eat, but you try to eat less. Preserve enough sanity to enable you to remind us through the long dark period ahead, that we are mad. Tell us often. The time will come when we are sane again'.

Hasidic.

....

Besides me there is no god. My arrows will be drunk with blood and my sword sated with flesh.   Deut 32:39,42

They shall make tools out of their swords and spears ; nation will not take up sword against nation nor ever again be trained for war.   Isaiah - 2:4

Not by strength, nor power, but by my spirit, says the Lord.   Zechariah - 4:6

Would that you knew the things that lead to peace.   Jesus - Lk 19:42

Those who live by the sword, die by the sword.   Jesus - Mt 26:52

Do you suppose that I came to establish peace everywhere? No, I will inevitably cause conflict.   Jesus - Lk 12:51

Blessed are those who make peace.   Jesus - Mt 5:9

There are three classes which are exempt from bearing arms; bards, judges, graduates in law or religion. These represent God and his peace, and no weapon must ever be found in their hands.   Triads of the Druids

All bloody principles and practices we do utterly deny, with all outward wars and strife and fightings for any end or under any pretence whatsoever.
                                        Declaration of the Society of Friends 1661

We are met on the broad highway of good faith and good will — all is to be openness, brotherhood and love.   William Penn - to native Americans 1682

It is not enough that we should die for our country, we must learn to love our enemies and executioners too.   Edith Cavell
        (who stayed behind to nurse wounded prisoners - and was executed 1915)

He who does not want to fight in this world, where eternal struggle is the law of life, has no right to exist.   Hitler

It is a higher glory to stay war with a word than to slay men by the sword; to maintain peace by peace, not by war.   Augustine

We shall match your capacity to inflict suffering by our capacity to endure suffering.
                                                              Martin Luther King

....

Friend, if I wert thee I would move, for I am about to shoot where thou art.
                                        - apparently said by a Philadelphia Quaker to a burglar!

In early centuries, the Christian churches were pacifist because:
- military service could entail worship of the emperor
- the end of the world was expected
- the new ethics of the Kingdom appeared to exclude warfare.

In succeeding centuries, power was sought by, or was thrust upon the Church, which was no longer legislating for its members alone. As in most ages, some church leaders fanned the flames of war but many tried to dampen them. "Holy" wars like the crusades [61] were exceptional. Religion could be used as an excuse for war but it often defined a people and became a rallying point against oppression. The shame is there but the fault lines are not always easy to judge. The great genocides of the 20C — by Atatürk, Stalin, Hitler, Mao and Pol Pot — were not inspired by established religion.

Christian thinkers from Tertullian to Aquinas built on Plato's and Cicero's efforts to alleviate the horrors of war. At the Synod of Birr in Ireland (697) Adomnan secured agreement for 'The Law of the Innocents'. This protected non-combatants and was agreed by rulers of the Celtic kingdoms of Britain. Innocent II (12C.) banned the crossbow as too lethal. In Europe the doctrine of the 'Just War' was continually redefined. Francisco de Vitoria in the 16 C. proposed war *as a last resort* if there was:
- failure of all peaceful means of resolution
- declaration by a lawful authority
- a limited objective to counter wrong done
- sincere intention
- a reasonable prospect of victory
- no intent to harm civilians
- assurance that the force used would not be disproportionate.

The pacifist witness was chiefly borne by minority groups and the **Quakers** have been outstanding in this. It was never for them a negative matter but a positive spirit of peace and reconciliation. They have won trust where others did not dare to go and proved excellent mediators, as well as ministering to the victims of war.

The Fellowship of Reconciliation founded in.1914 by Henry Hodgkin (Quaker) and Richard Roberts (Presbyterian) calls *'for the enthronement of love in personal, social, commercial and national life'* and for the acceptance of the risks involved in the belief that :
"the Power and Love of God stretch far beyond the limits of our present experience".

....

The whole of the law of nature was right save for the faith and its entitlement.
St Patrick - on the old religion - 5C.

All these the Irish willingly received and saw to it to supply them with food day by day
without cost, and books for their studies, and teaching free of charge.
Bede - on foreign students fleeing the Great Plague of 664

Almost all of Ireland, despising the sea, is migrating to our shores with a herd of
philosophers.   *Heiric of Auxerre (France) - 870*

People believed they were sent to Ireland to be anti-Irish and discharged their proper
duty by remaining so.   *Lecky*

Ireland is a woman risen again from the horrors of reproach.
- ode to Niall Mor O'Neill, king of Tir Eoghain - 1364

I burned all along the Lough within four miles of Dungannon and killed one hundred
people, sparing none of what quality, age or sex soever, besides many burned to death.
Sir Arthur Chichester - 1599

This oppression did of force and necessity make the Irish a craftie people; for such as are
oppressed and live in slavery are ever put to their shifts.
John Davies, Irish poet - 17 C.

The Irish were browbeaten, plundered and despised.   *J.H Plumb on the 18 C.*

Ireland is like a half-starved rat that crosses the path of an elephant. What must the
elephant do? Squelch it — by heavens — squelch it!   *Thomas Carlyle - 19 C.*

We must change their course of government, clothing, customs, manner of holding land,
language and habit of life. It will be otherwise impossible to set up in them obedience.
Sir George Carew
(who had Gaelic manuscripts cut up to cover English language primers.)

The courtyard's filled with water / And the great earls where are they?
The earls, the lady, the people / Beaten into the clay.   *Kilcash*

Preserve that which is living, and help the two Irelands, Gaelic Ireland and Anglo-
Ireland, so to unite that neither shall shed its pride.   *W B Yeats*

....

The conflict in Ireland was never simple. Religious divisions undoubtedly contributed to the tragedies of Irish history but the deeper issues were those of colonialism.

In Celtic times, Ireland was not one and Ulster was a separate kingdom. In the ninth century the Vikings settled Dublin and spread into the Irish heartland. In 1166 Dubliners invited Henry II to intervene in their internal wars (Norsemen and Normans being one and the same). The Anglo-Normans came to dominate the eastern counties by the 15C.and most of Ireland by the 17th. In the North, the natural links of Ulster with Scotland together with deliberate colonial policy led to widespread Scots settlement.

The London government alternated between bouts of reform and periods of neglect, but was always alarmed when foreign intervention threatened. The English break with Rome complicated everything. The friars through the provision of schools and welfare had gained the hearts of the majority of the people — 'the old English' remained Catholic and Anglican administrators were brought in over their heads. Successive revolts were aided by Spain and France. Each revolt brought atrocities — in Ulster 2,000 Protestant settlers were killed and thousands dispossessed; each revolt also brought repression — not least that of Cromwell, who massacred the citizens of Drogheda and Wexford.

Catholics and Presbyterians suffered discrimination and supported one other — Protestants helping to finance the first Catholic church in Belfast. Both called for unity and civil rights — Wolf Tone of the United Irishmen was Protestant. After the nightmare of the potato famine, Parnell — also Protestant — won the backing of the Catholic Church for Home Rule and in 1885 secured 85% of the votes. But the Protestant working class of Ulster was swept along by fundamentalist crusades, which demonised the Catholic Church.

In the late twentieth century:
- leaders of the mainstream churches cooperated constantly
- communities like Corrymeela challenged prejudices
- Ruth Agnew and Monica Patterson formed Women Together
- Sister Anna pioneered integrated education
- Denis Bradley (Catholic) and Roy Magee (Presbyterian) with others, acted as go-betweens with terrorist organisations.

The extremists lost ground to committed politicians and thousands of ordinary people who strove for a better future.   [see 78, 145]

The list given below is only a sample of major charities. Many grew from Christian inspiration and tens of thousands of Christians express their faith in such voluntary work. No exclusive claim is made here. There are men and women of many faiths and none who share the same concerns.

1824 **The RNLI** committed to providing a lifeboat service for those at risk. 300 lifeboats are manned by volunteers, saving 400 lives a year.

1824 **RSPCA** f. by Rev Arthur Broome - Anglican - with William Wilberforce, Elizabeth Fry and others, to promote respect for animals.

1835 **Mission to Seafarers** - f. by Rev John Ashley - Anglican - a social and welfare support network for seamen across the world.

1844 **Shaftesbury Society** - working for the disabled and disadvantaged - following the great 19C.Evangelical reformer.

1844 **Young Men's Christian Association** — YMCA (and the YWCA in 1855) to support young people in need.

1862 **The Red Cross -** f. by Henri Dunant, the Swiss banker, who was inspired by the work of the 100 Camillan brothers with 36 nurses, tending the sick on the battlefield of Solferino. They wore red crosses.

1865 **The Salvation Army -** f. by Gen.William Booth — fomerly a Methodist minister — now running 3,000 hospitals, schools and hostels in 103 countries, together with shelters, counselling and family tracing.

1866 **Dr Barnardo** – a London missionary, who opened boys' homes and a girls' village. Estimated to have helped 250,000 in his lifetime.

1869 **NCH Action for Children** - f. by Rev Thomas Stephenson - Methodist .

1881 **The Children's Society** f. by the Church of England to help vulnerable children and secure their rights.

1884 **NSPCC -** Congregational minister - Benjamin Waugh, together with Lord Shaftesbury, Dr Barnado & Cardinal Manning — drawing on earlier groups in Liverpool & New York.

1887 **St John's Ambulance Brigade** - in the tradition of the 11C. Order of St John of Jerusalem providing on-site care long before there was a statutory service.

1898 **The National Trust** - f. by Canon Rawnsley, Octavia Hill and others. Caring for 200 historic houses and large areas of unspoilt countryside.

1919 **Save the Children** f. by Eglantyne Jebb on seeing starvation in Vienna following the war...'*every war is a war against the child*'.

1928 **The Flying Doctor Service** in Australia — f. by the Rev John Flynn to bring medical help to remote areas.

1935   Alcoholics Anonymous - f. by Dr Bob & Bill Wilson in Ohio - self-help groups now numbering 3,000 internationally.
1940   Age Concern - a federation of 1,400 groups concerned with the care of the elderly.
1942   Oxfam f. by an Oxford vicar and students to provide emergency relief in Greece. Now world-wide and promoting long-term development..
1948   Christian Aid f. by the British Council of Churches for the relief of refugees and to finance development in the third world - working through local churches and other organisations on the ground.
1948   Cheshire Homes f. to help those disabled in war.
1950   The Samaritans f. by Rev Chad Varah - Anglican - as a befriending and listening service for the troubled and suicidal.
1953   Sue Ryder Homes f. by Baroness Ryder of Warsaw, former secret agent in Poland - to help the psychological victims of war.
1956   International Voluntary Service — f.by the Bishop of Portsmouth to provide volunteers in areas of need across the world.
1958   Voluntary Service Overseas was established by to assist countries overseas by the provision of skilled personnel.
1958   CRUSE f. by Margaret Torrie (Quaker) to help widows.
1959   The Hospice Movement — inspired by Cicely Saunders, for the care of the dying. Over 80 hospices in the UK. Earlier hospices included that of Trinity, Clapham f. by William Hoare - 1891.
1961   Amnesty International f. by Peter Benenson, Eric Baker (Quaker) and others working for prisoners of conscience across the world. Thousands have now been helped by moral and practical support.
1962   CAFOD .. now titled the Catholic Agency for Overseas Development with a wide remit in the developing world.
1964   Child Poverty Action Group f. on the initiative of Harriet Wilson (Quaker) to raise concerns about poverty in Britain and to campaign for welfare rights.
1965   Shelter f. by Rev Bruce Kenrick for those homeless or in poor housing.
1968   Tear Fund giving integrated spiritual and material support to the world's poorest, backed by many evangelical churches.
1971   Médecins sans Frontières f. by Bernard Koucher - humanitarian - doctor and former French Minister of Health - to provide specialist help across frontiers.   --------------

I myself shall tend my flock, says the Lord God. I shall search for the lost, recover the straggler, bandage the injured, strengthen the sick, leave the healthy and strong to play, and give my flock their proper food.   *Ezekiel - 34:15*

THE CHURCH TODAY

We have only clay jars in which to hold this treasure.   *Paul - IICor 4:7*

We know where the Church is, we do not know where it is not.   *Basil of Caesarea*

I will put up with the church until I see a better one; and it will have to put up with me, until I become better.   *Erasmus*

The Church is a mystery of the inauguration of the Kingdom of God in the world: the mystery of the incarnate Son of God still present in the world.   *Roman Cholij*

Just as God became visibly present and united to us in the visible, material humanity of Christ, so he remains visibly present and united to us in the structures and sacraments of the Church.   *Graham Leonard*

We bishops, popes, priests — we need someone to be a prophet for us too, for we must not set up the Church as untouchable.   *Oscar Romero*

To be of no Church is dangerous. Religion, of which the rewards are distant, will glide by degrees out of the mind, unless it be invigorated by external ordinances, by stated calls to worship, and the salutary influence of example.   *Samuel Johnson*

The Church exists for the sake of those outside it.   *William Temple*

My love for an institution is in proportion to my desire to reform it.   *J S Mill*

I have never seen a good outcome to any synod ... rivalries and manoevres always prevail over reason.   *Gregory of Nazianzus — Epistle 130. C4*

The Church of Christ is not an institution; it is a new life with Christ and in Christ, guided by the Holy Spirit.   *Sergius Belgakov*

The Church has neither the wish nor the obligation to extend her space to cover the space of the world.   *Bonhoeffer*

The Church is not possession of the kingdom, it is struggle for it.   *The New Catechism*

....

Don't stay away from church because there are so many hypocrites. There's always room for one more.   A R Adams

Some of the foregoing suggests the question — 'Can Christianity be rescued from the Church?' A reminder is therefore in order, that no attempt has been made to achieve a balance. The topics chosen are simply those that may be of current interest. What lies hidden is the wealth of teaching and caring which has flowed from a multitude of faithful pastors and people in every generation.

How should Christians regard the Church?

> **a lifeboat** — to rescue the perishing from an evil world — an 'ark of safety'
> **a Kingdom** — reared above all earthly kingdoms — impressively imperial in power and splendour
> **a base camp** — for training and refreshment — 'moveable' as befits a pilgrim people
> **a holding environment** — for the vulnerable, the hurting and the marginalised
> **a holy place** — for praise and adoration — set apart by God and for God
> **a foreshadowing community** — looking to what can become a reality for all
> **a heavenly community** — at one with the 'communion of saints' — a gathering of all Christians before and after death
> **the body of Christ** — closely identified with Christ himself.

All these ideas are to be found within the Church but which should shape Christian thinking? The last image is often used today and points to the presence of Christ in the common life of Christians. The metaphor is powerful in Paul, and gave rise to the very term 'member - ship' now applied to all human organisations. It did not feature much in Roman Catholic theology until Karl Adam (1924) and it then tended to become much more than a metaphor — it suggested a second incarnation. This was seen to give the Church a guarantee of infallibility. It was not that the Church regarded itself as flawless but that it would be prevented from betraying the Gospel in any fundamental way. It still meant that the living image of the body was shrunken and stretched onto the frame of an institution.

Jesus' criticism of the religious establishment of his day is radical and Christians need to take his warnings very seriously. The Church has no monopoly of faith, no absolute power over the individual, no control over the work of God and no exclusive authority. It is at most a witness and a servant.

....

*Uninquiring submission to external authority is neither God's method with man nor a
desirable method of human obedience.*   John Oman

*Every authority that is not confirmed by true reason seems to be weak, whereas true
reason does not need to be supported by any authority.*   John Scotus - 9C.

*If Holy Tradition is accepted as a source of faith, its immutability must be recognised.
Loyalty to tradition does not simply mean slavish attachment to the past and to external
authority, but a living connection with the entire past experience.*   Panagotis

Tradition is like the 'soul' that unites a person in his old age to his infancy.
                                                                              Roman Cholij

*Only in the general conscience of the Church can the essence of the faith be dynamically
re-interpreted. The Council is merely the instrument through which is expressed the
infallibility of Christ.*   Gerasimus Papadopoulos

The Bible is the Church's book. It can only be read profitably from her holding hands.
                                                                           Gustave Weigel

*They laid this stone trap / for him, enticing him with candles, / as though he would
come like some huge moth / out of the darkness to beat there.*   R S Thomas

*Those with this ministry of oversight, assisted by the Holy Spirit, may together come to
a judgement which, being faithful to Scripture and consistent with apostolic Tradition,
is preserved from error.*   ibid

The Roman Church has never erred and according to scripture will never err.
                                            Gregory VII - Dictates of the Pope - 1075

*A living, organically growing tradition is better expressed by the image of the Meeting of
the Waters, where streams and currents encounter each other in a mutually enriching
swirl of energy.*   Mary Grey

No morality can be founded on authority, even if the authority were divine.   A J Ayer

Man cannot accept certainties, he must discover them.   Middleton Murray

....

Tradition — to give over — that which is handed on.

The search for authority stems from the longing for certainty as we struggle to fathom the ways of God.

After Jesus' death, the earliest Christians found their authority in the apostles and those who recorded their testimony. Yet different interpretations were there from the start — as, naturally, everyone sees through their own eyes.

Orthodox Christians look first to the creeds and councils of early centuries. At this time the Church felt that it had to define and defend itself against imaginative speculation and a bewildering variety of creeds.

The Church of Rome claims a continuing development of tradition embodied in itself and increasingly expressed through the hierarchy and ultimately the pope himself. The primacy of respect, once accorded naturally to Rome as one of the capitals of empire, was the foundation for future expectation of universal obedience. This was thought essential for the unity of the Church but, more than any other factor, it helped to shatter that unity. The Church, as the body of Christ, seemed to look not to Christ as its head but to the pope — the vicar of the absent Christ.

Protestants sought safety in the sole authority of scripture — that is, in the records of the early Christians accepted as normative by the early church councils. These records came to be used with a rigidity and uniformity that was untrue to their nature.

Many Christians look within for their authority to conscience as the place where we can hear the voice of God. Of course, conscience itself is fashioned by heredity and community and can be hijacked by foolish imaginings and dark motives. Yet it can be examined in the light of reason, faith, scripture, tradition and experience, and it can be informed and cross-checked by the experience of the community. In the life of the church this community must include the lay as well as the cleric, the oppressed as well as the powerful, women as well as men, the married as well as the celibate. Then, it can indeed lay itself open to the influence of the Spirit of God.

When Jesus was questioned as to the source of his authority, he simply spoke of the Father. In this sense, there is only one authority — the Author of all things. In another sense, there is no authority, as truth authenticates itself.

The Year: 325 AD   **The Place: Nicaea**

Constantine strode into the Council like "some heavenly messenger of God, clothed in shining garments, which flashed with glittering rays of light". The assembled bishops were awed and gratified as they took their seats at the great feast, celebrating the day in York 20 years before, when Constantine was proclaimed Caesar by his soldiers. Now, seated in his imperial palace, he was at the height of his power. Tough and ambitious, he had removed his rivals, including members of his own family, and was Emperor of both east and west. In keeping with the warrior God, who had undoubtedly blessed him in battle, he ensured that all persecution of Christianity ended and its leaders enjoyed his personal favour.

He would, of course, require their loyalty, and their help in rooting out all division and dissent. Uniformity in religion and politics was ever the goal of an absolute monarch. It made for peace.

This Council was dominated by eastern bishops, with only a few from the west. Sylvester, the bishop of Rome, was not among them. The favoured churchmen had been given free passage to Nicaea but unknown to them, the Emperor's spies had been listening to their conversations at resting places on their journey. When they arrived at the palace, they were surrounded by ranks of soldiers standing with drawn swords. On entry, they were given rich presents. The times had indeed changed.

It was a useful tidying up exercise. After some days, the final communique, including the carefully worded 'Nicene Creed', was taken to each delegate by imperial notaries for signature. Bishops who refused to sign would be exiled. Theological dissenters were formally cursed and heresy was born.

Matters didn't end there. Constantine himself had no very settled opinion. Though baptised late in life, we cannot be sure that he became a convinced Christian. His son called a council in 359, which abandoned the creed, but his successor, the Emperor Theodosius, forced through an amended version at the Council of Constantinople in 381. He used it as the touchstone of orthodoxy, when savage persecutions were unleashed on all church dissenters —
— persecutions which may have played no small part in the welcome given by many Christians to the advance of Islam.

The Nicene Creed was not used widely in public worship for some 400 years but is now commonplace and still a standard text of orthodox belief.

The creed agreed by the bishops meeting near Izmir in modern Turkey has indeed lasted. Is that because of its undoubted worth or because it has been fenced against all criticism? It is possible, after all, to disregard the imperial trappings and judicious intimidation and still argue that the teachings there agreed should continue to be the norm of the Christian Church. Who would want to open up again the controversies which preceded it? The answer may be that thinking Christians in the 21st century would want to do so.

It is not my purpose at this point to argue for a different set of conclusions but it is time for the fence of orthodoxy to be torn down. We could welcome a free-range Christianity, which allows us to enjoy a rich diversity of understanding and to cast our faith into fresh language without incurring the old cry of heretic — though the word at first simply implied choice rather than betrayal.

The Nicene Creed does pose a number of difficulties. We have seen that it was drawn up in problematic circumstances nearly 300 years after the event that it seeks to enshrine. That is equivalent to our looking back to 1700 AD and setting in stone our interpretation of the events of that time. We have seen too that the creed was a political as well as a religious document, produced by Eusebius, the court theologian, so that Constantine could establish some kind of conformity across the Empire. There are parallels with the Acts of Uniformity in England between 1549 and 1662. A further difficulty involved language. Like many an international document, this declaration was interpreted differently according to the backgrounds of those involved; in this case, by theologians who came from either Greek or Latin churches.

The content too is scarcely balanced for Christians today, in that the whole of Jesus' ministry, both teaching and healing, is passed over. The imagery employed also has its challenge for us today. How should we interpret phrases like "he came down from heaven" and "he ascended into heaven"? The version we use today is that which was amended at Chalcedon in 451 and it has its place as a way of honouring tradition — but its concepts are confusing and the case for re-opening such credal statements is strong.   PTO

COUNCILS AND CREEDS

The Nicene Creed

We believe in one God, the Father, the almighty,
maker of heaven and earth,
of all that is, seen and unseen.

We believe in one Lord, Jesus Christ,
the only Son of God, eternally begotten of the Father,
God from God, Light from Light, true God from true God,
begotten not made, of one being with the Father.
Through him all things were made.
For us and for our salvation he came down from heaven;
by the power of the Holy Spirit he became incarnate of the Virgin Mary, and was made
man.
For our sake he was crucified under Pontius Pilate;
he suffered death and was buried.
On the third day he rose again in accordance with the Scriptures;
he ascended into heaven and is seated at the right hand of the Father. He will come
again in glory to judge the living and the dead, and his kingdom will have no end.

We believe in the Holy Spirit, the Lord, the Giver of life,
who proceeds from the Father and the Son.
With the Father and the Son he is worshipped and glorified.
He has spoken through the Prophets.

We believe in one holy catholic and apostolic Church.
We acknowledge one baptism for the forgiveness of sins.
We look for the resurrection of the dead, and the life of the world to come.

....

A **creed** is a statement of belief. The Nicene Creed was based on one used in
Caesarea and presented by Eusebius, the imperial court theologian, to the Council
of Nicaea in 325. It was designed to counter the teaching of Arius, over which a
split was developing in the Church. Arius appeared to present a more distant God
with Jesus as a bridge between humanity and God. The Council wanted to stress
that God himself was truly in Christ.

There were two major complications:

> A political one, in that it was the Emperor Constantine who controlled the
> Council and drove through its conclusions.
> The terminology used was ambiguous and interpreted differently in
> Greek and Latin — the confusion was evident for the next 50 years. The
> wording we have is a revision made by the Council of Chalcedon in 451.

The Apostles Creed was presented by Marcellus, bishop of Ancyra, to the bishop of Rome in 340. It may be based on an early baptismal confession, and was (doubtfully) attributed to the apostles in Jerusalem. The version now used was only fully developed in 750.

The Athanasian Creed is a fourth century canticle. It is not a creed nor written by Athanasius, though it is in keeping with his theology.

A creed was first called a *sumbolon* (symbol) — used by the army for a password that distinguished friend from foe. Creeds defined the outer limits of Christian teaching but had little part in public worship. The Roman Church did not use a creed in the Mass for a thousand years and some Protestant churches gave up using creeds altogether, although they feature prominently in Orthodox and Anglican worship. The World Council of Churches encouraged their use as a way of establishing common ground in ecumenical liturgies.

....

Judaism maintains that man's creed is that he believes in God, and therefore in mankind, but not that he believes in a creed.　　　　　　　　*Leo Baeck*

Wherever there is a creed, there is a heretic round the corner or in his grave
　　　　　　　　　　　　　　　　　　　　　　　　　　　A N Whitehead

A twentieth century African Creed:

We believe in the one High God who out of love created the beautiful world and everything good in it. He created man and wanted man to be happy in the world. God loves the world and every nation and tribe on earth. We have known this High God in the darkness and now we know him in the light. God promised in the book of his word, the bible, that he would save the world and all the nations and tribes.

We believe that God made good his promise by sending his son, Jesus Christ, a man in the flesh, a Jew by tribe, born poor in a little village, who left his home and was always on safari doing good, curing people by the power of God, teaching about God and man, showing that the meaning of religion is love. He was rejected by his people, tortured and nailed hands and feet to a cross, and died. He lay buried in the grave, but the hyenas did not touch him, and on the third day, he rose from the grave. He ascended to the skies. He is the Lord.

We believe that all our sins are forgiven through him. All who have faith in him must be sorry for their sins, be baptised in the Holy Spirit of God, live the rules of love and share the bread together in love, to announce the good news to others until Jesus comes again. We are waiting for him. He is love. He lives. This we believe.　　　　　　　　　　　　　　　　　　　　　　　　　　　Amen.

....

Clothe Aaron with sacred vestments, anoint him, and consecrate him as my priest.

Ex 40:13

Beware of the scribes who like to walk the streets in their long robes and to be greeted with deference... in foreign nations, kings hold sway over their subjects; and those in authority take the title ' Benefactor'. It must not be like that with you: on the contrary, the greatest among you must not be above the newest members.

Jesus – Mark 12:38, Lk 22:25

They appointed elders in each congregation. *Luke - Acts 14:23 - (see Nu 11:16)*

Jesus Christ counts us all as priests of his God and Father. *Rev 1:6*

You are obliged to look upon the bishop as the Lord himself. *Ignatius*

The priest is the same Christ Jesus, whose sacred person is represented by his minister.

Pius XII

Christ our Lord took upon him the form of a servant, how can his servant ... take upon himself the form of a Lord? *Milton*

Shamans and priests are Wizards of Oz who use special effects from sleight-of-hand to sumptuous cathedrals, to convince others that they are privy to forces of power and wonder. *Steven Pinker*

There is scarce perhaps to be found anywhere in Europe a more learned, decent, independent and respectable set of men than the greater part of the Presbyterian clergy

Adam Smith - 1776

But I gae mad at their grimaces
Their sighin' cantin' grace proud faces
Their three mile prayers, and half mile graces. *Robert Burns*

Go to the people; live amongst them; start with what they have; build on what they know; and when the deed is done, the mission accomplished; of the best leaders, people will say, 'We have done it ourselves'. *Lao Tzu - 6 C.BC*

....

Words: **minister** = 'lesser' or 'inferior' and therefore 'servant'.
priest = presbyter - the word for an 'elder'. **clergy** = a 'lot' or 'share' — that is in the ministry of the church. **bishop** = 'one who is given oversight'
pope = papa — father. a **lay person** = any one of the people of God.

Jesus saw himself in the role of a servant, and taught his disciples to think of themselves in the same way. In Paul, the emphasis is on the charismatic community — where functions are shared according to gifts which are there to be discovered in everyone. There is no suggestion of superior and inferior status. All are soul-friends for one another, all are stewards, carrying the keys of the Kingdom for one another, and all are priests — bringing one another to God and God to one another.

It is doubtful whether Peter was ever head of the church in Rome and there is no suggestion in the New Testament that he would have a successor. The apostolic succession is that of the whole church — even as all are thought of as saints ('consecrated to God').

Forms and structures are inevitable in any organisation and leadership has to be focussed in certain individuals but flexibility is healthier than rigidity and leaders are called to serve and enable. The Celtic church used the symbol of the wild geese to illustrate an ever-changing ministry — just as the leaders of a skein of geese change places regularly to share the advantages of the airflow passing along the formation.

In the second century, the clergy developed into a distinct order and were distinguished from the laity. By the fifth century bishops had adopted the trappings of royalty (the throne, crown, ring and kiss persist to this day). By this time too, the popes had adopted the title of Supreme Pontiff — originally a pagan title of the chief priest in Rome. Such power and status was believed to safeguard the unity and strength of the church but it lay in contradiction to the teaching of Jesus and was as likely to promote weakness and disunity.

No hierarchy ('holy rule') is spoken of in the early church for 400 years. Bishops or elders had oversight in *local* congregations — cities had such *overseers* for public worship before Christianity. In Augustine's time (4-5C.) there were 420 bishops in North Africa alone. In classical Roman society, those 'ordained' were the senators and knights. Ordinatio was signalled by the *raising* of hands — a ceremony rather different from the New Testament *laying on* of hands, which was first associated with healing. When the laying on of hands was used for ordination, it was the bishop *together with other presbyters* who used this symbol on behalf of the whole church.

Celibacy became a requirement in the Western church in 1139 but not in the Eastern church.   [see 54]

....

God is spirit, and those who worship him must worship him sincerely and truthfully.

Jesus - Jn 4:24

God is in heaven and you on earth, so let your words be few.   *Eccles 5:1*

Two that are sitting and occupied with the words of Torah, the Shekinah is among them. (Torah = the Law, Shekinah = the presence of God)   *Rabbinic*

When two or three meet together as my disciples, I am there among them.

Jesus - Mt 18:20

I need those who care, not those who offer sacrifices.

Jesus - Mt 12:7 - after Hos 6:6

First go and be reconciled with your brother.   *Jesus - Mt 5:24*

The sky is my throne and the earth is my footstool. So where will you build a house for me?   *Isaiah - 66:1 - quoted by Stephen - Acts 7:48*

Religious observance imparts structure to daily life, gives rhythm to the calendar, injects warmth into family celebrations, and creates solidarity during times of sadness and crisis.   *David Shatz (Jewish)*

Who, having been called to be a preacher, would stoop to be a king?

Thomas Carlyle

The General Confession with its repeated and elaborate protestations of guilt looks like a desperate attempt to persuade God to accept us on the score of our eating the maximum dust possible.   *H A Williams*

Your prayers have been for us like a ring of fire.

Desmond Tutu - on the struggle to end apartheid in South Africa

Do you think I would have danced it if I could have said it?   *Anna Pavlova*

Ceremonies are the hedge that fences the substance of religion from all the indignities too commonly put upon it.   *William Laud*

Fighting the dull rust that habit puts on the wonder of things.

Hermann Wouk (Jewish)

Men have banished the Deity; they have relegated it to a sanctuary. Madmen that you are! Set God free; see him everywhere where he is, or say that he does not exist at all.

Diderot

....

.

Worship is an awareness and a response. The word has to do with appreciation or the recognition of worth — 'worthship'. It is a word that belongs to all — not just those narrowly defined as religious.
It carries with it a sense of wonder and reverence, and should therefore be reserved for that which deserves such a response.
It could be used of the natural world, or of a great work of art, or an outstanding person, but Christians usually keep the term for God alone.

Being what we are as individuals and members of communities we seek to capture and repeat our deepest and most formative experiences — to recreate or re-member them. Certain times or places may help us in this and become sacred for us. We build a fire in the hope that the flame will come again.

Jewish worship stems from the home, and Muslim worship on the rhythm of every day. Others choose a sacred building — running the risk that religion may become a compartment of life. But all faiths insist that life is all of a piece — the sacred and the secular, work and prayer, earth and heaven, are one.

Christian worship is centred on God and patterned on the life of Jesus. Within each service and across the year a drama is re-enacted. The variety of form ranges from the holy space of silence, through the rites of repentance and forgiveness, to the elaborate celebration of incarnation and resurrection. It may be private — the intimacy of the spirit before its Maker — but often it is shared: the interflow of a fellowship that is more than the sum of parts.

There is a tension between past and future. The past claims us because Christianity is rooted in history, because the flame comes to us in the cresset of old forms, and because an older generation have handed it on to us. Then the future calls us into creative freedom, to explore the silence, to rediscover the sacredness of the commonplace and to turn old rigidities into dance.

Dangers crowd on every side — the empty husk of formalism, the habitual routines, the flattery of the Byzantine court, the repetition of magic formulae — but beyond all is a searching and a commitment, and always the curtain may be drawn aside, so that we become aware of One who never loses his awareness of us. It is for this that worship exists and with which it must never be confused.   [see 40, 118]

God who created the world and everything in it does not live in man-made shrines.

Paul - Acts 17:24

God deals with men through chosen individuals; particular acts in particular places for the benefit of all.

Graham Leonard

When I bring clouds to cover the land, the rainbow will appear in the clouds. Then I shall remember the covenant that I made with you and with all living things.

Gen 9:14

Whenever the red hunter comes upon a scene that is strikingly beautiful or sublime — a black thundercloud with the rainbow's glowing arch above the mountain, a white waterfall in the heart of the green gorge, a vast prairie tinged with the blood-red of sunset — he pauses in the attitude of worship.

Ohiyesa (Sioux)

This is a shot-silk universe, spirit and matter, inside and outside, divine and human, shimmering like aspects of one reality, which cannot be separated.

John Robinson

If you do not recognise God, at least recognise his signs.

Al-Hallaj (Sufi)

I love the rites and ceremonies of the Church. But I see, well pleased, that our great Lord can work without them.

John Wesley

The symbolic actions of former and present times which, because of their pertaining to divine things, are called sacraments.

Augustine

No ordinary meal — a sacrament awaits us
On our tables daily spread,
For men are risking lives on sea and land
That we may dwell in safety and be fed.

Scots prayer

There is not a single thing in the world of sense that is not a symbol of something in yonder one.

Al-Ghazzali (Muslim)

Whatever we see, wherever we look, we cannot touch or handle the things of earth and not, in that very moment, be confronted with the sacraments of heaven.

C A Coulson (scientist)

Just as the soul exists wholly everywhere in the body, so God exists wholly in each and every thing.

Aquinas

God's creation is sacramental in itself — that is, the finite speaks of the infinite. More than this — since God is present in his creation, then the finite becomes an actual *experience* of the Infinite.

This wider vision breaks out of the narrow confines that the church has often imposed upon it. The purpose of focussing Christian worship on certain sacramental acts is always to point beyond themselves. Churches differ as to how many 'sacraments' are appropriate. Up to thirty have been suggested (Hugh of St -Victor 12C.) but seven have become traditional: — *baptism, confirmation, eucharist, penance, extreme unction, ordination and matrimony.* Protestant churches acknowledge just two: *baptism and the Lord's supper (eucharist)* as these are most clearly instituted by Jesus. Quakers and the Salvation Army do not use any. (Should foot-washing appear in these lists? — Jn 13:3f.).

Christians have traditionally taught that:
>   the spiritual can be conveyed by the material
>   God directly acts through the human personality
>   the Christian community shares responsibility for building up the faith of the individual.

Unfortunately these teachings went hand in hand with narrow, exclusive and somewhat mechanical interpretations. Emphasis was placed on right materials, words and actions, obscuring the personal nature of our relationship with God. Preoccupation with validity — a legal term related to the giving of authority restricted God's freedom to deal with his own. Too often the use of the sacrament became indistinguishable from the practice of magic (hence the phrase *hocus pocus* — from the Latin "This is my body"*)*. It could even become an instrument of oppression — for example, the forcible baptism of 70,000 Jews in Spain in 1497 — which was assumed to be valid despite the coercion involved.

The use of sacraments is not unique to Christianity. In Greek and other 'mystery religions' the use of the elements of wine, bread and water were often understood as a way of achieving union with a god. There was little ethical content in the faith being practised. For a Roman soldier the 'sacrament' was the oath of allegiance sworn to the Emperor — the symbol of which was carried on the standards. For Christians too, the sacraments can and should symbolise the same whole-hearted commitment to the service of God.

....

I will sprinkle clean water on you and you shall be clean.   *Ezek 36:25*

He will baptise you with the spirit of holiness and with fire.
                                        John the Baptist - re Jesus - Mt 3:11

*Everything God has created is good — it becomes holy through God's word and by
prayer.*   *Paul - I Tim 4:5*

*It is by God's kindness you are saved through faith; there is nothing you can do. It is
God's gift.*   *Paul - Eph 2:8*

All sins have been annihilated with the sacrament of baptism: all of them entirely.
                                                Augustine

Baptism washes away the whole guilt of punishment belonging to the past.   *Aquinas*

Baptism is not the washing away of dirt but a sincere appeal to God.   *IPeter 3:21*

Baptism points back to the work of God and forward to the life of faith.   *J A Motyer*

Christ, not baptism, is the way to the sheepfold.   *John Bunyan*

You have made it so that children and babies sing your praise.
                                        Ps 8:2 - quoted by Jesus - Mt 21:16

*When we were baptised into union with Christ Jesus, we were baptised into his death,
so that, as Christ was raised from the dead, we might set out on a new life.*
                                                Paul - Rom 6:4

*Wash away, Waters, whatever sin is in me, what wrong I have done,
what imprecation I have uttered, and what untruth I have spoken.*
                                        Rig Veda 10.9.88-9

*Slowly, against the water light of the stars, emerged the outline of a woman holding out
a child high above her head, and singing something with her own face lifted to the sky.
'She's asking the stars up there,' he whispered,' to take the little heart of her child and to
give him something of the heart of a star in return — the heart of a hunter.'*
        — from Laurens van der Post describing a !Kung San family in the Kalahari

....

BAPTISM

Baptism passed into the Christian tradition because:

> Jesus himself was baptised
> his disciples, but perhaps not Jesus, baptised others — Jn 4:1
> Jesus commissioned his followers to do so — Mt 28:19
> (these words are likely to be a late addition to the gospel)

It is a sign of:
1. cleansing — as in many religions.
2. death and rebirth — dramatised by full immersion in water.
3. the outpouring of God's Spirit.

The reality to which it points is God's activity in human life. The faith of those baptised *is* the blessing, and the sacrament is a recognition, a commitment and a celebration of belonging to the Christian community. This is not to say that it is a *mere* sign nor was Jesus' baptism an empty gesture, rather it is the making visible of that which is invisible. Jesus' baptism was completed at Calvary —Lk 12:50 — when he shared the anguish of his people even to death. So his disciples, in baptism and in the eucharist, 'show the Lord's death' — but its meaning is realised by living it.

Infant baptism arose because converts became Christians as a whole family. The emphasis is on God's call to new life and on the hope of future faith. This understanding was corrupted when the doctrine of original or inherited sin was developed and baptism was seen as the antidote. The belief that the unbaptised were condemned to hell illustrates how far the church had departed from Jesus' view that children belonged to the kingdom — Mt 19:14.

Churches which baptise only adults stress the importance of a mature response. The gift of faith that the candidates have received is God's confirmation of their calling — now gladly acknowledged. For those baptised in infancy, Confirmation is the name given to the ceremony of completion — the fulfilment of a sacrament of hope. Those confirmed are *received* as members, not *made* members. This formal act should not be treated as the dividing line between Christians and non-Christians, the committed and the uncommitted.   [see 22]

....

Words: **Baptism** means 'to immerse'. The Hebrew word underlying the account of John's baptisms suggests that the believers baptised *themselves* in the presence of John. **Christening** is the giving of a *Christian* name. Converts wanted to give themselves a new name at the beginning of a new life — especially if their old name was a pagan one.

I am the bread of life.   Jesus - Jn 6:48

Life comes from the spirit, the flesh can create nothing.   Jesus - Jn 6:63

They knew him by the way he broke the bread.   Luke - 24:35

It only reflects upon himself if he eats without appreciating the person that it represents.
                                                                                       Paul - I Cor 11:29

It is your own mystery that lies there on the table.   Augustine

Religion with its masterpieces is one thing, Christian faith is another.   Karl Barth

*Colour, sound, movement, are united and bound together in a context of splendid,
stylised archaism around this altar, barely lit with a few candles, to produce one of the
wonders of religious history.*   Eugene Masure

Sacramental communion is bound up with the memory of real events.   C H Dodd

We are really anticipating the day when the whole human race will be home.
                                                                                          D S Cairns

*The Eucharist is the perpetual externalisation in human ritual of the self-suffering of
Christ, which was externalised on Calvary, but is ever real in the inward and heavenly
sphere.*   Oliver Quick

*The very giving of ourselves to God is a receiving of Him, and the very receiving of Him
is already a giving of ourselves.*   Donald Baillie

*Where there is no priest, there is no Eucharist; and where there is no Eucharist, the
Church is not present.*   Brendan Chomiskey

By consecrating bread, their priests could turn it into the very body of their god.
                                                        James Frazer – describing the beliefs of the Aztecs

It is the Last Supper that makes Calvary sacrificial.   A E J Rawlinson

As long as anyone is hungry, our Eucharist is incomplete.   Pedro Aruppe

The Eucharist is the silence of God.   Carlo Caretto

The Eucharist is a drama:
> - a remembering of Jesus' giving of himself
> - a realisation of the presence of God
> - a celebration of freedom — linked with the Passover
> - an anticipation of future fulfilment
> - and a challenge to work for that fulfilment.

The focus is Jesus himself — not the elements of bread and wine. The Aramaic words would be *'This — my body, is given for you'*, where *'body'* means the whole person. The meaning is clear — he is giving himself for his friends. As Jesus was present in the upper room, there was no question of the disciples confusing the material bread with the physical body of Christ.

Equally, the wine would not be seen as drinking real blood, which would have horrified Jews. An ancient Hebrew covenant ritual involved two tribes making peace by their members passing between two halves of a carcase, and the blood being sprinkled upon the warriors. This powerful symbolism spoke of a new kinship — as blood was life. We should not perpetuate an imagery, which does not belong to our history and which falls back into crude literalism.

In the *Didache* – now recognised as a first century training manual – worshippers are not offered 'body and blood' but invited to give thanks for Jesus as 'the vine' and for the 'life and knowledge' revealed in him.

Paul says that God is known in the things which he has made — Rom 1:20. Christians traditionally brought bread from home — in fact this sharing, this mutuality, was *the* characteristic of early Christian meals. The bread did not have to be changed, as God was known in creation and in the community of faith. The doctrine of transubstantiation was used at the Lateran Council of 1215 as an attempt to guard against a crude and magical interpretation of the sacrament, but today it promotes this very interpretation.

Words: Eucharist = 'thanksgiving' — as this service was a celebration of the life of Jesus. **Mass** = a 'sending out' — emphasising commitment and commission. **Communion** — with God and with other believers. The **Lord's Supper** — because the invitation lies in the hands of Christ, not the church. **Transubstantiation** — based on Aristotelian metaphysics, now outdated. It asserted that the real presence of Christ 'stood under' and *beyond* the material, not a local presence within the elements.
"Hocus Pocus" = **'this is my body'** !

Go therefore to everyone.   *Jesus - Mt 28:19*

The world is our cloister.   *Francis*

The world is my parish.   *John Wesley*

When you are my witnesses, I am God, and when you are not my witnesses, I am not God.   *Rabbi Simeon ben Yohai*

There is only one God, who is God of all the peoples, Indians, heathen, Greeks, barbarians. You employ violence and fury, overwhelming everything with fire and flame. The conquest was a great wrong.
F.Bartolome de Las Casas - to the Conquistadores

Neither Christianity nor the Church has a mission to make men happy, their mission is to tell them the truth.   *Jacques Maritain*

We are the first generation of Christians to discern God's mission to mankind, the Buddhist, the Hindu, the Muslim, as well as to the Jew and the Christian.
Wilfred Canterell Smith

The Church's task is to assist its people in plumbing the depths of their own humanity, where transcendence, being, and even love are discovered, and to bring these qualities, found in the centre of life, into the world. I name that centre of life God.
John Shelby Spong

Mission is often described as if it were the planned extension of an old building. But in fact it has usually been more like an unexpected explosion.   *John V Taylor*

The purpose of life is not in the far future, nor, as we so often imagine, round the next corner, but the whole of it is here and now, as fully as ever it will be on this planet.
Herbert Butterfield

For the spreading of the gospel I am ready to go to the ends of the earth.
Charles de Foucauld

Fr Foucauld inspired the Little Brothers and Little Sisters of Jesus, who live among the very poor of the world. They neither preach nor run schools or hospitals. John Taylor says of them: 'Out of sight, out of mind of the church as a whole, way below the poverty line, scattered in their twos and threes across the face of the earth, they do not work for their neighbours, they work with them. Their role is that of prayer and of a silent, hidden presence of love.'

When all the criticisms have been made, the Christian community throughout many countries remains the most widespread, the most inclusive, and the most in touch of any organisation. Its caring, its integrity and its very diversity make it a sign of hope for the future.

The church's mission is still that of Jesus — to witness to and to make real the Kingdom of God [47]. It is set in the context of God's mission — the ever-creating, ever-renewing work of God, which is everywhere and in everyone. It seeks the future through healing, through justice, and through community.

Christ is proclaimed as the revelation and incarnation of God at work. Here is the pattern and example, and the very nature of love. The mission of the church embodies his inspiration. It cannot, and should not, remain exclusive. It is there to serve *all* humanity. It is there to serve and not to dominate, to love and not to intrude, to unite and not to divide. And being what we are, the mission is also to ourselves, addressing our own failures to ensure that we are not marked by self-righteousness. God has many things to say to us through those who do not use the word Christian.

Yet the mission is urgent and the warnings real that must be given. There is too much evil, too much inhumanity and too fearful a prospect, if greed and callousness prevail in our world. All humanity is called to work with God through science, through medicine, through preaching, through every calling — but always through love — to hold back the forces of destruction and free the forces of creation. And this is Gospel — good news above all for the poor, the oppressed, the diseased and the captive.

Nor should Christians imagine that the mission to which they are called exhausts God's mission to humanity. He who called the Philistines from Caphtor and the Syrians from Kir (Amos 9:7)
will enable all kinds of people to speak truth to one another. Mission is always therefore a shared enterprise.

....

Moses: *Lord, I have never been a man who can talk easily, never in my life, not even now that you have spoken to me; I stumble over my words.*

God: *Who is it that makes a man able to talk? Who makes him deaf or dumb? Who makes him sighted or blind? Is it not I, the Lord? Go now; I shall help you to speak and tell you what to say.*   *Ex 4:10*

Liberation theology developed during the last decades of the 20C. It was forged in the struggle of local Roman Catholic clergy in Latin America against military dictatorships. It was then developed across the world, wherever the churches found themselves defending human rights against injustice or challenging the political and economic structures that oppressed the poor.

It was underpinned by a fresh realisation of the powerful implications of the Bible for political and social action. The Exodus, the Hebrew law and the prophets, the promise of the Magnificat, the inauguration of Jesus' ministry at Nazareth, and several of the parables, all pointed to the requirement that the gospel must be good news for the poor in every sphere of life.

The election of a Polish pope (1978) strengthened the church in its opposition to totalitarian communism but the Vatican was more ambivalent in supporting resistance to right wing dictators.

....

Human liberation, not God talk, is the primary focus of Christianity.

Elizabeth Tapia

It is not our role to bless or oppose a government. We are not for someone or against someone. We are for Christ, and we should contribute our actions so that things go in accordance with the Gospel.

Mgr Santos - criticising the rule of General Pinochet in Chile

We have to look for a way of change. Immorality has become 'amorality' — people are losing the sense of right and wrong.

Mgr Banks - opposing the injustices of General Stroessner in Paraguay

Already the Party is assuming a totalitarian role. It claims to speak for the people and yet does not allow the people to give their views.

Roman Catholic bishops to President Moi of Kenya

To our certain knowledge the army has brought about the maiming and death of hundreds and hundreds of innocent people who are neither dissidents nor collaborators.

Zimbabwe bishops on operations in Matabeleland under President Mugabe

The church is maturing. It is gradually learning to accept its moral responsibility and to condemn the Mafia as being totally opposed to all notions of Christianity.

Fr Fasullo — Sicily

....

LIBERATION !

On the front line — 20C.

Nicolai Baranov
— *founder of The Path — dedicated to Christian democracy in Poland. He spent 23 years in labour camps and psychiatric hospitals.*

Fr Calciu
— *founder of the Free Trade Union of Romanian Workers. He served long prison sentences under President Ceausescu.*

Fr Laurinavi≠ius
— *member of a group in Lithuania* **monitoring** *the Helsinki agreement. Murdered in 1981.*

Cardinal Arns
— *encouraged the* **base communities** *of poor people in the cities of Brazil. These were Bible study and pressure groups tackling local issues of water, drainage, health, lighting etc. 'The aim of interpretation is no longer to interpret the Bible, but to interpret life with the help of the Bible'.*
He accused the government of torture and murder in the 1973 manifesto: 'I Hear the Clamour of my People.'

Bishop Juan Gerardi
— *who spent 8 years cataloguing the human rights violations in Guatemala: 150,000 dead, 50,000 disappeared, 200,000 orphans and 40,000 widows. He was murdered in 1998, 3 weeks after the publication of his report.*

Cardinal Henriquez
— *founded the Vicariate of Solidarity to be alongside the families of the 'disappeared' under the rule of General Pinochet in Chile.*

Archbishop Rivera y Damas
— *persistent critic of the army in El Salvador and of the failure to investigate human rights violations. Called for 'the inescapable duty to see justice done.'*

Abbot Mpundu
— *opponent of the corrupt rule of President Mobutu in Zaire.*

Bishop Carlos Belo
— *condemned the Indonesian army over the East Timor massacres of 1991.*

Professor Heyns
— *moderator of the Dutch Reformed Church in South Africa. He was shot soon after the Church had finally condemned apartheid as a sin against God.*

Fr Edicio de la Torre
— *founder of the Federation of Free Farmers in the Philippines. Repeatedly detained.*

This list could be extended indefinitely. Those named were usually supported by many others, who had little status to protect them
and who often, therefore, took greater risks. The advantage of the church as an institution is clear, when it is able to speak for the powerless.

....

May they be one; as you Father are in me and I in you.   *Jesus - Jn 17:21*

Doctrines divide but service unites.   *— slogan of the United Bible Societies*

To plant in each non-Christian nation one undivided church of Christ.
The World Missionary Conference - 1910

An appeal for reunion:

The time has come, we believe, for all the separated groups of Christians to agree in forgetting the things that are behind and reaching out towards the goal of a re-united Catholic Church ... We believe that the visible unity of the Church will be found to involve the whole-hearted acceptance of:

- *The Holy Scriptures as the record of God's revelation of Himself to man, and as being the rule and ultimate standard of faith; and the Creed commonly called Nicene, as the sufficient statement of the Christian faith, and either it or the Apostles Creed as the Baptismal confession of belief.*
- *The divinely instituted sacraments of Baptism and the Holy Communion, as expressing for all the corporate life of the whole fellowship, in and with Christ.*
- *A ministry acknowledged by every part of the Church as possessing not only the inward call of the Spirit but also the commission of Christ and the authority of the whole body.*

May we not reasonably claim that the Episcopate is the one means of providing such a ministry? We would urge that it is now and will prove to be in the future the best instrument for maintaining the unity and the continuity of the Church.

We do not ask that any one Communion should consent to be absorbed by another. We do ask that all should unite in a new and great endeavour to recover and to manifest to the world the unity of the Body of Christ for which he prayed.   *— extracted from the letter- 'To All Christian People'*
- the Lambeth Conference (Anglican) – 1920

One cannot adhere to Christ as Head of the Church without loyal allegiance to his Vicar on earth.   *Pius XII – 1943*

These ecclesial communities which, specifically because of the absence of the sacramental priesthood, have not preserved the genuine and integral substance of the Eucharistic Mystery, cannot ... be called 'Churches' in the proper sense.   *Vatican Edict 2007*

....

The word 'ecumenical' (= 'world-wide') was used of the church councils in the early Christian centuries. It is used now of the movement to bring the mainstream churches together.

The early vision was caught by Presbyterian ministers — Thomas & Alexander Campbell in the early 19C. but its time had not yet come and the Churches of Christ emerged as a separate body. The modern movement began at the World Missionary Conference in Edinburgh — 1910. The 'scandal' of Christian divisions was obvious in non-Christian countries, where missions competed with one another. The totalitarian challenges of the 20C. added to the conviction that only a reconciled church could bring about reconciliation in the world.

John Mott and Dr Visser't Hooft were among many who inspired the formation of the World Council of Churches in 1948. This brought the Orthodox churches into regular dialogue with those of the Reformation. The Roman Catholic church kept apart until the second Vatican Council affirmed that Christ's Church was not identical with that of Rome, though seen to 'subsist' in it. It now participates actively but not as a member Church.

Several churches have united in the last hundred years — notable examples being that of the United Church of Canada (1925), the Church of South India (1947) and in England, the United Reformed Church (1969). The 'Week of Prayer for Christian Unity' goes back to Fr Pallotti in 1835 and is now observed widely.

The Anglican communion sees itself in a midway position — both Catholic and Reformed — and therefore seeks to be a reconciling factor, but the ordination of women priests is a stumbling block to Rome. It, in turn, presents several stumbling blocks — to give but one example, Eamon Duffy, though Catholic, has described the papacy as *"the most divisive institution in Christendom"*

The search for institutional unity has proved impossible. It has been the heart's desire of some fine Christians but, tragically, the efforts have been misdirected. It is not only that fears of inflexibility and uniformity are justified but also that a single institution could never do justice to Christian diversity. Thankfully, this will not prevent 'grass-root' Christians from shedding prejudices, speaking together in love, and working for the common good. This 'bottom-up' model is the better way forward. A healthy Christian movement requires the greatest freedom.   [see 55]

Orthodox: The Eastern churches — Greek, Coptic, Russian, Syrian, Armenian etc. They are independent, national churches with their own patriarchs but look to Constantinople for spiritual counsel. They preserve a 5-6C. form of Christianity. Doctrine is more mystical and flexible than that of Rome; worship centres on the incarnation and resurrection rather than on the cross. There is a great sense of the communion of saints and the nearness of eternity. As national churches they are close to government.

Roman Catholic: The Western church alienated that of the East by the claims of the papacy. Final separation occurred in 1054. The church of Rome is the largest and most international of the churches — rich in variety, tradition, and the affection it inspires. Its structure has favoured reform as well as abuse. Highly centralised, it has defined new doctrines that present difficulties for other churches.

Lutheran: Arising from the protest of Martin Luther in 1517 seeking to reform the abuses he saw in the church of Rome. He was a German, Augustinian monk, whose revolt was both theological and moral. The new churches were nourished by Luther's vernacular translation of the Bible. They are strongest in Germany and Scandinavia and both episcopal and non-episcopal (i.e. no hierarchy of bishops). They counsel obedience to secular authorities, encourage a personal faith based on salvation by faith alone, and stress scholarship and preaching.

Reformed: or **Presbyterian** churches were created by the followers of John Calvin — a French scholar who settled in Geneva. They are widespread in Europe and the USA. The Church of Scotland is Presbyterian and established but unlike the Church of England decides its affairs without reference to Parliament. Most Reformed churches are non-episcopal, with elders and ministers having an equal part in government. The sovereignty of God is stressed and there is strong emphasis on scholarship and social concern.

Baptist: Baptist churches can be traced back to various groups of Anabaptists ('re-baptisers') in the 16 C. The first English Baptist church was formed in exile by an Anglican clergyman — John Smyth — and this moved to Spitalfields in 1612. The Baptists were strong advocates of religious and political liberty and flourished in America. All practise believer's rather than infant baptism and are evangelical and missionary. Congregations are independent and members can perform all the functions of ministry.

... those that co-operate with one another. *(for statistics, see before the index)*

Anglican: Brought about by Henry VIII's break with Rome in 1535, the Church of England was a historic compromise. It remains a 'broad church' with Evangelical and Anglo-Catholic wings. The Church of England is one member of an Anglican communion that spread across the world. Its establishment in England means that certain aspects of its life are subject to Parliamentary or Royal assent.

Methodist: An 18C. foundation based on the work of the Wesley brothers. The name is a nickname arising from the 'methodical' discipline adopted by its early members. John Wesley was an Anglican all his life but travelled thousands of miles on horseback and preached in the open air. Early Methodists attended their local society and the parish church but the old structures failed to accommodate the new movement and it became a separate body. This was a church for all social classes, which thrived because of its close knit fellowship, local preachers and social concern.

Quakers: or **Friends** of the Truth were founded by George Fox in the 17C. He believed in the 'inner light' or 'that which is of God in everyone'. Simplicity and integrity are seen as the marks of Christ's followers. There are no clergy, creeds or sacraments. Worship is characterised by a quiet waiting upon God. Small in numbers, Quakers have been of great significance in national life and prominent in the international search for peace.

Salvation Army: Created by the inspiration and organisation of William and Catherine Booth in the 19C. William was a Methodist minister who, following Wesley, took the gospel to the streets. Its military style, enthusiastic music and evangelistic passion won the hearts of rich and poor alike and its social work gained worldwide respect for its care and effectiveness.

Pentecostal: — valuing baptism of the Spirit, speaking in tongues and faith healing, American pentecostal churches began with Charles Parham and William Seymour. The largest are the **Assemblies of God** and the **Church of God in Christ.** The **Apostolic Church** grew out of the Welsh revival of 1904-5 and the ministry of T D Barratt, in Sunderland in1907. The **Elim Foursquare Gospel Alliance** was created in 1915. The 'foursquare' refers to Jesus as Saviour, Healer, Baptiser and King.

Jehovah's Witnesses: The Bible Student Movement founded by C T Russell of Pittsburgh (d.1916) was developed by his attorney, Judge Russell, into the Witnesses. They proclaim the near end of the world. Michael and Lucifer are said to be the sons of God, with Michael becoming incarnate as Jesus. The movement appears close to anarchism and strongly attacks other church, business, and government institutions. Also known as **The International Bible Students** and the **Watchtower and Bible Tract Society.**

Seventh Day Adventist: William Miller of Massachusets had prophesied the Second Coming in 1844, then 1845. When it did not occur, he renounced his beliefs. Ellen White then established a new organisation, which became distinctive among Christians in observing the sabbath (Saturday). The Adventists promote healthy living without the use of drugs.

Christadelphian: = 'followers of the brethren of Christ'. Another group with a preoccupation with the end of the world. They developed from the teaching of Dr Thomas, a member of the American Churches of Christ and subsequently disowned by them. They accept the verbal inspiration of the Bible but question some of the doctrines that mainstream churches have derived from it.

Christian Science: Founded by Mary Baker Eddy of New Hampshire - b.1821. She established a method of faith healing based on the principle that matter is an illusion. In 'Science and Health as the Key to the Scriptures' she advocated right thinking as the answer to sin, suffering and death. This book is read alongside the Bible. It has little to do with real science. Teaching and administration is in the hands of a small self-perpetuating group.

Mormonism: or **The Church of Jesus Christ of the Latter Day Saints.** Founded by Joseph Smith in America in 1830. He claimed to have translated 'The Book of Mormon' from golden plates that related how the Americas were populated by Israelites and visited by Jesus after his resurrection. The book is very dependent on the language and content of the King James Bible. Smith was murdered but one group of his followers were led by Brigham Young to Utah and built Salt Lake City. Despite problems arising over polygamy and accusations of racism, the Mormons prospered and now run like a successful business organisation. The tracing and baptising of ancestors is a major preoccupation.

... groups more and distinct from the mainstream.

Spiritualism: Under this heading come various groups that seek to establish communication with the spirits of the dead. The nearest group to mainstream Christianity is the **Churches of the Greater World Christian Spiritualist League** founded in London - 1931.The chief spirit guide is said to be 'Zodiac', who is identified with the scribe who approached Jesus in Mk 12:28. The older **Spiritualists National Federation** was inaugurated in 1890. It teaches the fatherhood of God and regards Jesus as the special teacher of the Western world. The practice of seances is generally condemned by mainstream churches on scriptural and psychological grounds. Clearly the possibilities for fraud are legion but members of the Society for Psychical Research take the phenomena seriously.

Pluralism in America:

Religious diversity is characteristic of America. In earlier years, immigration, environment and Protestant teaching combined to promote individualism and independence. The insecurity of a new country (to Europeans) served to strengthen local communities and congregations, but often it fostered a mistrust of the outsider — in religion as in much else.

In 1800, 85% of the ex-European population came from the English speaking Reformed tradition. They supported the separation of church and state for the protection of both. Dissent flourished and there was always land in the west for unconventional communities.

Pluralism may, or may not, bring tolerance. Increasing diversity was usually accommodated through conflict, opposition and negotiation. Not only was one denomination suspect to another but Protestant feared Catholic, Evangelical feared Liberal, and each religion feared the 'corruption' of other faiths. For some, pluralism was an evacuation of belief; for others, it was an opportunity struggling to be born. Many now believe that pluralism need not involve the abandonment of deep convictions but it does require respect for all and full participation of women, native Americans, African Americans — in fact, of everyone.

Our concern now is whether American pluralism is just a reflection of the competing market-place or whether it offers hope that the human quest can sustain its values in a diverse world.

New Communities:

Many new communities and networks lie at the heart of the new search for spirituality. Among the best known are:

IONA This island lies off Mull in the West of Scotland. It has long been a sacred place — perhaps even before Columba landed there to found a Celtic community. The later Benedictine abbey was in ruins when George MacLeod of the Church of Scotland founded the Iona Community in 1938. The building was restored by ministers and others working *under* the direction of unemployed Glasgow craftsmen and is now a meeting place for the community and a place of international pilgrimage. The Community is an interchurch network of those who accept disciplines of prayer, work and giving. They are committed to a Christian witness of justice, healing and reconciliation, wherever they live and work.

TAIZÉ This is a community of worship and service near Macon in France. It was began in 1940 when Brother Roger created a sanctuary for Jewish refugees during the war. From 1959 it grew spontaneously to become a place of ecumenical prayer and pilgrimage. Brother Roger now welcomes some 6,000 visitors — especially young people — to worship here each week.

CORRYMEELA This residential centre at Ballycastle in Northern Ireland is the focus of a widespread community dedicated to confront the pain of Irish divisions and bring healing to the Catholic and Protestant communities. Under its founder — Ray Davey — it brings together six to seven thousand people each year for holidays and discussion programmes.

Celtic spirituality is a good example of 'far-away thinking come down on the long stream of time' (Alexander Carmichael †1912 who collected hymns and prayers from the highlands and islands of Scotland). Kenneth MacLeod records that:

One evening, a venerable Islesman, carried out of himself for the time being, allowed Dr Carmichael to take down from him a singularly beautiful 'going into sleep' rune; early next morning, the reciter travelled twenty- six miles to exact a pledge that his 'little prayer' should never be allowed to appear in print. 'Think ye,' said the old man, 'if I slept a wink last night for thinking of what I had given away. Proud indeed shall I be if it give pleasure to yourself, but I should not like cold eyes to read it in a book.' In the writer's presence, the manuscript was handed over to the reciter to be burnt there and then.

The search for a renewed spirituality is a widespread movement within and without the Christian Church. It defies definition but a loose description gives some idea of its scope:

- it draws on all religions and sources of human inspiration
- it appeals to the world of feeling, imagination and intuition
- it is optimistic and always ready to celebrate the good
- it shows a new appreciation of the earth and all creation
- it forms and reforms networks and communities but is inhibited by static institutions and creeds
- it develops personal health and well- being, whilst knowing that relationships are an important part of spiritual growth
- it values the quiet places but sees that true vision must be worked out among the noise and the crowds
- it commits itself to the search for justice and reconciliation.

Such a 'patchwork' faith raises fundamental questions:
- does it sit lightly to the ultimate coherence of faith and practice that must match reality?
- does it devalue the role of reason?
- does it face up to the nature of evil?
- does it overlook the value of forms and structures?

On the other hand, though it may lack the steadiness and safety which continuity offers, it is open to that spirit which enables the bones of old religion to live again. Like the old it can be indulgent but it can be challenging too and it is prepared to take the risks that reformation demands. It may have no present home but its home is everywhere and with everyone. Without the baggage of hierarchy, of power, of orthodoxy or frontier, it can bring freshness and renewal.

This is an old story expressed in new ways. Not the least striking thing about the Christian church has been its ability to renew itself. Old monastic communities have welled into new life, tired institutions have experienced revival and one reformation has led to another. Sometimes the new seeps like lava through the cracks of the old; sometimes it is a fresh eruption on the margins. It may be welcomed and it may be resisted but it is a testimony that the church does not belong to itself but to the Spirit who breaks and remoulds as need requires.

Day by day, in every way, I am getting better and better.   Emile Coué

THAT'S MY BOY!

Translating the Bible is no easy matter, so which translation shall we use? One describes Jesus' baptism in these words: *"A pigeon flew down and perched on him. Jesus took this as a sign that God's spirit was with him. A voice from overhead was heard saying: "That's my boy! You're doing fine!"".* This may be an inspired use of colloquialism, suitable for an edition of the Bible for teenagers, but it rather takes from the dignity of God! He sounds like a proud father watching his son play for the Chicago Bulls.

It is a more serious problem in mainline translations, for they are deeply influential. Take, for example one questionable version (QV) that stems from a stable that believes:
➤ that the Bible is the Word of God
➤ that Jesus is proclaimed as God in the New Testament
➤ that obedience is a chief requirement for Christians
➤ that we will go to hell if we do not acknowledge Jesus.
A few examples of QV translation are here compared with the Revised English Bible (REB) — one that is recommended by all the mainstream churches and Bible Societies in the UK.

IITim 3:16: This is the great conservative evangelical proof text. The QV has: *"Everything in the Scriptures is God's Word. All of it is useful for teaching."* You would not guess from this that Paul's reference is to the Jewish scriptures or that there were no capital letters used in the Greek. In any case it is a mistranslation. The REB has:
"All inspired scripture has its use for teaching the truth."

Phil 2:6:
QV *"Christ was truly God. But he did not try to remain equal with God".* REB *"He was in the form of God; yet he laid no claim to equality with God".* The Greek word 'form' (morphe) has occasioned much debate but verse 7 goes on to speak of Jesus 'assuming the form of a slave'. It does not mean that he literally became a slave nor does the earlier use of 'form' necessarily mean that Jesus *was* God. The QV's use of 'remain' is not in the Greek and presents a different meaning from the REB. The QV uses the same terminology in the Prologue to John's Gospel: *"The Word was with God and was truly God."* (John 1:1). This compares with the REB: *"and what God was, the Word was".* The distinction here may seem rather fine but it is nevertheless important. The use of 'Wisdom' in Philo suggests that it is rather the expression of God than that which belongs to the essence of God's being. The near-equivalent 'Logos' in Stoic philosophy points to the rational principle that can be discerned in all creation.

John has held back from simply writing that the Word was God. The only unambiguous statement in John is put into the mouth of Thomas (20:28), which lies therefore at one remove.

The 'I am' sayings: The QV provides a note on these:
"John also refers to himself as 'I am'; a phrase which translates the most holy name for God in the Hebrew Scriptures. He uses this name for himself when he makes his claim to be the life-giving bread, the light of the world, the good shepherd, and the true vine.". Whether this is an allusion to the name YHWH has been widely debated. It is by no means certain that the name can be translated in this way. The QV refers to this uncertainty in its note on Ex:3:14. It is a pity, therefore, that one opinion is given prominence in the introduction to John's gospel.

Mtt 11:23:
QV - *"People of Capernaum ... you will go down to hell!"*
REB - *"You will be brought down to Hades!"* 'Hades' is the Jewish synonym for death. The passage uses the symbolism of Sodom from the Old Testament to warn that the people of Capernaum are courting disaster. The saying is stern enough but the Greek is clear and does not carry the modern implications of the word 'hell'.

Mtt 6:10: The Lord's Prayer - and therefore of critical importance:
QV - *"Come and set up your kingdom so that everyone on earth will obey you."* REB - *"Your kingdom come, your will be done."*
Conservative evangelicals find the patience of God rather trying. There is no suggestion in Matthew's Greek that the purpose of the kingdom is to make everyone obey God. Jesus invited us to seek justice and peace, and by our love to become the kingdom. Our prayer is that God's purpose will be fulfilled and his kingdom come and that we will play our part in bringing about justice and peace.

I am not suggesting that the translators wilfully manipulate the texts. The scholars involved in both versions are, in part, conditioned by their presuppositions and tend to veer one way or another. For myself, however, I am inclined to trust the REB translators rather more for one very good reason: they seek to set aside their personal faith and to be guided by the manuscripts as handed down to us. For the authors of the QV *"translating the Word of God ... is something that grows out of their faith commitment to Jesus Christ.".* Surprisingly, it is those who count the scriptures as having all authority who are less likely to be true to them.

BELIEF TODAY

That which is called the Christian Faith existed among the ancients and never did not exist, from the beginning of the human race till Christ came in the flesh. It was then that the true religion (which never did not exist) began to be called Christianity.

Augustine

It is the nature of man to believe and to love: if he has not objects for his belief and love, he will attach himself to the wrong ones.   *Pascal*

Beware what you set your heart on, for it shall surely be yours.   *Emerson*

If one regards oneself as a sceptic, it is well from time to time to be sceptical about one's scepticism.   *Freud*

When men cease to believe in God, they will not believe in nothing, they will believe in anything.   *G K Chesterton*

Happy is he who bears a god within — an ideal of beauty, of art, of science — and who obeys it. All are lighted by reflection from the infinite.   *Pasteur*

I believe because it is impossible.   *Tertullian*

I don't need to believe, I know.   *Carl Jung*

Sir, I believe, help my unbelief.   *Mk 9:24*

When the great Rabbi Israel Baal Shem-Tev saw misfortune threatening the Jews, he used to go into a certain part of the forest to meditate. There he would light a fire, say a special prayer and the miracle would be accomplished and the misfortune averted. Later, when his disciple, the celebrated Magid of Mezritch had occasion, for the same reason, to intercede with heaven, he would go to the same place in the forest and say: *Master of the Universe, listen: I do not know how to light the fire but I am still able to say the prayer.* Again, the miracle would be accomplished. Still later, Rabbi Moshe-Leib of Sasov, in order to save his people once more, would go into the forest and say: *I do not know how to light the fire nor do I know the prayer but I know the place.* It was sufficient and the misfortune was averted. Then it fell to Rabbi Israel of Rizhyn to overcome misfortune. Sitting in his armchair, head in hands, he spoke to God: *I am unable to light the fire, I do not know the prayer and I cannot find the place. All I can do is tell the story and this must suffice.* And it did suffice!
........as told by Elie Weisel

A well-bred man keeps his beliefs out of his conversation.   Maurois

Before considering belief today, we should be reminded of tendencies which are only too common — to stifle spontaneity, fossilise the living, legalise the free, and 'be-little' the great. The dangers are ever present in our thinking. It has been said that beliefs are passed on like coconuts — the husks need cracking. We can recognise:

➤ that the mystery of God is here before us — in human life and in creation — not distant and nebulous. We do not need to look away from earth towards heaven in order to find God

➤ that the small leads to the great, the visible to the invisible. The sacraments fail if we do not see beyond them. The priest fails if he does not point away from himself. The church likewise is but a shadow of the real. It is God who draws us to himself. Our temptation is to downshift and imprison God in an image but the greater is not found in the lesser — the lesser is found in the greater

➤ that God comes to us freely as he wills and when and where. We cannot control the Spirit or dispense Christ

➤ that we need no fences, no defining barriers. We wrong the Gospel if we condemn the outsider, the outlaw and the heretic. They may have new truth for us

➤ that we have no need to guard the truth. Free debate, openness, honest doubt and searching criticism may put us at risk but never the truth itself.

This is not to say that there has been no past revelation or that tradition counts for nothing. On the contrary, we can sift the great insights of the past and 'bring forth treasures old and new'.

We stand before the greatness of reality without pretence and without the cloak of authority. We are the debtors of all who have gone before, travelling in their footprints. They knew the Master of the Universe *(see box opposite)*. The greater tragedy lies with those who know how to light the fire and say the prayer and can find the place in the forest, but who have forgotten whom to address.

....

Good news from a far country is like fresh water to a thirsty soul.   *Prov 25:25*

You that bring good news; get up to the top of the mountain. If you have good news, shout out to Jerusalem, ' God is here!'   *Isaiah - 40:9*

How wonderful it is to welcome to the mountains of Jerusalem the herald who has news of deliverance and proclaims the reign of God.   *Isaiah - 52:7*

I bring you good news, news of a great joy for everyone.   *Lk 2:10*

Jesus came to Nazareth and went to the synagogue. He stood up to read the scroll and found the passage that says:
'The spirit of the Lord is upon me. He has chosen me and sent me to announce good news to the poor, freedom for prisoners and sight for the blind. The broken victims will go free, because the year of the Lord has come'. "Today" he said "these words have come true".
     - Lk 4:14f. (Jesus read Is 61:1-2 but did not complete v 2)

Jesus travelled throughout Galilee, teaching in the synagogues, bringing the good news of the kingdom, and healing every kind of illness.   *Matthew - 4:23*

Go and tell John what you hear and see: the blind recover their sight, the lame walk, lepers become clean, the deaf hear, the dead are raised to life, the poor receive good news — happy are those who do not find me an obstacle to faith.   *Jesus - Mt 11:5*

To me, less than the least important of God's people, he has granted the privilege of bringing to foreigners the good news of the limitless riches of Christ. May you too, with all God's people, be able to understand what is the breadth and length and height and depth of Christ's love, and to know it, though it is beyond knowledge.
     Paul - Eph 3:8,18

The son of David embodies the ideal of the future in a personality of flesh and blood; he can, as a living person, show men what will be. He is the Messiah.
     - Leo Baeck - speaking of the continuing Jewish hope of the Messiah

It was there right from the beginning. We declare to you the true life which was with the Father and is now made visible to us.   *IJohn 1:1,2*

I don told you we is with you all the way — but even if we ain't with you, God's gonna take care of you.   *Old Mother Pollard to Martin Luther King*

....

What is the Gospel?

> ➤ it is news of a Kingdom where we can be free; where justice and compassion prevail; where the power of evil and disease can be overcome; where fulfilment becomes possible — for ourselves and those about us

> ➤ it is news of God, revealed more fully and more understandably in the life of Jesus than ever before

> ➤ it is news of an invitation to respond to the love of God as revealed in Jesus by loving him and our neighbour

> ➤ it is news of power — the Spirit of God active to bring about a transformation in the hearts of men and women

> ➤ it is news, therefore, of a summons — a divine imperative that requires us to choose, in the knowledge that our future and the world's future are held in the balance

> ➤ it is news that evil and death will not prevail — that God's purpose will outlive and outlast all that would destroy it

> ➤ it is news especially for the poor, the downtrodden and the dispossessed, for they have the most to gain

> ➤ it is news of life lived to the fullest potential — a life compared to which what we have so far experienced is but a shadow — life overflowing and eternal.

Some old news is good news:

'This is the good news,' said an old violin teacher, sounding a tuning fork, — 'this is A. It was A yesterday, it will be A next week, it will be A for a thousand years.'

Note: The English 'god spel' (= 'good / God story') is a translation of the Greek 'euangelion' meaning 'good tidings'. In Isaiah, this refers to the news of freedom and national salvation after the nation's exile. The apostles were seen as messengers ('angels') who carried the good news of Jesus Christ and of the Kingdom of God. Written records were not called 'Gospels' until the second century.

....

All secrets belong to God: but what is revealed belongs to us and our children always.
Dt 29:28

I was a hidden treasure and desired to be known.   *- of God in creation - Sufi*

Why do you not tear open the heavens and come down, so that when you appear the mountains might tremble?   *Isaiah - 64:1*

Can you fathom the mystery of God, or trace the limits of the Almighty?   *Job 11:7*

I thank you, Father, for hiding these things from the learned and revealing them to ordinary people.   *Jesus - Lk 10:21*

The Spirit assures our spirits that we are God's children.   *Paul - Rom 8:16*

The merely rational man laughs at all things, the man of reason at nothing.   *Jewish*

When Nothing descends into Something, every creature is a theophany.
     ('theophany' = 'one who reveals God')   *Duns Scotus*

He who knows himself knows his Lord.   *Sufi*

To prove is to eat soup with a fork.   *Orthodox proverb*

In all who have faith in Christ, reason shall be killed; for reason fights against faith.
Luther

All religions take astonishingly lightly the duty to tell the truth: they as yet know nothing of a Duty of God to be clear in the manner of his communications.
Nietzsche

Far from receiving enhanced vitality, philosophic certainty, and a dynamic sense of mission, I at first experienced confusion, alienation, and a considerable amount of stress.
Susan Howatch - on her experience of God

Never once did I receive a revelation without thinking that my soul had been torn away from me.   *Muhammad*

The curtain will separate the Holy Place and the Holy of Holies.   *Ex 26:33*

Jesus died; and the curtain of the temple was torn apart.   *Mk 15:38*

....

The Christian experience is that God — supreme but hidden — reveals himself through what is immediate. Nor is this just a Christian experience, for many have sensed this Greater lying behind the lesser. Truth, beauty, goodness, and love, all have this quality of 'givenness'. They carry no authority but their own. This is the beginning of all knowledge. Before ever we can weigh evidence or experiment, we have to start with trust.

Reason comes into its own when it has something to work on. It is like a storekeeper receiving a delivery, able then to describe and assess what is given. That which is received by faith can be explored by reason — and should be. Luther's killing of reason (see opposite) opens the door to folly.

If we choose to hand over this task of discrimination to others and to regard them as infallible for us, that is our choice. It will leave us passive and vulnerable — prone to intolerance and exploitation.

All revelation is special. There is no need to distinguish between that which comes to us through the Bible and that which comes through botany, or between that which comes to us through a priest and that which comes through a philosopher. Insofar as it is a revelation of truth, it is a revelation of God. A book, a person, an event, an experiment — any one may play its part — and, like as not, we will need both reason and imagination to receive it.

Christians will look to the Bible and to the church community for understanding, but find in Jesus himself the most deeply personal revelation of God. Even when we have searched diligently, we will know that it is not we who have found God but God who has found us. We look to the Spirit who is the inspiration of all reality. Then we will also become aware of what we do not know and cannot yet receive — when all is done, we will still be like children before the mystery of being — and if we cannot name that Being, so be it.

> As I had always known
> he would come, unannounced,
> remarkable merely for the absence of clamour -
> I looked at him, not with the eye
> only, but with the whole
> of my being, overflowing with
> him as a chalice would
> with the sea.   R. S. Thomas 'Suddenly'

God was passing by and a great wind came, shattering rocks before him. Then there was an earthquake, but God was not in the earthquake. and then fire, but God was not in the fire; and finally the sound of thin silence. When Elijah heard it, he wrapped his face in his cloak.   I Kings 19:11

Show us the Father.   Philip - to Jesus - Jn 14:8

No one shows a child the Supreme Being.   Ashanti (African)

No one knows a name by which to call him. His names are without number.
           - ancient Egyptian

I AM - that is my name.   Ex 3:14

The one 'I am' at the heart of creation.   Shivatashvatara Upanishad

The ocean of unlimited existence.   Aquinas

An ocean of infinite qualities.   Sankara (Hindu)

He who describes me sees me not; he who sees me describes me not.   Egyptian

Who can make an image of God?
He has no body. He is a Word that comes out of your mouth. That Word! It is no more.
It is past, and still it lives. So is God.   African

God and the Son of Man are immense, recurrent and daily transforming activities in the soul of each one of us.   Jung

I am an atheist but I do not say that there is no God; and until you tell me what you mean by God, I am not mad enough to say anything of the kind.
           Charles Bradlaugh

That God does not exist I cannot deny — that my whole being cries out for God I cannot forget.   Sartre

We are no longer the atheists who dare to assert that there is no God — we are only those who assert that if there is a God, he is greater than the one you have shown us.
           Prof. Schäf - Polish marxist

....

We are doing God this term — please send information.
           — a pupil's letter to the Archbishop of York

God — *He who is* —can be known but not described without loss:

> - we can use images from the natural world — an animal, a tree, wind, fire and sun — but they may deceive
> - we can use human images — king, shepherd, father, and mother — but God is more than human ... and more than masculine and feminine. This anthropomorphism suggests that 'God is made in the image of man', but it is even more of a problem to use terms which are less than personal
> - we can use concepts — wisdom, being, mind, cause — but they hide the personal
> - we can associate God with special days, buildings, priests, sacraments — but they hide God's universality
> - we can give God a thousand names and forms — but then God's unity is lost.

"In him we live and move and have our being" Acts 17:28, where Paul was quoting Epimenides.

Some prefer to speak through negatives — saying only what God is not — symbolised by the utter simplicity of the Holy of Holies (Jewish) or the K'abah (Muslim) or the 'little hut' (Buddhist). Therefore some fall silent, as is true of Confucianism and of much Buddhist teaching, preferring to speak only of things which can be more clearly known.

Christians turn to Christ as the revelation of God, but the enigma remains — 'veiled in flesh the Godhead see'.

This need not disturb us. Analogy is common in all disciplines — not least in science. What we must do is look beyond the language, because words, whether simple or sophisticated, will not do justice to the reality. The same applies to the words used for the divine surroundings. It may be traditional to think of God as 'up there' but it is equally true to speak of God as 'down there' or 'within'. He/She is found in the depths of created being as much as in the heights, and in the secret places at the heart of being, as well as in the far reaches of infinity.

....

Note: There should be no need for the simple confusion that arises because we speak different languages. God may be spoken of as Zeus, Allah, Brahman, Yahweh and a thousand other names. It does not mean that different gods are worshipped.

The difference between the many gods and the One God is not a mere difference of number — but a difference in essence. Leo Baeck

God is not one of the things that are. Dionysius

Mind includes in itself all states of being of the phenomenal world and the transcendental world. Asvaghosa - Buddhist

Man at last knows he is alone in the unfeeling immensity of the universe, out of which he has emerged only by chance. Jacques Monod

It is very important not to mistake hemlock for parsley but to believe or not in God is not important at all. Diderot

The working hypothesis of God makes sense of the universe. Arthur Peacocke

In the absence of any other proof, the thumb alone would convince me of God's existence. Isaac Newton

God has nowhere and nowhen that he comes to an end. Ila (African)

Three things God alone can do — endure the eternities of infinity — participate in all things without changing — renew all things without annihilating them. / Self-born, untaught, motherless, unshaken. Celtic

God is the place of the world but the world is not his place. Rabbinic

If I were to know him, I would be him. Rabbinic

Of the Great Spirit we know nothing. It comes from itself, is known by itself, and goes out of itself. It is not for us to know. Senthulo (African)

What is impenetrable to us really exists, manifesting itself in the highest wisdom and the most radiant beauty. Albert Einstein

Devout men see God in themselves. The Gita

The nature/supernature dichotomy is not a timeless given John Hedley Brooke

God is not a being to whom I seek access but a presence discovered in the very depths of my life. John Shelby Spong

How can I believe in God when just last week I got my tongue caught in the roller of an electric typewriter? Woody Allen

Does belief in God matter? Yes — because our ultimate beliefs will shape our lives and characters, and affect those about us. We all have that which is of ultimate concern to us — the issue is, is our concern great enough to deserve our commitment?

There are many things we cannot *prove* in life — even less can we prove the existence of God. There can be no measure great enough. That does not mean that such belief is unreasonable. Whether theist or atheist, the same challenges are set before us. To dispense with belief in God does not dispense with the search for explanations or the need to know where we stand. We can ignore this need and limit our thinking. There may be no *need* for the hypothesis of God or of mind or beauty or of laughter — but we would be the poorer if we were to be small minded in such things. Always we are challenged:

➤ by the order, unity and coherence of the universe
➤ by human consciousness and the mystery of mind
➤ by the problem of evil and the problem of goodness
➤ by love in all its forms.

The thoughtful theist should not use God just to plug the gaps in our knowledge. There is a mystery of the known as well as of the unknown, and little that cannot be counted miraculous. Belief in God is an all or nothing affair.It is tempting, but simplistic, to see progress in our understanding of God. Primitive man could have had just as profound a vision and his images may be no cruder than ours. If I use the masculine pronoun for God, it is only because the impersonal is even less adequate and we have no unifying personal word. Our inadequacy is apparent in so much clse — if God is **omnipotent** (all powerful), it can only be in the sense that S/He can achieve the end in view and knows the means necessary; if S/He is **omniscient** (all knowing), it can only be in a manner that lies outside time itself and is therefore unimaginable to us; if S/He suffers with creation, it is something hidden in the nature of love itself.

Each of these raises questions of how God gives us space and freedom to grow — for the mystery of humanity parallels the mystery of God. Sometimes God is known in His absence, His withdrawal, and His silence. Perhaps if this were not so, creation would cease to be.

Voltaire had little use for religion. He was out walking with a friend when they passed a church and Voltaire raised his hat. 'I thought,' said his friend, 'that you did not believe in God.' 'Oh,' said Voltaire, 'we nod, but we do not speak.'

....

He shall be called 'Emmanuel' meaning 'God is with us'.   Mt 1:23 (Is 7:14)

If you have seen me, you have seen the Father.   Jesus - Jn 14:9

I am returning to my Father and your Father, to my God and your God.
Jesus - Jn 20:17

I speak of Jesus of Nazareth, one specially chosen by God.   Peter - Acts 2:22

The creative principle of God became evident — clearly seen among us.   John - 1:14

He reflected the nature of God, and yet laid no claim to equality with God.   Phil 2:6

Christ's head is God.   Paul - I Cor 11:13

God chose to dwell in him in all his fulness.   Paul – Col 1:19

Who, for his immense love's sake, was made that which we are, in order that he might perfect us to be what he was.   Irenaeus

He was humanised that we might be deified.   Athanasius

The Greek theologians did not envisage the Son of God becoming man in any simplistic way; rather they envisaged humanity being absorbed into the divinity.
Karen Armstrong

God is not a baby three days old.   Nestorius

You may see the disc of divinity quite clearly through the smoked glass of humanity, but not otherwise.   Coventry Patmore

The Self, smaller than the small, greater then the great, is hidden in the heart of every creature.   The Upanishads

We use the word 'divine' because the word 'human' is not big enough.
Leslie Weatherhead

The Incarnation is not the glorification of the flesh but its supreme disparagement.
Hyam Maccoby

Through this knowledge and love of Jesus, I have come to know and love and live with God. As to going further, it seems a presumption and an impiety.   Bernard Canter

....

INCARNATION ?

We need now to develop the themes explored in 21 and 46. The challenge is well illustrated from a recent article:

"Jesus does not simply direct us to God. The astonishing fact is that those who were living in Palestine in the first century were able to see the living God for themselves and hear him speak".

Now, wherever this comes from, it does not come from the Bible.
.

Incarnation means 'to embody'. The temptation is to imagine a divine intervention that could have happened anytime, anywhere, but Jesus is not presented in the gospels as an alien visitation but as a fulfilment in history. He has a real family. He belongs to a real inheritance. He is truly human — one that emerges 'in the fulness of time'. This is precisely why the idea of a virgin birth is a distraction from the unfolding of the purpose of God.

Christ or Messiah is a title for one chosen by God. It does not imply divinity. Jews not only spoke of their own kings as 'messiahs' but also the non-Jewish, Persian king, Cyrus (Is 45:1).

logos (word) is used by John in the prologue of his gospel as a way of drawing together both Stoic and Jewish thought. The image describes the mind of God made known in creation. All that came to be was alive with the mind of God and Jesus embodies it in the flesh.

'son of God' was used by the Jews for anyone recognised as a true servant of God. It is an image and not a biological statement. It is not necessarily exclusive.

'son of man' means 'human' and is a term that Jesus seemed to prefer. Even the heavenly 'son of man' figure in the book of *Daniel* is interpreted in the Jewish tradition as an ideal human figure — one who can be what the nation has failed to be.

divinity in the culture of Greece and Rome moves easily between the gods and men. It is not so in Judaism. Although New Testament writers use several images that emphasise the closeness of Jesus to God, it is not baldly stated that Jesus *is* God. When Jesus is accused of blasphemy, it is usually when he appears to trespass on God's territory in matters such as forgiving sin or keeping the sabbath. To be acclaimed as Messiah also invited the charge of blasphemy.

The writer of John stresses the unity of will between Jesus and the Father but this is because he works with God and can hardly be taken as a statement about the nature of Jesus.

INCARNATION

Various words and images stress Jesus' closeness to God but we cannot ignore the sayings that emphasise his separateness. Jesus makes no claim to equality with God, saying:

- ➤ that he could do nothing by himself because he was not the source — Jn 5:19,14:10
- ➤ that the Father is greater — Jn 14:28
- ➤ that God alone is good — Lk 18:19
- ➤ that sins against himself and those against God's Spirit are not the same — Lk 12:10.

At the turn of the Millenium , many churches displayed posters announcing that this was the 2,000[th] birthday of Christ, and added peremptorily: *"Worship him here, now"*. How could Christians have travelled so far from Jesus' teaching, when he himself was quite clear that God alone is to be worshipped. His clear statement in the Temptation story should be enough to warn us off the usual interpretation that Jesus was tempted to exercise divine powers [see 22]. Our difficulty is that the later conclusions of the Christian church are read back into the text.

A more difficult example is that of the 'I am' sayings in John chapter 8. The writer creates these long speeches and we do not know how much historical weight to give to them. This is a late document that appears to reflect later disputes. Although we are bound to recall God's reply to Moses on Sinai: *"I am what I am"* the argument is to do with Jesus and Abraham, not Jesus and God, whom Jesus distinguishes from himself.

The scriptures do not speak with one voice. Peter, in his Pentecost sermon speaks of *"a man sent from God"*. Paul speaks in *Philippians* of one *'"who did not grasp at equality with God"* 9 2:6)— a reference going back to the story of Eden, where Adam did grasp at equality with God. The words that follow: *"though he was in the form of God"* are no more literal identification than is the phrase: *"found in the form of a slave"*. This is powerful imagery that illustrates how Jesus saw himself. It should not be taken to be a statement about his nature.

In the non-Pauline *Colosssians*, the claims are great but still present Jesus as the *"image of the invisible God"*. Certainly, it is said that *"the fulness of God"* dwells in him but the New Testament uses the same language in promising that the fulness of Christ will dwell in us. In a similar way, John records of Jesus: *"I and my Father are one"*. but in the same way, Jesus prays that we might be one.

Whatever conclusions orthodoxy may later reach, it is not the Bible that teaches that Jesus is God. We only have to see how many times Jesus speaks of God as one separate from himself. In the cry of desolation from the cross: *"My God, my God, why have you deserted me?"* (Mk 15:34), it cannot be God speaking to God. Even in John's Gospel, the words to Mary could hardly be clearer: *" I am returning to my Father and your Father, to my God and your God".*

We imagine that we know what God is like — what divinity is — and that we can fit Jesus into our template. It is better for us to see what Jesus is like and then realise, like the first disciples, that we can see something of the very nature of God in him. Donald Baillie, the Scots theologian, explored a paradox that can be helpful. He suggested that the more fully human we become, then the nearer we draw to the divine, and the more it can be seen that God is incarnate in us. As we make love our own, then God, who is love, is found in us. Jesus' friends found this perfectly expressed in him.

It is difficult to find the right words. Weatherhead suggests that we are driven to use the word 'divinity' because the word 'human' is not enough but with Baillie's help, we could argue that the word human will one day be enough — are we not meant to bear the image of the Creator? In Romans 8, does not God ordain that we should *" share the likeness of his son, so that he might be the eldest among a large family"* ?

This may not be what we have been taught. We want, like Thomas, to proclaim Jesus as 'Lord and God' — but Thomas was prone to fly to extremes. We may wish to say: that Jesus is the heart of the faith, the centre of everything, the one saviour — but it is God who lies at the heart of all. God is the centre and soul of all things. God is the Saviour. This is what Jesus taught.

We can have a sense of God in the depths of our being but there is nothing by which we can measure God and then apply that measure to the man, Jesus. It is enough to say that Jesus knew God at the heart of his being: *"I, yet not I, but the Father"* ... *"I can do nothing of myself"* and that even as God inspired and brought to fulfilment his life, so God can inspire us and bring us to fulfilment.

This is incarnation. It begins with creation and calling — it ends with renewal and salvation.

....

God's spirit was bringing order out of chaos.   *Gen 1:2*

The God fashioned humanity from the dust of the ground and the inspiration of life.
                                                                   Gen 2:7

When you remove their spirit, they die, and return to the dust from which they came.
When you return your spirit, they are created.   *Ps 104:29*

My Father has never stopped working, and I do the same.   *Jesus - Jn 5:17*

I will pour out my spirit on all humanity.   *Joel - speaking for God - 2:28*

It is the spirit that creates life; by itself the flesh can do nothing.   *Jesus - Jn 6:63*

The Father will give you another to stand by you, who will be with you for ever — the
Spirit of truth.   *Jesus - Jn 14:16*

All who are guided by the Spirit of God are children of God.   *Paul - Rom 8:14*

The winds are invisible though the effects are plain; the soul of man is itself unseen;
therefore despise not the unseen but honour God.   *Socrates*

We must not think of ourselves as cut off from the source of life; rather we breathe and
consist in it.   *Plotinus*

The final stuff of the world is mind-stuff.   *Eddington*

The negative gravitational energy cancels the positive energy that created matter. The
total energy of the universe is zero.   *Dennis Overbye*

The energy of God and the energy of nuclear power seem equally remote from daily
experience — both are proven by experience.   *Barbara Ward*

....

Spirit or **Ghost** in Latin and Anglo-Saxon carries images of wind and breath, just as the Hebrew word does. The Navajo also used to speak of the 'Holy Wind' or the 'Windhorse'.

Inspiration = to breathe into — all human inspiration was regarded as the activity of God's spirit.

Although Pentecost is celebrated as the birthday of the Christian church, the first Christians did not mean that the Spirit had not been present until then — see John 5:17. God's Spirit is the 'Wisdom' of Jewish literature; it is the rational principle – the mind – that informs the cosmos (the 'Logos' of John 1:1); it creates awareness and reveals God in humanity. The Spirit should not be restricted to the sacred for the sacred and the secular are one. It does not belong exclusively to ecclesiastical rites and privileges nor to those who have experienced 'a second baptism'. The realm of the Spirit includes all human society and not just the church.

So we are not talking of some strange, religious entity but of the very power and energy of God. It is God giving life to creation. The Holy Spirit has always been present and knows no bounds of space or time — *"the wind blows wherever it wants — you do not know where it comes from or where it is going to"* (John 3:8). The concept of the Spirit frees God from remoteness in space, and Jesus from remoteness in time. This is the brooding over chaos, the nurturing wisdom, the muse of the artist and the genius of the craftsman. This is the word of the prophet and the Word incarnate — the 'other self' of Jesus (John 14:16,26).

Because God is not distant — seeking to influence from afar — but around and within, Christians and Jews have spoken in personal terms of the Spirit as 'He' or, better still, 'She'. The bringing to birth of new things is best approached through the female principle. Our dilemma now is whether or not to use terminology which draws attention to gender or whether to lapse back into the impersonal.

The imagery of the Spirit is rich, commanding and personal — the gentleness of the dove, the refining fire, the breath of our own identity and the wind in its freedom. And we have tried to tether and control God's activity — to channel her gifts and control her fruits. But the gifts of the Spirit (I Cor 12) and the fruits (Gal 5) are found everywhere, nor can they come from any other source. Wherever they are found, God is present. No wonder that the 'sin against the Holy Spirit' is so serious — Lk 12:10 — for we can cut ourselves off from the spring of life itself.

....

O God, make clean our hearts within us
And take not thy Holy Spirit from us.   *Book of Common Prayer*

....

Baptise them in the name of the Father, and of the Son, and of the Holy Spirit, and
teach them to follow everything I have taught.   Jesus - Mt 28:19

I am going to my Father and your Father, to my God and your God.   Jesus - Jn 20:17

Stephen was inspired; it was a s though he could see the glory of God, and Jesus
standing on the right hand of God.   Luke – Acts 7:55

We utter the name of Person with dread when we speak of divine matters, and use it
because we are obliged.   Augustine

Ideas must be distinct before reason can act upon them; and no man ever had a distinct
idea of the Trinity.   Jefferson

The Father as the Absolute is incomprehensible; he became comprehensible through the
Logos — the expression of God's nature.   Origen

God's immortal being as Holy Trinity is a mystery that is inaccessible to reason alone.
                                                Roman Catholic catechism 1994

Only what is visible of God may be depicted in images.   John of Damascus

From its oneness it became manifold, while yet remaining within itself.   Dionysius

The presence of the Godhead is not the same as the presence of the Merciful One, nor the
Sovereign Lordship.   Al-Ghazzali - Muslim

It is not a divinely revealed 'mystery' but a doctrine worked out in various ways after
centuries of Christian speculation.   Nathaniel Micklem

How presumptious it is of us mere men, of insect stature on this unimportant speck of
dust amid all God's glittering worlds, to imagine that with human words, like those
about the Trinity, we can express the being and doings of that awe-ful and majestic
being in whose unfathomable mind this vast universe was once an idea.
                                                Leslie Weatherhead

Christians are, in the practical life, almost mere 'monotheists'. We must be willing to
admit that, should the doctrine of the Trinity have to be dropped as false, the major part
of religious literature could well remain virtually unchanged.
                                                Karl Rahner

....

Christian teaching makes a great deal of the Trinity — the idea that God is 'three persons in one' —Father, Son and Holy Spirit. It arises from the paradox of ascribing divinity and humanity to Jesus but it reduces mystery to mathematics. Confucius and the Buddha believed that there was little we could say about God. Christians try to say too much and then use the resulting formula not only to divide faith from faith, but even Christian from Christian.

Does it work? We can indeed speak of our *experience* of God — as creator, as present in Jesus, as present within us but we cannot claim to present an ultimate statement of the very being of God without transgressing the warning about images. We presume too much and in our efforts to enlarge our vision, we truncate it instead.

The New Testament proposes no geometric solution to the nature of God and 'trinitarian' references are generally a reading back of later dogmatics. Athanasius saw a defensive purpose — believing the doctrine to be 'a signpost against all heresies', as though free and marginal thinking could be blocked out by one all encompassing statement. Can we imagine Jesus holding forth on the nature of God in such a way?

If there are serious disadvantages to this doctrine, should we not abandon it? It is confusing because much of the associated terminology is redundant today. It is misleading because it has the appearance of a 'done deal' and closes down further exploration. It is divisive because it is a grave stumbling block to the seeking of common ground in inter-faith dialogue. .

Other religions have touched on this problem in different ways. Judaism speaks of the Creator, the Divine Wisdom or Holy Spirit, and the Son of God or Messiah. Hinduism speaks of eternal unchanging Being, the revealing Lord and the Self of all. Even Islam has had scholars who have reflected on the manifold nature of God who is yet one. Yet that is enough. We should not dare to go further. When we speak of body, mind and spirit in human beings, we know that such categories fail to trap what is elusive. How much more when we speak of God.

Surely it is time to be honest. This doctrine goes beyond the Bible and beyond what can be said. It is enough to speak of God's varied revelation of himself.

....

God's creativity has to be seen as permeating all time and space.   Russell Stannard

Natural laws are not chains about the living God but threads which he holds in his hands.   Bishop Alexander

Pure chance, absolutely free but blind, is at the very root of the stupendous edifice of evolution.   Jacques Monod

As ridiculous and improbable as the proposition that a tornado blowing through a junkyard may assemble a Boeing 747.
                    Fred Hoyle - on the idea that chance can explain all

The odds against a universe like ours emerging out of something like the Big Bang are enormous.   Stephen Hawking

The origins of life appear to be almost a miracle, so many are the conditions that would have to be satisfied to get it going.   Francis Crick

The lots may be cast into the lap, but the issue depends wholly upon the Lord.
                    Prov 16:33

The universe knew we were coming.   Freeman Dyson

Mathematics is the language in which God wrote the universe.   Galileo

The universe shows a beauty and a deep mathematical structure that strongly suggests an underlying mind, the mind of God.   Eugene Wigner

Astronomy is an impossible science — all you've got is opinions.   Sandage

There is no such thing as a philosophy free science.   Daniel Dennett

The elementary particles embody the symmetry. They are its simplest representations, but they are the result of the symmetries.   Heisenberg

Why is there something rather than nothing?   Leibniz

Man is equally incapable of seeing the nothingness from which he came, and the infinite in which he is engulfed.   Pascal

Mystery includes the known as well as the unknown.   Laurens van der Post

If I did not work — these worlds would perish.   The BhagavadGita

....

God is alive — he just doesn't want to get involved anymore.   - graffiti

Theorists calculate that when the universe was 0.01 seconds old, the temperature was 100,000 million°K and the density 4 billion times that of sea water. Only one particle in a billion would survive the first few seconds — all matter arising from barely more than nothing. This is said to be 13.7 billion years ago. The stars came 1 billion years later and our planet perhaps 4.6 billion years ago, with modern humans arriving in the last 100 thousand years. The science is superb and the scenario awesome.

Unless we take Genesis literally [8], we needn't argue about naïve alternatives like 'God or the Big Bang' (the idea of the 'Big Bang' was first proposed by Georges Lemâitre, astrophysicist and priest). Human thought cannot *prove* or *disprove* the existence of God — but we can ask what is reasonable. The choice seems to be between:

Alternative 1: That time and space, stars and planets, life and laughter, Beethoven and Einstein, arose from initial ingredients:
a pinprick of matter — a ripple of energy — a principle of order, behind which lay ... nothing.

Alternative 2: That this transient universe has arisen out of the eternal and enduring; that the marks of purpose, intelligence and design reflect the Mind which has given birth to all that is. God would then be seen to be:
  ➢ one who is an initiating *and* sustaining agency
  ➢ one who balances order and chance to allow a universe of possibilities — open to the future
  ➢ one who relates equally to all time and space
  ➢ infinitely greater than often envisaged.

Concepts like matter, energy and order pose their own problems. Are matter and energy the same? Can we speak of order — or law — or the symmetries, as something apart? And in what context does this birth take place? Is there none, or is there another kind of space or time? As for chance — it is a slippery notion, and a negative, which in normal experience can do nothing of itself. We know that the universe is one and coherent, that it is unfolding, that it is comprehensible and that it is fine-tuned as if 'it knew that we were coming'. Given the deep awareness of God that is characteristic of humanity, chance is a poor substitute for a creator in such a drama.

....

What is mind? No matter.   What is matter? Never mind.   - graffiti

....

Know me — eternal seed of everything that grows.   *Hindu*

Matter is potentiality.   *Aristotle*

*Evolution has no room for the supernatural. The earth and its inhabitants were not
created, they evolved.*   *Julian Huxley*

*There is no more design in the variables of natural selection than in the course the wind
blows.*   *Charles Darwin*

Not so much the survival of the fittest as the fitting of as many as possible to survive.
                                                                   T H Huxley

We have no scientific purchase on the special extra ingredients that give rise to sentience.
                                                                 Steven Pinker

*An impersonal, unreflective, robotic, mindless little scrap of molecular machinery is the
ultimate basis of all the agency and hence meaning, and hence consciousness, in the
universe.*   *Daniel Dennett*

*God created only the germs and causes of life, which then slowly developed over long
periods of time.*   *Gregory of Nyssa – 4C*

Darwinian theory is so loose, that it can incorporate anything scientists discover.
                                                                 Noam Chomsky

Any jackass can kick down a barn but it takes a carpenter to make one.
                                                                 Sam Rayburn

The genes are more like a recipe than a blueprint.   *Richard Dawkins*

Stasis, not change, is the hallmark of evolution.   *Matt Ridley*

Evolution cannot move a step without the creature's purpose and functioning.
                                                                   John Oman

We can rebel against the selfish tyranny of the replicators.   *Richard Dawkins*
          (that is genes which pass on copies of themselves.)

*What makes us special is that we, alone among species, can rise above the imperatives of
our genes.*   *Daniel Dennett*

....

Count me in. Your friend, Herbie.   *-- children's letters to God*

Darwin poses no insuperable problems for the Christian faith [65]
but there are several issues to disentangle:

- ➤ is the magnificent sweep of evolution God's way of providing both growth and freedom?
- ➤ our descent from the ancestors of apes is hardly humiliating — we come from dust and shall return to it — and science confirms it.
- ➤ design may not be apparent in chance but the whole system incorporates law as well as chance, continuity as well as change. It is what it is and not other — implying creative choice and an explanation that lies beyond itself.
- ➤ The fact that genetic survival is a precondition for human life does not make it the sole end of existence.
- ➤ Scientists who use evolution to *deny* creation or the God's existence have gone beyond their discipline and speak as philosophers.

Honest agnosticism may stay within the bounds of what is verifiable and if the myriad small steps of development, sifted by natural selection, are felt to be a sufficient explanation of life, so be it. Even the emergence of life and consciousness may have a simple atomic history but does this end our quest? The whole story requires different levels of explanation — the molecular, the genetic, the conscious organism — and does one *explain* the other? A book may be explained in terms of pen and paper or neuron activity or creative imagination — and each level of explanation is valid. As for the author — search as we will, we cannot *prove* from within the pages, that that there is one.

Does evolution do away with design? If we look for the designer of the car and see only robots and computer programmes, we do not discount the designer. Why should God not sustain a world that searches out its own future? When scientists look for patterns in the information received from space — patterns that might indicate intelligent life elsewhere — they know what to look for. Are there not patterns all about us that suggest cosmic intelligence?

Questions still remain — is mutation indeed random? — what is our own part in natural selection (as we too are part of the environment), — how *can* we rise above the 'imperatives of our genes'? And what of free will — does that exist? — and how do we face up to the suffering and waste which is so evident in the history of evolution? We will come to these in due course.

What is man that you make so much of him — only to test him every hour of the day?
Job 7:17

What is a human being, that you should notice him at all? Yet you have made him little less than a god.
Ps 8:4

Who are we here on this puny mud-heap spinning in space? I have not the slightest idea.
André Maurois

Either a beast or a god.
Aristotle

Bare, forked, shivering creature — so long a child, so vulnerable a man, so swift a decline.
- adapted from Shakespeare by source untraced

You're nothing but a pack of neurons.
Francis Crick

Upon the most exalted throne in the world, it is still our own rump that we sit on.
Montaigne

We really know nothing about the nature of man.
Jung

The scientific study of man is a myth — perhaps the most dangerous of all myths. Ultimately the psychologist, the psychiatrist, the sociologist, must each confess that his work must be prefaced by 'I believe' and not by 'I have proved scientifically'.
David Horrobin

You and I are one with the primordial, protean speck of life.
Alister Hardy

There is nowhere in all this life where we haven't been.
Seán Ó Ríórdáin

The human being is only a reed, but he is a thinking reed.
Pascal

Every man is an exception.
Kierkegaard

The wise man beholds all men as things made for holy uses.
Lao -tse

Man is the measure of things.
Protagoras

The soul is no nearer to the mind than it is to the body.
Kürtmeyer

Well did he know what was in human nature.
John - of Jesus - 2:25

I love mankind. Its people I can't stand.
Schultz

We are beginning to understand our biological history, and it will, beyond all doubt, teach us a great deal. We cannot grasp the full implications of this knowledge nor should we jump to quick conclusions — for example, if we share 98% of our genes with apes, it doesn't follow that we are 2% human. Genes do seem to provide a pool of possibilities rather than a blueprint. Even so, we are likely to be ruled by our genetic inheritance far more than we may care to admit. It must also be true that 1 million years as hunter-gatherers has had immense influence on human character and behaviour.

The nature and importance of humanity will always be debated. We can make out a case fairly easily for our unimportance if:
> genes are primary and organisms like us merely secondary
> in the vast stretches of time, we are a fortuitous late blip
> bacteria are counted as more successful (there are more E coli bacteria in the one person's gut than people in the world)
> we find no substantial self amidst the teeming information in the human brain and believe that 'there is no one at home'.

One of the lurking problems here is that of 'nothing buttery' — are we *nothing but* a collocation of atoms, or a pack of neurons, or a naked ape? It may be, on the other hand, that we are important because:
> we are among the most complex objects known
> because we alone can reflect and measure.

Does it matter where we stand in the nature of things? We cannot prove whether we are meant to be here, or whether we are 'Nature's wild card' and just happened along to complicate things. Biblical teaching does not dwell on our *relative* importance — all things exist to glorify God in their own right. What is emphasised is our responsibility, and that we have:
> a true self called into being by God and, in some sense, carrying the divine image
> a continuing relationship with God, who calls us into a fullness of being, which can now only be guessed at
> sufficient freedom to enable us to respond to God creatively and to become partners in his creating
> physical and spiritual natures (however inseparable), both of which have their origin in God
> a frailty bounded by impotence, sickness and death
> a destiny hidden with God, to whom 'all things are possible'.

....

.

You are free to eat from any tree in the garden except from the tree of the knowledge of good and evil. Gen 2:16

It is a strange desire to seek power and to lose liberty. Francis Bacon

I summon earth and sky to witness against you this day: I offer you the choice of life or death, blessing or curse. If you choose life, you and your descendants will live. So love the Lord your God, obey him and be loyal to him. Moses - Deut 30:19

Freedom is that which was written on the two tables on Sinai. Rabbinic

Others gain authority over you if you possess a will distinct from God's will. Rabbi Nahman

He enabled them to become children of God. John - 1:12

When he rediscovered his true self, he said, 'I will rise and go back to my Father' - the wayward son - Lk 15:7

Between cause and its so-called effect, there falls a cosmic shadow. Out of this shadow, man can accomplish a transfiguration of his own, however minutely, in an act of universal creation. Jung

It would be very singular that all nature, all the planets, should obey universal laws, and that there should be a little animal, five feet high, who in contempt of these laws could act as he pleased. Voltaire

Man is but an automaton in motion. Jean Rostand

I go the way fate has pointed me like a man walking in his sleep. Hitler

A living organism is an active player in its own destiny, not a lumbering robot responding to genetic imperatives. Sreven Rose

I have seen the Fates stamp like a camel in the dark; those they touch they kill and those they miss live on to grow old. – an early Arab poem

Liberty, what crimes are committed in your name." Mme Rolande, at her execution, 1792

All theory is against freedom of will; all experience for it. Samuel Johnson

....

It is difficult to see how the debate over freedom and determinism can ever be settled. Some theologians, in the Calvinist tradition, who stressed the sovereign power of God tended to see all human life as determined, and each person as either elected to salvation or condemned from the start, yet the general Christian view has been that God has left room for choice and responsibility. Now we are faced with the challenge of biological determinism, and some striking studies — for example of identical twins — seem to suggest that we are all automata. And yet indeterminacy — randomness and unpredictability — is very much in season. Theists can lose out both ways — the determinists see no room for God to 'interfere', and the indeterminists see plenty of room but no evidence of 'supernatural' intrusion.

The Christian case today is that God is within as well as without, and that the universal laws give space for the slow emergence of choice and therefore of free will. Freedom, of course, is an abstract; it can only operate where there is structure, much as footballing excellence is only possible where the rules of the game prevail. We have to discern the universal rules of the game and the scope for individual possibility within those rules. In practice, the determinist often qualifies his position or provides an escape for himself personally. The consequences of thorough-going fatalism are far reaching: ought and obligation, praise and blame, punishment and reward would have no place but they would be tools for conditioning, directed towards the survival of the species, with utility value but no intrinsic value — certainly very different from the prevailing sense we have of them.

What then of the Christian paradox — *'being in God's service, live in freedom'* — I Pet 2:6 ? At a deeper level it is a question of responding in love to the love of God. Only God can give us the scope, the opportunity, and the space in which to do justice to ourselves. To settle for less is to risk bartering away our freedom for real slavery — even as a drug-taker exercises his freedom one last time before becoming a slave.

Our evolution is underpinned by the raw material which is given, by chance which is inescapable, and by the environment which we relate to at every point but we are active participants and God has presented us with the possibility of growth into freedom. With his help, we can realise that possibility.

Know, O Man, by whom the universe is upheld. I am the producer and destroyer of the whole universe. There is nothing else.   The BhagavadGita

The eternal silence of those infinite spaces fills me with terror.   Pascal

My own suspicion is that the universe is not only queerer than we suppose, but queerer than we can suppose.   J B S Haldane

There is at bottom no design, no evil and no good, nothing but blind, pitiless indifference.   Richard Dawkins

Man knows that he is like a gypsy camping on the edge of the universe where he must live. The universe is deaf to his music and as indifferent to his hopes as to his suffering or his crimes.   Jacques Monod

Our environment is not indifferent to our lives but belongs to them. Nature is a healing and beneficent influence in the whole environment to the furthest depths of space.   J B S Haldane

And now we are saved absolutely, we need not say from what, we are at home in the universe.   Bernard Bosanquet

If man found that the Universe could love, he would be reconciled.   Camus

To consider the Earth the only populated world in infinite space is as absurd as to assert that in an entire field sown with millet, only one grain will grow.   Metrodorus - Greek - 4C. BC

Come quickly — as soon as these blossoms open, they fall. This world exists as a sheen of dew on flowers.   Shikibu

*In all your life have you ever summoned the dawn
or sent the morning to its place?
Have you taught it to seize the fringes of the earth
and banish the Dog-star from the sky,
to bring up the horizon in relief as clay is moulded by a seal,
until everything stands out like the folds of a cloak,
Have the doors of death been revealed to you
And have you seen those who guard the doors of darkness?
Do you know the rules that govern the heavens
or determine the laws of nature?*   Job 38:12f & 31. 4C.BC

As you wander down life's highway, don't forget to eat the roses.
— cow philosophy!

The far reaches of space and time are truly awe-some and few can fail to be excited by them. It is sad if some feel terror or despair. We are scarce coming to terms with the great discoveries of modern astronomy. Nevertheless, we should not imagine that people of long ago did not share the same feelings in the face of immensity — the infinite mystery of things was well appreciated by the writer of Job.

Today the mysteries are still apparent. We do not know what the beginning means nor what the nature of dark matter is nor dark energy nor whether our 'universe' is a mere locality of a greater universe and many of our laws of nature mere by-laws.

We know that we may be able to claim no special place in the scheme of things. True, some suggest that we could be a rare planet indeed — the conditions for evolution are not easy to match. Others believe that there may be uncountable planets that can sustain life. Christian teaching is that God is in relationship with all creation and doubtless can reveal himself to his own in a myriad ways:

If we are unique, it does not give us value. If we are one of a multitude, it does not deny us value. If we matter to God, that is all that matters, even if this home is temporary, suspended between darkness and darkness. If God is not, then we have only our own estimate of ourselves. Those who believe in a Creator are reminded that he must be immeasurably beyond our furthest imagining.

Do not address your mind to criticism of the Creator, do not pretend to know his categories,
Do not take his Universe in your hand, and point out its defects with condescension.
Do not think he is a greater potentate, a manner of President of the United Galaxies,
Do not think because you know so few human beings, that he is in a comparable though more favourable position.
Do not think it absurd that he should know every sparrow, or the number of the hairs of your head,
Do not compare him with yourself, nor suppose your human love to be an example to shame him.
He is not greater than Plato or Lincoln, nor superior to Shakespeare and Beethoven,
He is their God, their powers and gifts proceeded from him.
In infinite darkness they pored with their fingers over the first word of the Book of Knowledge.
        Alan Paton

....

God looked on everything and knew it to be very good. Gen 1:31

The Good must be the beginning and the end, even of all evil things. Dionysius

Evil is not wholly evil, it is misplaced good. Samuel Alexander

Nothing can be evil except something good. Augustine

I enquired into the nature of evil and found no substance there. Augustine

I couldn't stand it; I was overcome with nausea. Eichmann
(The architect of the Holocaust on visiting the extermination camp at Auschwitz)

Sheer evil is impossible. Aquinas

There is no not-holy; there is only that which has not yet been hallowed.
Martin Buber

What terrifies me is not the explosive power of the atomic bomb, but the power of wickedness of the human heart. Einstein

The future of mankind very much depends on the recognition of the shadow. Evil is terribly real. Jung

It is in our hearts that evil lies, and it is from our hearts that it must be plucked out.
Bertrand Russell

We have to find our good in the survival of our species. Peter Atkins

Only God is good. Jesus - Mt 19:17

Is God willing to prevent evil but not able? — then he is impotent. Is he able but not willing? — then he is malevolent. David Hume - after Epicurus

The existence of ethics is conditioned by that of theodicy, for if there is a distinction between good and evil, if evil exists, justification of God is inevitable.
(theodicy = 'God's justice') Nicolas Berdyaev

Without the diseased, there would be no real health. Jung

The maunderings of the drunken reveller proves the existence of the cup-bearer. Rumi

Goodness is the miracle that turns the tumult of chaos into a dance of beauty.
Tagore

....

Goodness has no independent existence. It is not a substance but a description of the very nature of God. This nature is reflected in what he has created — not least, in human beings. This is a difficulty for us. Creation does not seem to be good, and humanity may be judged to be far from good. We presume to know what goodness is and to measure all things by it. A possible answer to this dilemma is that we have a sense of what creation is trying to become — and what we can one day be. Such a sense can only exist because we have some direct apprehension of God, 'who alone is good'. The word, after all, is associated with 'godliness'. We may have to re-think, therefore, what goodness means — it cannot be an unfeeling or censorious or shallow goodness but something which is complex, passionate and stern in its resolve.

Evil has no independent existence, nor could it have. It has neither substance nor centre. It is the shadow of the good — not it's opposite. It is part of the unrealised, the falling short. It is the risk and the pain, the chaos and the chasm out of which good emerges and into which it could fall back. It is the returning darkness, the destroying flood, the crucifying of oneself and others. The fact that it ultimately has no substance does not make it less terrifying.

We who live in the midst of struggle can hardly conceive of a world without it. Our heavens are bloodless affairs and we turn again to the challenge of the elements. Earthquake, flood, wind and fire are life destroying and life creating. They belong to a world of free possibilities and of independent becoming. What kind of tame and sterile world would we make in which to enjoy ourselves?

It is natural for us to rebel, but by our rebellion, we have enlisted on the side of the good. Our very protest, which would dismantle all knowledge of God, turns out to be an acknowledgement that there is an ultimate good — that He is. So the 'problem of evil' leads into the problem posed by our sense of the Good.

We search our hearts and find that evil comes from self-doubt and fear. Hatred, jealousy, betrayal — these thrive upon our fears. Nietzsche counsels us to rise above good and evil by an act of will. Buddhist thought counsels detachment from good and evil, even as the lotus flower floats on the water but is unattached to it. Carl Jung counsels us to meet the Shadow — to accept ourselves and others as we and they really are. In Christian thought, if God can accept us, then we can accept ourselves.

....

The wicked are caught by their own wrongdoing — entangled by their own sin.

Prov 5:22

In the desert one must not whistle, for whoever whistles calls the demons together.

Musil

There is a satan in every one of us, of whose promptings we should be aware.

Muhammad

True spirituality consists in believing in the power of good rather than that of ill, in God rather than Satan. *Nicolas Berdyaev*

Our fight is against some devilry that lies in the very process of things, against something we might even call demonic forces existing in the air. The forces get men into their grip, so that the men themselves are victims in a sense, even if it is some fault of their own nature — they are victims of a sort of possession.

Herbert Butterfield - historian

God does not need an anti-God to be God. *Hans Küng*

They should remember that Hitler was a human being and was capable as such of his monstrous crimes. *Albert Speer*

The devil's might is all locked in God's hand. *Lady Julian of Norwich*

....

Notes:

The Snake: in the Garden of Eden and elsewhere is later linked with the devil, but in earlier times, often represented wisdom and is portrayed as guarding the threshold of life.

Lucifer: = 'light-bearer'. The passage in Isaiah (14:12) refers, not to a fallen angel, but to the King of Babylon.

Beelzebul / Beelzebub: This is probably a mocking description of a pagan god -- the 'Lord of Syria'. His title is altered to mean ' lord of the flies' — i.e. of decay and rubbish.

Satan: is a servant of God, who appears in Job and elsewhere as the prosecuting counsel or accuser. In Islam, he is a more human figure who will finally be forgiven.

Devil: from a Greek word meaning 'to throw apart' or 'disintegrate'. He came to be thought of as a mischievous Pan figure, spreading gossip and slander.

....

Lead me not into temptation. I can find the way myself. Rita Brown

The devil should not be dignified by the use of a capital letter. The concept was imported into Christian teaching from outside, although it had hovered around the margins of Judaism. Jesus does not teach that there is an alternative focus of power to God. The devil was a useful player in parable stories and a traditional shorthand way of summing up the reality of temptation — Peter taking on that role, when he tries to persuade Jesus to turn back from Jerusalem — Mk 8:33.

Our idea of the devil is a composite — an 'identikit' picture drawn from quite independent strands of thought. The tempting serpent, the dethroned gods of polytheism and the accusing figure from the court of heaven are brought together in a questionable way. Speculation about an angelic fall is a colourful attempt to explain the existence of evil. Several religions have been dualistic — believing in opposing good and evil forces. Zoroastrianism was one of these, as also its offshoot Mithraism, which was popular among Roman legionaries. (Zoroaster / Zarathustra was a religious reformer in Persia BC5-6C.

The devil has little importance in early Christianity and does not appear in the creeds. Among the influences which led to his (but not her?) greater prominence were:
  - ➢ the intense solitariness of hermits and monks wrestling with temptation
  - ➢ the imaginations of peoples facing plague and pestilence
  - ➢ the zealotry of those who sought conversions through fear
  - ➢ the need for visual representations of evil in art and acting. The secular guilds were more prominent than the churches in presenting Miracle Plays — with a terrifying devil for dramatic effect.

The profoundest objections to the existence of a personal devil are:
1. it is inconceivable that God would create pure evil *or* a being capable of becoming pure evil.
2. it makes the struggle of good and evil one which 'goes on over our heads' and we become pawns in the drama.

....

The identikit picture of the devil includes the wild animal, the horns typical of fertility gods, the dragon (ancient symbol of war and chaos), the trident (symbol of power), and the goat's hooves of Pan. (It is sometimes suggested that the goat imagery comes from the unclean animals of Judaism — but the goat is not a forbidden animal in Jewish tradition.)

You are a man and not a god.   *Ezekiel - 28:2*
              (said in condemnation of the ruler of Tyre)

O the mind, the mind has mountains, cliffs of fall,
Frightful, sheer, no man fathomed.   *Gerard Manley Hopkins*

Without the Fall, there would have been no human drama and so no literature, no art,
no suffering, no religion, no laughter, no joy, no sin and no redemption.
                                                      Malcolm Muggeridge

Until Christ, the damned lump of humanity was lying prostrate, no, was wallowing in
evil.   *Augustine*

I don't feel bitterness or hatred but I do not believe in the goodness of man.
              Eva Geiringer - sister of Anne Frank, victim of the Nazis

Heavier than the darkness was the burden each was to himself.   *Wisd 17:21*

They asked, 'Why does your master eat with outcasts?' Jesus heard it and said, 'It is
not the healthy that need a doctor, it is the sick.'   *Matthew - 9:11*

Everyone has sinned and fails to reflect the divine glory.   *Paul - Rom 3:23*

My sins are not scarlet — they are grey, all grey.   *William Temple*

We are told first to leave evil and then to do good. If you find it difficult, you may first
do good and the evil will depart.   *Rabbi Yitzhak Meir of Ger*

Sins truly repented, which God has forgotten, 'tis no business of ours to remember.
                                                      Meister Eckhart

Christianity resolved to find the world bad and ugly and has made it bad and ugly.
                                                          Nietzsche

Too much self-examination is as bad as too little.   *Theresa of Lisieux*

He who says day and night 'I am a sinner, I am a sinner' verily becomes a sinner. One
must have such burning faith in God that one can say: 'What? I have repeated God's
name and can sin still cling to me? How can I be a sinner any more? How can I be in
bondage any more? Have faith in God.   *Sri Ramakrishna*

God, in creating man, overestimated his ability.   Oscar Wilde

It is time for to re-evaluate what we mean by sin. We may believe in free will and personal responsibility, but the area of choice can be vanishingly small. We need to listen to those who unpick our genetic inheritance and recognise that our roots lie deep in the past; to listen also to those who explore our evolutionary history and show us that a million years as hunter gatherers has a lot to do with our levels of aggression and tenderness, competition and cooperation. This is not 'The Fall' of tradition [see 9]. It may be better to jettison the word 'sin' — it has become too 'religious'. Better to say what we mean in common parlance.

Free-range Christianity means breaking away from the burden of guilt bequeathed by Paul and Augustine. Paul, with the blood of Jesus' followers on his conscience, cried out: *"who can free me from the body of this death?"* (Rom 7:24). Augustine was haunted by his promiscuous past and feared God's judgement but, like Paul, felt trapped by his disordered nature. This morbidity infected the Christian tradition. It manifested itself in asceticism and the rejection of normal sexuality. It is there in Toplady's hymn *"Rock of Ages"* —
"Naked, come to thee for dress; helpless, look to thee for grace; foul, I to the fountain fly — wash me, saviour, or I die".Toplady, close to mental breakdown, argued savagely with John Wesley over the latter's belief that Christians could strive toward perfection.

This is not to dilute the problem of evil but to see it clearly and deal with it realistically. The great wrongs of the world are terribly real and should be fought. Certainly we need to be 'right with God' but that is more likely to come about when we practise love and forget ourselves in the fight for justice and mercy.

The church of Rome systematised renunciation, confession, penance and repeated absolution. Fundamentalist Protestants developed the doctrine of penal substitution, where Paul's thoughts about Jesus taking our sin upon himself — based on Is.53 — became an all-pervading doctrine of atonement. Most of our communion services image God as an oriental despot, whose mercy we abjectly seek: *Lord, have mercy; Christ, have mercy; Lord, have mercy"*. — never quite believing that we are secure in the love of God. There are many in our society who, rarely valued, are already convinced of their own worthlessness and who should not be faced with the idea that they are altogether depraved in order to make them fit for salvation. In the story of the lost son, the father is too busy welcoming his son home to hear his confession.

They murder the widow, the stranger, and the fatherless, and they say, 'God takes no notice'.   Ps 94:6

What a book a Devil's Chaplain might write on the clumsy, wasteful, blunderingly low and horridly cruel works of nature.   Darwin

The pain passes but the beauty remains.
                    Renoir - the artist - whose hand was crippled with arthritis

Your pain is the breaking of the shell that encloses your understanding.   Kahlil Gibran

If a misfortune falls, it is the fruit of your own labours.   The Qur'an 42:28

Pain is a priceless, essential gift.   Dr Paul Brand – pioneer in the treatment of leprosy.

Do you not see how necessary a world of pains and troubles is to school an intelligence and make it a soul?   Keats

The whole created universe cries out like a woman giving birth.   Paul - Rom 8:22

It was a belief in the goodness of man that died at Auschwitz not belief in the goodness of God.   Herbert McCabe

Freedom for us would mean being able to weep again.   Elie Wiesel

No one knows what grief is for.   Steven Pinker - on evolutionary biology

The only excuse for God is that he does not exist.   Stendahl

When the people of Israel set out into exile, God went with them.   The Zohar

I have risen against His justice, protested His silence, and sometimes His absence, but my anger rises within faith not outside it.   Elie Wiesel

And Aaron was silent.   (nb. the context) Lev 10:1-3

A prayer written by an unknown prisoner at Ravensbrück:
O Lord, remember not only the men and women of goodwill, but also those of ill will. But do not remember all the suffering they have inflicted on us. Remember the fruits we have bought thanks to this suffering: our comradeship, our loyalty, our humility, our courage, our generosity, the greatness of heart which has grown out of all this; and when they come to judgement, let all the fruits which we have borne, be their forgiveness.

The fact of suffering is a constant challenge to belief in the goodness of God. Both the pain that is inescapable in the natural world and the horror of human cruelty should dismay us. In the dread light of the holocaust, we are warned that all theology should take account of burning babies — and some will conclude that no theology is possible. For those who wish to pursue the quest:

➤ we acknowledge that we bring much suffering upon ourselves — but this does not account for all by any means
➤ we understand that the downside of free will is the ability to hurt others, but we also find ourselves assailed by outside forces
➤ suffering can be ennobling but it can be simply stupefying
➤ suffering in others creates deep wells of compassion within us.

Paul pictures the whole of creation as a bringing to birth. We see this clearly now — stars, planets, continents and all forms of life are born in the convulsion of titanic forces. Should it be different in the world of the spirit? There is more to be said:

➤ the same forces that bring suffering also give rise to beauty, goodness and love
➤ an alternative world is scarce conceivable, even if it is purely for enjoyment, much less if it is to forge strong, free personalities
➤ if only 'evil' people suffered, would there be any virtue in choosing to do good?
➤ our very cry of outrage witnesses to the reality of the good
➤ the Christian conviction is that God is not a God of coercive power but one who is present in the travail of his creation
➤ time and again, against all reason, we find that the human spirit can triumph. It is given only to a few to transmute suffering into joy and yet, as with Beethoven's later music, the possibility becomes an unbelievable certainty.

For most of us, Christian or non-Christian, the problem will remain. We may meet it with anger, or grief, or acceptance... all these are legitimate and are recorded of Jesus. Carl Jung taught that neurosis is always a substitute for legitimate suffering — an escape into unreality. This cannot be our response. There is suffering to be faced and there is reason to believe that faith and hope will have the last word.

....

It would have been better not to have been born. But how many are so lucky? Not one in a thousand!

Jewish

....

I am the your God who freed you from Egypt, out of the land of slavery.   Ex 20:2

Everyone who commits sin ends up as its slave.   Jesus - Jn 8:34

If one of your own countrymen becomes poor and sells himself, he is to keep the rights of redemption. One of his brothers may redeem him, or his uncle or any relation or he may even redeem himself.   - from Lev 25:47f

Aaron is to bring forward the goat. Laying both hands on its head he must confess over it all the sins of the Israelites and drive it away into the wilderness.
      - from Lev 16:20f.

The Spirit drove Jesus into the wilderness.   Mark - 1:12

Old people and children, invalids and hunters — everyone throws his or her sins on the vine, and the chief's nephew drags the whole collection outside the village and puts it at the feet of the sore tree.   - the Gbaya of Cameroun

In Carmarthenshire, the sin-eater used to rest a plate of salt on the breast of the deceased and place a piece of bread on the salt. After saying a prayer over the bread, it was consumed by the sin-eater and it was thought that with it he ate the sins of the dead
      - trad.

For this son of man came to serve, not to be served, and to give his life so that others may be freed.   Jesus - Mk 10:45

There is no greater love than this, that a man should give up his life for his friends.
      Jesus - Jn 15:13

He was not content with sending someone to deliver them. He came himself and redeemed them in his love and pity.   Isaiah - 63:9

World history has not been turned upside down to its very foundations. The world is not yet redeemed. The church must understand this sense of ours that we are not redeemed.
      Martin Buber - as a Jew to Christians

Show me that you are redeemed, then I will believe in your redeemer.   Nietzsche

Often the condemned is the burden bearer for the guiltless and unblamed. You cannot separate the just from the unjust, for they stand together before the face of the sun.
      Kahlil Gibran

....

REDEMPTION **114**

The imagery of redemption is rich and powerful. To redeem a slave from bondage was cause for celebration and a path to freedom. For the Hebrews, a kinsman could pay the price; for the Greeks, the slave might be freed by a temple and become the property of a god.

Jews celebrate the liberation of the people from slavery in Egypt as one of the great formative events of their nation. Christians see the cross as a manifestation of God's liberating power for humanity. There are many kinds of bondage:

- political and social oppression
- the prison of poverty and the slavery of wealth
- the entrapments of power and of self-righteous religion
- the assaults of sickness and isolation
- the burdens of sin and guilt
- the gnawing away of fear — especially the fear of death.

To destroy such slavery Jesus demonstrated the power of faith and love — allied to action to build the kingdom of God — and he gave that power to his followers.

The insight that underlies the sacrificial rituals of sin-bearing is that love is costly. This is true in so much human experience and it is true in the very experience of God. But the idea of cost must not be pressed too far. It is not that payment is made to the devil, much less is it a ransom made to God himself — *"We have put our faith in the living God, who is the saviour"* (ITim 4:10). Nor is it a transaction made 'over our heads' but it is a release of love that has the power to win us to freedom. Ignorance, idolatry, addiction, fear and guilt — such things can be overcome and left behind by those who walk unafraid as children of God.

Nor is this only a matter of individual redemption. The Jews have seen their mission as restoring the sparks to their divine source and so redeeming the world. Christians too seek the realisation of God's image in all humanity and become part of the same mission. The scope of the mission takes in nothing less than the whole creation which waits 'with eager expectation' — Rom 8:19. If evolution runs from the past to the future, redemption can be seen as running from the future to the past — claiming and reclaiming of all that has been alienated from God.

It is said that in Isaiah's day, a debtor would have a list of his liabilities nailed up in a public place. Sometimes a rich friend would take out the bottom nail, double the parchment, fasten the folded document at the top nail, and sign it as a pledge that he would redeem the debt.

....

The purpose and aim of all creation is atonement.   Rabbinic

All atonement is the reconciliation of the earthly and the infinite.   Leo Baeck

Therefore he will sit alongside the great and rank with the powerful, because he faced death as a criminal. He took the brunt of human injustice yet spoke up for those who wronged him.   Isaiah - 53:12

The sinner himself is to turn to God, since it is he who turned away. No one can atone for him.   Leo Baeck

God declares: 'Good and bad are among them; let them be joined together in a single bundle, that the one may atone for the other.'   The Talmud - re Gen 18:26f.

God allowed him to share the alienation of humanity, so that through him we might again reflect the goodness of God.   Paul - II Cor 5:21

Christ offers himself to be God's loving forgiveness for our sins.   I Jn 2:2

Christ died for us while we were still clearly in the wrong.   Rom 5:8

Outrage is offered to the moral justice of God by supposing him to make the innocent to suffer for the guilty, and it is loose morality and low contrivance to suppose him to change himself into the shape of a man in order to make an excuse for himself for not executing his supposed sentence on Adam.   Tom Paine

God chose to live in him, and through him to reconcile everything to himself.   Paul - Col 1:19

The gods take no interest in mankind.   Epicurus

All this has been God's work. He reconciles us to himself through Christ, and calls us to share in this ministry of reconciliation, for God was in Christ reconciling the world to himself.   Paul - II Cor 5: 18

He can never therefore be reconciled to your sin, because sin itself is incapable of being altered: but He may be reconciled to your person, because that may be restored: and, which is an infinite wonder, to greater beauty and splendour than before.   Thomas Traherne

....

ATONEMENT

The ideas of redemption, atonement and salvation overlap. Atonement can refer to unity and reconciliation ('at-one-ment") or it can refer to the means of bringing that reconciliation about. Early Hebrew thought is bound up with sacrifice and the powerful ceremonial of the Day of Atonement — Lev 16. The dramatic elements may appear crude:
> that God's holiness is physically dangerous (see Ezek 44:19)
> that God's anger could be appeased by animal sacrifice
> that sin could be hidden by a smokescreen (of incense)
> that guilt could be transferred to an animal (the scapegoat).

The obvious reaction is to say — 'surely God can simply forgive sin?' This might be true of personal offence, but we are talking here of destructive acts against God's creation. Anger against the child abuser, the racist thug or the ruthless tyrant is appropriate for God and for us. The scriptures speak of God's wrath against all that threatens his creatures or corrupts his purpose.

The Hebrew ceremonial is a reminder that evil:
> has to be taken seriously
> is costly in its effects, and in the price it exacts
> causes the innocent suffer

The innocent appreciate better than the guilty what evil means — at the trial of the officers in charge of the Auschwitz/Birkenau extermination camp, it was the survivors who felt most guilt and the defendants who, at times, seemed amused. It is the innocent who bear the burden and the cost of recreating the good.

Christians stress that God takes the initiative. The images of Judaism — the lamb of sacrifice, the scapegoat, and the servant who suffers for his people — are applied to Jesus. God identifies with his people (as Jesus did in his baptism, ministry and death). He knows the earth's distress from the inside out, shares the pain and degradation and reaches the lost with liberating power. What is altogether abhorrent in Christian theology is changing the idea of a sacrifice offered to God into a sacrifice demanded by God. Equally, the suggestion that a loving God sacrifices his only child for the sake of humankind is a moral absurdity that prevents a true understanding of the significance of Jesus for our time. It is noteworthy that the cross was not used as a Christian symbol for the first 400 years.

In face of such unconditional love, our identity is secure. We can afford to admit our guilt, to turn to God for help, and to join the struggle for reconciliation.

We must now face up to the fault-line that plagues some forms of traditional Christianity. It effectively side-lines God as Creator who must, as it were, be rescued by God as Redeemer. Some theology suggests that the first Creation has manifestly failed. Although everything was claimed to be good, it has been frustrated by humanity, whose 'fall' has corrupted it. The destructive effects are so far-reaching that the earth has to be destroyed in the Flood, with only one family miraculously preserved. This family too soon fails to fulfil God's purposes and the grim story continues in a litany of disobedience. Israel fails again and again and a remnant is left. The remnant too fails and is cast aside to await one individual. Then, in the Christian story, God himself cuts across all that has gone before, descends into a wicked world, sacrifices himself and then ascends triumphantly to heaven. He takes the saved with him. Everyone else and everything else is destroyed.

Critics will complain that this account is a travesty. I submit that it is near to the truth of what is often taught, once much of the secondary detail has been stripped away.

Let us consider the alternative. God's work of creation and renewal is seen to be all-of-a-piece. The evolution of the universe and then of life itself is a slow emergence over vast periods of time. The complexity and growing awareness characteristic of human life is akin to the shaping of raw material — very much creation in the making. In some senses the world makes itself but ever sustained in being by God who, through the interplay of chance and circumstance, of freedom and inheritance, builds an ever deeper relationship between himself and what he has made.

Moral awareness and a sense of the divine emerges in humanity, though beset by limitations and by the confusion of being in an environment that is both provident and demanding. The call of God is received by individuals and peoples, whether it is recognised or not. The perception of goodness, of beauty and of truth inspires and lures us on. Our natural experience of failure and guilt is met with a gradual realisation of the love of God, that protects, supports, redeems and saves, even as parents guide their children into self-realisation and independence. Into this developing history, the Christian is one who discovers in Jesus a revelation of the authentic nature of God.

These two very different viewpoints yield serious consequences. In the former view, it is only too easy for the physical to be seen in separation from the spiritual and devalued accordingly, because it belongs to a failed dispensation. Our animal natures therefore become suspect and celibacy is preferred above sexuality. Environmental and political issues take second place to the pursuit of eternity, for this world is passing away. The truth is narrowed to that which witnesses to the saving intervention that renders all the rest of history meaningless.

The latter view is of an integrated whole — the physical and the spiritual bound together; time and eternity profoundly inter-related — and truth is welcomed from any and every source.

One of the Reformation cries was: "Let God be God". The reason is that human minds are always prone to "be-little" God. We cannot easily cope with immensity. Pascal said of the universe: *"The eternal silence of those infinite spaces fills me with terror"*. How much more could be said of God! Yet for many those 'infinite spaces' will evoke, not terror, but excitement and awe. The 'fear of the Lord' should not be the kind of fear that paralyses and dismays.

The Jewish commandments warn us not to belittle God — it can be done by physical images and it can be done by the images we hold in our minds. Such images can often restrict and constrain God, as though we are trying to bring Him under control. We do not succeed, of course, but in the attempt we impoverish ourselves.
It is natural that we have to work with categories, but we should know that all our statements are tentative and provisional. We may speak of 'He' but God is beyond all gender. We may speak of God 'out there' or 'here at hand' or 'within' . All are true in part. One Celtic saying, translated from old Welsh, is cast in triadic form:
"Three things God alone can do — endure the eternities of infinity, participate in all things without changing, renew all things without annihilating them".
But this needs to be balanced by the Hindu: *"Devout men see God in themselves"*. A rabbinic saying combines both aspects of 'here' and 'there': *"God is the place of the world but the world is not his place"*.
Some will not use the word 'God'. In one sense it matters little. It was Einstein who said: *"What is impenetrable to us really exists, manifesting itself in the highest wisdom and the most radiant beauty"*.

....

Look to me and let the whole world be saved.   Isaiah - for God - 45:22

I have not come to condemn the world but to save it.   Jesus - Jn 12:47

The disciples: *Who on earth can be saved?*
Jesus: *Everything is possible for God.*   Matthew - 19:25

I am to acknowledge humanity in the man of evil and in the enemy of God to find the divine.   Leo Baeck

If we take people as they are, we make them worse. If we treat them as if they were what they ought to be, we can help them to become what they are capable of becoming.   Goethe

It is impossible to doubt that the wills of men are incapable of resisting the will of God.   Augustine

God misleads whom he will and guides whom he pleases.   The Qur'an

He has to be brutal to save the world.   J B S Haldane - speaking of Stalin

Bodhisattvas take a vow that one will liberate all sentient beings, down to the last one, no matter how long it takes.   Asvaghosa - Buddhist

Only on the foundation of unyielding despair can the soul's habitation be safely built.   Bertrand Russell

An atheist, who lives by love, is saved by his faith in God, whose existence (under that name) he denies.   William Temple

Not everyone who claims to follow me will enter the kingdom of heaven but those who do the will of my Father.   Jesus - Mt 7:21

We need to work out our salvation — this is where science comes in.   Roger Williams - discoverer of vitamin substances

Man, with all his science and all his power, cannot change his fate if he doesn't change himself.   Dr Pecci - financier

You must work out your own salvation, for all the time it is God who is working in you.   Paul - Phil 2:12

There is no salvation for anyone unless there is salvation for everyone.   Jewish

....
..

Salvation is a spacious idea full of promise and fulfilment. A saviour is one who can bring about such a victory — God himself, or someone inspired by him. The Roman world used the title for a victorious emperor but the full New Testament meaning includes healing and renewal, for body and soul, for individuals and nations, both now and in the future.

Then, as now, the idea of salvation can fall back into lesser meanings:
> - as in the mystery religions, where the initiate is united with the deity through sacramental ritual
> - as in the kind of mystical thought, where the enlightened can achieve all knowledge through asceticism
> - as in passive forms of Christianity, where God elects as he wills and one can only wait for salvation 'as one paralysed' (the phrase is Luther's)
> - as in cruder forms of personal religion, which see salvation as booking a place in heaven.

The full Christian understanding is neither passive nor as individualistic as this, nor is it so neglectful of the world. We are enlisted in the service of others and of God's Kingdom. It is true that God secures and safeguards us in our inner being but there is much to be worked out in practical living.

In our present understanding of evolution, we see its incompleteness, its struggle — and only in part its possibilities. We continually risk falling back into bondage, but God sets us free and ever freer, and inspires us with the spirit of reconciliation and service. It is all very practical and manifold:

- the Hebrews are saved when they escape from Egypt
- a crippled woman is saved from many years of bondage
- Zacchaeus is saved when he redistributes part of his wealth
- Paul is saved from mistaken fanaticism
- thousands are saved from bondage to doubt, to guilt, to despair, to evil and to death.

As for the ultimate outcomes, these are largely hidden with God, to whom all things are possible.

Words: there are several associated words that illustrate the many sidedness of the word 'salvation' — salve, salvage, safety etc.

....

Do not fret over what you are to eat, what you are to drink, what you are to wear. Your heavenly Father knows that you need these things.   Jesus - Mt 6:31

This son of man is going the way set out for him, but grieve for the one by whom he is betrayed.   Jesus - Lk 22:22

It is best for you that I go away.   Jesus - Jn 16:7

God does not use violent means to obtain what he desires.   Irenaeus

The historical mission of science has been to teach us that we are not the playthings of supernatural intervention.   Steven Weinberg

A miracle is a violation of the laws of nature; and as firm and unalterable experience has established these laws, the proof against miracle is as entire as any argument from experience can possibly be imagined.   David Hume

The fundamental problem is not about miracle but about transcendence.   Mary Hesse

If the scientific order of the world can make room for human freedom and human volition without disrupting its own procedures, so too it can make room for divine freedom and divine volition.   Peter Baelz

From the standpoint of the physical sciences, the maintenance and reproduction of a living organism is nothing less than a standing miracle.   J B S Haldane

The unexpected and the incredible belong to the world.   Jung

Miracle is the most intensely personal of all the categories of man's personal relationship with God — it is God knowing one in some sense by name.   H H Farmer

"We pray thee, O Lord, not that the wrecks should happen, but that if any wrecks should happen, Thou wilt guide them into the Scilly Isles for the benefit of the poor inhabitants."   An island prayer

If I did not work, these worlds would perish.   The BhagavadGita

....

A man complained to a rabbi that life was unbearable — his family of nine had to live in one room. The rabbi advised him to take the goat into the room for one week. Incxredulous but obedient, he came back after a week: "We cannot abide it – the goat is so dirty". "Go and put the goat out again", said the rabbi. A week later, the man returned – "Life is beautiful, rabbi. No goat, only the nine of us".

The word 'providence' covers all God's relationship with his creation — from the everyday to the miraculous (the two may be one). If God is an absentee landlord or an impotent spectator, he has little credibility. If he only 'intervenes' once in a while then creation loses credibility.

The full Christian view is a paradox — on the one hand, the universe is independent or, at least, possesses some freedom of its own — on the other hand, everything is dependent on the sustaining power of God. The reality we imagine and the laws we describe represent a partial understanding of God's activity. On this view, God underpins the known and the unknown. The known is more subtle and less machine-like than previously thought, and the unknown doubtless still holds many surprises.

Because humanity has developed greater awareness, God may be present with us in deeper and more personal relationship. In fact, this awareness may itself be a sign of God's greater indwelling. Some religions speak of identity here but Christians see a free and open relationship, such as a good parent has with a child growing into maturity. It may be that such an open relationship is true of all creation. We sometimes imagine a closed and fixed system and a time when every fact will be known and the jigsaw complete. But matter too may have personal and spiritual properties and all things may be open to possibilities that we can hardly guess at.

Science is rightly honoured for its exploration of the regularities — of likenesses — of the measurable. It will talk of 'laws' which are descriptions of the normal, the routine and the repeatable. But there is another world that we all can recognise, of the variable and personal, of beauty and inspiration, wetness and warmth. We all belong to both worlds for ultimately they are one.   [see153]

Agobard of Lyons 9C, was typical of Christians who fought against magic and superstition. The way was prepared for exploration by science and reason of a universe based on the rational activity of God himself. That is not to suppose the laws of nature are fully known or as rigid as Hume suggests (see opposite). We have room in which to manoeuvre. How much more must this be true of God, whose providence is over and under all that he has made.

....

Called or not called, God shall be there.   *Greek*

I have often been driven to my knees in prayer because I had nowhere else to go
                                              Lincoln

People think that they pray before God. But it is not so. For the prayer itself is the essence of the Godhead.   *Rabbi Pinhas of Korez*

Me? Me find fellowship with that up there? I would as soon think of shaking hands with the stars.   *- from an H G Wells novel*

In my arguments about the insolubility of the problem of God I had never foreseen the possibility of a real contact, person to person, here below, between a human being and God.   *Simone Weil*

When I pray, coincidences happen; when I don't, they don't.   *William Temple*

He prays best who does not know that he is praying.   *St Antony*

Pray as you can and do not try to pray as you can't.   *Dom Chapman*

Modern matter is so mysterious and elusive, we know so little either of its nature or its properties. Certainly we are not in a position to assert that it cannot be acted upon by influences which are not material.   *C E M Joad*

His mind is untroubled by sorrow, longs not for joy — free from the sense of 'I' and 'Mine' he attains peace.   *The BhagavadGita — describing the yogi*

I wish, O son of the Living God, ancient eternal King
for a secret hut in the wilderness
that it may be my dwelling —
and for me to be sitting praying to God in every place.   *- 10 C. Irish*

(Buddhists also teach that the mind should become like a hermit's hut— simple and uncluttered, as a prelude to enlightenment.)

In the rush and noise of life, step home within yourselves and be still. Wait upon God, and feel his good presence; this will carry you evenly through your day's business.
                                           William Penn

Pray, pray very much, but do not tell God what you want.   *French proverb*

Prayer is the world in tune.   *Henry Vaughan*

....

Prayerfulness is a cast of the mind, an awareness of the presence of God, and prayer itself a conversation, with or without words. It can be as natural as breathing but time-hallowed disciplines, a heritage of other people's prayers, and practical aids may be of help. Such aids would be curious in an entirely human relationship, but this one is special. Even if we can come as readily as a child to one we can trust, there are riches to be shared from many traditions.

These need not be just Christian — the Hindu yogi, the Zen masters, the teachers of Tao and many another can join with the Christian mystics to instruct us. Where these are more concerned with self-fulfilment, we can still learn, and then pass on to developing a more personal relationship with God. The word 'meditation' has to do with medicine and healing. It is this healing and wholeness we seek as we recognise the presence of God within and without.

There need be no striving in prayer. God will be there, called or not called. It may be that we empty ourselves and wait for him, or it may be that he will address us through the crowded world of perceptions, pressures and people. There may be much listening and little talking as in some of the closest of friendships, it is enough to be together. And if we have withdrawn for a moment, there will be work waiting to be done, for such is the rhythm of our discipleship.

There are paradoxes and contradictions. When we come as a child, it may be with petitions and requests, knowing that not even a sparrow falls to the ground without God's knowledge. And yet there is an absurdity in presenting our list of wants, and so we may seek instead to ally ourselves to the will of God. One day we may understand how the realm of the spirit relates us all one to another, even those we do not know. Many have felt the power of these realms, drawn strength from them, and believed.

When there is no awareness of God but only an emptiness or a dryness, we need not be dismayed. We can quietly lay the ordinary before God — the momentary pleasures of each day — the anxieties and distractions which crowd our minds — the friends and loved ones who mean so much — the passing stranger — the name which stands out from the day's news. We can lay these out before God and be still — acknowledging that this is his work. And if there is deeper pain, we can cry out as readily as Jesus did in his torment and then against all odds still say, *into your hands I give my spirit.*

....

*May you find your eternity in your life, may your future be realised in the life of the
world to come.*   Rabbinic

*A thousand years are only like yesterday when they have passed — no more than a
night-shift.*   Ps 90:4

*Not heaven itself upon the past has power;
But what has been, has been, and I have had my hour.*   Horace

*That which sings and contemplates in you is still dwelling within the bounds of that
first moment which scattered the stars into space.*   Kahlil Gibran

We should say that time began with creation rather than that creation began with time.
                                                                                Augustine

Time — the moving image of eternity.   Plato

These are already dead to this life who do not hope for another.   Goethe

*The time is coming when you will long to see God's new world and you will not see it.
'Here it is!' somebody will say, or 'There it is!' Don't run after them. For as the
lightning lights up the whole sky God himself will light up the whole world.*
                                                                           Jesus - Lk 17:22

When that day will come, no one knows.   Jesus - Mk 13:32

God does not foreknow the future — he simply knows it.   Aquinas

I am the A to Z — the beginning and the end.   Rev 21:6

*God knows the past and future of each creature, not by memory or by foretelling but in
the same direct way that God knows the creature's present.*   Ernan MacMullin

The distinction between past, present and future is an illusion.   Einstein

The important time is now — now is the day of salvation.   Paul - II Cor 6:2

*The years like great black oxen tread the world, and God the Herdsman goads them on
behind, and I am broken by their passing feet.*   Yeats

*Within its depths, I saw ingathered, bound my love in one volume, the scattered leaves
of all the universe.*   Dante

....

Eternity is very long, especially towards the end.   Woody Allen

We have long been used to the idea that time flows onward in a straight line. It confuses us that Biblical writers can see history as repeating itself (as though time were cyclical) or speak of the immediate future and the end of the world in the same breath —
e.g. Mk ch.13. Scholars suppose that early Christians expected the end of the world in their lifetime and that references that take a longer view must be later material. Maybe, however, it is foolish to tidy up material which can have more than one interpretation (compare Mt 16:28 and John 8:51) or can relate to different notions of time held simultaneously. The writers often use 'chronos' of the plain time of clock and calendar but 'kairos' of sacred time — God's moment of opportunity — when eternity breaks into our lives.

So the New Testament speaks of Christ already in the world but yet coming into it; of going away and yet remaining. The Kingdom lies over the horizon and yet it is here. Salvation is future fulfilment and yet is here and now. If all this stretches our imagination, so does modern physics, which describes the relativity of time and accepts the influence of the observer. Time has moved from prose to poetry. It is possible to speak of it:
 ➢ as enfolded in each moment
 ➢ as each moment being simultaneously present
 ➢ as open to the future and influenced by it.

Christians, like Jews, trace an unfolding pattern and a meaning in history, and yet it is ambiguous, containing judgement and promise for each generation. Nor is one generation merely a stepping stone for those who follow. Just as the point of the symphony is not saved up until the last bar, then all times and all peoples stand equally in relationship to eternity. Each of us is indebted to the past — perhaps each of us is indebted to the future. Christians see Jesus as the firstborn among many and believe that the Kingdom we can know now is a foretaste of the Kingdom to come.

We shall not cease from exploration
And the end of all our exploring
Will be to arrive where we first started
And know the place for the first time.
Through the unknown remembered gate
When the last of earth left to discover
Is that which was the beginning.

T S Eliot

I have looked over the wall and I see the bodies floating in the river, and that will be my lot also.   Sumerian - c.2,500 BC

Death means knowing nothing at the dawn of a morning that will not come.
                                                                                                                                                                    Egyptian

I have spoken in many theatres, I have travelled far and wide, and now I have paid my debt and gone my way. All this is simply dust.   Gemellus - Greek actor

These are the tears of things and the stuff of our mortality cuts us to the heart.   Virgil

The world is a bridge – build no house upon it.
                                                                                                       - ascribed to Jesus on the Akbar Gate, N India

So thou art naught, O mortal life, naught but a road, a fleeting ghost, an emptiness, a cloud uncertain and frail, a shadow and a dream.   Columbanus

While you do not understand life, how can you know about death?   Confucius

Our days are like grass: like the wild flowers we flourish. When the wind has blown, they are gone. But the love of God is always there.   Ps 103:15

For to one that is born death is certain, and birth certain for one that has died; therefore the thing being unavoidable. thou shouldest not mourn.   The BhagavadGita

The dust goes back to the earth from which it came, and the spirit returns to God who created it.   Eccles 12:7

I was not, I have been, I am not: I do not mind.   an Epicurean epitaph

Though death befalls all men alike, it may be weightier than Mount Tai or lighter than a feather.   Szuma Chien - 2C. BC

When the angel of death comes, he is terrible — when he reaches you, he is sublime.
                                                                                                                                                                 Arab saying

The last enemy to be destroyed will be death.   Paul - I Cor 15:26

"We are in a desperate state – feet frozen etc., no fuel, and a long way from food, but it would do your heart good to be in our tent, to hear our songs and our cheery conversation .... we are very near the end."
                                                                — from Captain Scott's last letter to J M Barrie

The Hebrews were never a good example of religion as the wishful dream of 'pie in the sky when you die'. They knew the grimness of death and the greatness of God long before they developed belief in life after death. The place of the dead — Sheol — was a shadowy affair and the resurrection still disputed in Jesus' time.

Today, science takes us to the thresholds of birth and death but no further and we struggle to understand:
> ➢ the boundary between the inanimate and the animate
> ➢ the emergence of personality in an unborn child
> ➢ the interplay of mind and body.

We know something of the stream of atoms forever reconstituting the flow of genes down the generations, and of the coming together and the disintegrating of an organism, but even if we 'create life' in a test-tube, we shall have but channelled the mystery and redirected the miracle.

Christians puzzle over the undertones in the story of Eden — the tree of life and the beguiling promise of the snake. The message may be that life is only found within God's providence and not in illusory independence or futile rebellion.

Physical death is woven into God's creation — *'modern man forgets that Nature intends to kill man and will succeed in the end'* (a doctor). The teaching that it is a punishment surely cannot be sustained. It is essential for life and development — limiting evil, bringing oppressive power to nothing, and clearing a path for a new generation. If the wages of sin is death — Rom 6:23 — it is spiritual death which is to be feared.

Jesus believed that God was God of the living and by that he meant past generations — Mk 12:26. He wept before the grave of a friend and shrank from the death that he himself faced; yet he saw his life as something to be laid down within the purpose of God. In his life he risked much; in his death he risked all, but it was encompassed by his total trust in God — 'Father, into your hands I commit my spirit' — Lk 23:46. It is the same for us all.

....

Its not that I'm afraid of death, I just don't want to be there when it happens.
Woody Allen

Those who sleep in the dust will awake and sing for joy.   Isaiah - 26:19

God is not God of the dead but of the living.   Jesus - Mt 22:32

Whoever trusts he who sent me has eternal life.   Jesus - Jn 5:24

Why should it be thought incredible that God should raise the dead?   Paul - Acts 26:8

We know that if the physical frame that houses us today is demolished, we possess a building which God has provided — eternal and in heaven.   Paul - II Cor 5:1

Whether we live or die, we belong to God.   Paul - Rom 14:8

Dear friends, we are now God's children, though what we shall be is not yet known.
      I Jn 3:2

The resurrection is a revelation of that which exists, and the transformation of things, and a transition into newness.   - letter to Reginus - the Nag Hammadi texts

I am no more puzzled by the darkness into which I am going than by the darkness from which I came.   Hume

If it were shown that the universe is heading for an all-enveloping death, then this might be held to falsify Christian faith.   John MacQuarrie

The whole temple of man's achievement must inevitably be buried beneath the debris of a universe in ruins.   Bertrand Russell

As at the beginning, so at the end, there is a hidden, unimaginable, new creative act.
      Hans Küng

The beginning bears witness to the end and the end will at long last bear witness to the beginning.   Rabbinic

As dreamers wake from sleep, we wake from waking.   – untraced

It is the gospel, and the gospel alone, that has brought life and immortality to light.
      David Hume

The Messiah will come when all his guests have sat down at table.   Jewish

Jesus was a typical man, they always say they will come back but you never see them again.   - graffiti

RESURRECTION ?   [see 27]   **122**

The Biblical writers are fully aware of the natural course of death and decay, nor do they look for a merely physical resurrection. Jesus sides with the Pharisees against the Sadducees in believing in resurrection, but the ground of his belief is the nature of God, who is God of the living.

Immortality suggests an automatic transition from one life to another but resurrection includes the reality of death — a clear discontinuity — and relies on the free, creative act of God. Yet Christians see all of life in this way, so the distinction cannot be pressed.

When resurrection is dismissed as unnatural, we forget that the story of evolution chronicles the emergence of life from death, and we fail to see the sacramental significance of Nature's transformations. It may be that life/spirit weaves for itself a body, and when this 'building' is discarded, it will weave another. Even our present physical cells are replaced every seven years and we retain no material identity over a lifetime. A sense of the dimensions of reality can save us from becoming the new 'flat-earthers' of our time.

Paul believes in no crude reconstitution — 'flesh and blood cannot inherit the Kingdom of God' — I Cor 15:35f — but it is not that he despises the physical; on the contrary, he claims that the human body is a temple (Greek Orphic teaching described it as a tomb). Yet he longs for a new embodiment — a spiritual body, woven in the texture of God's glory. He looks, that is, for true personality — not a ghostly remnant as Sheol or Hades might suggest. So, as Jesus says, God is still the God of Abraham and Isaac and Jacob. Even if we are not concerned about the possibility of new life for ourselves, we remember those we love and realise that God places eternal value on them. Earthly contracts may then matter little — Mt 22:23f — but love will have its recognition and reunion.

The New Testament emphasis is not on individual survival but on the community in which, alone, we can be complete. This is the fullness of Christ — the real body —and so we can begin to understand the imagery of the Second Coming when Christ is 'realised' once again.. The relationship of Jesus' resurrection to ours poses no problem. The disciples believed, not so much in resurrection as such (that of Jesus or their own) but they believed and trusted in God, who can raise whom he will.

....

.

The pious among all nations will have a share in the life to come.   *Jewish*

God's Day will be darkness.   *Amos - 5:20*
          (Amos challenged the view that God's Day would ensure Israel's triumph.)

In life and in all that follows death, you will do and suffer exactly as it is meet you
should.   *Plato*

Know also that everything is according to reckoning; and let not your imagination give
you hope that the grave will be a refuge for you.   *Jewish*

The dead were judged by what was written in the books, that is by what they had done
          Rev 20:11

Read your book! Your soul suffices as a reckoner against you this day.   *The Qur'an*
He who does not answer to the rudder shall answer to the rock.
          - displayed in a US law-court

Anyone outside the Catholic Church will incur the eternal fire.
          The Council of Florence

It is not your heavenly Father's will that anyone, however unimportant, should be lost.
          Jesus - Mt 18:14

My compassion rises again within me. I cannot let loose my anger, for I am God, not a
man. I cannot destroy.   *Hosea - 11:9*

Those who do not believe judge themselves.   *Jesus - Jn 3:18*

Evil possesses by its very nature the quality of defeating and destroying itself.   *Kant*

The reward of duty is the duty and the punishment of sin is the sin.
          Simeon ben Azzai

The self is the maker and non-maker and decides its own condition.   *Jain*

God exercises vengeance in silence.   *African - Barundi*

There is plenty room in my Father's house. I go to prepare a place for you.
          Jesus - Jn 14:2
          (as a servant would go ahead to prepare a place at the next inn?)

....

Belief in 'Judgement' usually centres on the court scene representing the Last Judgement, when everyone receives reward or punishment according to what they have done with their lives e.g. Mt 25:31ff. The weakness of the imagery is threefold:
- ➤ it removes God's involvement to a future point in time.
- ➤ it loses sight of the teaching that goodness is its own reward and evil carries its own condemnation.
- ➤ it can become a negative image — teaching that all humanity deserves condemnation — a view that has often been handed down to us.

For the Israelites who knew what it was to be downtrodden and oppressed — God's judgement was usually seen as their liberation and they longed for the Day of the Lord.

To do good out of fear or desire for reward can seem unworthy to us, and yet it is part of Jesus' teaching as passed on to us — Lk 6: 23 and elsewhere. It is part also of all our morality. Total self-lessness may be an unreal ideal or simply wrong. Are we not stewards of our own lives as well with a duty to render them to God? *"Whoever would save his life must lose it"*(Mtt 16:25) still enshrines a paradox.

The strength of the idea of Judgement is that it testifies to a divine purpose that measures all that is done and ultimately brings it to a conclusion. There is a challenge therefore to those who insist that the universe is indifferent to, and careless of, all our aspirations. It can seem so if we hanker after an inbuilt bias — obviously rewarding goodness and making evil unprofitable — but what should a moral universe look like? Should it not:
- ➤ give equal scope for free will to lean one way or another,
- ➤ give us an inbuilt perception of right and wrong,
- ➤ present opportunities for amendment and restoration,
- ➤ set ultimate limits to tyranny?

And this is exactly what we have — the last point being met by the greater success of co-operative behaviour and ultimately by death itself.

Although it seems at times that evolution favours aggression, cruelty and loss, we can balance against this — love, co-operation and achievement. These too are woven into human survival and ultimately predominate [see 101]. Perhaps some ambiguity must remain or else the prospect of final reward skews our moral choice.

The main object of religion is not to get a man to heaven but to get heaven into him.

Thomas Hardy

You cannot go anywhere and find Paradise, but if you stay where you are, you might be able to find Paradise within yourself.
Thor Heyerdahl
(renowned for his use of reed boats to cross the Pacific)

Damnation is no foreign, separate or imposed state — it is the inborn, natural, essential state of our own disordered nature.
William Law

God casts no soul away, unless it casts itself away.
Jacob Boehme

Nor can we fall below the arms of God, how low soever it be we fall.
Penn

But of the heaven which is above the heavens, what earthly poet ever did, or ever will sing worthily?
Plato

It is not in heaven that we are to find God, but in God that we are to find heaven.
Godet

That the saints may enjoy their beatitude and the grace of God more abundantly, they are permitted to see the punishment of the damned in heaven.
Aquinas

The disciples said, 'Lord, do you want us to call down fire from heaven to burn them up?' But Jesus retorted, 'You do not know what you are saying'.
Jesus - Lk 9:54
While sin remains and souls in darkness dwell,

Can heaven itself be heaven, and look unmoved on hell?
Whittier

Hell is in heaven and heaven is in hell. But angels see only the light and devils see only the darkness.
Jacob Boehme

Do not create hell by thrusting the 'wicked' into it. Get rid of the instincts of vengeance which are projected into eternity. As a consequence of the dark freedom that has to be lived through, hell exists, anyway. The 'good' must take upon themselves the fate of the 'wicked', share their destiny and thus further their liberation. Hell is not a triumph for God — it is the triumph of non-being.
Berdyaev

When you talk about heaven, let your face light up with the glory of God; when you talk about hell, your ordinary face will do.
John Wesley

The imagery of heaven and hell — woefully inadequate as it is bound to be — is witness to the conviction that human life is a serious matter and has ultimate consequences. We picture **heaven** according to our dreams — a landscape, a garden, a city — the detail is unimportant but the markers we lay down are not. We look for freedom, fulfilment and growth (something more than an endless church service writ large). The greater knowledge of God is central to the Christian hope. It is not a baseless hope, for glimpses of the glory of God are found in human experience but the 'how' and 'where' of it all is not given to us.

Hell was once the cave-like place of shadows or the place of the utter annihilation of all that is evil and destructive, and it was symbolised by fire. The idea of a place of perpetual torment — a torture chamber of unimaginable horror — should not be entertained by any who claim the name of Christ :

> ➤ it is an import from neighbouring religion, which has left marginal traces in the New Testament
> ➤ it is utterly alien to the spirit of Jesus
> ➤ it suggests a God of monstrous injustice
> ➤ its appeal is solely to fear, and its strategy is that of coercion.

Belief in such a hell may have been an understandable reaction to the atrocities of Roman persecutors but it was not a Christian response, and it spawned an awful legacy, when torture was used to 'save souls' from endless divine torture. The demotion of hell does not destroy human responsibility. The choice of spiritual life or death is real enough. Our task is surely not undue preoccupation with the future but everyday concern for the wellbeing of all, knowing that God will provide opportunities for reconciliation and healing throughout our lives and beyond.

....

Words: **Heaven:** — probably first = the sky — the limit of human vision beyond which was imagined the dwelling of God.

Paradise: — Persian for an enclosed garden.

Hell: — a cave or covered place. Sheol /Hades - a twilight zone.

Gehenna: — the valley outside Jerusalem, where children were said to have been sacrificed to Moloch. Deliberately desecrated by Josiah and used for the burning of offal. The city's rubbish burned perpetually there.

Purgatory: — an interim state of refining or growth. The teaching is developed from fragments such as I Cor 3:13f and reflection on other doctrines. It gave point to prayers for the dead but was rejected by the Reformers, who saw heaven as pure gift which could not be earned.

....

There is a secret too great to be told. George Macdonald

There is a dream dreaming us. African

The universe is a dream woven of dreams: the Self alone is awake. Schuon

The Self, smaller than the small, greater than the great, is hidden in the heart of every creature. The Upanishads

You yourself are even another world and have within you the sun, the moon and the stars. Origen

The barrier between me and the rest of creation was broken down. The few phenomena, sky, ice, rock, wind, and I, now constituted life, were an inseparable and divine whole. I felt myself — as glorious as God and at the same time no more than a grain of sand. Herbert Tichy - on the summit of Cho Oyu

The external world of physics has become a world of shadows. Eddington

Like a vast tide, Being will have engulfed the shifting sand of being. Within a new tranquil ocean, each drop of which, nevertheless, will be conscious of remaining itself, the astonishing adventure of the world will have ended. Teilhard de Chardin

To Tao all under heaven will come, as streams flow into a great river or sea.
('Tao' is the ultimate harmony of all being.) Tao Te Ching - 6 C.BC

Civilisation will not achieve perfection until the last stone from the last church falls on the last priest. Emile Zola

There will be no pain or injury in all my holy mountain; for the land will be filled with the knowledge of God as the waters cover the sea. Isaiah - 11:9

I am creating everything new. The past will not be remembered nor ever brought to mind. Rejoice and be delighted at what I create. Isaiah 65:17

I saw a new heaven and a new earth, for the first heaven and the first earth had vanished. There shall be no more death, no mourning or crying or pain, for the old order has passed. They will not need the light of lamp or sun, for the God himself will be their light. Rev 21:1,4, 22:5

Things beyond our seeing, things beyond our hearing, things beyond our imagining, have been prepared by God for those who love him. Paul I Cor 2:9

....

The core of the Christian faith is trust in God based on experience of his creative and transforming power. Without that trust, any speculation about the ultimate future is foolishness. In any case, God's consummation lies beyond all human experience, imagination and thought. From science we know that the earth is likely to be swallowed up in the death throes of our star, and that the stars themselves may be swallowed up in the awesome returning of our universe to what it was at the beginning. But, even to the scientists, new births and unimaginable transformations are possible.

Perhaps we belong to a world of shadows, a dream yet to become reality. Certainly we seem just half-human — hung between the greatness of God and a grain of sand. The Christian hope is that we will be created anew, or perhaps, created for the first time — clean and free before the face of God. But this 'self-fulfilment' — this realisation of self — is bound up with the whole creation. The promise of a new heavens and a new earth takes us far beyond the transient worlds we know, subjected as they are to pain and death.

It must be that something of God's Kingdom will be realised in this world of time and space — and it will be that earth and heaven, time and eternity, will gather into one great consummation beyond all imagination.

> *But he will come again, it's said, though not*
> *Unwanted and unsummoned; for all things*
> *Beasts of the field, and woods, and rocks, and seas,*
> *And all mankind from end to end of the earth*
> *Will call him with one voice. In our time,*
> *Some say, or at a time when time is ripe,*
> *Then he will come, Christ the uncrucified,*
> *Christ the discrucified, his death undone,*
> *His agony unmade, his cross dismantled*
> *Glad to be so — and the tormented wood*
> *Will cure its hurt and grow into a tree*
> *In a green springing corner of young Eden,*
> *And Judas damned take his long journey backward*
> *From darkness into light and be a child*
> *Beside his mother's knee, and the betrayal*
> *Be quite undone and never more be done.*
>
> Edwin Muir - 'The Transfiguration'

....

God spoke and called the world into being from the rising to the setting sun.   Ps 50:1

Who summoned the generations from the beginning? I, the Lord, was with the first of them, and I am with all who come after.   Isaiah - 41:4

Reproduction is the sole good for which human beings are designed.   Matt Ridley

Those whom God knew even before they were born, he intended to be like his Son — it was for this he called them.   Paul - Rom 8:29

Return to the marketplace.   Gautama
(the Buddha's advice to those who experienced enlightenment)

True godliness doesn't turn men out of the world, but enables them to live better in it, and excites their endeavours to mend it.   William Penn

All are clear, I alone am clouded.   Lao-tzu

The older I have become, the less I have understood about myself.   Jung

It is not granted to you to complete the work nor are you entitled to withdraw from it.
Rabbi Tarfon

Nobody made a greater mistake than he who did nothing because he could only do a little.   Edmund Burke

To live is not enough.   Pablo Casals

God has called me to be faithful, not successful.   Mother Teresa

I saw no visions, I heard no voices, but somewhere deep inside me, I knew that God was calling me. I knew that this meant the renouncing of marriage, of medicine, and of my liberty. It was as simple and devastating as that. I hadn't asked to be called and I didn't want to be.   Sheila Cassidy - on her call to work in the shanty town area of Santiago

Every wrong thing seems possible today and is accepted — but I don't accept it, that's all.   Pablo Casals – speaking of his opposition to Franco

If God dishes your rice in a basket, do not wish to eat soup!   African - Mende

I have learned in whatever state I am, to be content.   Paul - Phil 4:11

....

Vocation is God's call to us. He called the world into being, the prophets to speak and the people to serve him. He called Jesus from the carpenter's shop and, through him, he calls all humanity into his Kingdom. It is the calling that creates the person and the answering which is the path to life.

The products of human manufacture are fixed and complete — their future determined by their origin. The products of God's creative work are free and fluid — called into an open future. Whatever truth there may be in genetic determinism; however much reproduction may be a law of evolution; these are but the platform upon which God builds his greater purpose. There is no 'sole good' but a varied sheaf of good possibilities. There is no single task to be performed but many vocations arising out of the one discipleship.

We cannot tell the mind of God. We can hardly tell our own minds. But the immediate and practical lies before us. Change and chance help to determine the conditions of our lives. God does not necessarily appoint those conditions but he calls us to serve him through them.

We cannot limit vocations to that of the priest or teacher or nurse. The mechanic, the hairdresser, the businessman and the clown each have their calling to be fulfilled with integrity and compassion. Like as not, we will know several vocations at the same time — motherhood, fatherhood, singleness (chosen or unchosen) and those touching family and neighbour, community and stranger. Above all we are called to measure up to our humanity — and 'the likeness of his Son' is a good measure of what that can mean.

....

What the church needs is fighting men of God, not hog-jowled, weasel-eyed, sponge-columned, mushy-fisted, jelly-spined, pussy-footed Christians.   *Billy Sunday*

Be known to everyone for your consideration of others ... then the peace of God that is beyond all understanding will guard both your hearts and your thoughts in Christ Jesus. And so my friends, all that is true, all that is noble, all that is just, all that is pure, whatever is lovely and attractive, whatever is excellent and admirable — fill your thoughts with these things — and the God of peace will be with you.

Paul - Phil 4:5f

....

God only made part of me. He made me when I was little; the rest I growed myself.   *- a child*

ETHICS

The three primary principles of Wisdom: wisdom to the laws of God; concern for the welfare of humanity; suffering with fortitude all the accidents of life.
- triads of the druids - early oral tradition

The proposition 'God is good' is not a tautology.   *Bertrand Russell*

Science has no methods for deciding what is ethical.   *Richard Dawkins*

God has delivered yourself into your own keeping.   *Epictetus*

For everything else we thank God, but the deed is our responsibility.   *Leo Baeck*

I do not agree with the view that to be moral, the motive has to be benefitting others. People like me only have a duty to ourselves.   *Mao Tse-tung*

Conscience is the most secret core and sanctuary of a man. There he is alone with God.
'Gaudium et Spes' - Second Vatican Council

Principles are only tools in God's hands, soon to be thrown away as unserviceable.
Bonhoeffer

The end will always justify the means — no action which is not justified by its results can be right.   *George Moore*

We have always control over the means and never over the ends. If one takes care of the means, the end will take care of itself.   *Gandhi*

The human mind has no more power of inventing a new value than of imagining a new primary colour.   *C S Lewis*

The Christian religion as organised by the churches has been and still is the principal enemy of moral progress in the world.   *Bertrand Russell*

I want my lawyer, tailor, valet, even my wife to believe in God. I think that if they do, I shall be robbed and cheated less.   *Voltaire*

The greatest good for the greatest number is a heartless doctrine.   *Gandhi*

In the New Testament, religion is grace and ethics is gratitude.   *Erskine*

You have need of the law, that love may be manifested; but if it cannot be kept without injury to the neighbour, God wants us to suspend and ignore the law.   *Luther*

If you love your neighbour, you have met every requirement of the law.   *Rom 13:8*

....

I feel bad that I don't feel worse.   *Michael Frayn*

For all people, the principles we live by are rooted in our beliefs. The ethics of the Ten Commandments derive from an ultimate view of reality [11] and so it is with all ethics — values cannot be plucked out of the air or easily negotiated. The practically minded may adopt a code and ignore its basis but such a course can easily become legalistic. The 'heavenly minded' can become so detached in their ideal world to be no earthly use. We can base ethics on:

- ➢ reason — *if* we know what is reasonable
- ➢ the happiness of the greatest number —if we know the secrets of happiness— and what of the few and their good?
- ➢ our emotions — but our biology may have an older agenda
- ➢ conscience — self talking to self or the community talking to us?

Luther's view of the blameless conscience (see opposite) is close to Augustine's 'love God, then do what you will' but it is also not unlike Machiavelli's teaching that politicians should be liberated from the restrictions of morality. Hitler welcomed this teaching as a 'cleansing of the mind'.

We can debate whether values can ever be absolute. Many, like liberty and equality, may be in conflict with one with another — but is not contempt for another or the rape of a child always wrong?

The golden rule — 'do as you would be done by' is echoed in most religions. It fits Darwinian ethics, if altruism is treated as another form of self-interest. Jesus would surely have accepted the weaving together of true self-interest with concern for others — he was ready to speak of reward as the just consequence flowing from a good action — e.g. Lk 6:23. Yet his teaching reaches beyond to that love which lies beyond calculation and judges all rules. This, above all, is why Biblical teaching gives no blueprint to be matched to every circumstance, but requires choice, responsibility and goodness of heart. It is one thing to know what is required but another to do it.

We seem to need not only values and motivation but also insight into the situation around us. It is quite apparent with political responsibilities that a clear eye for the possible is an essential if wisdom is to prevail. A realistic spirit need not imply betrayal as the cynics or idealists would have it. We have to have regard to the situation in which we are placed and still seek some correspondence between our transient kingdoms and the Kingdom of God.

ETHICS

....

The sacred rights of mankind are written by the hand of the divinity itself.
                                                                    Alexander Hamilton

It is better that one man should die for the nation.   Caiaphas - Jn 11:50

*There are three tests of Civil Liberty: equality of rights, equality of taxation, freedom to
come and go.*   - triads of the druids - early Celtic tradition

*If one made a find of any kind (e.g. a honey tree) and marked it, it was therefore safe for
him, no matter how long he left it.*   - native Australian

To no one will we sell, to no one will we refuse, right or justice. Magna Carta
         — declared null and void by Pope Innocent III 10 weeks later.

*By natural birth all men are equally and alike born to like propriety, liberty and
freedom.*   Robert Overton - 17C.

*We hold these truths to be sacred and undeniable; that all men are created equal and
independent, that from that equal creation they derive rights inherent and inalienable,
among which are the preservation of life, and liberty, and the pursuit of happiness.*
                                                        Thomas Jefferson - 1776
                    (- draft for the Declaration of Independence.)

*Men are born free and remain free and equal in rights. Social distinctions can
only be founded on general usefulness.*   Declaration of the Rights of Man 1789

*Equality of mind or body, as of worldly condition, is as inconsistent with the order of
nature as with the moral laws of God.*   William Buckland - Dean

*Both the love of man and the respect for his rights are duties, but the former is only a
conditional, while the latter is an unconditional.*   Kant

*The concept of property rights went back to biblical times and was transmitted and
transformed by Christian teaching.*   David Landes

*If a Roman soldier forces you to carry his baggage for a mile along the road, go two
miles with him.*   Jesus - Mt 5:41

*The defence of human rights has reached such extremes as to make society defenceless
against certain individuals. It is time to defend not so much human rights as human
obligations.*   Alexander Solzhenitzyn

....

The enshrining of human rights grew out of radical thinking — both Christian and non-Christian (Tom Paine was brought up as a Quaker). The values, if not the language, arise from Mosaic law. It is there saved from mere legalism by being embedded in God's covenant-commitment to the nation. Human rights today have to be argued on the basis of inherent worth and society's self-interest — a society of 6 billion people, with a history of struggle and waste. Perhaps ultimately there are no rights but a sketch-map of responsibilities that must suffice till love becomes possible.

A history of the philosophy of rights would the Stoic, Marcus Aurelius, who argued for equality and world citizenship, and Tertullian 3C, who fought against the exposing of children human sacrifice, political assassination and gladiatorial combat.In 17C. Britain, it would include Gerard Winstanley, the 'Digger' leader, — John Donne, the poet, —and the Quakers, George Fox and James Nayler, the first to speak of liberty, equality and fraternity. In revolutionary France there was ferment within the Church as well as outside it. The Abbé Gregoire became leader of the 'Constitutional Church' and perhaps 50% of clergy supported him; one reason, perhaps, why Pope Pius VI repudiated 'the abominable philosophy of human rights'.Pierre Bayle, Protestant, had gone so far as to defend the rights of atheists.In Britain a Bill was passed to keep clergy out of the House of Commons — they were too radical!

The United Nations Declaration of Human Rights stems from the writings of Jacques Maritain (Catholic philosopher), Eleanor Roosevelt and John Foster Dulles, and from the groundwork of American churches looking to the end of war.

Jesus' teaching goes beyond the law — involving the extra mile, the refusal to take offence and the possibility of unlimited forgiveness. There is little expectation of uniformity and no rigid equality but, as in a family, every expectation of respect, caring and generosity. If there is any bias, it is towards the poor, the sick and the vulnerable — including women and children, the accused and the convicted, the marginalised and the foreigner.

The earth will belong equally to all, undivided by walls or fences. Lives will be in common and wealth will have no division. .For there will be no poor man there, no rich, and no tyrant, no slave. .Further, no one will be either great or small anymore. No kings, no leaders. All will be on a par together. — the *Sibylline Oracles 2:313-38.*

(Jewish writing from Phrygia a generation before Paul).

....

Woman is as essential to man as man is to woman.   Paul - I Cor 11:11

Woman has the right to ascend the scaffold. She must equally have the right to ascend the speaker's tribune.   Declaration of the Rights of Women 1791

Sin began with a woman. It is because of her we all die.   Ecclus 25:24

As we have noted with vexation, contempt for divine truths reached such a level that even women, it is reported, serve at holy altars.   Pope Gelasius - 494

Women should remain at home, sit still, keep house, bear and bring up children.
       Luther

The Queen is most anxious to enlist everyone to join in checking the mad, wicked folly of 'women's rights."   - attributed to Queen Victoria

The creation pattern may be summarised thus: man to lead, woman to support; man to initiate, woman to enable; man to take responsibility for the well-being of women, women to take responsibility for helping man.   J I Packer - 20C.

There are many who desire Enlightenment in a man's body, but none who work for the benefit of sentient beings in the body of a woman — therefore I shall work in a woman's body.   - on Tara - the Loving Mother - Buddhist

The legal subordination of one sex to the other is wrong in itself and one of the chief hindrances to human improvement.   J S Mill

The fact that in Jesus' birth, human-male is excluded, connotes that a new human image, a new saving world, could no longer be sustained through a patriarchal order.   P S Kyung

Reason and logic are <u>not</u> masculine instruments of oppression. To suggest that they are is an insult to women.   Richard Dawkins

All structures of ministry should be so designed as to create and sustain with maximum force faith-knowledge that it is Christ himself who ministers to us.   J I Packer

The use of women's experience explodes as a critical force, exposing the classical theology as based on male experience rather than on universal human experience.   Rosemary Ruether – Catholic

....

Woman was God's *second* mistake.   *Nietzsche*

With some notable exceptions, Jesus' witness to God's valuing of both sexes has been betrayed. It is the tragedy of the Church that the image of God came to be been distorted by oppressive patriarchy. It is scarcely credible that John Cardinal O'Connor of New York could still be arguing for the 'maleness' of God in 1991.

Differences go well beyond reproductive biology and roles can be different yet carry equal dignity. The sexes have helped to fashion each other in the long course of evolutionary development. There is no simple dualism but perhaps the male is more unstable than the female, more criminal, more alienated and more in need of other voices to reach full humanity!

In the Eucharist , there a view that a man can best image for us the presence of Jesus but is this the only consideration? No one can adequately represent God's presence in the community of faith and, if there is priesthood, it is in the common sharing in which the true body is realised. If women could be witnesses to both cross and resurrection, how can we ask for other credentials?

The idea that 'a woman's place was in the home' was partly a Protestant reaction to the convent. We need now to look to a future where motherhood and fatherhood are honoured, difference is celebrated, and choice is widened for both sexes.

A women's **roll of honour** includes those greeted by Paul in Rom 16 and:
- women martyrs — **Blandina** - Lyons 177, **Perpetua & Felicitas** - Carthage 203.
- **Philoumene** - head of a school of theology in Rome - 2 C. **Hilda of Whitby** - 7C.
- leaders of the mediaeval church like **Hildegard, Birgitta & Catherine of Siena.**
- Quaker women persecuted for discussing theology in public — **Mary Fisher & Elizabeth Williams** in 1653, **Elizabeth Fletcher & Elizabeth Leavens** in 1654, **Mary Dyer** -- hanged in Boston, America - 1660.
- American feminist pioneers — **Emma Willard, Mary Lyon, Elizabeth Stanton, Susan Anthony and Elizabeth Blackwell.**
- British pioneers — **Mary Wolstonecraft, Josephine Butler, Elizabeth Anderson.**
- women doctors — **Elsie Inglis,** who formed the Women's Hospital Unit in the 1st World War, and **Helena Wright,** medical missionary and pioneer in family planning and sexual health (b.1887).
- the suffragettes — **Emily Davies, Emmeline & Christabel Pankhurst.**

Many, though not all, of these later pioneers were deeply influenced by their Christian background and convictions.

···

I will not give a woman a pessary to procure an abortion -- but I will keep my life and my art in purity and in holiness.   Hippocrates

You knitted me together in my mother's womb — my life was fashioned before it had begun.   Ps 139:13,16

Before I formed you in the womb I knew you and before you were born I chose you.
Jer 1:4

We drown children who at birth are weakly and abnormal. It is not anger but reason that separates the harmful from the sound.   Seneca

You shall not kill by abortion the fruit of the womb.   The Didache - 1C.

The systematic killing of unborn children in huge numbers is part of a general disregard for human life that has been growing for some time. We are crossing lines, at first slowly, and now with rapidity. Abortion has coarsened us.   Judge Bork - USA

No parents will have a right to burden society with a malformed or mentally incompetent child.   Bentley Glass - geneticist - 1999

Directly willed and procured abortion to be absolutely excluded as a licit means of regulating birth.   Papal Encyclical - 1968

If you deny that life begins with the fusion of sperm with ovum, the big bang, an explosion of energy, when does it begin?   Jack Scarisbrick - founder of Life

The potentiality concerned is not that of becoming something else but of becoming what it essentially is.   Thomas F Torrance

We believe that the right of every woman to control her own fertility is a fundamental human right.   National Abortion Campaign

No one can be in favour of abortion. Humanists regard abortion as better than bringing unwanted babies into the world.   Humanist Dipper

We believe that abortion is an evil — and that abortion on demand would be a very great evil. But we also believe that to withhold compassion is evil, and in circumstances of extreme distress or need, a very great evil. Christians need to face frankly the fact that in an imperfect world the 'right' choice is sometimes the acceptance of the lesser of two evils.   The Church of England – 1988

···

The background to this issue is God's order of creation, where there is uncountable waste. The majority of fertilised eggs do not implant and 50% of those that do then miscarry. Then there is a 'biological imperative' in the animal world and in poorer human societies, which makes survival dependent on every means of population restraint. We who have better contraception and live in wealthier societies should not dismiss this too easily.

Should compassion be the ruling principle? We are not dealing just with the irresponsible but with women in genuine distress, who face the consequences of rape or are clearly unready or unable to take on the responsibility of a child — particularly if handicapped. Resort to back-street abortion, with its risks, is a measure of the distress.

It is understandable that churches, believing that God places infinite value on human life, should make a stand on the principle that all life is sacred from conception. Yet there is no scriptural or rabbinic condemnation of abortion and Aquinas held that there is no 'person' in the early embryo. For many centuries the Catholic Church regarded 'ensoulment' as later than conception and Gregory XIV decreed that penalties for abortion should only apply after the first 40 days. This accords well with scientists who argue that personality can only come with the formation of the nervous system. This depends though on the assumption that the physical gives rise to the spiritual and not vice versa. It also means that the legal moment has to be fixed somewhat arbitrarily.

Christians might agree that this is not simply an individual matter for the mother. The child is not part of her; the father is more than a spectator; and doctors and nurses face their own moral dilemma. It is, and must be, a matter of both public and private concern, especially if there is truth in the charge that we have created a 'culture of death'.

If this is a case of 'the lesser of two evils', then it will rank with many other tragic dilemmas. But it could be argued that a decision born out of love is wholly good because good and evil lie in the will and not in the action. Is such love possible if the issue is purely utilitarian — selection on the grounds of convenience, or gender, or used to weed out defective babies?

Once pregnant, tragedy may be unavoidable — it is time once more to invest the moment of intercourse with greater seriousness.

In vitro fertilisation:
Judaism is opposed to the use of donated sperm or ova. This breaks the genetic connection between parents and child and introduces confusion at the most basic level of identity and relationship.　　　　　*Rabbi Dr Nisson E Shulman*

One in eight couples are infertile. Infertility, whilst not life threatening, causes severe anguish and anxiety. It eats at self-esteem, is a severe blow to sexuality and may cut into the deepest marital bonds. Of course, it is nobody's right to have a child, but incurable infertility causes a form of prolonged grieving and mourning. For many IVF is the final hope.
　　　Prof Robert Winston - the Infertility Clinic, Hammersmith Hospital

Embryo research:　　　*(permitted in Britain 0 - 14 days)*
After years of research using human embryos immediately after fertilisation in the laboratory, it has become possible to distinguish between male and female embryos within 36 hours of fertilisation. There are many genetically inherited diseases which afflict only boys. A family with a history of such diseases could therefore now choose to have their children by means of in-vitro fertilisation.
　　　Mary Warnock

Most infants with congenital malformations and chromosomal disorders are now born to healthy young women with no identifiable risk factor. There is no evidence that such rare sporadic disorders can be detected or prevented prior to pregnancy.　　　　*The Royal College of Physicians - 1989*

Sex selection:
If it is feared that people might whimsically decide to go through the risks and hazards in order to have a boy rather than a girl, it is perfectly possible to introduce regulations to specify the family conditions under which sex selection will be permitted (and this in my view might properly include the selection of a male baby for those with hereditary titles).　　　　*Mary Warnock*

Surrogacy:　　*(commercial forms of surrogacy are illegal in Britain)*
The danger of exploitation of one human being by another appears to the majority of us far to outweigh the potential benefits, in almost every case.
　　　The Warnock Report

He was just the same as my other kids when they were born. The difference was I was giving him away. I just felt empty. When you have a baby you're happy, tired and so relieved it's all over. But I felt sick inside.
　　　- a surrogate mother

Clearly there can be no exclusive Christian insight into issues of this kind but simply a commonly shared concern for the family and the intrinsic value of an individual human life.

In vitro fertilisation poses little difficulty if the egg and sperm are that of the couple concerned. If a donor is involved, Catholics have condemned the practice as 'mechanical adultery' — but even the terminology presupposes a rather legalistic and mechanical view of marriage itself. More concern should surely be directed towards the problem of identity — an area of human psychology as yet little understood. There is also an issue of health priorities if IVF remains an expensive procedure.

More controversial still is the use of early embryos for research. They are capable of arrested development by deep freezing — is this an indication that they are not yet true life forms? Or if we say that they are undoubtedly human and alive, does that mean that they should be treated as personalities? They cannot feel or think; they have no notion of themselves; they have no desires or volition. To make use of them for other ends is not like using a developed human being for such ends — and yet the doubts remain that our technological expertise is outrunning our moral and spiritual capacity. Parliament recently gave approval for stem cell research in the hope that future sufferers from degenerative diseases would benefit.

Researchers can use the surplus 'pre-embryos' inevitably created by the practice of IVF. These are normally destroyed after 5 or 10 years and have no prospect of life beyond that which they already possess.
Is this better than mere disposal? Many Christians and non-Christians have grave doubts about the creation of embryos *solely* for research as well as doubts about the nature of some experiments. With our new genetic knowledge, it is difficult to see far ahead and easy to tell ourselves to 'stop playing God', though we have been doing this ever since we learned to play with fire. Advances in stem cell research will help to allay some of our present doubts and fears.

....

Words: cell / embryo / foetus / child — an area such as this makes very clear how our opinions are reflected in our use of language.
in vitro fertilisation — strictly 'in glass fertilisation' i.e. 'test tube babies' where the sperm and egg are brought together in the laboratory.
In **surrogacy,** a woman bears a child for an infertile woman.

ETHICS

....

The Lord gave; the Lord has taken away; may his name be blessed.   Job 1:21

An adult person suffering from a severe illness, for which no relief is known, should be entitled by law to the mercy of a painless death, if and only if, that is their expressed wish.   The Voluntary Euthanasia Society

I do not think that we can assume that God wills the prolongation of torture for the benefit of the soul of the sufferer.   Dean Inge

A sure and certain faith in resurrection to eternal, spiritual life is incompatible with making the prolongation of physical existence, regardless of the cost to the patient, an over-riding priority.   Lewis Stretch

The fear of the future lies like a black cloud over everything. I dread beyond words that I may become senile and helpless, a burden and a responsibility to others. If I could know that I was able to lay down my life at my own wish and will, it would give me freedom and relief, and enable me to enjoy infinitely more the many pleasures life can still give me.   — letter to the press

Before the Nazis took over a propaganda barrage was directed against the traditional compassionate nineteenth-century attitudes towards the chronically ill, and for the adoption of a utilitarian point of view. Euthanasia of persons with chronic mental illness was discussed at a meeting of Bavarian psychiatrists in 1931. By 1936 extermination of the physically or socially unfit was openly accepted..........(275,000 persons were put to death in the Aktion T-4 programme — half of the early victims came from church institutions.... most were gassed but children were often starved to death) ......the victims were the mentally defective, psychotics, epileptics, and patients suffering from infirmities of old age and from various neurological disorders such as infantile paralysis, multiple sclerosis and brain tumours.

Whatever proportions these crimes finally assumed, it became evident to all that investigated them that they had started from small beginnings. The beginnings at first were merely a subtle shift of emphasis in the basic attitude of the physicians. It started with the attitude that there is such a thing as a life not worth living.
     Dr Leo Alexander - office of the Chief Counsel for War Crimes at Nürnberg

I came here (to St Anne's Hospice, Manchester) to die with cancer. You have shown me how to live with cancer. I thought of going to Lourdes. I find that here Lourdes has come to me.   — a patient

....

There is general agreement that life should not be prolonged unduly, although in practice the decision may not be an easy one. Euthanasia — literally 'good death' — is about compassionate killing; that is the intent to end a life which has become, or appears to be, intolerable. There is a strong assumption in most religions that life and death are matters for God alone, and yet the same traditions have accepted measures to increase fertility and have allowed the taking of life in some circumstances. In the Christian tradition:

> ➤ life is sacred — simply a *deduction* from the Bible?
> ➤ there is a powerful case for compassion where extremes of pain and futility are experienced

Suicide posed a particular difficulty but we know now that it may spring from courage as well as from despair. A request for euthanasia may not indicate lack of faith or obedience and it may contain a strong element of regard for others.

The greatest danger is that of abuse. It is not only the shadow of Hitler's policies that must make us pause but also the possibility of eroding trust in a hospital environment, of undermining the integrity of medical staff, and of testing to destruction the motivation of relatives. Even if the commitment of the patient has been made long in advance, and has been re-affirmed, it may be that we are not wise enough or good enough to take this responsibility upon ourselves. If the protection of the law remains, clear guidelines can still allow loving discretion in marginal cases.

An alternative approach is that of Cicely Saunders, leader of the modern hospice movement. She, like others before her, demonstrated that the control of pain and caring support can enable the dying to experience calm and dignity in cheerful and dedicated surroundings. The hospice she opened in Sydenham in 1967 treated the whole person — physical and emotional, social and spiritual. Many have followed its example.

Euthanasia has been legalised in **Holland** in 2000. Although illegal for the previous 17 years, doctors who followed strict guidelines were protected from prosecution.
Studies showed that: — 25,000 terminally ill patients considered euthanasia each year,   — 9,000 requested it and 3,000 received it,
                — 11% of doctors would not administer it.
A significant number of cases were non-voluntary — these included handicapped infants. There were also several hundred doctor assisted suicides each year.

....

He created them male and female.   Gen 1:27

My lover is mine and I am his;
he grazes his flock among the lilies.
while the day is cool and the shadows are dispersing.
Turn my beloved, and show yourself a gazelle or a young stag
on the hills where aromatic spices grow.   Song of Songs 2:16

Amnon hated her with exceeding hatred; for the hatred he had for her was greater than
the love he had once had.   *- a story of love, rape and revulsion - II Sam 13*

We may eventually come to realise that chastity is no more a virtue than malnutrition.
Dr Alex Comfort

I think teenagers should be promiscuous.   *Dr Martin Cole*

Any belief in the permanence of human feeling for a single human being is an illusion,
and therefore exclusivity of sexual community is a lie.
-- attributed to Otto Gross, who profoundly influenced Jung

In the past two thousand years Christianity has done its work and has erected barriers of
repression, which protect us from the sight of our own 'sinfulness'.   *Jung*

Far from an enemy of sex, the Judeo-Christian sexual code is a guide to getting the best
out of sex. It was a code for 'safe sex', sex which harms nobody, which cements
relationships, cultivates love, builds moral maturity and secures family life for children.
Clifford Longley

Christian women undoubtedly welcomed the restraints which Christianity imposed on
men.   *Mary Kenny*

When a husband and wife share intimacy it is rewarded and a blessing from Allah.
Hadith - Muslim

The act of intercourse has been traditionally regarded as a biological act. This is a
mistakenly narrow interpretation. It is a body language, through which couples talk to
and do things for one another. When couples make love they rejoice in each other's
presence and the pleasure they exchange. Thus sex is a recurrent act of thanksgiving.
Jack Dominian

....

Repressive attitudes towards sexuality have appeared many times in Christian and non-Christian thinking. Sometimes Greek and Indo-Persian teaching — that the spiritual must free itself from the material — has been responsible. Sometimes it was the practice of asceticism that turned people away from family and society. Sometimes the practical problems of sexual licence brought about a reaction (see, for example, the disastrous Soviet experiment of the 1920's when sexual licence was encouraged).

As so often the Biblical picture is complex :
- ➤ Biblical material is often positive — as in the Song of Songs
- ➤ violent exploitation and the practice of temple prostitution underlies much of the Biblical condemnation of fornication
- ➤ Jesus has far more to say about injustice and hypocrisy than about sexual misdemeanour (the word for lust in Mt 5:28 implies a direct intent to sin).

Our biological roots testify to the power of sexual instinct for creation or destruction and all societies have developed rules and guidelines for the control of sexual behaviour — control that should not be identified with repression. The 'repressive' attitudes that we identify with the Victorians arose largely from doctors, who were wrestling with the problems of syphilis and mental illness.

The evolutionary origins of sexuality are much debated — it may have originated as a defence against disease. It now serves more than one purpose and Christians should have no difficulty in accepting it as both gift and responsibility. Nor should there be any difficulty in recognising, with Freud, a sexual element in all our loving.

Virginity in the Jewish tradition is associated with young marriageable women and the promise of fertility rather than with the passionless purity conveyed by later Christian teaching. In earlier days, it was bound up with property rights — Ex 22:16. **Pre-marital sex** is not condemned in scripture as some assert. We may count it unwise at times but our chief concern should surely be whether it occurs in the context of responsible love and sincere commitment. Casual sex (paid or unpaid), divorced from any true relationship, is always a sad betrayal. The uncoupling (so to speak) of sex from the procreation of children by **contraception** is still sadly described as 'inherently evil' in a recent papal encyclical. This is not to ignore the fact that the promotion of 'safe sex' as the *sole* answer to unwanted pregnancy or AIDS is not an adequate response.

....

If a man lies with another man as with a woman, both of them have committed an abomination; they shall be put to death.   *Lev 20:13*

Their women gave up natural intercourse for unnatural ... and the men, gave up natural intercourse and were consumed with passion for one another..
           Paul - Rom 1:26

AIDS is not just God's punishment for homosexuals, it is God's punishment for the society that tolerates homosexuality.   *Jerry Falwell*

Jesus went out of his way to declare forgiven, and to reintegrate into society in all details, those who were identified as 'sinners' by virtue of the accidents of birth, or biology, or economic desperation.   *Walter Wink*

Certain people in every generation are attracted to their own sex, and especially to the young of their own sex. These priests, teachers, scoutmasters and team coaches:'have been 'father' or 'mother' to everyone's children. What remains of that most valuable of human resources, when the element of sexual prohibition has been removed?
           Roger Scruton

In 1954 Alan Türing committed suicide. He should, for his role in breaking German codes, have been fêted as a saviour of his nation. Instead, this gentle, stammering, eccentric genius was destroyed for a 'crime', committed in private, that harmed nobody.
           Richard Dawkins

I didn't want anything to do with him. I didn't even want to hear his name mentioned. I just wanted him to disappear.   *— a mother*
(— after learning that her son was homosexual. After 18 months she decided that 'trying not to love my son wasn't going to work'.)

The acceptance of our erotic choices depends on the degree to which society is willing to affirm sexual expression itself as a form of play — positive and life enhancing. What we should now be trying to 'liberate' is an aspect of the personal lives of everyone's sexual expression.   *John D'Emilio*

How can acts, designed to underpin and develop love, be intrinsically morally wrong? Is the omnipotent, omniscient, omnipresent Father terribly concerned with transient anatomical interactions or is He likely to be more concerned with love, warmth and charity?   *Andrew Miles*

....

Words: Homosexual = 'same sex'. (**Lesbian** originally one who comes from the island of Lesbos.)
         Homophobia = 'fear of sameness' (not 'anti-male')

It is thought that perhaps 5% of the human population are homosexual but this may vary for reasons not yet understood. In any case, we are not dealing with opposites but a spectrum of sexuality in which there are many variables. Researchers have pointed to a number of physical differences that can accompany male homosexuality and some studies suggest that this may be inherited through the female line. One theory suggests that homosexuality is a side-effect of genetic differences that otherwise enable a woman to have higher quality offspring. In animals generally, there seems to be a link with overpopulation but it is hard to explain any anti-reproductive strategy in evolutionary terms.

Christians have a choice — either to condemn such practice as deserving execution (as with adultery and the reviling of parents — Ex 21:17) or to interpret Jesus' teaching for our time, believing that his ethic of love requires us to reappraise the issue.

A papal letter of 1986 described homosexuals as 'disordered in their nature and evil in their love' believing that intercourse should always be in the context of marriage and open to the transmission of new life. But James Boswell has shown that there were Orthodox and Catholic liturgies for same sex unions up to the 14C and Ailred — 12C Abbot of Rievaulx — saw such love as one key to understanding the love of God. Freud commented that *the only unnatural sexual behaviour is none at all* (as with compulsory priestly celibacy?).

The Bible has no one sex ethic. It shares the instinctive reaction against homosexuality which springs from the powerful urge to reproduce. The Hebrews believed that the male seed carried the whole child and that wasting it was tantamount to murder (there were no laws against lesbianism). Paul saw it as unnatural, whereas we may see it today as a natural variant. He perhaps associated it with exploitation, promiscuity or child abuse — equally condemned among heterosexuals. There is a link with AIDS — anal intercourse may carry particular risk — but most sufferers are heterosexual. In any case the idea that AIDS is a divine punishment is abhorrent.

Whatever we make of Roger Scruton's argument (opposite) we can celebrate the achievements of Newton and Halley, Michelangelo and Botticelli, Schubert and Tchaikovsky — all homosexuals.

The 1967 decriminalisation of homosexuality in Britain was fore-shadowed by the Church of England report of 1954.

When a man is newly married, he is not to be liable for military service — he must remain exempt for one year to be happy with the wife he has taken.   *Deut 24:5*

God the Father — every family in heaven and on earth is named after him.
Paul - Eph 3:14

The family! Home of all social evils, a charitable institution for indolent wives, a prison workshop for the slaving breadwinner, and hell for children.   *Strindberg*

There remain no legal slaves, except the mistress of every household.   *J S Mill*

Be subject to one another. The husband must give the wife what is right for her, and equally the wife must give the husband what is right for him.
Paul - Eph 5:21, I Cor 7:3

We marry none; it is the Lord's work, and we are his witnesses.   *George Fox*

Marriage frees you to love people outside it in a clear way.   *Libby Purves*

Love can never be domesticated.   *Kathleen Raine*

A wise man ought to love his wife with judgement not affection.   *Seneca*

Let there be spaces in your togetherness and let the winds of the heavens dance between you.   *Kahlil Gibran*

It is not your love which sustains the marriage but the marriage which sustains your love.   *Bonhoeffer*

A ruined world is rebuilt with hearthstones.   *William Soutar*

The man has to find his feminine side in the woman, and the woman her masculine side in the man. The exterior marriage is for the sake of the interior marriage. In Christ there is neither male nor female.   *Bede Griffiths*

Jewels and precious stones, sons and wives form strong fetters. These drag men down. Men who have destroyed such bonds, who are free from longing, go forth and retire from the world.   *- Gautama - the Buddha*

For better, for worse, for richer, for poorer, in sickness and in health, to love and to cherish, till death do us part.   *- the Marriage Service*

Christians didn't invent marriage! Shifting customs and underlying values regulate it in every society and, no doubt, it has grown out of our biological need to nurture our offspring. Christian marriage today sees love as finding its full freedom in an exclusive relationship:

- that involves unconditional commitment
- that gives the greatest opportunity for development
- that presupposes an equality of respect
- that gives children a stable and loving environment
- that teaches us healing, forgiveness and renewal
- and that frees us for wider friendships, becoming the foundation of a good society.

Such a list is dismaying, as normally 'life's not like that'! Yet we can hold such ideals with humility and humour, and with God's help, may achieve a 'good enough' marriage, with no great regrets. This is not to devalue the functional side of marriage. There remain practical advantages in the close, working partnership of a man and a woman.

The founding of a family is not a private matter, and both civil and religious ceremonies recognise the new reality. The Christian ceremony is an occasion for two families coming together to share:

- thanksgiving and celebration
- a solemn and unqualified commitment
- the 'bereavement' experienced by parents letting their 'children' go
- the promise of God's continued blessing.

The ceremony does not of itself constitute the marriage (it is only in more recent times that church and state have sought to insist on a strict distinction). Love and commitment are in themselves signs of God's blessing already given. What can make a relationship 'sinful' is exploitation, not it's legality. Nor is it ideal that everyone should marry. Single people can find fulfilment in other ways. Jesus' difficult saying — Mt 10:37 — would suggest that family life itself needs to be caught up into a greater vocation.

....

A 1631 edition of the King James Bible rendered Ex 20:14 as ' Thou shalt commit adultery'. Unfortunately, this edition was withdrawn.

....

Let no one be unfaithful to the wife of his youth.　　　　　　　　*Mal 2:15*

Do not commit adultery.　　　　　　　　　　　　　　　　　*Ex 20:14*

Jealousy is worse than adultery.　　　　　　　　　　　*Bertrand Russell*

Do not separate those whom God has joined together.　　　*Jesus - Mt 19:6*

If the unbelieving partner wants a separation, it should be given.　　*Paul - I Cor 7:15*

Go and bestow your love on a woman loved by another man, an adulteress; love her, as I the Lord love the Israelites.　　　　　　　　　　　　　*Hos 3:1*

Seldom, or perhaps never, does a marriage develop into an individual relationship smoothly and without crises; there is no coming to consciousness without pain.　　*Jung*

Divorce should be possible only when a marriage has broken down beyond the power of restoration.　　　　　　　　　　　*Methodist Conference 1980*

There can be little reason for keeping within the bonds of legal marriage two people between whom no spiritual marriage exists.　　　*Society of Friends 1949*

If a wife fears cruelty or desertion on her husband's part, there is no blame on them if they arrange an amicable settlement between themselves; and such a settlement is the best way.　　　　　　　　　　　　　　　　　*The Qur'an*

The only ground for divorce which is appropriate is that the marriage has irretrievably broken down.　　　　　　　　*Lord Mackay - the Lord Chancellor*

Cohabitation meant marriage. What was, and still is, condemned was any relationship that was adulterous or incestuous.　　　*Rabbi Jonathan Romain*

I decided very early on that it was no use relying on anyone but yourself, so any relationship that implied giving anything of yourself away was bound to be frightening. I think that's modified itself now to a lingering conviction that nothing nice can last for long.　　　　　　　　　　*Jean - 25 yr. - whose parents divorced*

....

Annulment:

The Catholic Church does not allow divorce but an annulment can be obtained if it can be shown that the marriage bond did not exist: i.e.

- if there was no real consent or understanding of the implications,
- if the marriage was never consummated, or
- if there was a lack of intention — e.g. to have children.
  (60,000 annulments are granted each year in the USA)

Society is bound to recognise the reality of marriage breakdown. The attempt to preserve marriage by legal means alone perpetuates what is, in fact, an empty shell. Yet all societies discourage casual unions and try to ensure that family responsibilities are not lightly discarded.

In Jesus' teaching there is a clear ideal but also a recognition of human weakness. The church faces the same dilemma — encouraging its members to seek demanding goals, whilst recognising that they may fall short. It is the underlying reality that is important here, not the public, legal face of the marriage. In the Middle Ages, the church ceremony was the *confirmation* of the marriage not its inauguration. The older Christian tradition was that marriage was a matter of mutual consent regardless of lawyers. The relationship might develop by degrees and include pre-marital intercourse as the couple felt ready. Church lawyers changed this at the Council of Trent — 16C. (in 1753 in England). Only then did 'living in sin' become possible as an accusation.

When we have grasped the fact that that the ceremony does not *create* the marriage, or bring God into it for the first time, then we can put the issues into perspective. When a marriage is broken, the vows are already redundant, made so by countless failings In the light of a faith that promises new life, a new relationship can be sought, with the same goals expressed in vows to a new partner.

The task of church and society is to offer preparation, help and mediation as appropriate and to give support and understanding to existing marriages, especially when under strain. If common values cannot be agreed, then there should be alternative ceremonies for differing standards (Paul accepts that such differences will arise — I Cor 7:15). When a marriage is ended, the task is to ensure that proper responsibilities are not shelved in respect of property, finance and, above all, children. We are more conscious today of the continuing duties of both parents towards their children (in Islamic law, the father retains complete responsibility for their maintenance).

If divorce has become 'easier' in Britain (until 1857 it needed an Act of Parliament for one divorce), it should not follow that the great challenge of marriage has been abandoned. Christians will continue to draw attention to the misery involved in promiscuous and selfish relationships, and the high calling of, and richness to be found in, a totally committed, lifelong relationship.

ETHICS

To have a child is the nearest we come to the creativity of God.   *Rabbi Jonathan Sacks*

Let the children come, for they belong to the Kingdom of God.   *Jesus - Mk 10:14*

Young people now love luxury; they have bad manners, contempt for authority; they contradict their parents and tyrannise their teachers.   *Socrates - 400BC*

When a man has a son who is out of control, then his parents are to bring him to the elders, after which the men of the town must stone him to death.   *- from Dt 21:18f*

Break his will betimes; begin the great work before they can run alone, before they can speak plain — break his will now and his soul will live.   *John Wesley*

Children, obey your parents — fathers, do not cause your children to turn against you.
Paul - Eph 6:1

What children expect from grown-ups is not to be 'understood' but to be loved.
Carl Zucker

Women are entitled to become mothers by artificial insemination.
UK Human Fertility and Embryology Authority

Fatherlessness is extremely bad news for children, precipitating them into poverty and lasting emotional problems.   *Valerie Grove*

When my mother and my father reject me, then God will adopt me.   *Ps 27:10*

Do not kill your children in fear of poverty. We will support them and you.
The Qur'an - Surah 81:8

Train up a child in the way you should have gone yourself.   *Charles H Spurgeon*

A child is not a vase to be filled, but a fire to be lit.   *Rabelais*

You are the bows from which your children as living arrows are sent forth. Let your bending in the Archer's hand be for gladness.   *Kahlil Gibran*

It needs courage to let our children go, but we are trustees and stewards and have to hand them back to life — to God. We have to love them and lose them.   *Alfred Torrie*

If your parents take care of you up to the time you cut your teeth, you take care of them when they lose theirs.   *Akan proverb - Ghana*

The biological imperative is to produce children but today we can easily underestimate the instinctive drive to provide offspring — particularly male — for the survival of family or community. The preference for males was a matter of power and protection — they were, biologically speaking, more dispensable (in time of war). We are now able to value both sexes alike.

Scripture does not insist that intercourse must be linked with procreation — I Cor 7:5 — and however high a calling parenthood may be, there seems to be no requirement to bear children without restriction. Birth control can be part of responsible parenthood and involve the sincere recognition of divine providence just as surely as leaving conception entirely to chance. Likewise, in-vitro fertilisation may lead us further down a road which regards babies as a kind of consumer product but it can also be part of the long co-operation between human and divine creativity that need not jettison reverence and gratitude.

The greater threat to vocational parenthood may come from the disordering of priorities that places wealth, and therefore work, before the welfare of children. It may come too from underestimating the demands of parenthood. It is no reflection on single parents to say that the parental sharing of love and responsibility gives a child greatly increased chances at all stages of growing up, as well as making independence an easier step when the time comes. It is questionable whether anyone should *choose* to have a child outside such a stable relationship. At the same time society needs to do its utmost to support those who have no choice in the matter.

The rediscovery of the family becomes ever more urgent. It is here that we should learn accepting and giving, self-regard and regard for others, discipline and forgiveness, inherited identity and fresh opportunity. It is here that we learn to discover ourselves and glimpse something of the reality of God.

Statistics (Great Britain):
- 25% of children are in one parent families (8% in 1971).
- over 2% of children are with mothers who never married.
- fewer than 2% of children are with lone fathers.
- 30% of couples are childless at the time of survey.
- household size has dropped from 2.91 people to 2.36 in 7 years.
- 29% of households are one person (17% in 1971).

General Household Survey 1998.

ETHICS

....

Disease is very healthy. The immune system is designed to cope with it.
Dr Paul Pearsall

The advent of civilisation dealt a blow to man's health from which he is only now recovering.
Prof James Neel

Stress is necessary and can hold a structure together.
Dr David Lewis

I have learned to be content whatever my circumstances.
Paul - Phil 4:11

If it should ever prove possible to find some means of making people gentler and wiser than heretofore, I believe that means will be found in medicine.
Descartes

If God had decreed from all eternity that a certain person should die of smallpox, it would be a frightful sin to avoid and annul that decree by the trick of vaccination.
Timothy Dwight - 19C. President of Yale University

Value the services of a doctor for his calling comes from God and his skill from the Most High.
Ecclus 38:1

Sometimes corporal disease proceeds from sin and when the soul is healed, the corporal malady is more wholesomely treated.
Statutes of the Synod - Exeter 1287

One doctor writes of a case where a man's happiness and that of his wife and family, his affections, and even his religious belief and faith in God were imperilled by the fact that he was not drinking enough water to keep up his blood pressure.
Leslie D Weatherhead

We know a great deal about how to patch up many of the most common killers of Western society, but much less about how to prevent them and, in many cases, almost nothing about their causes.
David Weatherall
- President of the British Association for the Advancement of Science

We belong to one another like parts of one body.
Paul - Eph 4:25

I did nothing much, I listened to her fairy tales, danced with her a little, took her on my knee, and the job was done.
Jung - on healing a disturbed girl

In the end, only the wounded physician heals.
Epidaurus

....

EASE AND DIS-EASE [see 23,72] **138**

The challenge of medicine today is to hold together all the healing arts from the chemical laboratory to the psychiatrist's couch; from the surgeon's knife to spiritual advice; from the counsellor to the healing community. The holistic treatment of earlier times can now be allied to the great discoveries of scientific medicine. We can now:

- ➢ look at physical and spiritual needs together
- ➢ test and evaluate remedies more surely than ever before
- ➢ appreciate the value of positive beliefs in sustaining health
- ➢ value nursing and caring skills equally with diagnosis and drugs
- ➢ seek to understand 'wellness' and its relationship with environment and community.

The ideals of Hippocrates and the practice of Christian compassion are as valid as ever — not least in treating the old, the addicted and the mentally ill. The commercial health industry would screen from us the loss of vigour and youth so that expectations give way to indignation and litigation when we feel denied. There was some virtue in cultivating resignation to the will of God, but Jesus fought the ravages of sickness. Can we continue to do this and yet discover the secret of Paul's contentment?

Disease is surely not to the fore in the will of God, yet he has allowed it to exist in a world that has much to teach us. Buddhists believe that sickness results from the passions that are unreal creations of the mind. If we do not share this view, we can still recognise that we have much to learn about the interplay of mind and matter. We gratefully use the doctor's skill against physical enemies but the longer term search for health may well be a spiritual battle against ignorance, folly, sin and the 'dis-ease' that underlies much illness.

Health is not just an individual matter and we are not in the business of allocating blame — it is a matter for the community seeking to discover afresh the need for faith, hope and love, and a purpose for living. Without such saving graces, we inevitably erode our well-being. Is it not significant that, with all the means at our disposal, we have not rolled back the enemies that face us. Perhaps this is simply that the evolutionary 'arms race' will always be in balance, or perhaps it is because we have not realised sufficiently the healing community — our way of living and our relationships, one with another, continually show that all things are connected in the web of life. We are, for better or for worse, members of one another.

....

Do you not know that your body is a temple where the spirit of God lives?

Paul - I Cor 6:19

Doubtless I am free to do anything, but I will not let anything make free with me.

Paul - I Cor 6:12

Be careful that this freedom does not become a problem for the weak.   *Paul - I Cor 8:9*

Almost every culture in the world has felt the need for an escape route from mundane reality, or for a direct line to the supernatural.   *Jancis Robinson*

Who has trouble? Who has remorse? Who has quarrels and anxiety? Who gets the bruises without knowing why? Whose eyes are bloodshot? He who lingers over the wine.

Prov 23:29

Those who govern should not crave strong liquor. They will forget the law and trample on the rights of the defenceless.   *Prov 31:4*

Lord, my God, you are indeed great. You make grass for cattle and plants for humanity — producing grain from the earth and wine to cheer the hearts of the people.

Ps 104:1,14

Allah has cursed khamr (alcohol), those who produce it, those for whom it is produced, those who drink it, those who serve it, those who carry it, those it is carried to, those who sell it and those who buy it.   *Hadith - Muslim*

The lack of inner values, the narrow outlook, the inability to live life (in the highest sense of the term) are what have given us hard drinking.
- article in a Moscow atheist magazine on 'spiritual emptiness' - 1981

I am convinced that wide use of cannabis would in the long run cause terrible psychological and social devastation.   *Andrew Wilski - consultant psychiatrist*

The campaign against smoking has certainly caused more crippling illness and premature death than if it had never begun.   *Woodrow Wyatt*

Herein is a great contempt for God's good gifts, that man's breath should be wilfully corrupted by this stinking smoke.   *King James - 1598*

....

Work is the curse of the drinking classes.   *Oscar Wilde*

Apart from medicinal uses, drugs have been used throughout human history for recreation, conviviality and heightened awareness. Alcohol is an excellent social drug and tobacco a source of comfort and relaxation. Younger generations look to a range of drugs for pleasure and excitement and we have to acknowledge the positive aspects of some of these, before we can helpfully tackle the negative side. There is an over-reaction of age against youth, well illustrated by government and media over ecstasy deaths:

> ➤ several hundred deaths each year are attributed in the UK to ecstasy, cocaine and heroin but
> ➤ Sir Richard Peto estimates that 5 million of today's smokers will die from tobacco in the next 50 years.

It is the abuse of alcohol, in fact, which is the greatest danger for the young — far more serious than the toll taken by illegal drugs. Tens of thousands will die from cirrhosis of the liver. As many again will be deeply affected by alcoholism. To this should be added the related problems of work loss, crime and road accidents.

The global drug trade probably began when Britain developed opium growing in India, in order to sell to China. We created Hong Kong as a world centre for drug trafficking, and it has remained a scourge of the West ever since. Other countries heavily involved in drug production have first been ravaged by poverty or war (Colombia and Afghanistan). This is a stark warning to us all.

But if warlords and drug barons target the streets of wealthy nations, the latter are no less culpable. Tobacco barons have turned to aggressive marketing in the third world and sought, under the banner of free trade, to prohibit all restrictions linked with health campaigns. There are immense profits to be made from human misery, whatever the legalities or illegalities may be.

We can distinguish between the damage caused by certain chemicals and the degree of vulnerability to addiction, which varies between individuals. Addiction brings loss — of responsibility, of freedom and of self. All forms of addiction may indicate a spiritual malaise. It is commonest in disintegrating communities where identity and purpose are hard to find. It could be a displaced native community or a crumbling housing estate. It could equally be a broken family or some inner despair or the empty indulgence of the bored rich. The best defence against the abuse of drugs is a faith to live by, recognition from others, and the opportunity to face the future with cheerfulness.

ETHICS

....

On his doorstep lay a poor man named Lazarus.   *Jesus - Lk 16:20*

Whoever has been given a lot, much will be expected of him.   *Jesus - Lk 12:48*

Some labour under an enormity of clothes, others perish with the cold.
Some are inundated with delicacies and feast like Dives, clothed in purple, and Lazarus
dies of hunger at the gate.   *Alcuin - to the king of Northumbria*

If He who created us had ordained that one part of the human race should grow rich
and fat on the sighs and sufferings, the tears, the toil and the blood of the other, then we
should bend the knee to our fate — but we utterly deny the blasphemous doctrine.
         James O'Brien - 1833

The few rich are the cause of the many poor.   *Bp Fastidius 5C*

I should welcome the poor to my feast, for they are God's children.
I should welcome the rich to my feast, for they are God's joy.
         Brigid of Kildare - 5C.

There will not be any poor among you if you obey the Lord your God.   *Deut 15:4*

The gods only laugh when people ask them for money.   *Japanese saying*

There are three conversions necessary — of the heart, the mind, and the purse.   *Luther*

A man who dies rich, dies disgraced.   *- attributed. to Andrew Carnegie*

Let your alms sweat in you palm until you know to whom you are to give. The Didache

When you give of your possessions, you give but little.   *Kahlil Gibran*

There is no possible help for the poor if they will not help themselves. It is to a rise and
reformation in the habits of the peasantry that we look for deliverance and not to the
impotent crudities of a speculative legislation.   *Thomas Chalmers*

Be neither miserly nor prodigal, for then you should either be reproached or reduced to
penury.   *The Qur'an - surah 17*

It is scarcity, not sufficiency that makes people generous.   *E Evans-Pritchard*

What good is the moon if you cannot buy or sell it?   *Ivan Boesky - speculator*

When you are down to your last two loaves, sell one and buy a lily.   *Chinese*

....

All wealth is gift. It is the earth itself — flowing with milk and honey. It is God's promise of prosperity to a community that obeys his laws. If we together cultivate the earth, profit from its resources and enjoy it, then this is part of God's intention. To respect wealth is to respect the earth and our community upon it. If we plunder the earth and ignore community, then we abuse the gift.

Part of the problem of poverty is that of exclusion from the community — it is the rejection that comes from the denial of relationships and lack of opportunity. The absolute poor may be rich in community — the relative poor may be far better off but marginalised. In wider economic terms both capitalist monopoly and state socialism can be a denial of true personhood — the reduction of worker or consumer to an object.

Some historians now suggest that money originated first to build up relationships and create friendship, and only as a secondary objective to facilitate trade. The free flow of gifts and mutually beneficial exchange fostered common interest and created peace.

Money, as such, is neutral but it's use becomes the occasion for vice and virtue, greed and generosity. Instead of being a servant, it becomes a master and 'no one can serve two masters' (Mt 6:24). If our priorities are wrong, money seduces us and becomes our god. Then we have to submit to iron economic laws or live for the vagaries of chance — forgetting our true 'weal', the wealth of all priceless things, which belong to life.

Wealth not only builds community; it is usually created by the community. The wealth creators, contrary to some opinion, are rarely the small minority who are conspicuous by what they 'own'.
All wealth is the product of original resource, past creativity and present industry, for which stewardship we are answerable to God.
The issues of wealth are always: how was it created, at whose expense, and for whose benefit?

The sharing or redistribution of wealth becomes a matter of justice and a matter of relationship, not a matter of charity. The old Jewish and Christian prohibition of usury was born out of the fear of exploitation based on excessive interest. Today we are faced with the challenge as to whether an economy based on debt can lead to true community, or whether its long-term instability must force us to search for new solutions.

ETHICS

....

God put humanity in the garden of Eden to cultivate it and look after it. Gen 2:15

Only by the sweat of your brow will you have bread. Gen 3:19

The gods have ordained sweat as the price of all things precious. Hesiod

Let those who are lazy learn the ways of the ant and gain wisdom. Prov 1:6

Craftsmen maintain the fabric of this world — their craft is their prayer. Ecclus 38:34

A scholar's wisdom depends on having ample leisure. Ecclus 28:24

What reward does anyone have for all his work and toil here under the sun?
  Eccles 2:22

We worked for a living rather than be a burden to any of you. Paul - II Thess 3:8

The poor without employment are like rough diamonds, their worth is unknown.
  John Bellers

Through work we are able to attain Buddhahood. Suzuki Shosan - 17C.

Work is not only a means of life but itself life's prime want. Karl Marx

Let me not live to be useless. John Wesley

There can be no joy of life without joy of work. Aquinas

When Adam delved and Eve span, who was then the gentleman? John Ball

Intelligence has beamed upon the mind of the bondsman that all wealth, comfort and produce, everything valuable, useful, and elegant have sprung from the palm of his hand. The Great Charter - 1842

To maintain the Christian quality in the world of business and of domestic life, and to maintain it without pretension or hypocrisy, was the great achievement of these extraordinary people. G M Trevelyan - on the Quakers

If Christians agreed that the primary purpose of industry is the stewardly care of God's creation, we should act more wisely. A B Cramp

....

Judaism honoured daily work and its rabbis followed a trade. This tradition passed through Jesus the carpenter and Paul the tentmaker into Christianity. Benedictines, Cistercians, Carthusians and other orders set work alongside contemplation as part of their service to God. Neither Greek philosophy nor aristocratic influence could turn Catholic or Protestant away from this work ethic.

In Genesis, man has a vocation to cultivate the untamed earth in co-operation with God. Work is not 'the curse of Adam' [9]. It is human disobedience that brings disharmony between humanity and the environment. If the earth is subject to humanity, it nevertheless follows God's order, and will repay greed and exploitation with 'thorns and thistles'. Eden is not meant to lose its joy nor should work be just drudgery and all consuming. Despite this:

- there is nothing romantic or unreal about the Jewish understanding of work. Its attitude is practical and down to earth — recognising the necessity of work for survival
- leisure too is essential — see the sabbath laws — the rhythm of work and rest contributing to life's wholeness (holiness)
- work builds community and is a service we render to each other. Human interdependence is recognised by the writer of Ecclesiasticus, and this is as true today, when every industry should exist for the service of others
- in such community, choice is enhanced and purpose readily discovered. The tragedy of the unemployed is not just financial but also spiritual since their place in the community, together with their personal self-esteem, is undermined.

The **parable of the labourers** - Mt 20:1-16 - may be Jesus' way of saying that Gentiles coming late into the Kingdom would be treated the same as his own people. It illustrates, nevertheless, the tension between the values of the Kingdom and the requirements of economics. Casual workers may be fairly paid by the hour but God (represented by the owner) responds to their *needs*.

The Friends

The Quakers are remembered most for their pacifist witness but Trevelyan celebrates their contribution in business. The Darbys, Frys, Cadburys, Rowntrees, Lloyds, Barclays, and others built their success on industry, integrity and the respect shown to their employees. Together with humanist pioneers like Robert Owen, they set standards in business, which can command universal respect. Add to this the Quaker contribution to education, welfare, the anti-slavery movement, prison reform and political reform, and we have a record of social service unsurpassed by any group of comparable size.

....

*The poor will always be with you, and that is why I command you to be generous
towards any who are in poverty and need.*   *Deut 15:11*

The poor will always be there.   *Jesus - Mk 14:17*

*When you reap the harvest — what is left is for the stranger, the orphan and the
widow.*   *Deut 24:19f.*

*Speak for those who cannot speak for themselves — and stand up for the wretched and
the poor.*   *Prov 31:8-9*

*They began to sell their property and possessions and share with everyone according to
his need.*   *Luke - Acts 2:45*

From each according to his abilities: to each according to his needs.   *Marx*

*If anyone does not make provision ... for his own family, he has denied his faith and is
worse than an unbeliever*   *Paul - I Tim 5:8*

*Not from your own do you bestow upon the poor — for what has been given is common
for the use of all.*   *Bp Ambrose of Milan - 4C.*

Anyone who will not work, should not eat.   *Paul - II Thess 3:10*

*Here is thy footstool and there rest thy feet, where live the poorest, the lowliest and the
lost.*   *Tagore*

Bread for myself is a material question: bread for my neighbour is a spiritual question.
         Berdyaev

*There is no possible help for the poor if they will not help themselves. It is to a rise in the
habits of our peasantry that we look for deliverance and not the impotent crudities of a
speculative legislation.*   *Thomas Chalmers*

*I must refuse to insult the naked by giving them clothes they do not need instead of
giving them work which they sorely need.*   *Gandhi*

*It is but equity that they who feed, clothe and lodge the people should have such a share
of their own labour as to be tolerably well fed, clothes and lodged.*   *Adam Smith*

*Poverty is an anomaly to rich people: it is very difficult to make out why people who
want dinner do not ring the bell.*   *Walter Bagehot*

....

THE STATE OF WELFARE [see 75,81] **142**

The Christian (and human) responsibility for the welfare of all requires especial concern for the poor and needy, children and elderly, sick and disabled, the stranger, the refugee and the prisoner.

It seems a straightforward matter. Perhaps it was, when family and local community took care of their own, when almsgiving was accepted by all and temple or church was the centre of welfare. Maybe their dilemmas were just the same but on a smaller scale. In fact, welfare is fraught with difficulty. We know that:

➢ generous help can create debilitating dependence
➢ an open door for refugees can cause social breakdown
➢ compassion for prisoners may undermine the salutary nature of punishment
➢ the efficiency of state welfare can sink into impersonality.

The problems of power and the intractability of human nature mean that hard choices are inescapable. The tensions are already there in the New Testament, as a comparison of the idealistic note in Luke's account of early communism (Acts 2:44f.) with the practical advice given by Paul to Timothy (I Tim 5:3f.) clearly shows. Utopian visions have failed again and again but world-weariness is not a Christian option. The striving for new models of co-operation and community building is an urgent Christian calling as we reach towards the values of the Kingdom of God. — but they have to be well earthed.

The created order is not indulgent and demands effort and struggle. Out of this comes the right balance of dependence and independence. Our Welfare State is committed to the same search. In these things also we have to 'work out our own salvation' — Phil 2:12. One of our first calls is to honour the work of managers and politicians who pursue the art of the possible with integrity.

Some of our guiding principles might be:
➢ support the family as the primary unit of welfare
➢ to give every encouragement to charitable and voluntary work as this has the great advantages of being both flexible and personal
➢ to seek self-help initiatives and solutions wherever possible, as these encourage dignity and responsibility
➢ to provide a safety net which permits more than survival
➢ to build paths out of poverty and dependence
➢ to tackle the social causes of deprivation
➢ to renew the faith of the despondent in themselves.

ETHICS

....

Put God's Kingdom and his justice first.   Jesus - Mt 6:33

Life for life, eye for eye, tooth for tooth.   Deut 19:21

I thought of all the acts of oppression perpetrated under the sun; I saw the tears of the oppressed, and there was no one to comfort them.   Eccles 4:1

If anyone causes the downfall of one of these children, it would be better for him if he were to have a millstone hung round his neck and be drowned in the depths of the sea.
Jesus - Mt 18:6

Laws human must be made according to the general laws of nature, otherwise they are ill-made.   Richard Hooker - 16C.

The country's planted thick with laws from coast to coast and if you cut them down, d'you really think you could stand upright in the winds that would blow then?
Thomas More - in Robert Bolt's 'A Man for all Seasons'

It was said to the men of olden time: him whom the court condemns, the court shall put to death. But I say unto you, if a court puts to death only one man in 70 years, that court is a court of murderers.   The Talmud

The first care must be to find a good man for a gaoler; one that is honest, active and humane.   John Howard 1777

It is better that ten guilty persons should escape than that one innocent suffer.
Sir William Blackstone - 18C.

If only there were evil people somewhere insidiously committing evil deeds, and it were necessary only to destroy them. But the line dividing good and evil cuts through the heart of every human being.   Solzhenitsyn

Whoever has never done any wrong may cast the first stone.   Jesus - Jn 8:7

If you and I plain truth must tell, everything human we comprehend, only too well, too well!   Walter de la Mare

Criminality and serious psychological disorder are part of the price we pay for the society we have.   Dr Masud Hoghughi - clinical psychologist

Revenge must be left in my hands, says the Lord.   Deut 10:7

Justice is worth as much as there is love in it.   The Talmud

....

Christian thinking begins with the bedrock of laws drawn from Jewish tradition and arising from the principles of the Ten Commandments. The cry for justice, whether on behalf of an oppressed people or an oppressed individual, must never be lost in an over-sentimental view of human nature. It is right that there is both anger for the wrong done and compassion for the victims.

Yet justice must be limited — an eye for an eye and no more, setting limits to hate and vengeance. And it must be impartial, with punishment decided accordingly. Punishment is not sub-Christian. It is a recognition of responsibility over against the kind of determinism that robs an individual of dignity. A modern dilemma is that diagnostic psychiatry can usually state a case for diminished responsibility and treat the offender as patient rather than criminal — an *apparently* humane course, which undermines true personhood.

Retribution is to repay a debt that is owed. Church and law courts throughout the ages have tried to assess that debt and require just payment, but decisions seem often far removed from the injured party. It may be that Truth and Reconciliation Commissions, such as that convened when apartheid ended in South Africa, may teach us more about a restorative justice which gives due place to the victims.

Christians also recognise a corporate responsibility. None of us is 'without sin', and all of us are accountable to God. Often enough our society has a duty to address the situation that contributed to the offence. If society is sick, it is manifested in its casualties, which include both victims and offenders. This is not to say that all the blame attaches to the social environment but that it cannot be, and should not be, discounted. At the moment it is commonplace for 'white-collar crime', which may defraud thousands of their savings or pensions, to be treated more leniently than theft by those of lesser social status. Yet there may be less excuse for the former — much should be expected of those who have received much.

Ultimately there must be place for compassion — and no grudging compassion at that. It is recognition of one who is yet a child of God and who, by will or circumstance, has become other. The claim of forgiveness — of restoration — does not mean that a debt must not be paid. It does mean that the search for reform and rehabilitation becomes a necessity. No one is beyond redemption. We could start with the root and branch reform of our prisons.

The Year: 949 BC   The Place: Jerusalem

The procession moved slowly from the great throne room of the palace, through the state hall, lined with 600 shields of beaten gold, and across the courtyard. The Cilician horses, harnessed to their chariots below the walls, snorted and threw out their necks as the trumpets rent the air. Solomon, with his Egyptian wife, daughter of the Pharaoh, moved with the long line of priests into the vestibule of the Temple and into the main hall. At the far end, the great winged cherubim guarded the entrance to the Holy of Holies. Twenty years into his reign, the king had fulfilled the dream of his father, David.

The trumpets died away but outside the noise of oxen and sheep was indescribable and soon the massive altar would run with blood and a pall of smoke would ascend in a cloud of flies. Then the king knelt and his voice rang out:
"Lord God of Israel, there is no God like you in heaven above or on earth beneath, keeping covenant with your servants and showing them constant love while they keep faithful to you with all their hearts". Billows of incense accompanied the great prayer and eddied around the roof timbers.

"Can God indeed dwell on earth? Heaven itself, the highest heaven, cannot contain you; how much less this house that I have built! Yet hear, Lord the cry which your servant makes before you this day, that your eyes may ever be on this house night and day, this place of which you said: 'My name will be there.' Hear the request of your servant and your people Israel when they pray towards this place. Hear in heaven your dwelling and when you hear, forgive."

And so for seven days the prayers and celebrations continued, and on the eighth day Solomon dismissed the people.

And yet … so often the vision is lost and so often human striving becomes ensnared in ambiguity. Lesser priests and bureaucrats will have their way and God is enclosed in cedar and gold, entombed in marble and stone, locked away in temple and church. As for Solomon himself; he fulfilled the dire warnings of Samuel, when the people asked for a king, even as the nations round about had kings:

"This will be the kind of king who will reign over you. He will take your sons and make them serve in his chariots and with his cavalry, and they will run before his chariot. Some he will appoint officers over units of a thousand and units of fifty. Others will

plough his fields and reap his harvest; others again will make weapons of war and equipment for the chariots. He will take your daughters for perfumers, cooks and bakers. He will seize the best of your fields, vineyards and olive groves, and give them to his courtiers...... There will come a day when you will cry out against the king whom you have chosen; but the Lord will not answer you on that day."

I Sam.8:11f.

Whether these words were written with foresight or hindsight, they sum up the king who sponsored arts and scholarship and became known for his wisdom, and yet was an oppressor. Thousands of slaves worked for him in the mines of Arabah and in the copper refinery at Ezion-geber. Thirty thousand young men were conscripted into forced labour. Inequalities grew and taxation bore down on the poor. Himself the issue of David's greatest crime — the murder of Bathsheba's husband — Solomon showed even less regard for the laws of God and paved the way for the ruin of his kingdom:

"Your songs, your sayings and your proverbs were wonders of the world. In the name of the Lord God ... you amassed gold and silver like so much tin and lead .... You stained your reputation and tainted your line. You brought God's wrath upon your children and there was outrage at your folly."

ben Sirach: Ecclus. 47:20f.

And the priests? They naturally fell into line. The king whose palace walls overshadowed their quarters was more immediate than the one who was sovereign of heaven and earth. Their status and their power lay with Solomon. Was not the Lord with him? In the days when the Hebrews were still nomadic, God was one who called from the mountain tops and from the desert, who belonged to the star-lit sky and the storm. Solomon recognised this but there is ambiguity here. The palace was built first and only then was the Temple added — effectively a royal chapel. This was the kind of alliance which Constantine would seek in another age. The glory of the king would enhance the worship of God and the glory of God would serve the glory of the king. Here in Jerusalem the people would meet with both and marvel. It was a far cry from the simple Tent of Meeting, where Moses *"spoke with God face to face".*

So the stage was set for the further separation of the sacred from ordinary life and the priesthood from ordinary men and women. Here too would begin the long warfare between the divine right of kings and the prophetic voices which recalled the people to a lost vision.

PTO

GOVERNMENT

This is Babylon the Great which I have built by my mighty power and for the honour of my majesty.   *Nebuchadnezzar - Dan 4:30*

A tomb now suffices him for whom the whole world was not sufficient.
                                                            - anonymous epitaph for Alexander the Great

Communism aimed at making gods of men.   *David Landes*

Men must choose to be governed by God or they condemn themselves to be ruled by tyrants.   *William Penn*

It is not possible to found a lasting power upon injustice.   *Demosthenes*

A model of a transformed society must begin from the material structures that are given to us at this time in history.   *I Young*

Patriotism is not enough. I must have hatred for no man.   *Nurse Edith Cavell*

Civil community is spiritually blind and ignorant. It has neither faith, nor love, nor hope. Civil community can only have external, relative and provisional tasks and aims
                                                                            Karl Barth

If you have sacrificed my country to preserve the peace of the world, I shall be the first to applaud you. But if not, gentlemen, may God have mercy on your souls.
                         Jan Masaryk - Czech leader - to Neville Chamberlain 1938

We leave to others the passions and politics of the world, and nothing will ever be taught, I trust, in any of our halls, which shall have the remotest tendency to disturb the existing order of things.   *Thomas Chalmers*
            - a founder of the Free Church of Scotland which opposed the establishment

Do not listen to those who say: 'The voice of the people is the voice of God'. The inconstancy of the people is always near to madness.   *Alcuin*

I am as much for government by consent as any man but if you ask how it is to be done, I confess I do not know.   *Cromwell*

The statesman's task is to hear God's footsteps marching through history and to try to catch on to his coat-tails as he marches by.   *Bismarck*

Politics and the pulpit are terms that have little agreement. No sound ought to be heard in the church but the healing voice of Christian charity.   *Burke*

....

How can you govern a country with two hundred and forty six varieties of cheese?
                                                                    Charles de Gaulle

Can we solve the problem of power — whether of large organisations, trans-national corporations or countries? It could be argued that Jesus is of little help to us. He did not seek power for himself and he sided with the powerless. He acknowledged Pilate's authority and the rights of Caesar. He did not ask the tax collector or the centurion to abandon his post. Yet Christians can argue that:

➤ power belongs to God and leaders can claim no final authority
➤ all are answerable to God and to the law
➤ power does not justify arrogance or contempt for others
➤ it is best characterised by the ideals of service.

Democracy can make possible the rightful use of power but we know well how it can be abused, both by those who manipulate public opinion and by the 'inconstancy of the people'. Among those who sought to restrict government by separating law from private morality were the Lutherans, August Francke and Christian Thomasius.There is justification for the way in which democratic states develop several power centres and ensure that one is always subject to the scrutiny of another. The churches themselves are a valuable part of this structure — criticising and being criticised.

Democracy in trans-national corporations and finance houses is far from a reality. Increasingly they are run by a self-selecting elite — a new world aristocracy — networking across financial and business institutions. Individual shareholders of independent spirit face a hard task to influence powerful investment groups, which themselves are run by a similar elite. Consumer power, galvanised by campaigning groups, may be a sign for the future and the strongest governments can still use regulatory powers effectively but will modern communications assist the dispersal of power or will it escape all government control?

Idealistic Christians seek more than patriotism and support greater communities and the United Nations. A vision of falling barriers and international brotherhood is part of the dream of the Kingdom but alongside that is the hard reality of human fallibility. Few large conglomerates look inspiring at close quarters. The warning remains that *'small is beautiful'* (E F Schumacher) and that the local, the personal and the known are preferable to distant authority.

Where government overreaches itself and creates a new Babylon, our duty may be to oppose it in the name of God. The challenge is to do this without creating a mirror image of the oppressor.

....

It was I who created the smith to fan the coals in the fire and forge weapons for every purpose; and I created the destroyer to deal out havoc.   Is 54:16

When the Lord God delivers them into your power, you must exterminate them.
                                                                        Deut 7:2

War is part of God's arrangements for the world.   Helmuth von Moltke

The Pathan is never at peace except when he is at war.   Afghan saying

Cain rose up against his brother Abel and killed him.   Gen 4:8

The same honour waits for the coward and the brave. They both go down to Death.
                                                                Homer - The Iliad

Was it for this the clay grew tall?   Wilfred Owen

Rachel was weeping for her children, and refused to be comforted, because they were no more.   Mt 2:18 - after Jer 31:15

Better to be among the victims than among the killers.   The Talmud

Unless there is some point at which you are prepared to fight, all principles become flexible and all ends in themselves disappear.   Isaiah Berlin

Of all our human hallmarks, the one that has been derived most straightforwardly from animal precursors is genocide.   Jared Diamond

The geological record is full of cases where the development of enormous horns and spines has been the prelude to extinction.   J B S Haldane

Fight for the sake of Allah those who fight against you, but do not attack them first.
                                                                The Qur'an 21

What terrifies us is not the explosive power of the atomic bomb but the power of wickedness of the human heart.   Einstein

War does not determine who is right; only who is left.   Bertrand Russell

The roaring of lions, the howling of wolves, the raging of the sea, and the destructive word are portions of eternity too great for the eye of man.   Blakes

You will hear of wars and rumours of wars. Do not despair.   Jesus - Mt 24:6

....

The world is a long way from being able to police itself other than by the alliance of its strongest powers pursuing their own interests. Not only the aberrant dictator but also the mutual distrust of peoples and the terrorist fringe of the deprived threaten the security of all. There are no guarantees possible in such a world. Neither ultimate deterrence, nor international groupings, nor unilateral disarmament, can give such assurances.

Technology races ahead and we can become either victor or victim through the power it affords. The restraints of chivalry, the principles of just warfare and the values agreed in human conventions fail easily in an age, when civilians still suffer alongside combatants and future generations bear the consequences of the sins of their parents. Nor is it any reassurance that democratic countries built on Christian culture have not only used atomic bombs but also chemical weapons (agent orange in Vietnam) and created yet more radiation sickness by the use of depleted uranium in shells (the Gulf War).

The search for clean, surgical military action will go on, and will probably elude us — even supposing that the world can be divided into the sinners and the righteous without qualification. Mistakes, atrocities and lies surround every action, and once the dogs of war are slipped, no one can predict the full consequences.

Even our longing for justice becomes a temptation — creating the cry that 'something must be done' and putting our faith in a military solution rather than doing nothing. The truth is that once peace has collapsed, the scope for truly moral action may have vanished too. Peacemaking must be done when the wood is green — Lk 23:31.

As it is, our fears distort the politics and economics of the world. The armaments bill prevents much else being achieved. 50% of scientists are said to work on defence-related projects. When military action is needed, unlimited resources are found and herculean efforts made. Can we not summon the same resolve for the work of peace? — or must we retreat behind ever-rising barricades from the despairing people of a hungry world?

For 250 years the Christians of Urakami had survived persecution. On August 9th. 1945, the atomic bomb exploded 500m. from their cathedral and thousands of them were among the 70,000 who perished in Nagasaki.

Sometime they'll give a war and nobody will come.   Carl Sandburg

....

Live in the virtue of that life and power that takes away the occasion for all wars.
George Fox

There is no bravery greater than a resolute refusal to bend the knee to an earthly power no matter how great, and that without bitterness of spirit and in the fullness of faith that the spirit alone lives, nothing else does.
Gandhi

He who has no power of resisting war may take part in war.
Gandhi

Where there is a choice between cowardice and violence, I would advise violence.
Gandhi

The Christian doctrine of love, operating through the Gandhian method of non-violence, is one of the most potent weapons available to an oppressed people in their struggle for freedom.
Martin Luther King

We shall match your capacity to inflict suffering by our capacity to endure suffering.
Martin Luther King

True peace is the way of agony.
Shimon Peres

Suppose you pay back evil with kindness. Then what are you going to repay kindness with?
Confucius

It takes the quiet of a suburban home for the birth of the thesis that non-violence corresponds to God's refusal to judge. In a scorched land, soaked with the blood of the innocent, it will invariably die.
Miroslav Volf

But what if I should discover that the very enemy himself is within me, that I myself am the enemy who must be loved. What then?
Jung

If the government reaction is to crush by naked force our non-violent struggle, we will have to reconsider our tactics.
Nelson Mandela - May 1961

Peacekeeping is no job for a soldier but only a soldier can do it.
Dag.Hammarskjold

Are we still of any use? We have been silent witnesses of evil deeds; we have learned the arts of equivocation and pretence — will our inward power of resistance be strong enough for us to find our way back to simplicity?
Dietrich Bonhoeffer

What misery, what destruction! But human nature is such that the human mind can wake up and find an alternative.
Tenzin Gyatso - the Dalai Lama

....

THE PEACEMAKERS

The resort to violence, even if it is a last resort, perpetuates hatred and division, obscures the true objectives, and degrades everyone concerned. Even if, at that moment, there seems to be little alternative, there is often the recognition that we did not recognise soon enough ' the things that make for peace'.

If Christians, together with all men and women of goodwill, mobilised all possible resources, we could build peace. If nations devoted the same energy and resource in times of quiet as in time of war, we could ensure that most conflict was stillborn. If we took a long-term view and held steadily to humanitarian goals, we could break the cycle of violence.

None of this is easy — evil is very real and evildoers can be utterly unscrupulous. Nothing will be achieved in one bound and God alone knows whether a peaceful world is achievable. Can we, nevertheless, set ourselves some guidelines?

➤ to honour the vocation of responsible armed forces but use them in constructive roles whenever possible.
➤ to honour the pacifist traditions in many faiths and learn from their witness.
➤ to develop the rule of international law and the use of such sanctions as will uphold justice without impeding reconciliation.
➤ to call governments and other powerful bodies to account.
➤ to develop the disciplines of non-violent resistance as exemplified by Gandhi and Martin Luther King.

This last may well be the most important. Oppression can best be challenged from *within* the community — external force being clumsy and often counter-productive. The challenge has to come from ordinary people but it can only do so if they become extraordinary by their insight, unity and endurance.

Ultimately peace-making is a spiritual struggle and a harnessing of spiritual power. It needs teaching in our churches, it needs the common effort of the great faith communities; it needs vision, and it will claim casualties. Meanwhile, we have all to work out our individual vocation. It is said that Sir William Penn, in the early stages of the Quaker movement, asked George Fox whether he should still wear a sword. The answer came, 'Wear it as long as you can'. In the wisdom of that reply lies our duty to 'work out our salvation' (Phil 2:12). Our personal choices may differ, but we can share the overall aim — 'to take away the occasion for all wars'.

P.S. The circus-owner, Mr Barnum, kept a lion and a lamb in the same cage as an experiment. When asked, "Was it successful?", he replied, "Quite successful, except that from time to time, one has to renew the lamb."

ETHICS

If your brother Israelite is reduced to poverty you must help him as you would an alien or a stranger.   Lev 25:35

Have nothing to do with the people of this land or with foreign wives.   Ezra 10:11

Blessed be Egypt my people, Assyria the work of my hands, and Israel my inheritance
                                                                                     Is 19:25

I now understand how true it is that God has no favourites.   Peter- Acts 10:34

So peaceful are these people that there is not a better nation in the world.
                                                       Columbus on the native Americans - 1492

The Indian must be exterminated. He has no right to usurp the land that God intended us to make fruitful.   Frank Skimmerhorn - Colorado - 19C.

In the dust where we have buried the silent races and their abominations, we have buried so much of the delicate magic of life.   D H Lawrence

Gypsies wished to be slaves, because this would raise them, if not to the level of human beings, at least to a par with good domestic working animals.
                                                                     Dr Wickenhauser - 19C.

In the aversion which people feel towards strangers, we recognise the expression of self-love.   Freud

The result is an illness — the illness of those estranged from those to whom they belong.
                                                                              Kyle Haselden

Among the young Nazis judged as the living incarnation of concepts detested by humanity, were some of the best human beings in a humanitarian sense.
                                       Col Henry Faulk - involved in the re-education of German prisoners

An influx of men and women of alien race would be very undesirable.
                                                                         Arthur Bryant 1963

When we let freedom ring, when we let it ring from every village and hamlet, from every state and every city, we will be able to speed up that day when all of God's children, black men and white men, Jews and Gentiles, Protestants and Catholics, will be able to join hands and sing in the words of that old Negro spiritual, 'Free at last! Free at last! Thank God almighty, we are free at last!'   Martin Luther King

Prejudice (to 'pre-judge') can affect all kinds of relationships, where human differences may lead to discrimination or outright hostility. We have an innate preference for our own kind and a distrust of the stranger. We seem also to react to frustrations by projecting blame on to outsiders so as to safeguard our own self-worth. It is not difficult, therefore, for power-seekers to play upon our natural fear as a matter of expediency.

The Jewish people were, at times, driven in upon themselves in order to survive, and their exclusiveness then became an excuse for prejudice. Yet Jewish teaching was hospitable to the stranger — it was sympathy for a fellow Israelite that could not be taken for granted in Levitical law. The story of **Ruth** may well be a liberal tract against narrow nationalism, for Ruth, the Moabitess, was to be the great grandmother of King David.

Jesus praised both Romans and Samaritans as examples of faith and he recognised no social boundaries in his ministry. Peter led the way in ensuring that the Gospel was taken to the Gentiles (lit.'foreigners') as well as to his own people. Christians are surely called to confront prejudice by an honest assessment of the past — for example:
➢ that even as the US constitution welcomed the oppressed of Europe, the Supreme Court ruled that native Americans were 'aliens by birth'
➢ that in 1764 there were 20,000 black servants in London alone
➢ that half a million 'gypsies' died in the Great Devouring (as the Roma call the Holocaust).
Then by a better assessment of the present — realising that while many need to be freed from oppressive discrimination, we all need to be freed from the fears which restrict our humanity. This too is no easy road for most societies to travel. It can help if we recognise the universal parenthood of God and see that our calling and salvation is bound up with that of all humanity.

This is where, as we saw earlier, we can rescue the wonderful cartoon story of **Jonah** from literalism. The key to the story lies in Jonah's prayer — 2:2-9 — which is often ignored as an afterthought. The disaster is the ruin of the nation at the hands of a mighty empire that swallowed it up — see e.g. Jer 51:34f. In a text dated 21C. BC, Nineveh is represented by a great fish. The storm and chaos of waters adds to the drama with typical imagery [37]. Israel, through the understandably reluctant prophet, is commanded to care about the very people who are oppressing them — a vivid commentary on the teaching of Isaiah (see opposite).

....

Our material needs are the same as other people's, our children are as good as theirs; yet we have to force our sons and daughters into slavery.   *Nehemiah - 5:5*

May trouble come upon those who add house to house and field to field until everyone is displaced and they are left in sole possession of the countryside.   *Isaiah - 5:8*

The Indian's maps are in the way of the white men's dreams.   *Hugh Brody - 1981*

Free trade is God's diplomacy and there is no other certain way of uniting people in the bonds of peace.   *Richard Cobden*

World hunger will be eradicated within ten years.   *Henry Kissinger - 1974*

To search for solutions is not an act of benevolence but a condition of mutual survival.
The Brandt Report

Trade carried on with far-off foreign nations is often replete with cheating and extortion, and no limit is set to the profits.   *Calvin - notes on Is 2*

It is science alone that can solve the problems of hunger and poverty.   *Nehru*

If it took half the world to develop Britain, how many worlds will it take to develop India?   *Gandhi*

The gift of material goods makes people dependent. The gift of knowledge makes them free.   *Fritz Schumacher*

History tells us that the most successful cure for poverty comes from within.
David Landes

The little that one produces with a broken hoe is better than the plenty that another gives you.   *Buji proverb - Nigeria*

Tell them we still have a choice; to go the way of 1931 in competitive enmity, finishing up in darkness, death and war; or in the way of 1947, when the Marshall Plan was a symbol of co-operation between those with surpluses and those with deficits.
Barbara Ward - spoken in her final illness

Every noon at twelve in the blazing heat God comes to me in the form of two hundred grams of gruel.   *anon - India*

Humans are designed to do a lot more than survive.   *Muhammad Yunus*

....

We are one world — one people — one web of life. The welfare of all is our welfare. If conscience fails to convince us, then migration, violence and environmental degradation will make it all too clear.

It is said that charity begins at home, which is natural, though we do not always practise it. But charity should then ripple outwards until it takes in the whole world. Then, can we abandon the illusion that we are the world's benefactors, dispensing largesse out of our generosity? We are an integral part of the world and its peoples and we are as indebted to them as they to us — but the former debt is greater, as wealthy nations, wittingly or unwittingly, plunder the world and still hold it in bondage.

We have the resources; we can produce the food, and scientific skill will not desert us. UN studies suggest that we should be able to cope with population growth. But agriculture alone, technology alone and science alone will not solve the problems. What we still need is spiritual regeneration and the down-to-earth wisdom that will translate principles into practical politics.

We have seen immense waves of compassion and ready response to natural disaster. We have understood the need for long-term aid, sustained by the goodwill of many, and we have seen the darker problems of manipulation and corruption by both givers and receivers. We know that aid can be abused, that it can create dependency. Now we are beginning to recognise that there are major structural problems:
> - trade is often far from mutually beneficial
> - power and monopoly remain with the rich nations
> - debt becomes slavery for many.

The challenges are immense but so should be our resolve:
> - can we move beyond exploitation to sustainable development?
> - are the simplistic alternatives of free trade or protectionism blinkering our understanding of particular needs?
> - can we guarantee fair returns to third world producers?
> - can we ensure that trans-national corporations become the servants of national dignity and democracy?

These are spiritual matters no less urgent than the Christian call to personal regeneration — not least because Christians themselves need to understand and practise more fully the radical demand of their faith and to seek justice for all peoples.

The poor give aid to the rich:
The net flow of money *from* the third world to the first over a period of eight years after all profits, payments and aid is taken into account, is estimated at **$400 billion** — equivalent to six Marshall Plans. (The Marshall Plan brought American finance into the reconstruction of Europe after the second world war.)

Third World Debt: 1980 — $560 billion
⠀⠀⠀⠀⠀⠀⠀⠀⠀⠀⠀⠀⠀2005 — $2,740 billion (after huge repayments)
Debt servicing p.a. $500 billion. Official Aid: $100 billion.
Countries cannot go 'bankrupt' nor, unlike developed economies, can they call on taxpayers to help during a recession.

Sub-Saharan debt: 1962 — under $3 billion
⠀⠀⠀⠀⠀⠀⠀⠀⠀⠀⠀⠀⠀2005 interest payments $23 billion p.a.

The World Bank: reviewed 18 *of its own projects* that had been approved between 1980 and 1995. Only 3 of these were found to be able to repay their debts in the prescribed period.

Philippines: The Bataan nuclear power station was built in an earthquake zone by Westinghouse who admitted to giving a $14 million bribe to a close friend of President Marcos to secure the contract Cost $2.3 billion. Last payment: 2007 - $16.7 million. The power station has never been operational.

Sustainable debt: Experts now wish to reduce debt repayments for poor countries to 20-25% of overseas earnings. 'Heavily Indebted Poor Countries', whose repayments exceed 150% overseas earnings, have had some debts cancelled. Bangladesh is judged to have 'sustainable' debt, although 84% of the population live on less than $2 a day. (Germany's reparation payments after 1945 were 5%.)

Help given has made a difference: Malawi has 4,000 new teachers, Tanzania - 3 million more children in primary schools, Mozambique - 1 million children vaccinated.

....

It is doubtful whether we should benefit politically from making the poor countries richer than they are now — as the gap narrowed, we of the rich, would lose much political power.⠀⠀⠀⠀⠀⠀⠀⠀⠀*Lord Sudeley - House of Lords 1972*

It is a scandal that we are forced to choose between basic health and education for our people and repaying historical debt.⠀⠀⠀⠀⠀⠀⠀*President Mkapa of Tanzania*

....

If, in the wealthy world, the scale of debt has proved our undoing, how much more, can be the ruin suffered by the third world, where invisible chains keep whole peoples in bondage. Of course, debt is not the only problem — war, corruption and mismanagement exact an awful toll. Sometimes the injuries have been self-inflicted but sometimes too the rich countries have fostered the wars, created the corruption and imposed the mismanagement. Countries weakened by colonialism, disasters and internal strife have been unfair game for the inducements and coercion of the powerful outsider. Even well meant advice and investment has been found to be utterly misguided. How hollow, in the 1970's, the World Bank's assurance: 'there is no general problem of developing countries being able to service debt'. And how scorned any suggestion that the 'developed' countries would prove unable to do so in 2008/9.

Our naïve response is to blame poor for accepting credit. Some believed the promises, some had to survive, and some were committed by their dictators. They couldn't know how interest rates would rise dramatically and commodity prices fall. Now they find that they have lost their country's resources, their skilled personnel and their future — and still the debt-collector is at the gate.

Organised charity can only do so much. **Christian Aid, CAFOD, Tear Fund** and others harness the giving of the world church, avoid abuses by using local communities to administer aid and work for the long term — but much more than charity is needed. The **Jubilee Debt Campaign** made a real difference but the achievements are marginal as yet. (The campaign is based on Hebrew laws of debt limitation — Lev 25 — *Hallow the fiftieth year and proclaim liberation in the land* — v 10). Debt forgiveness runs up against the 'moral hazard' of encouraging the spendthrift to borrow without obligation but there is a far greater moral hazard — the fearful 'innocence' of the rich who cannot see why children are dying. The challenge is to:

> ➢ create international regulations which prevent exploitation,
> ➢ lend under mutually agreed constraints which limit liability,
> ➢ ensure that debts incurred by dictators are paid by them or die with them,
> ➢ enable the poor to help themselves — they will stand up if we get off their backs,
> ➢ limit the opportunities for capital flight (corrupt leaders of some 18 countries are estimated to have robbed their people of £123 billion, much of it now in Western banks) .

ETHICS

....

It is God's earth.   *Ps 24:1*

Be fruitful, spread across the world and take responsibility for it.   *Gen 1:28*

Glory to man in the highest, for man is the master of things.   *Swinburne*

The gentle shall inherit the earth.   *Jesus - Mt 5:5*

The meek shall inherit the earth but not the mineral rights.   *John Paul Getty*

The land is mine, and you are strangers and tenants of mine.   *Lev 25:23*

The land is a mother that never dies.   *Maori*

The monk who tills the soil must do penance.   *Buddhist*

The earth is empty and waste and stripped bare — the earth itself desecrated by those who live on it, for they have violated the everlasting covenant.   *Isaiah - 24:3,5*

Only when the last tree has died and the last river poisoned and the last fish been caught will we realise that we cannot eat money.   *Cree - American*

Now your way of life is no longer working, you are interested in our way. But if we tell you our way, then it will be polluted, we will have no medicine and we will be destroyed as well as you.   *Buffalo Tiger - Miccasukee American*

We don't have to protect the environment. The Second Coming is at hand.
   US Secretary of the Interior to President Reagan

All over the world today, long-established communities that grew organically, that are ecologically sustainable and that give people a feeling of belonging and meaning, are being torn apart.   *Larry Rasmussen*

Things fall apart; the centre cannot hold;
Mere anarchy is loosed upon the world,
The blood-dimmed tide is loosed, and everywhere
The ceremony of innocence is drowned.   *W B Yeats*

Nature cannot be commanded except by being obeyed.   *Francis Bacon*

While the earth exists, sowing and harvest, cold and heat, Winter and Summer, day and night, shall not cease.   *Gen 8:22*

....

Care for the environment is a necessity of modern times, especially now we know how much we can damage the world's climate. Much less was known in Biblical times and yet relevant themes are there:

- ➤ the recognition of the wonder and beauty of creation
- ➤ the ancient covenant covering the entire natural world — indicating that it does not just exist for humanity
- ➤ the 'cursed ground' of the Eden story re-emerging elsewhere in the Bible as the consequence of pride and disobedience
- ➤ humanity answerable to God — as tenants of the earth.

This last puts into perspective the call in Genesis to subdue ('lead') or dominate ('ensure a home for') — Gen 1:28. It does not allow us to exploit or degrade the natural world. Sometimes religion has been ultra-conservative — holding back development through reverence for the earth, but Christianity distinguished the Creator from the creation and allowed science to flourish. This was a breakthrough but it could be used to justify the plunder of the earth.

Modern dilemmas were already apparent in the 19C. Eleanor Ormerod — entomologist — pioneered the use of 'Paris green' in agriculture and apparently implored farmers to 'drench Nature in a slurry of poison'. Edward Norman and Henry Doubleday, both Quakers, advocated instead the use of insect predators to counter pest damage. Since then we have recognised the fragility of planet earth and the dangers of rampant exploitation. We know ourselves to share a common evolutionary heritage with all living things, and to belong to the same web of life, yet still we treat this wounded world as if it were our own property. (In British law, land is technically leased from the Crown, who is answerable to God.)

The first stark choices of the nuclear age have brought home to us the responsibilities hidden in all our choices. The romantic and the realist now speak with one voice. We need the age-old insights — humility to offset our pride, appreciation to replace our carelessness, and an urgent realisation that only the meek are fit to be caretakers of the earth.

Population increase is judged by some to be the *greatest* threat to the environment and in some areas it is currently the most obvious. Yet UN studies suggest that the world's population can level off at c.12 billion and that this is sustainable. Growth is slowing significantly in parts of the world and Christians should accept family planning as one helpful measure to aid in this. Nevertheless Catholics are right that contraception is no panacea — a fairer world economy is paramount to offset the need for large families.

....

God created all the wild animals and brought them to the man to see what he would call them.　　　　　　　　　　　　　　　　　　　　　　　*Gen 2:19*

When an animal is named and described, it becomes a possession forever, and the value of every individual of it is enhanced.　　　　　　*William Kirby - scientist*

Tyger, tyger, burning bright in the forests of the night
What immortal hand or eye dare frame thy fearful symmetry?　　　　　*Blake*

You must not work on the sabbath — neither you nor your oxen.　　　*Ex 20:10*

You are not to muzzle the ox that is treading out the grain.　　　*Deut 25:4*

We remember with shame that in the past we have exercised the dominion of man with ruthless cruelty, so that the voice of the earth, which should have gone up to thee in song, has been a groan of travail.　　　　　　*Basil the Great – 4C*

The question is not can they reason? Can they talk? But can they suffer?　　*Bentham*

Until he extends the circle of his compassion to all living things, man will not himself find peace.　　　　　　　　　　　　　　　*Albert Schweitzer*

We are all netted together.　　　　　　　　　　　　　　　*Darwin*

It is a generally received opinion that all the visible world was created for Man — yet wise men nowadays think otherwise.
　　　　　　　　　John Ray - the 'father of natural history' - 17C.

Mounting the horse was a more than human gesture, the symbolic act of dominance over the total creation.　　　　　　　　　　　*J Bronowski*

If we still slaughtered our own beasts for food, we would not find the details of blood sacrifice too shocking to admit of a spiritual interpretation.　　*John V Taylor*

The Chesapeake hunters with swivel guns killed 1,500 ducks in eight hours. Soon the sound of wild life grew faint. A silence fell upon the land.　　*John Stewart Collis*

What is man without the beasts? If all the beasts were gone, men would die from a great loneliness of spirit, for whatever happens to the beasts also happens to man.
　　　　　　　　　　　　　　　　　　　　　Chief Seattle - 1855
　　— this quotation is taken from **Chief Seattle's Speech,** *sometimes claimed to be fraudulent. It has been through several interpretations but does appear to be based on notes taken at the time.*

....

ANIMAL WELFARE

Even though Judaism began in a harsh, semi-nomadic economy, there are signs of concern for animals in various scriptures:

➤ the salvation theme of Noah's ark included the animal world
➤ the sabbath law required that working animals should rest
➤ and that the ox should be allowed to eat whilst threshing.

We are still naming the animals — Gen 2:19 — classifying and seeking to understand the richness of the living world, and we are still called to accord dignity to all creatures. Our debt is incalculable — not just for food but for the revolutions brought about by the first working dog, the first mounted horse, and the first ox harnessed to the plough. It is difficult to argue that such partnership and companionship is unwarranted interference in Nature, even if it has been imposed by one side.

It is true that we have used and abused the rest of the animal world and that we forget that we belong to it. Nature has always been a stern arena of competition but human plundering has often outrun human need. The challenge of vegetarianism remains for various reasons. Is it time to step back from our age-old assault upon the animal kingdom? We may be healthier for it and we may feed the world better if we use grains directly, instead of wastefully through the guts of animals. Yet where is the line drawn? At fish? At milk? (cows will not give milk unless a calf is born first — what happens to surplus calves?)

There are many questions we have yet to answer:

➤ if we do not cut loose from our heritage and become vegetarian, can we raise animals in conditions of dignity?
➤ can we leave behind our evolutionary hunting instincts?
➤ is it possible to use animals for human health in testing medicines and in spare part surgery without abusing them?
In other words, is it right to use creatures as machines purely for their utility value? Is it necessary — if human tissue, and eventually, human organs can be grown in the laboratory
➤ can the rich of the world give practical help to enable all people to shoulder responsibility for the management of wild habitats with all their flora and fauna?
➤ is the sentiment attached to many animals disproportionate to the just claims of our human neighbours?
➤ can we pass on to future generations the joy and humility which the wonder of creation should evoke?

....

Only one is wise, the Lord most terrible, seated upon his throne. It is he who created wisdom, observed and measured her, and infused her into all his works. To everyone he has given her in some degree, but lavishly to those who love him.   Ecclus 1:10

Give me a firm place to stand, and I will move the earth.   Archimedes

Do not say, 'I am self-sufficient; nothing can go wrong for me'.   Ecclus 11:24

I see no reason to suppose that these machines will ever force themselves into general use.
The Duke of Wellington - re steam locomotives

One machine can do the work of fifty ordinary men. No machine can do the work of one extraordinary man.   Elbert Hubbard

The machine threatens all achievement.   Rainer Maria Rilke

The new electronic interdependence recreates the world in the image of a global village.
Marshall McLuhan

We are now splicing, recombining, inserting and stitching living material into economic utilities. Our very sense of ourselves and society will likely change.   Jeremy Rifkin

Part of our revulsion against cloning originates in the fear that what is uniquely ours could be shared by another. The single-minded obsession of the genes to do their own determining in their own body is our strongest bulwark against loss of freedom to external causes.   Matt Ridley

I believe the strength and soundness of Christian sensibility, the meaning of love and charity, have changed the world at least as much as technological development.
Robert J Oppenheimer

The notion that to be human, some would say to exist in the image of God, is to be called on to participate responsibly in the ongoing work of creation, is a persuasive one, though not to be taken lightly.   Michael Reiss

When you destroy a blade of grass / You poison England at the root.
Gordon Bottomley

What I have been taught unselfishly, I pass on freely.   Wisdom 7:13

We have seen only a fraction of his work; there remain many mysteries greater still.
Ecclus 43:22

....

Sometimes Christians have been suspicious of technology — anxious to conserve and conscious of human arrogance. Sometimes they have been of a questing spirit, supported by the understanding that we are called to be partners - however junior - in creation. It is hardly helpful now to reopen old arguments about not interfering with nature or to retreat to a world long vanished. We are part of nature and our impact has already been immense.

The onrush of technological progress today will excite and dismay us. No sooner have we come to terms with our mastery of the inorganic world than we are plunged into the technology of living things. What happens when we introduce and recombine genes in plants to satisfy our palates, or to "outflank Nature", or to manufacture new materials? What happens when we insert new characteristics into animals according to our requirements — or use animals to carry human tissues and organs for repairing our own bodies? What happens if we alter our own genetic make-up or decide to clone human beings? In principle what can now be done is not so radically different from past selection and breeding — or from nature's own methods of mutation and cross-breeding. We can now deliberately break down the barriers between species but viruses routinely transfer genes from one species to another. Are there hidden costs? Nature is infinitely subtle and patient. By comparison, with all our extraordinary skill, we are amateurish and impatient.

Our greatest problem, as always, is human failing. Can we trust ourselves? The answer will be — sometimes yes, and sometimes no. There are serious issues of power and greed. Once more we reach out for the fruit of knowledge but this time to patent and profit.

> ➤ can we trust scientists to live up to their own highest standards of integrity when they are given an 'infinitely malleable construction set'?
> ➤ can we ensure sufficient control of commercially driven technology? — and who will control the controllers?
> ➤ can we produce wise enough leaders who can comprehend, let alone cope with, the speed and range of advance?
> ➤ can we ensure that voters and consumers help to shape the future without falling prey to manipulation and false fears?
> ➤ can we distribute fairly the benefits of new technologies whilst ensuring that the initiators take full responsibility for the risks?

Only a broad vision, a humane heart, and supreme sensitivity can chart our future course wisely.

CONNECTIONS

Prove all things — keep that which is good.   Paul - I Thess 5:21

You have set everything in order by measure and number and weight.   Wisdom 11:20

Throw them in the water. If what they contain is right guidance, God has given us better. If it is in error, God has protected us against it.
                    Umar bin al-Khattab - Muslim leader on the capture of scientific books

The scientists are the successors of the prophets.   Muhammad

We should not hold rashly an opinion in a scientific matter, so that we may not come to hate later whatever the truth may reveal to us, out of love for our own error.
                    Augustine

Most people say that it is the intellect which makes a great scientist. They are wrong: it is the character.   Einstein

There is but one source for science: it must come from the mediaeval insistence on the rationality of God.   A N Whitehead

You ask me if we could explain everything in scientific terms? Yes, it is possible, but it is as though one were to reproduce Beethoven's Ninth Symphony in the shape of an air pressure curve.   Einstein

Science tells us something about everything but not the whole truth about anything.
                    C M Joad

Why is science nonsense? Because it has answers.   Martin Heidegger

We feel that when we have answered all possible scientific questions, the problems of life remain completely untouched.   Wittgenstein

Science can never grow where the spirit of the universe is seen as hostile or capricious.
                    William Temple

Science itself is impossible without God.   Stanley Jaki

Let him who has scanned the heavens, go down to the depths of hell.
                    Bernard of Clairveaux

I was lucky enough to look over the good Lord's shoulder while he was at work.
                    Heisenberg

Science without religion is lame; religion without science is blind.   Einstein

Science and religion both seek to discern patterns but science prefers to explore those things that allow experimentation.

It is increasingly recognised that mediaeval Christian philosophy paved the way for modern science. Etienne Tempier, Jean Buridan, Nicholas Oresmé, William of Ockham, Robert Grosseteste and Roger Bacon belong to this roll of honour. Greeks and Arabs made vital contributions, but Christian thought, drawing on its Jewish heritage, set the basis for further development, by teaching:

➢ that all creation is governed by rational laws
➢ that the earth itself is not divine and is therefore open to exploration
➢ that the material world is good
➢ that optimism is justified by God's control of unfolding history
➢ that we can, and should, discover more
➢ that truth should be shared, and the gains used to bring relief to those in need.

The founders of the Royal Society in 1645 stood in this tradition, as do a significant number of scientists today.

Although the paths of science and faith seem very different in their approach to truth, closer examination suggests otherwise:

Everything we feel, think and do is necessarily a belief.   *Andrew Newberg*

Both are a vocation where openness and honesty are essential prerequisites of the search for truth. Both require a measure of trust and humility. Both involve reason and imagination — the heart as well as the mind. Both require us to 'prove all things and hold fast to that which is good'. Both are justified by the good that is brought to humanity.

There will still be tension, but that is because there is no greater enterprise than that of 'thinking God's thoughts after him' (Einstein). Reality is multi-levelled — it can yield to different levels of explanation. The particle, the atom, the cell, the person, all have their story. If we seek to explain someone's actions, we may describe their behaviour, their motives, their background, their genetic patterns — but few imagine that an atomic read-out or a personal mathematical equation would be wholly adequate. We could go on to speak of the context of their actions, the environment, the influence of others, their sense of God's guidance. Each description, each level, is part of the explanation — ' We only know in part — one day we shall know as clearly as we are known '— I Cor 13:12.

Note: The word 'science' in this sense is attributed to William Whewell 1840 — Prof. of mineralogy then of theology at Cambridge.

CONNECTIONS

....

What is referred to as the conflict between science and religion is very often a conflict between science and art.   John Macmurray

I don't see how studying a flower ever detracts from its beauty.   Richard Feynman

It is impossible to say where art ends and science begins.   Herbert Spenser

I have filled him with the spirit of God, making him skilful and intelligent, an expert craftsman and a master of design.   Ex 31:3

All that is true, all that is noble, all that is just and pure, all that is lovable and attractive, whatever is excellent and admirable — fill your thoughts with these things.   Paul - Phil 4:8

Art, since it begins with the infinite, cannot progress.   Whistler

A poet should have no opinions, no principles, no morality.   Keats

Popular Stage playes are sinfull, heathenish, lewde, ungodly Spectacles.   William Prynne - Presbyterian lawyer - 1632

All art is religion in the sense that every artist must believe that there is something worth glorifying.   Henry Moore

Man is a completely futile being. Art has become a game by which he distracts himself   Francis Bacon - 20C. artist

Man is only wholly man when at play.   Schiller

It is not as if the artist were a special kind of man; every man is a special kind of artist   Amanda Coomaraswami

Christian art is nothing special. It is sound, healthy, good art.   H R Rookmaaker

I arrange my subject as I want it, then go ahead and paint it like a child — I am no cleverer than that.   Renoir

Artistic creation does not copy God's creation, it continues it.   Maritain

Christ is more of an artist than any artist — he worked in living spirit and bodies — he made men instead of statues.   Vincent van Gogh

....

Christianity has a high view of the artist's vocation. All inspiration is God-given — 'breathed in' — and the skill of artist or craftsmen is a gift for the world's enriching. John of Damascus — 8C. saw icons as a continuation of the incarnation and the great Christian themes have produced a wonderful heritage. For centuries there has been a rich and fruitful partnership between the church and the artist. Art and architecture, sculpture, drama and literature witness to a depth and range of imagination that will seed the future with its inspiration. It can be argued that art clothes itself in the dominant culture and owes its achievement to other than its environment, but Stalinist Russia is sufficient reminder of how arid an ideology can be and how cramped the art which struggles beneath it.

The church indeed has been totalitarian at times. The Empress Irene (780-802) gave the clergy control of graphic art and believed that the artist should simply do the painting at their behest. There has been repression in Christian history but the issues are not always straightforward. The artist will often challenge and offend — maybe 17C. plays were sometimes 'lewde, ungodly spectacles' ! (see opposite). Is censorship *ever* justified? Art can be seriously subversive — if so, we have to ask in each case if it is subverting something good or something that deserves to be overthrown. Paul Klee once said, 'The more horrifying this world becomes, the more art becomes abstract.' Is this the mirror held up to our eyes? There is an old story of a Nazi officer looking at a Picasso painting and demanding, 'Who is responsible for this?' The answer came, 'You are!'

A Christian perspective might well challenge the slogan *"Art for art's sake"*, as though the artist had no responsibility whatsoever and existed in a vacuum. Art should criticise society including the church and religion — and it should be criticised in its turn, so that the wheat can be separated from the chaff, the uplifting from the debasing. It may sometimes be a distraction and a game, and there is a place for play but few artists have held such a diminished view of their vocation. It is not that art has to have a religious theme (in the narrow sense of the word 'religious'). It is that good art is gospel by its very nature — to warn, to reveal, to illuminate — to enable us to see. And that last point brings us very close to the mission of Christ.

John Constable was travelling by coach from East Bergholt, having been to see his native village for the last time. When they passed the vale of Dedham the artist remarked to his fellow passenger how beautiful it was. 'Yes,' was the reply, 'This is Constable's country.'

Serve God gladly, come into his presence with singing.   Ps 100:2

Everything we ever knew about the movement of the sea was preserved in the verses of a song. For thousands of years we went where we wanted and came home safe because of the song.   Nootka steerswoman

It is a higher revelation than all wisdom and philosophy.   Beethoven

One tiny boy is blind and deaf and has no palate. Communication seems impossible. Miss Godfrey put a record on the player and placed his hands on the table beside it. And with an expression of rapture on his face, he began a solitary dance to the vibrations he felt from the music   - from a special care unit

All metre and mystery
Touch on the Lord at last,
The tide thunders ashore
In praise of the High King.   Irish - 13C.

When I composed that, I was conscious of being inspired by God Almighty. Do you think I can consider your puny little fiddle when he speaks to me?   Beethoven - when a violinist complained that a passage was unplayable

My ideas come uncalled and go through my head singing and singing and storming until at last I have them before me as notes.   Beethoven

I have no need to think of new tunes . I have the greatest difficulty not to step on them when I get out of bed.   Bach

I write as a sow piddles.   Mozart

Is it not strange that sheep's guts should hale men's souls out of men's bodies?   Shakespeare

Music is your own experience, your thoughts, your wisdom. If you don't live it, it won't come out of your horn.   Charlie Parker

Mozart is the incarnation of the divine force of creation.   Goethe

I am tired before the concert, not afterward.   Rubinstein

Humanity is far more important than music. You can do much for humanity with music, with anything noble. But greater than all is love, love for all the living.   Pablo Casals

One cannot judge 'Lohengrin' from a first hearing, and I certainly do not intend to hear it a second time.   Rossini

Early Christian music drew on Jewish synagogue traditions and Greek modes. It responded to the needs of the liturgy and developed through plainsong to unaccompanied choral music to the towering heights of Bach's B Minor Mass and Beethoven's Mass in D. Ambrose, 4C Bishop of Milan, and then Pope Gregory (✝ 604) established the range and form of church music. This was greatly enriched through the work of monasteries, such as St Gall in Switzerland. The 11C monk, Guido d'Arezzo designed the stave and took 'Do-Re-Mi' from the first syllables of a Latin hymn.

The Reformation and later renewal movements widened the scope of hymn singing — Jan Hus and Martin Luther contributed many hymns in the vernacular and Charles Wesley wrote no fewer than 6,000. Sometimes there were strict rules as to what was appropriate in church. The Calvinists insisted on scriptural texts, using metrical psalms and paraphrases rather than 'human tunes'. The Puritans favoured simple, unadorned singing. They were not against music as such — Cromwell had 48 violinists at the wedding of his daughter, with 'mixed dancing and much mirth'. It was the Quakers and some Evangelicals who saw little place for music at all.

John Wesley wanted to hear the congregation. He abhorred 'drawling' and sought lively tunes, publishing the first hymn book to use a variety of sources — this in 1737 in Carolina.

Without doubt there are hymns of fine value amidst a great deal of dross — as well as some doubtful singing styles. One aberrant form was given to arbitrary repetition:
> *Bring down Sal -- Bring down Sal --*
> *Bring down Salvation from the skies.*   *!*

Hymns belong to the whole people of God. It is not easy to know which should be discreetly interred and forgotten. We can be too scrupulous in matters of language and doctrine and need a certain tolerance to match the catholicity of the Christian community.

Church Choirs: The performers are placed in a Single Seat. Here they form themselves into a round Ring, with their Backs to ye Congregation. Here they murder anthems, chuse improper Psalms, leave off in ye middle of a sentence, sing Psalms of all kinds to new jiggish tunes. If ye Minister offers to direct them, 'They will sing as they list or not at all.' They frequently leave their own Parish Church and go in a Body to display their Talents in other churches. I have known them stroll six or seven miles for this purpose, sometimes with a young female singer or two in their train.   - a Suffolk clergyman – 1764

....

In wonder all philosophy began; in wonder it ends.   *Coleridge*

What is a philosopher? Only a man who likes to see the whole.   *John Stewart Collis*

They breathe the thin air of the academy and wear the pale colours of mere wisdom.
                                        Leo Baeck - on the Greek philosophers

*Do not let principles be the rules of your existence. The Führer himself, and he alone, is
the German reality of today and of the future.*   *Martin Heidegger*

There is no nonsense but some philosopher has said it.   *Cicero*

*The principles of logic and metaphysics are true simply because we never allow them to
be anything else.*   *A J Ayer*

Religious motives have been on the whole a hindrance to the progress of philosophy..
                                                Bertrand Russell

Science is what you know, philosophy is what you don't know.   *Russell*

Errors in religion are dangerous; those in philosophy only ridiculous.   *Hume*

Fire is not material any more than life is material.   *Einstein*

The philosophers have only interpreted the world — the point, however, is to change it.
                                                Karl Marx

*One's task is not to turn the world upside down, but to do what is necessary at the given
pace and with due consideration of reality.*   *Bonhoeffer*

*Judging whether life is, or is not, worth living amounts to answering the fundamental
question of philosophy.*   *Albert Camus*

A thorough sceptic cannot live his scepticism.   *David Hume*

*A little philosophy inclineth man's mind to atheism, but depth in philosophy bringeth
men's minds about to religion.*   *Francis Bacon*

Be a philosopher but, amid all your philosophy, be human.   *David Hume*

....

My advice to you is not to enquire why or whither, but just enjoy your ice-
cream while it's on your plate.   *Thornton Wilder*

Philosophy is an ally to all clear thinking and honest religion. It exists within and without the Christian tradition and grapples with the same ultimate questions of life and meaning — seeking to see reality as a whole. There are alleged differences — that philosophy::

> ➢ promotes free enquiry over against the untouchable assumptions of religion — *"posing questions that cannot be answered, compared with answers that can never be questioned"*!
> ➢ requires honesty, not obedience
> ➢ seeks evidence, not blind acceptance
> ➢ recognises no supernatural revelation.

But these differences fade on closer examination:

> ➢ all thinking is based on assumed premises and there is no reason why Christianity should stifle debate, especially as it owes much to the questing spirit of rabbinic Judaism
> ➢ sincerity of heart and mind lies at the core of Jesus' teaching
> ➢ Jesus also asked people to open their eyes to the evidence before them and to read the signs of the times. He was far from requiring blind acceptance
> ➢ many philosophers have believed in God — revelation is the equivalent of discovery but seen, as it were, from the other side. The philosopher is bound to believe that there is truth to be revealed.

Philosophy shares with science and theology all the problems of human knowing, of language, and of the nature of the real. We see 'as through a glass darkly' and there is no unambiguous route to certainty and no neutral standpoint from which all the panorama of human existence can be surveyed. In itself, philosophy is not a body of knowledge but a method of thinking which can only be salutary and helpful to Christian thought.

Naturally, there will be teaching in certain philosophies that Christianity cannot accept, for example:

> ➢ if it empties the world of all meaning
> ➢ if it denies all human freedom and responsibility
> ➢ if it undermines all morality
> ➢ if it is so thoroughgoing in its scepticism that everything crumbles — including philosophy itself.

The Jews honoured Wisdom. Christians honour the Word — that principle of Reason and Wisdom which enlightens every human being. 'Philosophy' — the 'love of wisdom' unites us all.

CONNECTIONS

....

Does Job have no reason to fear God?   *Job 1:9*

God is a comforting illusion which must be abandoned.   *Freud*

I don't need to believe, I know.   *Jung*

The psychological mechanisms are the way in which God makes himself known.
                                                                 James Moray

The soul of man is a far country which cannot be approached or explored.   *Heraclitus*

I do not even recognise my own actions as mine.   *Paul - Rom 7:15*

Religious ideas are illusions, fulfilments of the oldest, strongest and most urgent wishes of mankind ... Judgements of values made by mankind are attempts to prop up their illusions with arguments.   *Freud*

In the depths of my heart, I can't help being convinced that my dear fellow men, with few exceptions, are worthless.   *Freud*

This poor old lady doesn't need us. What she needs is forgiveness. She needs to make peace with her soul. There must be a God somewhere, to help, to hear, to heal her.
                            Anna Freud – psycho-analyst - daughter of Sigmund.

The importance of consciousness is so great that one cannot help suspecting the element of meaning to be conceded somewhere within all the monstrous, apparently senseless biological turmoil.   *Jung*

The 'I' is not a combination of body parts or brain states or bits of information, but a unity of selfness over time, a single locus that is nowhere in particular.   *Steven Pinker*

Is there a lace here for the spirit? Is there time on this brief platform for anything other than the mind's failure to explain itself?   *R S Thomas*

Many humble people have done many things which all ordinary sources of evidence seem to set outside the range of unassisted humanity. When they say, 'It is God working through me', I cannot see that I have the right or the knowledge to reject their testimony.
                                                Frederic Bartlett – psychologist

....

Anybody who goes to see a psychiatrist ought to have his head examined.
                                                                 Samuel Goldwyn

Psychology is the study of the normal mind and psychiatry the treatment of mental disorder. Modern psychology is a challenge to the 'hard mysticism of science' — its impersonality and mathematical abstractions. From Paul onwards Christian thought has grappled with the complexities and vulnerability of human nature. It was well used to the conflicts and self-deceptions involved. Paul's words (opposite) are familiar to us all. It has been well said that mental health problems do not affect one in three persons, but one out of one. In fact, psychology developed out of 15C. theology and spiritual discipline.

What Christianity was unprepared for was the onslaught on all beliefs as the 'acceptable face of disreputable desires' — Freud. But he undermines all values and all judgements, including his own, and it is not surprising that he loses faith in the worth of humanity. To dismiss great areas of human thought as akin to a 'comfort blanket' should make us pause but it poses the question why we evolved to find comfort in false beliefs.

Psychology should be a critical ally in the re-examination of all Christian doctrine and practice. The love of power in church structures, the hidden meanings of Christian symbolism and the elements of wishful thinking in the dream of a forgiving Father and a compensatory heaven — these need our recognition. Realising that *all* human thought becomes suspect, we have a choice — either we are slaves of our instincts, and freedom, responsibility and identity are all betrayed, or else we can emerge with our deepest beliefs tested but intact. The challenge for psychiatry lies in Chesterton's observation that 'psychoanalysis is confession without absolution'.

There is much in common in psychology and Christian thinking:
- ➢ that we are all a mix of normal and abnormal
- ➢ that a balance of physical and spiritual is desirable
- ➢ that chemical and surgical treatment, counselling and befriending, are all appropriate in the treatment of disorders
- ➢ that acceptance, forgiveness, faith and love are life-giving
- ➢ that each church, hospital, and society itself needs to be a healing community.

....

Dr Yellowlees used to describe **Zacchaeus** as a classic case of inferiority — due to his stature? He chose an occupation where he could compensate by exercising unjust authority and climbed a tree to be above his colleagues. Jesus' cure was admirable psychotherapy. Salvation had indeed come to his house.   cf. Lk 19:2f

TRAVELLING TOGETHER

Humanism is the effort of men to think, to feel, and to act for themselves. Geoffrey Scott

A humanist argues both sides.   Protagoras - 1 C. BC

*We look on the same stars, the same heavens are above us all, the same universe
surrounds us. What matters it by what method each of us arrives at the truth?*
                                    Symmachus – a Jewish Christian to Ambrose 4C

The conversion of Europe to Christianity was one of the greatest disasters of history.
                                                                    Margaret Knight

*I am repelled by St Francis, in whom I feel my own humanity chilled, alienated,
impoverished.*   H J Blackham

I serve God, I believe in God, and I want it known.   Voltaire

We can become what we will.   Mirandola - 1486

My country is the world and my religion is to do good.   Thomas Paine

*The vast majority of humanists were patently sincere Christians, who wished to apply
their enthusiasm to the exploration of their faith.*   Diarmaid McCulloch

*Only on the firm foundations of unyielding despair, can the soul's habitation henceforth
be safely built.*   Bertrand Russell

*All the grand sources of human suffering are in a great degree conquerable by human
care and effort.*   J S Mill

One must be bound to the world by some bonds of love before humanism can help one.
                                                                        H J Blackham

*What the world now needs is not merely a rationalist denial of the old but a religious
affirmation of something new.*   Julian Huxley

*Those who live according to reason are Christians, even though they are accounted
atheists. Such were Socrates and Heraclitus among the Greeks.*   Justin - 2C.

*The excellencies of Socrates are shadows of virtues — not true virtues, but are to be
regarded as vices.*   Melanchthon - 16 C.

*Humanism in the stricter sense is justified by its production in every generation of its
quotas of just men.*   H J Blackham

....

Humanism is a tradition that focuses on the ideals, aspirations and welfare of humanity. It is represented strongly inside and outside the Christian tradition and has been a vital corrective to an intolerant church. It looks for inspiration to the Greeks, the Renaissance and the Enlightenment. Those who claim the label today are generally agnostic — replacing, it has been said, 'I AM THAT I AM' (Ex 3:14) with 'I AM'. It welcomes the principle that Bentham took from Francis Hutcheson — to seek the greatest happiness of the greatest number — and it has made great contributions to tolerance, law, public education and representative government.

Christians should welcome the common ground with Humanists. Luther may have thought Erasmus 'not devout' but he stands no less in the Christian tradition and even bitter critics like Voltaire have believed in God as well as in tolerance and humanity. Christian teaching from creation to incarnation should lead to the highest valuing of humanity.

It must be asked, nevertheless, whether there is an agreed basis for humanist thinking and whether it has the coherence and stamina to sustain a way of life. The optimistic strains of humanism can overlook the darkness in human nature and it can lead to an over-confident belief in progress. Kant (both Christian and humanist) continued to defend the French Revolution and to believe in the triumph of reason even when its ideals were being betrayed.

The pessimistic strain of humanism can come to treat people as 'conscious automata' (T H Huxley) or deliver them up to deterministic laws (Marx). In jettisoning God, we can move on to jettison our own humanity. Nietzsche wondered, 'Who will hereafter raise high the image of man?' The artist, Lyonel Feininger, said of Germany in 1935, 'Am I not right when I say that the people of today are sleep-walking into a dehumanised, mechanistic state?' In the face of such challenges, Christians hold to humanity made in the image of God and given infinite value. Can humanist agnostics offer an optimism that is as well grounded?

As for thoroughgoing scepticism, does it allow for any values at all? In overthrowing the supernatural, Hume acknowledged that he was undermining the natural — and advised us to take to backgammon! Perhaps Christianity and humanism do indeed need each other.

....

The **British Humanist Association** united the Rationalist Press Association and the Ethical Union in 1963. Its offices are in London.

TRAVELLING TOGETHER

....

Did none of them think to give praise to God except this foreigner?   Jesus - Lk 17:18

A heathen who occupies himself with the Torah takes as lofty a place as a High Priest in Israel.   The Talmud (The Torah is the law of God)

God has spoken to mankind through Judaism to the Jews, Christianity to Christians, Islam to Muslims.   Jonathan Sacks

Take neither Jews nor Christians for your friends.   The Qur'an 5:51

We have our own works and you have yours; let there be no argument between us. God will bring us all together, for to him we shall return.   The Qur'an 42:15

The pious of all nations will have a share in the life of the world to come.   The Talmud

If Christ were here now, he would not be a Christian.   Mark Twain

Like friends may we associate; speaking words in kindly spirit, going along the same wagon-pole.   Atharva Vedas - Hindu

Our ability to reach unity in diversity will be the beauty and test of our civilisation.   Gandhi

Our inmost prayer should be that a Hindu should be a better Hindu, a Muslim a better Muslim, a Christian a better Christian.   Gandhi

Vie with one another in good works, for to God you shall all return, and he will resolve your differences.   The Qur'an 5:49

Our religion is sublime, pure and beneficial. Theirs is mean, licentious and cruel.   William Wilberforce

Whoever honours his own sect and disparages that of another, does his own sect the greatest possible harm.   12th Edict of the Emperor Asoka

The differences between faiths do not reach up to heaven.   19C Russian Orthodox

No one can come to me unless he is drawn by the Father.
No one can come to the Father unless I draw him.   Jesus - Jn 6:44 / 14:6

Whoever learns from the Father, comes to me.   Jesus - Jn 6:45

....

All roads *don't* lead to the same place — some lead us into the high country and some into swamps. So it is with religions; yet it may well be that the spirit of God has enabled us to avoid the by-ways as the years have gone by. Jesus freely recognised faith in other than his own people and challenged the intolerant of his own tradition. It is therefore with humility that we meet one another. Religions do not exist in watertight compartments — they draw from one another, share insights, enrich one another, and increasingly experience the same environment and the same social problems.

Christians have nothing to fear from this dialogue and a great deal to gain — what is of God will endure. It does take time to win through the externals of a religion, couched as it is in the culture out of which it sprang. There are problems of language — so many different names for God. The differences are noticed first, especially if they seem to point to the darker side of another faith. What we need is an alliance of those whose beliefs are kindly, generous and open against all that is mean-spirited and destructive, then there can be honest exploration. There should be no room today for the assumptions commonplace in Wilberforce's time.

Jesus' words 'no one comes to the Father except by me' may or may not be faithfully recorded as they do not appear in earlier gospels. In any case, John has already identified Christ with the very mind of God (the Word)— *"which enlightens everyone"* - 1:9. It follows that everyone who discovers truth is, by definition (Jn 6:45) drawn to the Father, and so to the Son, who is truth. It is equally true that anyone who practises love knows the Father, and serves the Christ, as the parable testifies — Mt 25:31f. There is no room for the narrow interpretation that only Christians have access to God. Given Jesus' example, we cannot justify an exclusive and ungenerous faith.

> *My heart is capable of every form.*
> *A cloister for the monk, a fane for idols,*
> *A pasture for gazelles, the votary's Kabah,*
> *The tables of the Torah, the Qur'an.*
> *Love is the faith I hold: wherever turn*
> *His camels, still the one true faith is mine.*   *Ibn al Arabi – Muslim*

Honoured names from the past in this context include **Matteo Ricci, Schall & Verbiest** - founders of the Chinese Catholic Mission, **Judah ha Levi & Moses Maimonides** in Moorish Spain, **Leibnitz,** who suggested that Europe could learn from Confucian missionaries, and **Lessing** in his dramatisation of 'Nathan the Wise'.

....

CAUTION ! A twelve point check for would-be disciples:

....

1) Does the cult use an overload of scientific or religious jargon? Some specialist terms may be essential but many cults are simply out to impress.

2) Be careful if extravagant promises are made — that you will become wealthy or be free from all illness or find a wonderful partner or have a guaranteed ticket to heaven.

3) Are cult members excessively friendly — with much touching, hugging etc. We all want to be wanted but 'love bombing', as some call it, is a warning signal.

4) Is the group highly exclusive, given to denouncing those outside, and difficult to leave should you want to?

5) If prolonged meditation is practised, are there unusual features — sleep deprivation, hypnotic techniques or drugs?

6) Is there a great deal of secrecy — regarding signs and ceremonies or the leadership, and are all finances transparent and independently audited?

7) Is the leader, however inspiring, also autocratic — with instructions handed down from the top or control vested in a self-perpetuating leadership — backed up by a strict discipline of rewards and punishments?

8) Are members expected to hand over a significant amount of wealth through donations, tithing or charges for special courses?

9) Does the group seek to direct a member's family life or their use of money or their career?

10) Is sexual liberation part of the teaching and what is meant by this?

11) Is there talk of UFO's, aliens, other planets etc?

12) Does the group expect the end of the world in the foreseeable future?

....

There are cults that are beneficial and one of the above features is not enough to make a judgement but the more that do fit, the greater should be the caution shown.

The Cult Information Centre in London is helpful in such matters..

Our modern world is awash with cults of all kinds — there are several hundred in Britain. Some have leaders who are genuine and sincere: some have leaders who cynically manipulate and control others in order to gain power and great wealth. Many of us are trusting, especially in matters of religion, and utterly unprepared for the unscrupulous way in which someone may deliberately set out to found a religion and take advantage of the gullible — and all this behind a mask of benevolence and serenity.

No one expects that they themselves can be taken in and assumes that only the ignorant, the uneducated and the poor follow these 'messiahs'. The truth is the opposite — it is the intelligent, the well educated, the prosperous who are most likely to give up their freedom and their integrity to a fraudulent group. It may happen when we are most vulnerable — in teenage years, or when a relationship has broken down, or when our existing beliefs have been shaken. The fact that extreme groups can lead to mass suicide is a stark warning of the dangers.

Yet there is no clear dividing line between a cult and a religion and major religions may first have appeared as a cult. Some religions too, or groups within a religion may fail under the scrutiny of the list opposite. Life is never simple — except perhaps for those who, understandably, would sweep away all religions as fraudulent. A more thoughtful approach is to remember that mainstream political movements are also dogged by the power-hungry with false prospectuses — and that genuine medicine has to guard against the fringe of quacks and deceivers.

The best cults may simply be drawing on the riches available to us across cultures and faiths, bringing insights that can benefit us and techniques that can help us to heal ourselves and others. They are not exclusive and seek to share but not control. Their leaders or teachers do not seek status and wealth but share the spirit of the great masters. Moses was ambitious for his people but not for himself; the Buddha spoke of himself as simply 'a monk with a leaky umbrella'; Muhammad was quite adamant that honour should be given to God alone, and Jesus saw himself in the role of a servant.

It is good that the spiritual wealth of Eastern religions has become more available in the West; that science is revealing more and more to us; that technology makes it so much easier to share — but we need to be cautious if we are not to join those who 'stop their ears to the truth and turn to fables' — II Tim 4:4.

See, the people that live alone and do not reckon themselves among the nations.
Nu 23:9

I the Lord have called you and will hold your hand and will make you a light to the nations.
Is 42:6

In those days, when ten men from nations of every language summon up courage, they shall touch the robe of a Jew and say, 'We will go with you because we have heard that God is with you'.
Zech 8:23

Abraham is the Father of us all.
Paul - Rom 4:17

The gracious gifts of God and his calling cannot be revoked.
Paul - Rom 11:29

In the world of mere events, Judaism stands in solitude; in the world of history, it stands in the very midst of and together with other nations.
Leo Baeck

The Jew was the great nonconformist, the great dissenter of history.
Leo Baeck

The existence of the Jews is the best proof of the existence of God.
Marquis D'Argens to Frederick the Great

The law of dislike for the unlike will always prevail. The Jews bring the unlike into the heart of every community and must there defend a frontier as large as the world.
Israel Zangwill

We must overcome the superstitious terror with which we have regarded the Nazareth movement, a movement which we must place where it properly belongs — in the spiritual history of Israel.
Martin Buber - speaking as a Jew - with reference to Christianity

An anecdote:
Martin Buber is said to have addressed some Christian priests as follows: We all await the Messiah. You believe he has already come and gone, while we do not. I propose that we await Him together. When He comes, we can ask Him: were you here before? And I hope that I will be close enough to whisper in his ear, 'For the love of heaven, don't answer'.

Jews are just like everyone else, only more so.
Jewish saying

Judaism today isa historic faith and a living inheritance. It is shaped by the Talmud — a quarry of rabbinic interpretation edited in Palestine in the fourth century and in Babylon in the sixth century, but drawn from earlier sources. The Talmud is made up of the teachings of the rabbis in the Mishnah and then presents extended discussion and application of these teachings in the Gemara. Much of this teaching is profoundly humanistic. Neither the Bible nor the Talmud is seen as the final word — *"The truth is the considered judgement of the majority of authoritative interpreters in every generation"* — *Yerushalmi Sanhedrin 4:2*

As in any religion, there are conservative and progressive schools but Judaism has always been its own most searching critic. Legalism is a danger but many Jewish scholars do not see the Law as an end in itself but rather a ladder to draw closer to God and a means of sanctifying everyday life. Not since the fall of the Temple has there been any priesthood, and leadership depends on the consent of the people. Nationalism too is a danger but the Jewish calling is seen as that of a custodian and should not be exclusive. The Law is for all humanity, which has one unity and one destiny.

The relationship of Jew and Christian has been deeply tragic, shadowed by appalling moments of history and the imperialism of a church which claimed the Jewish heritage but often cast out the Jew.
Now we can be free to explore the Torah together, to respect Jewish family and community life, and to be reminded of the unity of the sacred and secular. Christians need the witness of Jewish scholars:
 — to aid our understanding of Jesus the Jew,
  — to challenge us to avoid a sentimental or romantic faith which
  puts its trust in a saviour but is little earthly use,
   — to teach us how faith can be sustained, when structures fall, and
  rituals fail, and God himself seems lost in darkness.

It may be then that Christians will be able to share their own distinctive understanding of God's work among us, of the fulfilment of the law in unexpected ways, and to give fresh insight into the way in which atonement is won out of guilt and suffering. Above all, it may be possible to acknowledge together the universal witness of Jesus the Jew, who belongs to both traditions and to all peoples.

Reform Jews usually adapt rabbinic teaching to the surrounding culture.
Orthodox Jews adhere more strictly to tradition.
Conservative Jews are conservative at home but more liberal in company.

TRAVELLING TOGETHER

There is no God but Allah, and Muhammad is his prophet.

I am no more than one who gives warning.   Muhammad

Nothing is said to you except what was said to the messengers who came before you.
                    God's messenger to Muhammad - The Qur'an 41:43

The unbelievers among the people of the Book and the pagans shall burn for ever in the fire of Hell.   The Qur'an 98:6

Be courteous when you argue with the People of an earlier revelation. Say: 'We believe what has been revealed to us and what has been revealed to you. Our God and your God is one'   The Qur'an 29:46

Believers; have neither Jews nor Christians for your friends.   The Qur'an 5:51

You will surely find that the nearest in affection to believers are those who say —'We are Christians'.   The Qur'an - 5:82

I am sent to you by Allah to confirm the Torah already revealed and to tell you of an apostle who will come after me, whose name is Ahmed (= Muhammad).
                    Jesus - according to The Qur'an 61:6

Unbelievers are those who say: 'Allah is one of three'. There is one God.
                    The Qur'an 5:74

Every novelty is an innovation, every innovation is an error, every error leads to Hell.
                    Islamic

It is clear that Muhammad walked in the path of the prophets.
                    Patriarch Timothy I 8C.

Religion is a falcon with which to hunt.   Arab saying

They did not kill Jesus, nor crucify him, but they thought they did.   The Qur'an 4:157

There should be no coercion in the matter of faith.   The Qur'an 2:256

The Muslim world has not been guilty of systematic forcible conversion, nor arbitrary ghettoisation, nor total and massive expulsion, nor genocide, nor a Holocaust.
                    Mohammed Talbi - Dean of Tunis University – 1997

Do not think you are going amongst infidels. Muslims have attained a salvation.
                    Pope Pius XI — to a missionary setting out for Libya

Islam (= 'submission' that is to Allah)) is the faith proclaimed by
Muhammad (570 - 632) as a renewal of age-old truth. He reformed the old
Arabian tribal religions, re-established strict monotheism, and brought
unity and social reform to the heart of the Middle East.

There is extensive common ground between Islam and Christianity:
- The Qur'an values much Jewish and Christian teaching — seeing Jesus as a
  prophet and his predecessors as true Muslims
- Christians, in turn, should be able to recognise Muhammad as a prophet, and a
  great deal of the Qur'an as inspired
- The clear, uncomplicated teaching of Islam is attractive. It acknowledges no
  priests or sacraments, no 'church' and no distinctions between members
- The outward discipline of prayer, fasting and pilgrimage is a helpful
  framework for inward spirituality
- Islamic teaching on almsgiving, equality, and justice deserves the respect of
  Western society.

There is also much pain in Christian-Muslim history and many differences
remain. True dialogue, which alone can win through to genuine
understanding, must be honest about these. It is not just the current
concerns over the position of women and the administration of justice —
Christians still have much to do in social matters — but also deep
differences of doctrine — for example:
- in the approach to the Qur'an and the Bible. Christians now practise a greater
  freedom in interpreting their own scriptures
- there are disagreements between the scriptures, as witness the Qur'an's
  declaration that Jesus was not really crucified – 4:157
- the Qur'an includes harsh condemnation of non-believers
- Islam may have a rather different vision of society
- any doctrine of incarnation or trinity is rejected by Islam.
  (the latter is assumed in the Qur'an to be Father, Mary and Son)
- the theme of eternal punishment plays a much greater part in the Qur'an than
  in Christian scriptures.
Yet, whatever these differences, in a world fractured by militancy, there is
an overwhelming need to foster mutual understanding and to work together
against those who would exploit religious division.

The Bahai have roots in Islam. Ali Muhammad was executed in Persia in 1850 for seeking
to reform Islam. Baha Ullah (Mirza Husein Ali) later became leader and messiah of the
movement, which opposed slavery, polygamy, jihad and the subjugation of women. It has
developed into a positive movement for peace, justice and equality.

What is but one, the wise will call by manifold names.

In the great teaching of the Vedas there is no sectarianism. *Thoreau*

In India I found a race of mortals, possessing everything but being possessed by nothing.
Apollonius Tynnaeus - 1 C.

India was the motherland of our race and Sanskrit the mother of Europe's languages.
India was the mother of our philosophy, of much of our mathematics, of the ideas
embodied in Christianity, of self-government and democracy. In many ways, Mother
India is the mother of us all. *Will Durant - American historian*

Among a thousand cows the calf finds its mother, so the deed once done follows after the
doer. *The Mahabharata*

As rivers flow and disappear at last
In ocean's waters, name and form renouncing,
So too the sage, released from name and form
Is merged in the divine and ultimate existence. *Mundaka Upanishad*

The Supreme Intelligence dances in the soul for the purpose of removing our sins. They
never see rebirths who behold this mystic dance. *the Unmai Vilakkam (mediaeval)*

A chapter which had a Western beginning will have to have an Indian ending. The
only way for mankind is the Indian Way. *Arnold Toynbee*

The Bhagavad Gita
Those who are born will surely die and the dead will be born again. 2:27

The wise look impartially on a learned brahmin, a cow, an elephant, a dog
and an outcaste. 5:18

In the powerful, I am their strength — free from desire and attachment;
in everyone, I am the desire which is not contrary to morality. 7:11

A man of action is superior to an ascetic, or a follower of the path of
knowledge, or one who blindly performs rituals. 6:46

Great souls who have become one with Me have reached the highest goal;
they do not undergo rebirth, a condition which is impermanent and full of
pain and suffering. 8:15

HINDUISM

HINDUISM

Hinduism is a broad river of ancient tradition — a hospitable family of religions. It contains a rich wealth of scripture, imagination, story and symbolism, which can make the Christian tradition appear austere, confined and limited. It is largely, though not always, tolerant — absorbing different ideas as aspects of truth. Krishna, the Buddha, and Jesus have all been seen as manifestations of the divine and Hindus visit the temples of their choice to suit their own devotion. There is unity lying behind the multiplicity but it is a diffuse kind of monotheism, which to outsiders appears to blur the boundaries of truth and falsehood, right and wrong.

To a Hindu, what we do now, sows the seeds of the future and the working out of this 'karma' may follow us through many incarnations. Sin is often a matter of ritual impurity but there is a seeking after inner purity, leaving behind all restlessness and desire. The disciplines which lead to inner peace may start with the forms of yoga now popular in the West but many of these are preliminaries to the greater yoga. This is a life-seeking discipline which brings release, and it may involve devotion or meditation or good deeds.

The positive Christian understanding of individuality, history and human society gives way to a communal culture of acceptance and absorption. The thrusting, missionary spirit is largely absent as for many there is no redeemer, no good news, and no great expectation that this world can be changed for the better. Nevertheless, there can be reform affecting women, marriage and caste, for these are cultural matters which do not belong to the heart of India's ancient wisdom.

Given such wealth, there is much for Christians to learn without needing to sacrifice our different truths.

....

Hindu = from the Indus. A Hindu calls his belief 'Sanatana Dharma' — the Way of Truth. **Jainism** — one of the many developments of Hinduism emphasises the sacredness of all life.
The **Caste** system seems to have developed as layer after layer of invaders pushed earlier inhabitants to the lower levels of society. It became associated with belief in karma -- an effective tool of social control as each person deserves, therefore, their place in society.
Yoga = yoke and therefore a discipline. Compare Jesus: 'Take my yoke upon you'.
The **International Society for Krishna Consciousness** or Hare Krishna movement springs from Hindu tradition but it is more clearly monotheistic, rejects all divisions based on caste, and is strictly vegetarian.

TRAVELLING TOGETHER

I have seen an ancient path, trodden by Buddhas of a bygone age.
Siddharta Gautama - the Buddha

The Eightfold Path — Right views, Right intention. Right speech, Right action, Right effort, Right mindfulness, Right concentration.
Gautama

A man shot with a poisoned arrow refused to take it out till he knew who had fired it and why. He died. So it is with those who want to find out all about God before doing something about their suffering and misery.
Gautama

I have gone round in vain the cycles of many lives ever striving to find the builder of the house of life and death. How great is the sorrow of life that must die! But now I have seen you, housebuilder; never more shall you build this house. The rafters of sin are broken, the ridge-pole of ignorance is destroyed. The fever of craving is past: for my mortal mind is gone to the joy of Nirvana.
Gautama

No doer is there; naught but the deed is found. Nirvana is, but not the man who seeks it; the path exists but not the traveller on it.
Visuddhimagga

All that we are is made up of our thoughts. If one speaks or acts with an evil mind, than pain follows, even as the wheel, the hoof of the ox.
The Dhammapada

All composite things decay. Diligently work out your own salvation. Whatever grounds there be for good works undertaken with a view to rebirth, all of them are not worth one sixteenth part of that goodwill, which is the heart's release. Goodwill alone shines and burns and flashes forth in surpassing them.
Ittuittaka

Generating one moment of love for one being is greater than making an ocean of offerings to a thousand Buddhas for a thousand ages.
Gautama

As long as space remains
So long as sentient beings' suffering is there
I will be there
To serve as much as I can.
Shantideva

I always believe that it is much better to have a variety of religions, a variety of philosophies rather than one single one. This is necessary because of the different mental dispositions of human beings. Each religion has certain unique ideas or techniques, and learning about them can only enrich one's own faith
Tenzin Gyatso - the 14th Dalai Lama

Gautama (448 -? 368 BC) was born as a prince in Northern India and became known as 'the Buddha' = 'the enlightened one'. His teaching is a development from Hinduism. He does not speak of God, as he felt that nothing could be said about the divine. The self also is indeterminate — rather close to Hume's 'nothing but a bundle of different perceptions' or to the conclusions of Daniel Dennett that all our sensations, perceptions and consciousness do not yield an unchanging, independent self.

Gautama sought to discover the wisdom that stills the pain of suffering. He came to believe that we can detach ourselves from all that is illusory and impermanent and be able to walk the way which leads to ultimate being and peace — the state of Nirvana. In contrast to Christianity, it is the All which matters and not the Self. So reincarnation is rather like one flame being lit from another until it is finally extinguished or 'as dew drops into the shining sea'.

Gautama was an itinerant preacher and similar to Jesus in his way of teaching, his temptations and his conflicts with authority. But Jesus sought out the poor, spoke prophetically to the powerful and saw purpose in his own suffering. Gautama was more solitary, more concerned with our inward quest and with a 'kingdom' reached by steady ascent rather than once for all entry. His creed was kindly and moderate, promoting reverence and humility. Later Buddhist teachers have developed the idea of 'bhodisattvas' — those who postpone the realisation of themselves to become saviours who help others on the road. Aung San Suu Kyi of Burma shows how activism for the sake of others is an authentic part of the Buddhist tradition.

There is no church but orders of monks lead disciplined lives and the wisest attract many pupils. They have a profound understanding of human psychology and an ability to cultivate serenity in a troubled world. Christians, in contrast, have much to say about God and about this world as the arena in which God is at work but the wealth of Buddhist teaching and practice can be helpful to Christian disciples.

Zen Buddhism was developed in Japan by Eisai (1141 - 1215 AD).. It emphasises *direct* experience — all scriptures and dogmas are avoided and even explanations are thought misleading. The ideal is to achieve experience and action without striving.

'What is Zen?'   *'Boiling oil over a blazing fire.'*   *Zen Mondo*

TRAVELLING TOGETHER

There is but one God. Truth by name, the creator, all pervading spirit, without fear, without enmity. Whose existence is unaffected by time, who does not take birth, self existent, who is realised through his grace.

— the Mool Mantra - the Sikh Creed

Why look for God in the forest when God is at home?   the Adi Granth - 684

You are immanent in all beings.   the Adi Granth 1291

If I could write with the winds everlasting, pens dipped in oceans of ink; yet must your glory transcend all my striving.   Guru Nanak

Gone is the burden we bring from our past, the burden we carry through death and rebirth. In the midst of God's faithful, our spirits are cleansed, set free by the Guru's grace.   Guru Arjan

The dawn of a new day is the herald of a sunset. Earth is not your permanent home.
Ravidas - Adi Granth - 793

Make mercy your mosque, righteousness your prayer mat, compassion your creed and your prayer.   Guru Nanak

I will make sparrows hunt down hawks;
I will turn jackals into fiercer lions;
And make one single Sikh fight a legion.   Guru Nanak

Strengthen me, O Lord, that I shrink not from righteous deeds, that freed from the fear of my enemies, I may fight with faith and win.   Guru Gobind Singh

Just as the castor oil plant imbibes the scent of the adjacent sandalwood, similarly even those who have fallen are freed by the company of the true ones.   the Adi Granth - 861

Why should one speak evil of women, they who give birth to kings?   Guru Nanak

Call no one high or low. God, the one potter, has made all alike. God's light alone pervades all creation.   the Adi Granth

All castes and special clothing are like dust.   Guru Nanak - Adi Granth 352

All men in reality are the same, none is separate; a single form, a single creation.
Guru Gobind Singh

Guru Nanak (1469-1539) was a poet and singer who grew up 40 miles from Lahore, India. He sought to renew Hinduism and Islam and bring them together by drawing on the best of each. His high monotheism was more personal than that of Islam — emphasising devotion to the Name more than obedience and giving greater place to the grace of God.

The rituals of place, time and ceremony were largely laid aside for a discipleship based on attitudes and action. There is little hierarchy in Sikhism — every gurdwara entrance being set a step lower than the outside to welcome the lowest of the low. The equality of all who come is celebrated in the common meals that follow worship. Karma and rebirth are taught but not in a fatalistic way. There is a balanced approach to ethics and a strong regard for human rights — the 9th Guru was martyred for defending the rights of *Hindus*.

The leadership was handed down through several gurus but the reconciliation of Hindu and Muslim was never achieved and severe persecution influenced the changes made by the 10th in line — Guru Gobind Singh. He formed the Khalsa — the order of Sikh warriors immediately recognisable by the symbols they wear and the turbans that wrap their uncut hair. This is a defensive order that now includes most adult males. The Guru from then on is said to reside in the Khalsa and the Adi Granth (the scriptures) rather than in a person.

Most Sikh teaching can be shared by Christians, and Sikhs themselves are admired for their very open witness to their faith. As in Christian history, the warrior image can be abused and turned to intolerance and coercion but this is only by turning away from the true teaching.

Sikh = disciple.
Guru = teacher.
The Adi Granth was compiled by Guru Arjan in 1604. It is the scripture of the Sikh faith and includes contributions from Hindu and Muslim holy men.
The **Gurdwara** is the temple.
Sikh men normally take the name **Singh** meaning lion.
Women often take the name **Kaur** meaning princess.
The symbols worn by men and women are referred to as the '5 K's'
kesh is uncut hair, **kanga** is a comb, **kachera** a style of breeches, **kirpan** a sword — which may be very small as it is the symbol which counts, and the **kassa** a bracelet.

I am a transmitter, a believer in and admirer of antiquity.
Master K'ung - Confucius

*With coarse food to eat and water to drink, and with no pillow but my bent arm, I can
still find happiness.* Master K'ung

*Respectfulness, without the rules of propriety, becomes laborious bustle:
carefulness, without the rules of propriety, becomes timidity,
boldness, without the rules of propriety, becomes insubordination;
straightforwardness, without the rules of propriety, becomes rudeness.*
Master K'ung

*If a man be without virtues proper to humanity, what has he to do with the rites of
propriety?* Master K'ung

While you do not understand life, how can you know about death? Master K'ung

A good man, it is not mine to see. Master K'ung

*It is very difficult to associate with the populace. These sort of men grow familiar and
insolent when we have too much correspondence with them: and because they imagine
they are slighted when never so neglected, we draw their aversion upon us.*
Master K'ung

To sin and not to repent is to properly sin. Master K'ung

Acknowledge your benefits by the return of other benefits, but never revenge injuries.
Master K'ung

Obey heaven, love your neighbour as yourself. Master K'ung

*Punishments are too common: that if the magistrates were good men, the wicked would
conform their lives to theirs.* Master K'ung

*You have been willing to hear us, O Ti, for you regard us as our Father. I, your child,
dull and unenlightened, am unable to show my feelings.*
- from the prayer used by the Emperor at the Altar of Heaven in Peking

Those who are great among men are those who do not lose their childlike heart.
Mencius - 372 - 289 BC.

Confucius was born in China in 551BC.He was a near contemporary of Socrates and the Buddha. His real name was K'ung Fu-tzu but he became known as Master K'ung. Much of his teaching was concerned with harmonious social relationships and he drew on the good from earlier traditions. His stress on propriety was certainly wedded to his class and the culture of his time but his general wisdom presents few problems for Christians. He doubted whether much could be known about the deeper truths of human existence and concentrated on what functioned well.

K'ung was reticent about God. Existing tradition spoke of Shang-Ti — the Supreme Ruler — and the Emperor would offer yearly homage to Shang-Ti on behalf of the people. K'ung preferred the less personal term 'Heaven' and described the ancient Way (Tao) as the Way of Heaven. He saw no need for priests or images but he did value ceremony — being referred to at times as 'that man of ceremony'. Everything had its rightful place in his ethical teaching and everyone was expected to show loyalty and trust to those placed above them and genuine care for those below them. In matters of justice, the emphasis was on deterrence rather than punishment — shame (loss of face) rather than fear.

The early Catholic missionaries — Matteo Ricci, Schall and Verbiest saw Confucianism as a preparation for Christianity but their openness was condemned by the Pope. The major difficulty was that of ancestor worship. The Seat of the Spirits was to be found in each home and the ancestors were believed to have power to bless the future. K'ung had accepted this tradition as a matter of due reverence but it was not of first importance for him — 'you are not yet able to serve men; how can you serve spirits?' In the same way he did not speculate about God's ways of reward and punishment but simply believed that, by and large, Heaven favours the good. K'ung's personal achievement was very dependent on whether the current ruler would listen to his advice. In the end, he felt that he had failed — 'the mountain is fallen, the high machine is demolished, and the sages are all fled'.

A later development in Confucianism is ascribed to Meng K'o (Mencius), who was born around 372BC. He believed that people are born innately good and that it is bad environment that produces bad people. He therefore stressed education as the key to a good society. Unlike K'ung, he encouraged the inner search or mystical side of religion.

**There is one thing that is invariably complete. Alone it stands and does not change.
I do not know its name. I call it TAO.**

25

The Tao that can be expressed is not the eternal Tao. 1

*Without going outdoors one knows the world. Without looking out of the window one
sees the Tao of heaven.* 47

*Why did the ancients so treasure this Tao? Is it not because it has been said of it,
'Whoever asks will receive; whoever has sinned will be forgiven?'* 62

*The world is a spiritual thing which must not be handled. Whoever handles it destroys
it, whoever wants to hold on to it loses it.* 29

The soft wins victory over the hard. The weak wins victory over the strong. 36

*Whoever knows their maleness and guards their femaleness, eternal Life does not leave
them and they become again as a child.* 28

*Whoever cherishes love acts but has no designs. Morality is the penury of faith and trust
and the beginning of confusion.* 38

*I have three treasures that I treasure and guard. The first is called 'love'; the second is
called 'sufficiency'; the third is called 'not daring to lead the world'.*

67

*So is the Man of Calling: he encompasses the One and sets an example to the world. He
does not lay claim to glory, therefore he accomplishes works.* 22

*So also is the Man of Calling: if he wants to stand above his people he puts himself
below them. If he wants to be ahead of his people, he stands back.* 66

*So spoke the Man of Calling: 'Whoever takes upon himself the misfortune of the realm,
he is king of the world.* 78

*As to dwelling, live near the ground.
As to thinking, hold to that which is simple.
As to conflict, pursue fairness and generosity.
As to government, do not attempt to control.
As to work, do what you like doing.
As to family life, be fully present.*

Lao-tse - Tao Te Ching

....

Lao-tse was an archivist at the Imperial Court in China and rather older than Master K'ung who met him briefly. Lao-tse is an epithet meaning 'the Old One' and he was also known as old 'long-ear' i.e. teacher. He died in 520 BC. and his sayings were later gathered into the Tao Te Ching. The idea of Tao = 'the Way' (pronounced more like 'Dao') was not new but Lao-tse deepened its meaning. The concept is close to that of the 'Logos' or divine Principle said to lie at the heart of all things.

Lao-tse taught that the Tao had to be known directly without striving. A disciple should be like a bamboo shoot — firm and resolute but empty within. In this void, receptivity would be complete and effortless. The Old One had little time for externals and artificiality — or for the ceremonies and proprieties held dear by Master K'ung. It was a more passive and inner approach to reality.

Christians will readily find parallels between the teaching of Lao-tse and that of Jesus even though Jesus' disciples are clearly called to a more active life of service. The 'Man of Calling' is very much akin to some Jewish teaching regarding the Messiah, as an ideal man beyond time. Lao-tse saw the Man of Calling as 'one who never acts yet nothing is left undone.' Life expresses itself through him — rather as Jesus is seen as one who emptied himself so that the Father was expressed through the Son. This example flows on into all human conduct — Lao-tse's teaching being an excellent antidote to the coercive, controlling tendency in much of Christian history. Even rulers were to rule as far as possible by not ruling.

If Confucianism was aristocratic, Taoism was egalitarian and a way for the common people to follow. Its popularity, however, led to its embrace of older animistic beliefs and its practice today is often bound up with belief in demons and nature spirits.

It was Chuang tse in the 4 C.BC. who developed the teaching of the two principles derived from the Tao of yin and yang. This is the polarity manifest in light and darkness, masculine and feminine, heaven and earth. Sometimes Confucianism and Taoism were seen as part of this polarity — being active and passive. Harmony with the Tao meant achieving a balance between all such polarities — so much so, that even good and evil seem to dissolve and the view emerged that we should let things be. The arrival of Buddhism in China led to further developments in Taoism and some of these took on imperial trappings and elaborated a pantheon of gods far removed from the original teaching.

There have been times of enriching dialogue between the great faiths.Eight generations of the Bakhtisho family were among the many Christians, who served the first Islamic rulers as physicians, translators and advisors. The 'heretical' Syrian Christians were midwives to the birth of Muslim culture and learning — persecuted by the Byzantine orthodox, they welcomed Muslim tolerance and their schools of learning flourished in Edessa, Seleucia-Ctesiphon and Gundeshapur. This last also gave refuge to pagan philosophers driven out of Athens by Justinian.

Muslims spoke of *itijihad* — the struggle for truth, through dialogue and reason. Christian scholars had translated Greek works into Syriac and were well placed to convert these into Arabic. Among them were Severus Sabkhut, Jacob of Edessa and Yuhanna bin Adi al-Tikriti.. Qanawati lists 60 translators linked to the 'House of Wisdom' in Baghdad of whom 58 were Christian. Its first Principal was a Nestorian Christian — ibn Masawah. His most famous pupil was the Christian, Hunayn bin Ishaq (809-873) who led a team of translators that relayed the works of Galen, Aristotle, Plato and Hippocrates to the Muslim world. Hunayn published a guide to accurate translation and laid the foundations of scientific and philosophical terminology in Arabic.

This was a time of public dialogue. Patriarch Timothy I debated with Caliph al-Mahdi; Hunayn with Yehya bib al-Munajim and Dinkha of Tikrit with al-Mas'udi. These were not dialogues of antagonists but of thinkers who respected each other. The Christian philosopher, Yuhanna bin Adi was taught by the Muslim thinker, al-Kindi, as well as by the Christian, Abu Bishr Matta.

In time, however, there was a hardening of Muslim attitudes. Christians suffered from discrimination, social exclusion and taxation.The *'gates of itijihad were closed'*.

In the tenth century, it was Córdoba in Andalusian Spain that was the centre of western learning. Established by Caliph al-Rahman, the largest library held 400,000 volumes, at a time when Christian Europe could scarce muster 400 in one place. The Great Mosque was shared by Muslims and Christians. Hasdai, a Jew, was Grand Vizier and Judah Halevi was celebrated as 'the greatest poet in Andalusia'. The Muslim philosopher, Ibn Rushd (Averrhoes) wrote his commentaries on Aristotle and the Jewish scholar, Maimonides his *"Guide for the Perplexed"*. The Christian, Peter Abélard, developed the 'yes and no' theology of Erigena Scotus.

The Christians of Toledo celebrated the Eucharist in Arabic and welcomed scholars from all over Europe. Peter, Abbot of Cluny, commissioned the first translation of the Qur'an into Latin. The greatest translators, like Robert of Ketton and Michael Scot were, in effect, explorers, discovering new worlds of learning.

So Muslim science and mathematics spread to Europe and mutual respect was such that, even in 1220, the crusading Emperor Frederick, who spoke Arabic, restored the Muslim call to prayer in Jerusalem.

In sixteenth century India, the Muslim ruler, Akbar the Great, set out to be 'emperor of all the faiths'. He married a Hindu and held weekly seminars, where Muslims, Hindus, Christians and others held dialogue. He abolished the poll tax on non-Muslims, ended slavery and gifted Amritsar to the Sikhs.

Why did these years of enlightenment end? A change of ruler, an invasion, social collapse — these could cause a resurgence of fundamentalism. In Andalusia, it was the fierce Berber tribesmen that fragmented the Muslim empire and the devastation of the Black Death that helped to pave the way for the 'triumph' of Christian orthodoxy in Spain, when Ferdinand and Isabella drove out the Jews and the 'Moors'.

Today, the world's fundamentalists would have the gates of *itijihad* firmly closed. They do not recognise God's insistence: *"are not these my people also?"*. The orthodox do not see the need to keep the city gates open (Rev 21:25) so that travellers from the open country may come and go. The tolerant may not mind, but too often, they are indifferent to those who pass through. It is the seekers and dissenters who can be truly catholic and welcome the inter-faith world, where the uniformities give way to the 'yes and no' of creative thought.

"Orthodox" means 'right opinion' and came to mean 'true glory', but beware, the truth cannot be gated and guarded. The 'true glory' transcends our lesser creeds. We can take courage, abandon our exclusive past and discover the inclusive will of God for all his people — each with the best of their own.

....

"We should not be ashamed to acknowledge truth from whatever source it comes to us."
al-Kindi

That's it then? We can't trust scripture — Jesus isn't God — the Trinity is redundant — the Church has gone off the rails — there's not much left, is there?

On the contrary: we can meet Jesus as if for the first time — Jesus the man — a man inspired — a man to inspire. Jesus, in whom, through whom, we can see God. Jesus, stepping out of the stained glass, off the sacred pedestal and into the crowded street. Jesus, as the first disciples knew him — a man of intense conviction, evident charisma and practical love. Jesus, who was not God but in whose company people found God.

It doesn't mean that God is found nowhere else. It doesn't mean that God is found in no-one else. Who has looked everywhere? Who has lined up the candidates, compared them and graded them? Enough! We have found what we have found.

In seeing Jesus, we look through the eyes of those who came after. We cannot be sure of the details, yet through their stories, he comes clearly into focus. What do we see?

We see someone who trusted people. He trusted his friends to stand by him; trusted his hearers to think for themselves; he trusted women to be as searching in their thinking as men; he trusted children to be worth encouraging. He took risks. He trusted the collaborators and the resistance fighter, the wealthy and the poor, the establishment figure and the outlawed, the mentally ill, the foreigner. Sometimes people let him down; sometimes they betrayed his trust but it did not put him off. He appealed to the heart. He sought and found "that of God in everyone" — to use a fine Quaker phrase. Let's not imagine that such trust is easy. He was not blind to human failing or to the awful possibilities of evil, but he was willing, if need be, to discount each person's past for the sake of their future — *"I came not to condemn but to save"* Jn 12:47.

All this was not a matter of personal preference. It was because Jesus was held by a vision of what God was seeking — a greater community, a Commonwealth of generosity and service. The realisation of this community required an openness, an inclusiveness, that knew no boundaries. In that society, at that time, it meant including the sick and disabled — though they were thought to be suffering God's punishment for their transgressions. It meant including the 'sinners' who could not fulfil the requirements of the law, because of occupation or circumstance.

It meant including the rabble (John 7:48) and the prostitutes. It meant including the Samaritans — despised because history is hard to forgive — and non-Jews of all kinds — even the Roman soldiers that held his country in an iron grip.

Such openness is not easy. Our instincts are to stay with the group, to fence ourselves in, to fear the outsider. To be open to all is to become 'defenceless' and the risks are real.

We should recognise the pull of loyalty and tradition in a Jewish community under serious threat. The land was not only occupied, it was increasingly colonised and there was every justification for patriotic hatred. Jesus' first priority may well have been to "the lost sheep of the house of Israel". It may even be that his own understanding was limited at first. His brother, James, who became leader of the Christian community in Jerusalem, appears to have remained in many ways a traditional Jew, as well as a Christian.

The first great crisis of the early church is illustrated by Peter's dream of the clean and unclean animals — a dream that helped to bring about the removal of the barriers between Jews and Gentiles. Yet that revolution was surely well-rooted in the everyday attitude of Jesus to those about him.

We have said that such openness is not easy. When we are hurt, when we are wronged, Jesus teaching is that we should forgive. This is a greater word than we often credit. It is not a 'letting off' nor a gesture that demonstrates our rightness and nobility. It is a recognition that we often stand where they stand — that "all fall short of the glory of God". The standard is God's forgiveness of us. It means unconditional acceptance and love — best illustrated by the forgiving father in the Prodigal Son story . The Lord's Prayer reminds us how to live in the quality of that forgiveness, and Jesus' words from the cross: "Father, forgive them, they do not know what they are doing", shows what it can mean in the greatest extremity.

Such extremity is a painful reminder that living the Kingdom of God is not a gushing, sentimental thing. It involves a struggle for justice. For Jesus, that meant challenging social division, the deep inequities of his society, the oppressive taxation, burdensome religious practice, and the exploitation of the poor. It was not for nothing that both the Jewish authorities and the Roman authorities saw him as subversive — or that "the common people heard him gladly". PTO

REDISCOVERING JESUS

He was disturbing the natural order of things, the 'God-given' order of things and the very basis of wealth and power. John the Baptist had already been imprisoned and executed, because he was seen as a threat. Jesus' teaching and popularity was more far-reaching in its scope and dangerous in its attack upon prevailing values. He was naturally restricted by the possibilities of his time and situation. How much more there is for us to do today in confronting injustice and oppression, for our opportunities are so much greater. For us too, it may involve sacrifice, as well as determination and struggle. Jesus' costly challenge to the corruption practised in the very temple courts rings down through the centuries.

The heart of Jesus' teaching is bound up with the word 'love' but this is an umbrella that embraces all of the above. It is more than family feeling based on kinship, more than sympathy for others. It is a deep and tough recognition of the value and potential of each person and the seeking of their highest welfare. The recognition is in seeing that everyone is "coined for himself" — a special creation of God, and in whom God is at work.

Such love can and does include love of self. Although the road of self-sacrifice is an important element in Jesus' teaching, there is no sign of the self-denigration that has sometimes been characteristic of Christian teaching. Tyndale's fine translation in the story of the Prodigal Son: *"then he came to himself"* is a reminder that we can overdo our advocacy of 'selflessness'. Jesus transmits without qualification the Jewish teaching "love your neighbour as yourself". But he also pushes the boundaries of neighbourliness. As we have seen, he recognises no boundaries and moves into new territory by teaching: *"love your enemy"* .

This last can be easily spoken when enemies are far away but alien settlers were everywhere in Galilee, and Roman soldiers frequented the streets of Judaea. Defence of our own interests, wariness of neighbours and fear of enemies is natural to us all, but the ethic of love means removing barriers and entering completely into the concerns of others. In Jesus' teaching, God enters our lives unreservedly. In the same way, we are asked to seek the welfare of every traveller we meet.

....

In this game of high stakes, God has declared what is trumps. Not clubs (sheer force), diamonds (the power of wealth) or even spades (dogged hard work) but hearts.

R C Walls

There is nothing rose-tinted in this. Jesus' 'defencelessness' is
symbolised by his baptism — with its unquestioning identification with
others and its overtones of death. This is a foreshadowing that is starkly
shown in the brutal end he ultimately suffered. This was a consequence
of his living ministry and it demanded courage. Unrelenting love may
need courage — the taking up of a cross, if it is the only way to see
through a mission. This is 'giving up the whole world to save one's
soul' — not in the sense of gaining a place in heaven but as a holding
on to complete integrity — being true to our selves, to our calling and
to God.

Such courage is derived from God and this is why it is difficult to
divorce 'living the good life' from faith in God. If we love God, we can
love our neighbour — but how do we love God? Better to say: 'if we
know that God loves us, we are able to love our neighbour and, maybe,
just maybe, our enemy'. Christians share a vision of the good with
very many others but they also possess a particular vision of God and
this has inspired and sustained so many over the centuries.

It is therefore possible to live without undue anxiety, without being
burdened by the passing of time, without being depressed by the power
of evil. We can know God as 'abba', 'Father'; we can be convinced:
*" that there is nothing in death or life, in the world as it is or the world as it
shall be, in the forces of the universe, in heights or depths — nothing in all
creation that can separate us from the love of God"* Rom 8:38f.
Despite the extremity that Jesus suffered, he could still say —
"Father, into your hands I entrust my spirit. "

All this is 'Gospel' — Good News for everyone. We need no more.
Theories about how our salvation is conjured out of Jesus' death are of
little relevance. Speculation about those who lived long before Jesus or
far away from any Christian contact becomes irrelevant. This is a
vision of the good and a vision of God — and the spirit of God
empowers us to live out these visions. Jesus embodies such truth —
'incarnates' it. He becomes the one enabling us to see when the tide of
unseeing retreats. He worked as God works. He is a 'saviour' because
he shows us God, the Saviour. He is the Word that is made flesh —
God's word to us. This is the Gospel.

THE WAY

This above all, don't lie to yourself.   Dostoevsky

A game is playing in which heads or tails may turn up. What will you wager? The true course is not to wager at all. Yes, but you must wager; this depends not on your will, you are embarked in the affair.   Pascal

My knowledge is pessimistic, but my willing and hoping are optimistic.
                                                      Schweitzer

It is nowhere forbidden to laugh or to eat one's fill or gain possessions or enjoy oneself with musical instruments or drink wine.   Calvin

I can't think that when God sent us into this world, he had irreversibly decreed that we should be perpetually miserable in it.   John Wesley

It is not entirely ignoble that faced with this unloving, impersonal universe, we make a little island of warmth and love and science and art for ourselves. That's not entirely a despicable role for us to play.   Steven Weinberg

To know whether a man is a good man, one does not ask what he believes but what he loves.   Augustine

You have been entrusted into your own keeping as if an orphan had been committed to your trust.   Epictetus

Being a part, we cannot grasp the whole; we are at its mercy. We may assent to it, or rebel against it; but we are always caught up by it and enclosed within it. Love is our light and our darkness, whose end we cannot see.   Jung

They all died in faith, not having experienced the promises, but having seen them far ahead, and were convinced and made them their own, and knew that they were strangers and pilgrims on earth.   Hebr 11:13

The way that can be named is not the Eternal Way.   Tao Te Ching

I have gone forward, not as one travelling in a road cast up and well prepared, but as a man walking in a miry place, in which are stones here and there, safe to step on
.   John Woolman

I am going on ahead to prepare a place for you.   Jesus - Jn 14:2

Don't worry, duckie, there will be plenty left for you to find out.

Mrs Crick - to her son, Francis - who jointly discovered the structure of DNA.

The Jewish prophets, Gautama, Master K'ung and Lao-tse sought out the ancient paths, so that we might travel wisely. Muhammad instructed his followers to 'be in the world like a traveller'. Hindus refer to their faith as 'the Way of Truth' and Jesus' disciples were known as 'Followers of the Way'. For pilgrims, it is an outward journey and a journey inwards — the Way is there before us, it is deep within us, and it is the manner of our going.

There will be a mixed company of wayfarers — many unrecognised by the names they bear — all who seek truth and are heartened by the wonder of it; all who seek humanity and are themselves of a humane spirit; all who practise the law of love which is no law but the very Spirit of reality. For the universe is not unloving and impersonal, even though God so respects our growing that we can only meet him as another 'wayfarer who turns aside to rest for a night' — Jer 14:8 & Lk 24:28. For God is indeed with us — 'Emmanuel' — though the manner of that incarnation will often elude our grasp.

There is a highway — a way of holiness, of wholeness and 'it shall be for the wayfarers' — Is 35:8. There will be green pastures but certainly there will be wilderness too. Often we will be tempted to turn back or to turn away from our companions but their salvation is ours and ours is theirs. We will break bread with them and we Christians will find Christ in them and it may be that they will find themselves, and Christ in themselves and in us. He, as ever, will travel on to prepare a place for us and we can ask no more. As to doctrines, it is best to travel light. Jurgen Moltmann has suggested that our theology should simply be a theology of the way, for it cannot yet be a theology of the home country.

And let there be laughter ....

'Tis a brave world — do not be afraid of it; do not calculate your chances so closely that you will miss your chance; do not pretend to know what you do not know. Work and laugh and give thanks for these three are one.

Erasmus

Mo shoraidh slan leat, 'sgoch ait an taid thu.

I said to myself 'I am determined to be wise' but wisdom was beyond my reach — all that has happened lies out of reach, deep down, deeper than anyone can fathom.

Eccles 7:24

STATISTICS

World religions:

Christians	1,600 million	——
Hindus	800	"
Muslims	750	"
Buddhists	325	"
Confucians	225	"
Taoists	50	"
Sikhs	20	"
Jews	15	"

USA:

Christians	106 million	——
Jews	5.8	"
Muslims	5.5	"
Hindus	1.3	"
Buddhists	1.0	"

UK:

Christians	5.2 million	——
Muslims	1.0	"
Hindus	500	"
Sikhs	300 thousand	
Jews	280	"
Buddhists	25	"

CHRISTIAN DENOMINATIONS:

Church of Rome	1	billion
Orthodox	300	million
Lutheran	70	"
Methodist	70	"
Reformed	70	"
Anglican	70	"
Baptist	40	"
Pentecostal	30	"

....

Baptist	33.5	million
Church of Rome	30.0	"
Methodist	20.5	"
Pentecostal	11.0	"
Lutheran	7.6	"
Orthodox	4.0	"
Reformed	3.6	"
Anglican	2.5	"

....

Church of Rome	1.75 million	
Anglican	1.5	"
Reformed	750 thousand	
Methodist	400	"
Baptist	200	"
Pentecostal	200	"
Orthodox	75	"
Salvation Army	60	"
Quaker	20	"

Caution: _These figures represent no more than an impression of a picture which is ill-defined and ever-changing, with boundaries open to challenge._

(Orthodox — also known as Eastern Orthodox. Reformed includes Presbyterian)

....

"I count myself a Hindu, Christian, Muslim, Jew, Buddhist and Confucian."
                                                                                            Gandhi

SELECTED DATES

28   **Pentecost**
60   The first gospel written
70   Roman legions recapture Jerusalem
79   Vesuvius erupts
120   Britain becomes part of the Roman Empire

250   Persecution of Christians under Decius

313   The Peace of Constantine makes Christianity an official religion
325   The Council of Nicaea
330   The conversion of Ethiopia
397   Ninian begins his mission in Whithorn, Galloway

410   Alaric sacks Rome

525   Benedict establishes a monastery at Monte Cassino
535   The eruption of Krakatoa affects world climate
565   Columba moves from Ireland to Iona
597   Augustine sent to Kent

612   Irish missions found communities in Italy
622   Muhammad moves to Medina

793   The Vikings plunder the monastery at Lindisfarne

930   The first true Parliament is established in Iceland

1054   The great division of the Eastern and Western Churches
1066   The Norman Conquest
1071   The Seljuk Turks from Asia capture Jerusalem
1099   The Crusaders capture Jerusalem

1172   The Irish Church accepts the authority of Rome

1204   The Crusaders capture Constantinople
1208   St Francis begins his vocation
1215   King John seals Magna Carta
1215   Dogma of transubstantiation proclaimed
1274   The "Summa Theologica" of Thomas Aquinas
1290   England expels the Jews

1321   "The Divine Comedy" of Dante
1347   One fifth of Europe dies in the Black Death
1378   Rival Popes are installed

1379 John Wycliffe attacks the Papacy
1381 The Peasants Revolt

1453 The Gutenberg Bible is printed
1483 Torquemada becomes the Grand Inquisitor in Spain
1486 Publication of "The Hammer of the Witches"
1492 Columbus crosses to America

1508 Michelangelo finishes the Sistine Chapel
1509 Erasmus satirises the Church
1517 Luther challenges Rome
1525 Publication of Tyndale's New Testament
1534 Formation of the Jesuit Order
1535 Henry VIII breaks with Rome
1538 Death of Guru Nanak
1542 Francis Xavier sails for the Far East
1543 Publication of "De Revolutionibus" by Copernicus
1560 Formation of the Church of Scotland

1605 Publication of the "Advancement of Learning" by Francis Bacon
1610 The Authorised Version of the Bible
1620 The "Mayflower" sails to America
1633 Galileo forced to recant
1637 Massacre of Christians in Japan
1638 The first Welsh chapel
1645 The Royal Society is inaugurated in London
1665 The Great Plague of London
1669 George Fox founds the Society of Friends
1687 Publication of Newton's "Principia"
1690 The Battle of the Boyne

1707 England and Scotland united
1721 Bach writes the Brandenburg Concerto
1739 The first Methodist chapel
1751 First part of Diderot's 'Encyclopédie' published
1767 James Cook lands in Australia
1776 The American Declaration of Independence
1776 Adam Smith publishes "The Wealth of Nations"
1779 Publication of David Hume's "Dialogues"
1783 Sunday Schools organised in England
1791 Thomas Paine publishes "The Rights of Man"
1797 The French Revolution
1797 Edward Jenner demonstrates vaccination
1798 Publication of Malthus'"Principle of Population"
1801 England and Ireland united
1807 Slavery abolished in Britain

1825 First public railway
1829 Equal rights given to Catholics in Britain
1832 The Reform Act extends democracy
1832 Livingstone sails for Africa
1833 The Oxford Movement
1840 The first Reform synagogue in Britain
1848 Publication of "The Communist Manifesto"
1859 Charles Darwin's "The Origin of Species"
1870 The First Vatican Council
1899 Publication of Freud's "Interpretation of Dreams"

1903 The first powered aeroplane
1908 The imprisonment of Emily Pankhurst
1916 Publication of Einstein's "Special Theory"
1917 Russian Revolution
1922 The partition of Ireland
1925 Publication of Hitler's "Mein Kampf"
1928 Fleming discovers penicillin
1940 The Holocaust
1945 The atom bomb is dropped on Hiroshima
1948 Formation of The World Council of Churches
1948 Creation of "The Baby" computer
1948 The National Health Service formed in Britain
1949 Chinese Revolution
1956 Launch of the contraceptive pill
1968 Death of Martin Luther King
1992 The Church of England ordains women priests

2000 First draft of the human genome published
2009 Election of President Obama in theUnited States

....

INDEX OF TEXTS

Adi Granth	"First Book" A Sikh collection of nearly 6,000 hymns compiled in 1604 and 1704.
Apocrypha	"hidden" writings not necessarily included in the canon. Jewish: 200BC - 100AD. Christian: 2C-3C.
Atharvaveda	Hindu hymns and magic spells drawn from the Vedas (1500 -1200BC). Reflecting folk tradition.
BhagavadGita	"Song of God" 1C - 2CAD — Hindu. Included in the Indian epic — the Mahabharata.
Bible	"Books" Jewish and Jewish-Christian literature written 6CBC - 90AD.
Dhammapada	"Way of Virtue" An anthology of Buddhist teaching compiled 1C - 2CAD.
Didache	"Teaching" a first century manual of church practice and morals — possibly from Syria.
Mahabharata	"Great Epic of the Bharata Dynasty" An Indian parallel to the Greek Iliad, with interpolations of religious teaching.
Nag Hammadi	2C-3C. papyri found in Upper Egypt. Gnostic Christian writings which emphasise revelation.
Odes of Solomon	Similar to the Psalms but usually thought to be Christian in origin. 1C - 2C.
Philip. Gospel of	One of many gospels of doubtful origin, perhaps reflecting the teaching of a Gnostic sect. 1C - 2C.
Qur'an	"Reading" A written compilation of the revelations given to Muhammad. Text established in the 7C.
Rigveda	A collection of hymns drawn from the Hindu Vedas (1500 - 1200BC).
Talmud	"Instruction" 1C - 6C.AD. The teaching of the early Jewish rabbis, together with extensive commentary and application.
Tao-te Ching	"Classic of the Way of Power". A Chinese philosophical work, variously dated from the 8C – 3C.BC.
Thomas. Gospel of	A fragmentary apocryphal writing emphasising secret revelation. 1C - 2C.
Upanishads	"Sessions" Hindu mystical and philosophic texts from 700 -500BC, which elaborate the ideas contained in the Vedas..
Zohar	"Splendour" A Jewish mystical work, perhaps attributable to Simeon ben Yohai 2C.

NAME INDEX

Reference numbers with an asterisk indicate further biographical details.

A

Addison. Joseph 1672-1719 English essayist and politician. **71**
Adelard of Bath. 12C scholar of Greek and Arabic learning. **1**
Adomnán. (Eunan) (625-704) Abbot of Iona. Biographer of Columba. **62**
Adorno. Theodor 1903-69 German social philosopher. **78**
Agnew. Ruth 20C Women's Peace Movement activist. **80**
Ahlstrom. Sydney (20C) American historian. **66**
Ailred of Rievaulx. 1109-1166 Cistercian teacher. **134**
al Ghazzali. Abu 1058-1111 Islamic philosopher in Baghdad. **87 105**
al Hallaj. † 922 Persian Sufi (Muslim) in Baghdad. **87**
al Kindi. 800-870 Arab philosopher in Iraq. **1**
Alcuin of York.c.737-804 Scholar. Adviser to Charlemagne. **72 139 143**
Alexander. Bishop. 1799-1845 - formerly a German Jewish rabbi. **105**
Alexander. Leo 20C psychiatrist — adviser at the Nuremberg trials. **132**
Alexander. Samuel 1859-1938 Australian philosopher. **110**
Allen. Woody b.1935 US film actor, director and comedian. **101 119 120**
Ambrose. 339-397 German Bishop of Milan. **62 63 142 155**
Anna. Sister, contemporary pioneer of integrated schools in Ireland. **80**
Anselm. 1033-1109 Italian philosopher. Archbishop of Canterbury. **6 64**
Antony c.251-356 Hermit in Egypt. f.of Christian monasticism. **61 63 119**
Apollonius c3 – c97 Greek philosopher from Cappadocia. **163**
Aquinas. Thomas 1225-74 Italian. Father of Roman Catholic theology.
    4 35 65 76 86 87 99 109 119 140
Arch. Joseph 1826-1919 Methodist social reformer and trade unionist. **74**
Archimedes c. 287-212BC Greek mathematician. **152**
d'Argens Jean Baptiste 1703-71 French writer and free-thinker. **161**
Aristotle 384-322BC Philosopher. f. the Lyceum in Athens. **62 67 106 107**
Arjun 1563-1606 fifth Sikh Guru. Compiler of the Adi Granth. **165**
Armstrong. Karen. b.1944 Writer & broadcaster. **1 26 102**
Armstrong. 1900-71 Jazz musician. **1**
Arnold. Thomas 1795-1842 English educationist and scholar. **73**
Asoka. 273-232BC Buddhist Emperor of India. **2 153**
Asser 850 - c.909 Celtic scholar and counsellor to Alfred the Great. **73**
Astor. Nancy 1879-1964 Viscountess. First woman MP. **39**
Asvaghosa c.80 -c.150 Buddhist poet and teacher. **43 101 117**
Athanasius 296-373 Theologian. Patriarch of Alexandria. **56 102 104**
Atkins. Peter. b.1940 Oxford professor of physical chemistry. **110**
Auden. 1907-73 Wystan Poet and writer. **31**
Augustine of Hippo 354-430 Theologian. (Augustine of Canterbury is 6C.)
    50 54 77 79 82 87 88 89 92 104 110 112 118 120 122 127 153 170
Augustus (Octavian) 63BC -AD14 Founder of the Roman Empire. **17* 21**
Aurelius 121-180 Emperor and philosopher. **128**

Averroës (Ibn Rushd) 1126-98 Spanish Islamic philosopher. **72**
Ayer. A J 1910-89 Oxford philosopher. **83 156**

B

Bach Johann S. 1685-1750 Celebrated composer & organist. Lutheran. **155**
Bacon. Roger 1220-92 English philosopher & scientist. Franciscan. **6 153**
Bacon. Francis 1561-1626 English philosopher. **1 32 108 150 156**
Bacon. Francis 20C English artist. **154**
Baeck. Leo 1873 -1956 Political leader of German Jewry under Hitler.
　　36* 5 7 20 34 38 47 50 84 98 101 115 117 127 156 161
Baelz. Peter b.1923 Oxford professor of theology. **118**
Bagehot. Walter 1826-77 English economist and journalist. **22 142**
Baillie. Donald 1887-1954 Scots Reformed theologian — brother of - **89**
Baillie. John 1886-1960 Scots Reformed theologian. **27**
Bak. Per contemporary writer. **3**
Bakunin. Michael 1814-76 Russian **32**
Balfour. Arthur James 1848-1930 British statesman and philosopher. **3**
Ball. John † 1381 Executed as a leader of the Peasants Revolt. **141**
Banks 20C Catholic priest in Paraguay. **91**
Barnado. Thomas 1845-1945 Physician. f. homes for homeless boys. **74**
Barrat T D 20C Methodist - Pentecostalist evangelist. **93**
Barth. Karl 1886-1968 Swiss Reformed theologian. **7 89 144**
Bartolomé de Las Casas 1474-1566 "Apostle of the Indians" **71 90**
Basil the Great 329-79 Renowned bishop of Caesarea. **61 72 151**
Bartlett. Frederick 1886-1969 Cambridge professor of psychology **157.**
Beattie. William 18C Pioneering doctor in mental health. **75**
Beckett. Samuel 19C clergyman. **75**
Bede. the Ven. 673-735 Anglo-Saxon theologian and historian. **79**
Bedel. Indian Sufi poet. **140**
Beethoven. 1770-1827 The great German composer and musician. **114 155**
Bell. Andrew 19C Anglican educationist. **73**
Bellers. John 1654-1725 Quaker social reformer. **141**
Benedict. c.480-547 Italian abbot. Founder of Western monasticism. **61**
Benedict XIV Pope 1740-58. Able and respected. Promoted learning. **67**
Bentham. Jeremy 1748-1832 English philosopher and social reformer. **151**
Berdyaev. Nicolai 1874-1948 Russian theologian. **111 112 124 142**
Bergson. Henri 1859-1941 French philosopher. **76**
Berlin. Isaiah Berlin 1909-1997 Liberal philosopher. **145**
Bernard of Clairveaux 1090-1153 French theologian and reformer.
　　28 50 63 64 82 153
Bierce. Ambrose 1842- c.1914 Misanthropic American writer. **41**
Bismarck. Otto 1815-98 German Chancellor **144**
Blackham. H J d.2009 f. British Humanist Association. **158**
Blackstone. William 1723-80 English jurist and codifier. **76 143**
Blake. William 1757-1827 English poet, painter & mystic. **5 75 145 151**
Boehme. Jacob 1575-1624 German theosophist and mystic. **124**
Boesky. Ivan b.1937 US financier and speculator. **140**

Boguet. Henri, early 17C Jesuit writer. **69**
Bohr. Niels 1885-1962 Danish physicist. **1**
Bolt. Robert 1924-95 English playwright. **143**

Bonhoeffer. Dietrich 1906-45 Lutheran theologian and anti-fascist.
58* 82 127 135 146 156
Boniface I Pope 418-22 Restored authority of the papacy. **54**
Boniface. (Wynfrith).680-754 Anglo-Saxon "Apostle of Germany". **69**
Booth. William 1829-1912 Methodist founder of the Salvation Army. **93**
Bork. Robert b.1927 US legal scholar and judge. **130**
Bosanquet. Bernard 1848-1923 Idealist philosopher at St Andrews. **109**
Boswell. James 1740-95 Scots man of letters. Biographer of Johnson. **134**
Bottomley. Gordon 1874-1948 English poet. **152**
Bradlaugh. Charles 1833-91 Social reformer and secularist. **100**
Bradley. Denis, contemporary Irish priest and worker for reconciliation. **80**
Bradley. Ian, contemporary historian. **74**
Brahe. Tycho 1546-1601 Swedish astronomer. **70**
Brand. Paul b.1914 Missionary and pioneer in the treatment of leprosy. **52 113**
Brandt. Willy 1913-92 German statesman and Chancellor. **148**
Brigid. (Bride) 453-523 Irish abbess. **140**
Bronowski. Jacob 1908-74 Polish -British mathematician.Humanist. **42 151**
Brooke. John Hedley contemp. British historian. **101**
Browning. Robert 1812-89 English poet. **49**
Brueggemann. Walter contemporary American N.T.scholar. **35**
Bryant. Arthur 1899-1985 English historian. **147**
Buber. Martin 1878-1965 Jewish theologian and philosopher. **110 115 161**
Buckland. William 1784 -1856 Dean. Oxford geologist. **128**
Buddha. The (Gautama) c.563-483BC Founder of Buddhism.
164* 45 126 135 160
Bulgakov. Sergei 1871-1944 Russian economist Orthodox theologian. **63**
Bultmann. Rudolf 1884-1976 Lutheran New Testament scholar. **28**
Bunyan. John 1628-88 Baptist tinker, writer and pastor. **88**
Burgman. Francis, 19C.? Dutch missionary in Kenya. **71**
Buridan. Jean c.1300 -58 French scholastic philosopher. **153**
Burke. Edmund 1729-97 Irish statesman and political philosopher. **38 126 144**
Burns. Robert 1759-96 Scotland's national poet. **85**
Butler. Nicholas 1862-1947 US educationist and philosopher. **41**
Butterfield. Herbert 1900-79 English historian. **47 90 112**

C

Caesar. Julius c.101-44BC Military leader and Roman dictator. **59**
Cairns. David 1862-1946 Scots theologian and Christian apologist. **89**
Caligula. 12-41AD Roman Emperor — unstable autocrat. **17**

Calvin. Jean 1509-64 French theologian. Reformer.
55 65 69 76 93 104 148 170
Camus. Albert 1913-60 French journalist, playwright & novelist. **110 156**

Canter. Bernard - contemporary Quaker. **102**

Caretto. Carlo contemporary Italian priest. **89**

Carew. George 18C English governor in Dublin. **80**

Carlyle. Thomas 1795-1881 Scots writer and historian. **80 86**

Carnegie. Andrew 1835-1919 Scots industrialist and philanthropist. **140**

Casals. Pablo 1876-1973 Spanish cellist and conductor. **126 155**

Cassidy. Sheila contemporary activist for civil rights. **126**

Cavell. Edith 1865-1915 English nurse in occupied France. **79 144**

Ceresole. Pierre early 20C French Quaker. **102**

Chacour. Elias. contemporary Palestinian Orthodox priest. **49**

Chadderton. Lawrence 17C English Puritan. **72**

Chadwick. Henry 20C Church historian. **56**

Chalmers. James 19C missionary in New Guinea. **71**

Chalmers. Thomas 1780 -1847 Scots theologian. **75 76 142 140 144**

Chamberlain. Houston 19C US clergyman. **78**

Chamberlain. Neville 1869-1940 British statesman & Prime Minister. **144**

Chapman. Dom 1865-1933 Abbot. NT and patristic scholar. **119**

Chesterton. G K 1874 -1936 Catholic critic, novelist and poet. **35 97**

Chichester. Arthur 16C English commander in Ireland. **80**

Cholij. Roman, contemporary Orthodox writer. **82**

Chomiskey. Brendan contemporary Orthodox writer. **89**

Chomsky. Noam b.1920 Linguist and political activist. **106**

Chrysostom. John 347-407 Archb.of Constantinople. Hymn-writer. **70 76**

Chuang tse. † c.275BC Leading exponent of Taoism. **167***

Churchill. Winston 1874-1965 British Prime Minister. **10 51 76**

Cicero. Marcus Tullius 106-43BC Roman orator and statesman. **70 156**

Cobbett. William 1763 -1835 English journalist and reformer. **75**

Cobden. Richard 1804 -1865 English free trade campaigner. **148**

Cole. Martin, contemporary doctor and sex educationist. **133**

Coleridge. Samuel 1772 -1834 English poet and journalist. **156**

Collis. John Stewart b.1900 Irish scientist & "poet" of ecology. **151**

Columbanus. c.550-615 Celtic missionary in Gaul and Italy. **61 121**

Columbus. Christopher 1451-1506 Spanish adventurer **70 147**

Comfort. Alex. b.1920 Physician and writer. Specialist in ageing. **133**

Confucius. (K'ung Fu-tse) 551- 479BC Moral teacher and social reformer.
165* 24 121 146 166 167

Conolly. 19C Enlightened reformer in mental health. **72**

Consilium. Richard Pablo, contemporary Catholic priest. **15**

Constable. John 1776-1837 English landscape painter. **154**

Constantine I. 274-337 Emperor who legalised Christianity. **53 71 84 105**

Cook. James 1728-79 English navigator and explorer. **66 83**

Coomaraswami. Ananda, contemporary US religious scholar & writer. **154**

Cooper. Vernon contemporary native American. **43**

Coué. Émile 1857-1926 French psychotherapist. **95**

Coulson. Charles 1910-74 Chemist. Methodist and ecumenist. **86**

Cramp. A B contemporary Christian writer. **141**

Crick. Francis b1916 English researcher into DNA. **105 107**
Cromwell. Oliver 1599-1658 Reformer and Lord Protector. **144**
Crowfoot. Isapwo † 1890 Chief. Leader of the Blackfoot Confederacy. **43**
Cyprian. 200-258 Bishop of Carthage. **51 82**
Cyril of Alexandria 377-444 Patriarch. **63**

D

Dalai Lama. (Tenzin Gyatso) b.1935 Spiritual leader of Tibet. **146 164**
Daley. Janet, contemporary journalist and writer. **134**
Damasus I. Pope 366-84 Commissioned Jerome to produce the Bible. **54**
Damian. Peter 1007-72 Cardinal Bishop of Ostia. **64**
Dante. Alighieri 1265-1321 Writer and national poet of Italy. **120**
Darwin. Charles 1809-92 Theory of natural selection. **77* 62 106 113**
Davey. Ray, contemporary founder of Corrymeela — Ireland. **95**
Davies. John 17C poet. **80**
Davies. Norman, contemporary British historian. **61**
Dawkins. Richard b.1941 British zoologist. **15 37 106 127 129 134**
Day. Clarence 1874-1939 American writer. **4**
Delacroix. Eugène 1798-1863 French Romantic artist. **5**
D'Emilio. John, contemporary social critic. **134**
Demosthenes. 383-322BC Greek orator and politician. **144**
Dennett. Daniel contemporary US scientist **6 77 105 106 157**
Descartes. René 1596-1650 French Catholic philosopher. **67 138**
Deschner. contemporary German expert on British social history. **74**
Diamond. Jared, contemporary evolutionary biologist. **145**
Diderot. Denis 1713-84 French writer and philosopher. **86 101**
Diocletian. Roman Emperor 284-305 Soldier. Persecutor of Christians. **59**
Dionoth. 6C Celtic Abbot of Bangor (Wales). **54**
Dionysius the Areopagite. 1C Athenian. cf.Acts 17:34. **101 104 111**
Dodd. C H 1884 -1973 Biblical scholar and Congregational pastor. **87**
Dominian. Jack b.1929 Catholic psychiatrist & marriage counsellor. **133**
Dominic. 1170 -1221 Spanish founder of the "Black Friars". **61**
Donne. John c.1572 -1631 English poet and preacher. **128**
Dostoevsy. Fyodor 1802 -81 Russian novelist. **1 20 65 170**
Doubleday. Henry 1808-1875 Quaker naturalist & horticulturalist **150**
Douglass. Frederick 19C escaped slave. Rights campaigner. **70**
Duffy. Eamon b.1947 Catholic church historian. **54**
Duncan. Robert 1919-88 American poet and playwright **148**
Duns. Scotus c.1265-1308 Oxford theologian. **99**
Durant. Will, contemporary US historian. **163**
Dwight. Timothy 19C President of Yale. **72 138**
Dyson. Freeman b.1923 English physicist. Prof. at Princeton. **105**

E

Eckardt. Alice & Roy — contemporary US Christian writers. **27**
Eckhart. John (Meister) 1260 -1327 Dominican mystic. **1 6 112**
Eddington. Arthur 1882 -1944 prof. astronomy in Cambridge. **103 125**

Eddy. Mary Baker 1821-1910 Founder of Christian Science. **94**

Eichmann. Adolf 1901-62 Nazi war criminal. **110**

Einstein. Albert 1879-1955 German/Swiss physicist of world renown.
5 37 101 110 112 120 122 156

Eleazar. 1C Jewish rabbi. **50 82**

Eleutherus 2C bishop of Rome. **59**

Eliot. T S 1888-1965 Anglo-American poet, critic and playwright. **2 140**

Elizabeth I. Queen of England 1558-1603. Settled the C of E. **53 55**

Emerson. Ralph Waldo 1803-82 American poet and essayist. **20 97**

Epictetus. c.50 -c.130 Stoic philosopher. **127 170**

Epicurus. c.341-270BC Greek philosopher. **115**

Epidaurus. 2C.BC Greek doctor? **138**

Erasmus. Desiderius 1466-1536 Dutch humanist theologian.**15 82 158 168**

Erigena. Johannes Scotus c.810-77 Celtic philosopher & theologian. **73**

Erskine. John 1721-1803 Scots Evangelical theologian. **127**

Euripides. 480-406 BC Greek tragic playwright. **105**

Eusebius of Caesarea 264-340 bishop. Church historian. **59**

Evans-Pritchard. Edward 1902-73 Prof.anthropology at Oxford. **140**

F

Fabiola. † 399 Roman benefactress and charity worker. **72**

Farmer. H H 1892-1981 Reformed theologian, preacher and pacifist. **118**

Falwell. Gerry US tele-evangelist **134**

Farrer Austin 1904-68 English theologian and Biblical sholar. **37**

Fastidius. 5C. British bishop of Sicily and ecclesiastical writer. **140**

Fasullo. contemporary Catholic priest in Sicily. **91**

Faulk. Henry English intelligence officer in 1939 -45. **147**

Feininger. Lyonel 1871-1956 American artist who taught in Germany.**158**

Feynman. Richard 1918-1988 American physicist. **154**

Finney. Charles G US evangelist who led the 1830 revival. **74**

Forster. E M 1879-1970 English novelist and essayist. **4**

Fortescue. Judge 15C Chief Justice of England. **34**

Foster. William 19C MP Educationist. **73**

Foucauld. Charles 1858-1916 French missionary monk and mystic. **90**

Fox. George 1624-91 f. of the Society of Friends. **93 128 135 146**

Francis of Assisi c.1181-1226 f.of the Franciscan Order. **6 55 61 64 90**

Frayn. Michael b.1933 Playwright, novelist and journalist. **127**

Frazer. James 1854-1941 Social anthropologist. **89**

Freud. Anna 1895-1982 f.of child psycho-analysis. Daughter of … **157**

Freud. Sigmund 1856-1939 Founder of psycho-analysis. **97 134 147 157**

Friedlander. Albert b.1927 Jewish professor & rabbi. **78**

Fry. Elizabeth 1780-1845 English prison reformer. **143**

G

Galen. Claudius c.130-201 Greek physician and writer. **72**

Galileo. Galilei 1564-1642 Astronomer &mathematician. **67* 1 105**

Gandhi. 1869-1948 Indian spiritual teacher and non-violent activist.
>**3 127 142 146 148 159 161**
Gaulle de. Charles 1890-1970 French General and President. **142**
Gautama. Siddharta c.563-483BC Founder of Buddhism.
>**164* 45 126 135 160**
Gelasius I Pope 492-96 asserted papal supremacy. **129**
Gemellus. Greek actor. **121**
Getty. John Paul 1892-1976 oil billionaire and art collector. **150**
Gibran. Kahlil †1931 Lebanese poet & mystic.
>**28 113 114 120 135 137 140**
Glanville. Joseph 1636-80 English philosopher and clergyman. **8**
Glass. Bentley, contemporary geneticist. **130**
Glinka. Mikhail 1804 -57 Russian composer. **155**
Gobind Singh. 1666-1708 Tenth Sikh Guru. Created the Khalsa. **165**
Godet Frédérick 1812-1900 Swiss Protestant theologian **124**
Gibbon. Edward 1737-94 English historian. **61**
Goebbels. Joseph 1897-1945 Nazi politician **1**
Goethe. 1749-1832 German poet, writer and scientist. **7 117 120**
van Gogh. Vincent Dutch artist. Pioneer of Expressionism. **154**
Goldwyn. Samuel 1882-1974 Polish -American film producer. **157**
Gollancz. Victor 1893-1967 Publisher, writer and philanthropist. **20**
Gosse. Philip 1810-88 English zoologist. Spec.marine invertebrates. **77**
Graham. James 1792-1861 British statesman. Home Secretary. **69**
Granville-Barker. Harley 1877 -1946 English playwright and producer. **4**
Gray. Asa 1810-88 American botanist at Harvard. **77**
Greer. Germaine b.1939 Australian feminist writer and lecturer. **135**
Gregoire. Abbé 1750-1831 French clergyman and revolutionary. **128**
Gregory of Nazianzus. 329–389 Theologian in Cappadocia. **82**
Gregory of Nyssa. 330-395 Bishop and theologian. **104**
Gregory VII (Hildebrand) Pope 1073-85. Fought secular control. **54 65 83**
Gregory X. Pope 1271-76 **78**
Gregory XIV. Pope 1590-91 **130**
Grey. Mary, contemporary Catholic feminist theologian. **83**
Grienberger. contemporary French Jesuit astronomer. **67**
Griffiths. Bede †1993 Benedictine inter-faith contemplative. **135**
Grosseteste. Robert 1175-1253 Bishop, scholar and church reformer. **153**
Grove. Valerie b.1946 Journalist. **137**
Gunton. Colin. contemporary British theologian. **27**
Gyatso. Tenzin The Dalai Lama b.1935 Spiritual leader of Tibet. **146 164**

H

Haisch. Bernard, contemporary astro-physicist. **8**
Haldane. J B S 1892-1964 Scots geneticist. **77 109 117 118 145**
Hammarskjold. Dag 1905-61 Swedish and UN statesman. **146**
Hanina. early Jewish rabbi **34**
Hardy. Alister 20C Australian biologist at Oxford. **6 107 124**
Haselden. Kyle, contemporary psychologist. **147**

Hawking. Stephen b.1942 Cambridge theoretical physicist. **106**
Heidegger. Martin 1889-1976 German philosopher. **153**
Heiric of Auxerre c.840-876 Teacher and hagiographer. **75**
Heisenberg. Werner 1901-76 German theoretical physicist. **105 153 156**
Henry IV. King of England 1399-1413. **55**
Henry VIII. King of England 1509-47 Broke with Rome 1534. **53**
Heraclitus. 5C.BC Greek philosopher. **157**
Herbert. George 1593-1648 Clergyman and poet. **36**
Heschel. Abraham 20C American Jewish scholar. **141**
Hesiod. 8C.BC Greek poet. **141**
Hess. Rudolf 1894-1987 German politician. Deputy to Hitler. **24**
Hesse. Hermann 1877-1962 German novelist and poet. **118**
Heyerdahl. Thor b.1914 Norwegian anthropologist and adventurer. **124**
Hilary of Poitiers c.315-368 Bishop and theologian. **4**
Hill. Gardiner 19C pioneer in mental health. **72**
Hippocrates. c.460-377BC Greek "father of medicine". **67 123 131**
Hillel. Early first century rabbi in Babylon and Judaea..**29 31**
Hitler. Adolf 1889-1945 German Führer. **6 78 108 127**
Hodge. Charles 1797-1878 American Presbyterian theologian.**15**
Homer. c.9C.BC Greek writer of epic poetry. **121 145**
Honorius I. Pope 625-38 Asserted the Roman Church in Britain. **54**
Hooft. Visser't 20C Dutch ecumenist. **92**
Hooker. Richard 1554-1600 Laid basis of Anglican theology. **76 143**
Hopkins. Gerard Manley 1844-89 English Catholic priest and poet. **112**
Horace. 65 -8BC Italian lyric poet and satirist. **120**
Horrobin. David, contemporary Christian writer. **107**
Howard. John 1726-90 English prison reformer. **143**
Howatch. Susan b.1940 Quaker. **99**
Hoyle. Fred. b.1915 English astronomer and mathematician. **8**
Hubbard. Elbert contemporary writer. **152**
Hughes. Thomas 1822-96 Liberal MP f. Working Men's Colleges. **74**
Hugo. Victor 1802-85 French playwright. **40**
Hume. David 1711-76 Scots empiricist & atheist. **110 116 118 122 156**
Hus. Jan 1369-1415 Bohemian reformer. **58* 55**
Hutcheson. Francis 1694-1746 Moral philosopher. Prof.Glasgow. **158**
Huxley. Julian 1887-1975 Biologist. UNESCO grandson of **106 158**
Huxley. T H 1825-95 Early exponent of Darwinism. **77 106 158**

I

Ibn al-'Arabi 1165-1240 Spanish Sufi (Muslim) theologian . **159**
Ibn Rushd (Averrhoës) 1126-98 Spanish Islamic philosopher. **72**
Ignatius of Loyala. c.1495-1556 Theologian. f.Jesuit Order. **1 6 70 85**
Inge. William 1860-1954 Dean of St Paul's. Philosopher. **98 132**
Innocent I Pope 402-417 Strong centralising pope. **54**
Innocent III Pope 1198-1216 Temporal and spiritual supremacist. **77**
Innocent IV Pope 1243-54 Political preoccupations. **65 78**
Irenaeus c.130 -200 bishop of Lyons. Greek Father. **9 56 63 102 118**

J

Jahn. Janheinz contemporary anthropologist. **4**
Jaki. Stanislaus contemporary philosopher of science. **153**
James VI 1567-1625 King of Scots — and England as **James I. 139**
James VII King of Scots and of England as **James II** 1685-8. **53**
Jeans. James 1877-1946 English astro-physicist. **8**
Jefferson. Thomas US President 1801-9. Statesman. **19 76 104 128 Jerome.**
342 -420 Croatian ascetic, scholar and translator. **61 65**
Joad. C E M 1891-1951 English philosopher & broadcaster. **119 153**
John of Damascus c.675-479 Theologian and hymn writer. **104**
John Scotus Erigena ("The Scot from Ireland") 810-77 Theologian. **73 83**
John of Monte Corvino 13C missionary to China. **61**
Johnson. Samuel 1709-84 English lexicographer, critic and poet. **108**
Josephus. Flavius 1st C Jewish historian and soldier. **20**
Joubert. Joseph 1754-1824 French Catholic philosopher. **73**
Julian Lady - of Norwich. c.1342-1413 English mystic. **6 111**
Julius. Johannes 17C victim of witch-hunts. **69**
Jung. Carl 1875-1961 Swiss founder of analytical psychology.
 108 110 113 118 126 133 136 146 157 170
Justin Martyr c.100-165 Samaritan philosopher in Rome. **158**
Justinian. Roman Emperor 527-65. Re-invigorated Rome. **51 65**

K

Kant. Immanuel 1724 -1804 German philosopher. **37 123 128 158**
Keats. John 1795-1821 Romantic poet and writer. **113 154**
Kempis. Thomas à 1379-1471 German Augustinian monk. **7**
Kennedy. Ian contemporary physician. **72**
Kenny. Mary contemporary journalist. **133**
Kierkegaard. Søren 1813-55 Danish theologian. **6 37 107 123**
Kilcash. Irish poet and balladist. **80**
King. Martin Luther 1929-68 Baptist civil rights leader. **58* 79 146 147**
Kingsley. Charles 1819-75 Cambridge historian, reformer & writer. **74 77**
Kirby. William contemporary entomologist. **151**
Kissinger. Henry b.1923 US Secretary of State and academic. **148**
Klee. Paul 1879-1940 Swiss artist. **154**
Knight. Andrew 19C Quaker missionary. **71**
Knight. Margaret 20C humanist and atheist campaigner. **158**
Kruschev. Nikita Russian Chairman 1958 -64. **33**
Küng. Hans b.1928 Swiss Catholic theologian. **21 27 36 111 122**
K'ung Fu-tse — see Confucius. **166* 24 121 146 167**
Kürtmeyer contemporaryAmerican writer? **107**
Kyi. Aung San Sun b.1945 Persecuted Burmese democrat. **164**
Kyung. P S contemporary Chinese feminist writer. **129**

L

Ladman. Cathy contemporary American comedian. **3**
Laqueur. Thomas 18C social commentator? **76**

Lancaster. Joseph 1778-1838 Quaker educator in Britain & America. **73**
Landes. David contemporary British historian. **75 128 148**
Lao-tse. 604-531 Chinese sage and teacher of Taoism. **160* 85 107 167**
Laplace. Pierre 1749-1827 French mathematician and astronomer. **163**
Las Casas. Bartolomé de 1474-1566 Spanish priest **73**
Latimer. Hugh c.1485-1555 Protestant bishop of Worcester. **73**
Laud. William 1573-1645 Archb.Canterbury. Absolutist. **86**
Lavigerie Cardinal 1825-92 Founder of the Anti-Slavery Society **70**
Law. William 1686-1761 English clergyman and writer. **42 126**
Lawrence. D H 1885-1930 English novelist, poet and writer. **53 147**
Leach Edmund 1910-89 English anthropologist **9**
Lecky. William 1838-1903 Irish historian and philosopher. **80**
Leiber. Justin contemporary specialist in linguistic anthropology. **4**
Leibniz. Gottfried 1646-1716 German philosopher. **100**
Lenin. Vladimir Ilyich 1870-1924 Russian Marxist revolutionary. **74**
Leo IX. Pope 1048-54 Schism with Eastern Orthodoxy. **55**
Leo X Pope 1475-1521 Excommunicated Luther. **66**
Leo XIII. Pope 1878-1903 Condemned Anglican orders. **55**
Leonard. Graham b.1921 bishop of London, then Catholic convert. **82 87**
Lewis. C S 1898-1963 Cambridge prof.literature & writer. **2 127**
Lewis. David b.1919 contemporary doctor and sailor. **138**
Lilburne. John 1614-57 Pamphleteer and Leveller leader. **34 76**
Lincoln. Abraham 1809-65 US President and abolitionist. **70 119**
Livingstone. David 1813-73 Scots missionary and explorer **71**.
Locke. John 1632-1704 Philosopher. English empiricist. **76**
Longfellow. Henry 1807-82 American poet and translator. **73**
Longley. Clifford 20C religious journalist. **133**
Louis XV. 1643-1715 King of France. Absolutist. **24**
Lowe. Robert 19C clergyman. **75**
Loyola. Ignatius 1495-1556 Founder of the Jesuits. **55**
Ludlow. John 19C Christian socialist. **74**
Luther. Martin 1483-1546 German reformer and hymn-writer.
      38 53 55 65 70 76 78 93 99 127 129 140

M

Macaulay. Thomas 1800-59 Essayist and historian. MP and peer. **63**
Maccoby Hyam b.1924 20C Jewish scholar **102**
MacCulloch Diarmaid 20C Reformation historian **158**
Macdonald. George 1824-1905 Scots religious writer, novelist & poet. **125**
McCabe. Herbert 20C Catholic writer. **113**
MacIntyre Alasdair b.1929 contemporary British philosopher **128**
Mackay. James b.1927 Scots jurist. Lord Chancellor. **136**
Mackenzie. George 17C defender of alleged witches. **69**
MacLeod. George 1895-1991 Christian visionary. f.Iona Community. **95**
McLuhan. Marshall 1911-80 Canadian writer. **152**
Macmullen Ramsay contemporary historian **57**
MacMullin. Ernan contemporary theologian. **120**

Macmurray. John contemporary British philosopher. **3 154**
MacQuarrie. John b.1919 Scots theologian & philosopher of religion. **122**
Machiavelli. Niccolo 1469-1527 Italian political philosopher. **76 127**
Madison. James US President 1809-17 "Father of the Constitution". **76**
Magee. 20C Irish Presbyterian minister. Worker for reconciliation. **80**
Maimonides. Moses 1138-1204 Jewish philosopher **7 72 126 159**
Mandela. Nelson b.1918 South African prisoner then President. **146**
Mao Zedong Revolutionary leader of China 1949 - 1976. **8 127**
Maraffi. Fr. 17C Preacher-General of the Dominican Order. **67**
Marcellinus. 4C Roman critic of Christianity. **56**
de la Mare. Walter 1873-1956 English poet and writer. **143**
Maritain. Jacques 1882-1973 Catholic philosopher & diplomat. **90 128 154**
Marx. Groucho 1895-1977 one of a family of US film comedians. **32**
Marx. Karl 1818-80 philosopher and political theorist. **3 74 75 141 156 158**
Masaryk. Jan 20C leader of Czechoslovakia. **146**
Masure. Eugene contemporary Catholic theologian. **89**
Maurice. F D 1805-72 Cambridge moral philosopher and theologian. **74**
Maurois. André 1885-1967 French writer and biographer. **97 106**
Mearns. Andrew 19C clergyman & social critic. **74 75**
Meîr. Rabbi 2C "The Enlightener". Compiler of the Halakhot (laws). **112**
Melancthon. Philipp 1497-1560 German linguist. Reformer. **158**
Melbourne. William British Prime Minister 1934, 35-41. **3**
Mencken. H L 1880 -1956 US philologist, editor and satirist. **2 37**
Mendel. Gregor 1822-84 botanist and founder of genetics. **77**
Meng-tzu (Mencius) 372-289BC Confucian philosopher and sage. **166**
Meolmud. Dynvall 5C.BC Celtic King in SW Britain. Legal codifier. **59**
Merton. Thomas 1915-68 French born Catholic monk **159**
Methodius. 825-85 Missionary to the Slavs (with his brother Cyril). **71**
Metrodorus. 4C.BC Greek philosopher. **109**
Miles. Andrew contemporary American theologian. **134**
Mill. John Stuart 1806-73 English philosopher & social reformer.
 2 82 129 135 158
Miller. William 1781-1849 US farmer. f. "Second Adventists". **94**
Milton. John 1608-74 poet. Defender of the Commonwealth.**76 124**
Minsky. Marvin contemporary American scientist. **6**
Mirandola. Pico della 1463-94 Italian Renaissance philosopher. **158**
Mkapa. President of Tanzania in 2005.**149**
Moltke. Helmuth von 1800-91 Chief Gen.Staff of the Prussian army. **145**
Moltmann. Jürgen b.1926 German theologian. **8 63**
Monod. Jacques 1910-76 French geneticist .**77 101 106 110**
Montaigne. Michel 1533-92 French essayist. **31 108**
Moore. Aubrey 1848–1890 Oxford canon. **77**
Moore. G E 1873-1958 Cambridge philosopher. **127**
Moore. Henry 1898-1986 English sculptor of organic form. **154**
Moore. James contemporary historian? **77**
Moray. James contemporary prof.of psychology. **157**

Morris. C S American black Baptist pastor **148**
Morris. William 1834-96 craftsman, poet and social activist. **74**
Mott.. John 1865-1955 American Methodist ecumenist. **92**
Motyer. J A contemporary Catholic theologian. **88**
Moule. Charles b.1908 Cambridge Biblical scholar. **51**
Mozart. Wolfgang Amadeus 1756-91 Renowned Austrian composer. **155**
Muggeridge. Malcolm 1903-90 Journalist. Catholic convert. **112**

Muhammad. c.570-632 Supreme Prophet of Islam.
    161* 38 63 64 99 111 153 156 160
Muir. Edwin 1887-1959 Scots poet and critic. **125**
Müller. Ludwig 20C Lutheran leader who collaborated with Nazism. **78**
Max Müller 1823-1900 philologist and writer. **3**
Murray. Middleton 20C theologian. **83**
Musil. Robert 1880-1942 Austrian novelist. **111**
Mussolini. Benito 1883-1945 Italian dictator. **1**

N

Nahman of Bratzslav †1810 Jewish Rabbi. **108**
Nanak. Guru 1469-1539 Founder of Sikhism. **166* 38**
Napoleon Bonaparte 1769-1821 French emperor **3**
Nash. Ogden 1902-71 American humourist. **36**
Nayler. James c.1618-60 Quaker colleague of George Fox. **128**
Neel. James contemporary professor of medicine? **138**
Nehru. Jawaharlal 1889-1964 India's first Prime Minister. **148**
Newberg. Andrew contemp. prof.psychiatry – Pennsylvania. **153**
Niebuhr. Reinhold 1892-1971 American theologian and activist. **45**
Nestorius. † c.451 Patriarch of Constantinople and 'heretic'. **102**
Newton. Isaac 1642-1727 Outstanding scientist and administrator. **101**
Nicholas I. Pope 858-67 Asserted church and papal authority. **55**
Nietzsche. Friedrich 1844 -1900 German philosopher and critic.
    2 31 99 110 112 114 129 158
Nightingale. Florence 1820-1910 English hospital reformer. **62**
Norman. Edward 19C Quaker entomologist. **150**

O

Oastler. Richard 1789-1861 Factory reformer. Tory churchman. **74**
O'Brien. James 1805-64 Chartist leader. Advocate of credit banks. **140**
Ohiyesa. 1858-1939 Sioux physician and author. **87**
Oman. John 1860-1939 English Reformed theologian. **83** and cover.
Oppenheimer. J Robert 1904-67 American nuclear physicist. **152**
Oresmé. Nicholas c.1320-82 French mediaeval philosopher. **153**
Origen. 185-254 theologian of Alexandria. **40 104 125**
Ormerod. Eleanor 19C entolomologist. **150**
Overbye. Dennis contemporary journalist. **103**
Overton. Robert c.1609-88 Independent leader in the civil war. **128**
Ovid. Publius 43BC-17AD Latin poet. **35**

Owen. Richard 19C. biologist in the British Museum. **77**
Owen. Robert 1771-1858 Welsh social reformer. **75 141**
Owen. Wilfred 1893-1918 English wartime poet. **139**

P

Pachomius. 4C founded monasteries in Egypt. **61**
Packer. J I contemporary evangelical theologian. **129**
Paine. Thomas 1737-1809 English revolutionary writer. **115 158**
Panagotis. contemporary Orthodox theologian. **83**
Papadopoulos. Gerasimos 20C Greek Orthodox monk & theologian. **83**
Pargeter. William 18C Anglican clergyman and psychologist. **3**
Parnell. Charles Stewart 1846-91 Irish nationalist politician. **80**
Pascal. Blaise 1623-62 French mathematician & theologian.
        29 97 105 107 116 170
Pasteur. Louis 1822-95 French microbiologist. **97**
Patmore. Coventry 1823-96 English Catholic poet. **102**
Paton. Alan 1903-88 South African writer and educator. **36 110**
Patrick. 385-461 British "Apostle of Ireland". **80**
Patterson. Monica contemporary peace campaigner in Ireland. **80**
Paul III. Pope 1534-49 First pope of the Counter-Reformation. **55 67**
Paul IV. Pope 1555-59 Leader of the Counter-Reformation. **65**
Paul VI. Pope 1963-78 Liberal ecumenist. **21**
Pavlova. Anna 1881-1931 Russian ballerina and choreographer. **86**
de Payen. Hugh - founder of the Templars. **64**
Peacocke. Arthur b.1924 Oxford theologian and scientist. **101**
Pearsall. Paul contemporary physician? **138**
Pecci. contemporary Italian financier. f.of the Club of Rome. **117**
Pelagius (Morien) Early 5C Celtic theologian. **57**[*]
Penn. William 1644 -1718 Quaker reformer and colonist.
        39 76 79 119 126 144 146
Pepys. Samuel 1633-1703 Diarist and naval administrator. **72**
Perkin. Harold English historian. **74**
Philip II. King of Spain 1556-98 Authoritarian Catholic. **65**
Picasso. Pablo 1881-1973 Spanish artist. Inspired cubism. **154**
Pierre. Abbé b.1912 Catholic priest. Worker for the homeless. **52**
Pinhas. Jewish rabbi in Korez. **119**
Pinker. Steven contemp. American psychologist. **5 45 85 106 113 157**
Pitt the Elder 1708-78 English statesman and orator. **76**
Pius VI Pope 1775-99 embattled by French Revolution. **128**
Pius IX Pope 1846-78 proclaimed doctrine of infallibility. **54 63**
Pius XI Pope 1922-39 Est. the Vatican State. **78 85 162**
Pius XII Pope 1939-58 controversial relationship with fascism. **78 85 92**
Plato. c.428-347BC philosopher. f.of the Academy in Athens. **43 120**
Pliny the Elder 23-79AD Roman scholar and historian. **17**
Plotinus. 205-270 Egyptian philosopher. f.of Neo-Platonism. **1 103**
Plumb. J H contemporary historian. **80**
Poi. 13C.BC Egyptian artist. **72**

Polkinghorne. John contemporary physicist and clergyman. **43 118**
Pollard. 'Mother' who encouraged Martin Luther King **98**
Pope. Alexander 1688-1744 English Catholic satirical poet. **28**
Popper. Karl 1902-94 Austrian philosopher. **1**
Porter. Roy contemporary physician and medical historian. **72**
van der Post. Laurens 1906-96 South African writer. **88 105**
Protogoras. c.490-421 Greek philosopher. **107 158**
Prynne. William 1600-69 Puritan pamphleteer then Royalist. **154**
Ptolemy. 2C.AD Greek astronomer and geographer. **67**
Purves. Libby b.1950 writer, journalist & broadcaster. **135**

Q

Quick. Oliver 1885-1944 Anglican theologian. **89**

R

Radbertus. Paschasius 785-860 Benedictine Abbot of Corbie **89**
Rabelais. (anag. **Alcofribas Nasier**) ? 1494-1553 Satirist **137**
Rahner. Karl 1904 -84 German Catholic theologian. **104**
Raine. Kathleen b.1908 contemporary English poet and critic. **135**
Ramakrishna. 1836-86 Indian Hindu teacher. **112**
Ramanuja. Srinivasa 1887-1920 Indian mathematician. **15**
Rasmussen. Larry contemporary ecological writer. **150**
Rawlinson. A E J 1884 -1960 bishop, theologian and historian. **89**
Rayburn. Sam, contemporary US industrialist. **106**
Reginus. unknown recipient of a Nag Hammadi letter. **122**
Reiss. Michael contemporary ecologist and writer. **152**
Renoir. Pierre August 1841-1919 French artist. Impressionist. **113 155**
Ricci. Matteo 1552 -1610 f. Jesuit mission in China. **71 159 166**
Richard I King of England 1189-99 Warrior crusader. **64**
Ridley. Matt. contemporary writer on human evolution **77**
Ridley. Nicholas 1500-55 bishop. Protestant martyr. **106 126 152**
Rieu. Emile Victor 1887-1972 Editor and translator. **15**
Rifkin. Jeremy contemporary journalist. **152**
Rilke. Rainer Maria 1875-1926 Czech poet. **120**
Riórdáin. Seán Ó 1916-77 Irish poet. **107**
Roberts. J M b.1928 world historian. **51 82**
Robinson. Jancis contemporary expert on wines. **139**
Robinson. John 1576 -1625 English separatist pastor in Leyden. **2 15**
Robinson. John 1919 -83 Biblical scholar. **87**
Rochefoucauld. François La 1613 -80 French classical writer. **29**
Roger. Brother b.1915 f. of the Taizé community. **95**
Rolande. Mme victim of the French revolution. **108**
Romain. Jonathan contemporary Jewish rabbi. **136**
Romero. Oscar 1917 -80 Archb.El Salvador. **58* 81 140**
Rookmaaker. H R contemporary art historian. **154**
Rose. Steven contemp. American evolutionary biologist. **108**
Roschini. Gabriele, contemporary Catholic writer. **63**

Rossini. Gioacchino 1792-1868 Italian composer. **155**
Rostand. Edmond 1868-1918 French poet and playwright. **108**
Rowntree. Joseph 1836-1925 Quaker industrialist and reformer. **74**
Rubinstein. Artur 1887-1982 Polish pianist. **155**
Rubinstein. Richard contemporary Jewish historian. **78**
Ruether. Rosemary b.1936 American feminist theologian. **129**
Rûmi. 1207 -1273 Persia's greatest Sufi (Muslim) poet. **110**
Russell. Bertrand 1872-1970 English mathematician and activist.
      2 110 117 122 127 136 145 156 158
Russell. Charles 1852-1916 Forerunner of the Jehovah's Witnesses. **94**

S

Sabellius. c.3C Roman or Libyan theologian. **59**
Sacks. Jonathan b.1948 United Hebrew Chief Rabbi. **intro. 3 37 137 159 161**
Sandage. Allan b.1926 American astronomer. **105**
Sandburg. Carl 1878-1967 American poet and biographer. **145**
Sankara. 8C Indian Hindu philosopher. **8**
Santos. Mgr. 20C Catholic priest in Chile. **91**
Sartre. Jean-Paul 1905-80 French philosopher, writer and activist. **100**
Sassoon. Siegried 1886-1967 war poet **4**
Saunders. Cicely b.1918 founder of the modern hospice movement. **132**
Scarisbrick. Jack contemporary f.of "Life" — rights of the unborn. **130**
Schäf. 20C. Polish marxist. **100**
Schall. Adam 1591-1666 Jesuit missionary and astronomer. **157 166**
Schiller. Friedrich 1759-1805 German historian, playwright and poet. **154**
Schulz. Charles 1922 -00 American strip cartoonist. **148 150**
Schumacher. E F 1911-77 German economist & ecologist. **137 141**
Schuon. Frithjof contemporary religious philosopher. **125**
Schweitzer. Albert 1875-1965 German missionary & musician. **2 151 170**
Scot. Reginald 16C opponent of witch-hunts. **69**
Scott. Robert Falcon 1868–1912 Antarctic explorer **121**
Scruton. Roger b.1944 Lawyer and philosopher. **134**
Seattle. Chief c.1790-1866 Duwamish. Catholic convert. **151**
Seneca. Lucius 5BC-AD65 Roman philosopher and statesman. **3 30 130 135**
Shaftesbury. 7th earl 1801-85 Evangelical social reformer. **74**
Shakespeare. William 1564 -1616 English playwright. **9 43 155**
Shammai (Ha Zaken) c.50BC-AD30 Jewish rabbi. **16* 39**
Shatz. David contemporary Jewish writer. **86**
Shaw. George Bernard 1856 -1950 Irish playwright and esayist. **15 31**
Shikibu. 11C Japanese poet. **109**
Shosan. Suzuki 17C Buddhist writer. **141**
Shulman. Nisson contemporary Jewish rabbi. **131**
Siculus. Didorus 1C.BC Roman writer. **60**
Simeon ben Azzai 2C. Jewish rabbi **123**
Simeon. ben Manasya Jewish rabbi. **49**
Simeon. ben Yohai 2C Galilean rabbi. **90**
Siricius. Pope 384 -99 fostered learning. **54**

Sixtus IV. Pope 1471-84 **65**
Skimmerhorn. Frank instigated the Sand Creek massacre 1864. **147**
Smith. Adam 1723-90 Scots economist and philosopher. **85 142**
Smith. Joseph 1805-44 f. of the Mormon church. **94**
Smith. Wilfred contemporary Christian writer. **90**
Smyth. John 16C Anglican who f. 1st English Baptist church. **93**
Socrates. 469-399BC Greek philosopher. **31 103 137**
Solzhenitsyn. Alexander b.1918 Writer and rights campaigner. **9 128 143**
Somervell. D C 1885-1965 church historian **29**
Song-ts'an. Zen Buddhist. **1**
Soutar. William 1898-1943 Scots poet and diarist. **135**
Spee. Friedrich von 17C German opponent of witch-hunts. **69**
Speer. Albert 1905-81 Architect and Nazi government adviser. **111**
Spenser. Edmund c.1552 -99 English poet. **154**
Spinoza. Baruch 1632-77 Dutch Jewish philosopher and theologian. **1**
Spong. Bishop contemporary US Biblical scholar. **90 101**
Spurgeon. C H 1834 -92 English Baptist preacher. **72 137**
Stafford-Clark. David 20C physician. **9**
Stalin. Josef 1879-1953 Georgian dictator of the USSR. **61**
Stannard. Russell contemporary writer on Christianity and science. **105**
Stapleton. Thomas 1535-98 Catholic writer and controversialist. **69**
Stauffer. Ethelbert 20C New Testament scholar. **37**
Stendahl (Marie-Henri Beyle) 1783-1842 French novelist and critic. **113**
Stevens. Joseph 19C.? Methodist minister. **75**
Stretch. Lewis contemporary physician. **25**
Strindberg. August 1849-1914 Swiss playwright **135.**
Sudeley. Lord 20C English peer. **149**
Sunday. Billy d.1935 US evangelist. **126**
Svetlana. Allilulyeva Daughter of Stalin. **62**
Swinburne. Algernon Charles 1837 -1909 English poet and critic. **43 150**
Symmachus. 4C Jewish Christian **158**
Szuma Chien. 2C BC Chinese philosopher. **121**

T

Tagore. Rabindranath 1861-1941 Indian poet and philosopher. **110 142**
Talbi. Mohammed contemporary Muslim philosopher. **162**
Tapia. Elizabeth contemporary Christian writer. **91**
Tarfon. Rabbi. 2C.? Jewish teacher. **126**
Taylor. John V contemporarybishop. Gen.Sec.CMS. **90 161**
Teilhard de Chardin. Pierre 1881-1955 Anthropologist and mystic. **125**
Tempier. Etienne French physician and philosopher of science. **153**
Temple. Frederick 1821-1902 Archb.Canterbury and liturgist. **77**
Temple. William 1881-1944 Archb.Canterbury. Ecumenist.
        3 35 112 117 119 153
Tennyson. Alfred 1809-92 English poet. **1**
Teresa Mother 1910-97 Albanian nun. f. Missionaries of Charity. **6 61 126**
Tertullian. 160-220 Latin theologian in Carthage.**2 15 62 97**

Reference numbers with an asterisk indicate further biographical detail.

The quotation at the end of 170 is Gaelic. It is the traditional farewell of the Hebridean mother to her son emigrating to America and probably seen for the last time. It translates:
> *"Whatever shores you sail to, may joy await you."*

....

I am silent, my throat is injured, O Sufi singer, you sing the rest. RÛMI

....

Graham Hellier is a Presbyterian minister who served in the Presbyterian Church of England and in the Church of Scotland. Also for many years Senior Master in an Anglican secondary school and a Methodist local preacher. He lives in Herefordshire, England.

....

Made in the USA
Middletown, DE
20 July 2016